Self, No Self?

Self, No Self?

Perspectives from Analytical, Phenomenological, and Indian Traditions

EDITED BY

Mark Siderits, Evan Thompson, and Dan Zahavi

OXFORD
UNIVERSITY PRESS

OXFORD
UNIVERSITY PRESS

Great Clarendon Street, Oxford OX2 6DP

Oxford University Press is a department of the University of Oxford.
It furthers the University's objective of excellence in research, scholarship,
and education by publishing worldwide in

Oxford New York

Auckland Cape Town Dar es Salaam Hong Kong Karachi
Kuala Lumpur Madrid Melbourne Mexico City Nairobi
New Delhi Shanghai Taipei Toronto

With offices in

Argentina Austria Brazil Chile Czech Republic France Greece
Guatemala Hungary Italy Japan Poland Portugal Singapore
South Korea Switzerland Thailand Turkey Ukraine Vietnam

Oxford is a registered trade mark of Oxford University Press
in the UK and in certain other countries

Published in the United States
by Oxford University Press Inc., New York

British Library Cataloguing in Publication Data
Data available

Library of Congress Cataloging in Publication Data
Data available

Typeset by SPI Publisher Services, Pondicherry, India
Printed in Great Britain
on acid-free paper by
MPG Biddles, King's Lynn and Bodmin

ISBN 978-0-19-959380-4

1 3 5 7 9 10 8 6 4 2

Preface

This work represents an attempt to begin a dialogue among philosophers who are interested in problems to do with the nature of consciousness and the self, but are situated in differing locations in the philosophical landscape. The project began with a mini-conference held at Columbia University in March 2008, featuring Georges Dreyfus, Evan Thompson, and Dan Zahavi, as well as John Dunne, speaking on the topic of the existence of a self and the question of consciousness' reflexivity. This event was organized by the Columbia University Seminar on Comparative Philosophy, and we wish to express our thanks to Chris Kelley, *rapporteur* for the Seminar, for all he did to make the event possible. The office of Columbia University Seminars is also to be thanked for its generous financial support of this and similar activities.

The event at Columbia represented a dialogue between phenomenology and Buddhist philosophy. A larger conference was organized by the Center for Subjectivity Research in Copenhagen in April 2009, featuring an expanded range of voices: phenomenology and Buddhist philosophy, but also Advaita Vedânta and analytic philosophy. Many of the papers in this collection first saw the light of day at this conference. Their present form owes much to the spirited and stimulating discussion that it sparked and helped foster. This event was made possible through the generous support of The Danish National Research Foundation and the Danish Ministry of Science, Technology and Innovation. We must also express our deep gratitude to Joel Krueger and Pia Kirkemann for all their help in making the event run smoothly and successfully.

Editing of this volume was made possible in part thanks to generous research support from the Korea Research Foundation. Thanks are also due to Peter Momtchiloff of Oxford University Press for his support, encouragement, and to Jennifer Lunsford and Angela Anstey-Holroyd for their able assistance in shepherding us through the production process.

Contents

Notes on Contributors

MIRI ALBAHARI is an Associate Professor in Philosophy at the University of Western Australia, where she has held a permanent position since 2006. She did her MA at the University of Otago (on the metaphysics of colour), and her PhD in philosophy from the University of Calgary in 2005. Her book, *Analytical Buddhism: The Two-Tiered Illusion of Self*, is on how the illusion of self is put together. She hopes to write a follow-up book on how the Buddhist Noble Eightfold Path, via virtue, meditation, and wisdom, could dissolve the illusion of self in a way that does not incur the types of pathology that are predicted by Western neuroscientists.

GEORGES DREYFUS was the first Westerner to receive the title of Geshe after spending fifteen years studying in Tibetan Buddhist monasteries. He then entered the University of Virginia where he received his PhD. in the History of Religions program. He is currently Professor of Religion of the Department of Religion at Williams College. His publications include *Recognizing Reality: Dharmakirti and his Tibetan Interpreters* (SUNY Press 1997), *The Svatantrika-Prasangika Distinction* (co-edited with Sara McClintock, Wisdom 2003), and *The Sound of Two Hands Clapping: The Education of a Tibetan Buddhist Monk* (University of California Press 2003), as well as many articles on various aspects of Buddhist philosophy and Tibetan culture.

WOLFGANG FASCHING teaches philosophy at the University of Vienna (Austria) and is presently working on a project about the nature of experiential presence. He is the author of *Phänomenologische Reduktion und Mushin: Edmund Husserls Bewusstseinstheorie und der Zen-Buddhismus* (Alber 2003).

JONARDON GANERI is Professor of Philosophy at the University of Sussex. His work is at the border between Indian and analytical philosophy. He has published three books: *The Concealed Art of the Soul: Theories of Self and Practices of Truth in Indian Ethics and Epistemology* (Clarendon 2007), *Philosophy in Classical India: The Proper Work of Reason* (Routledge 2001), and *Semantic Powers: Meaning and the Means of Knowing in Classical Indian Philosophy* (Clarendon 1999). He is currently working on the philosophy of mind in classical Indian thought, as well as on the philosophy of early modern India.

JOEL W. KRUEGER is a postdoctoral research fellow at the Danish National Research Foundation: Center for Subjectivity Research, University of Copenhagen. His research interests include issues in phenomenology and philosophy of mind, Asian and comparative philosophy, pragmatism, and philosophy of music.

MATTHEW MACKENZIE is Assistant Professor of Philosophy at Colorado State University. His primary research is in Buddhist philosophy, philosophy of mind, phenomenology, and metaphysics. He has published in journals such as *Philosophy East and West, Asian Philosophy,* and *Phenomenology and the Cognitive Sciences.* He is currently co-authoring, with Bradley Park, a book on enactivism and Asian philosophy.

CHAKRAVARTHI RAM-PRASAD is Professor in the Department of Religious Studies at Lancaster University. His research interests include Indian and comparative episte mology, metaphysics, and philosophy of religion. Recent publications include *Knowledge and Liberation in Classical Indian Thought* (2001 Palgrave), *Advaita Epistemology and Metaphysics: An Outline of Indian Non-Realism* (RoutledgeCurzon 2002), and *Indian Philosophy and the Consequences of Knowledge* (Ashgate, 2007).

MARK SIDERITS is currently in the philosophy department of Seoul National University. He previously taught philosophy for many years at Illinois State University. He is the author of *Indian Philosophy of Language* (Kluwer 1991), *Personal Identity and Buddhist Philosophy: Empty Persons* (Ashgate 2003), and *Buddhism as Philosophy* (Ashgate and Hackett 2007), as well as numerous articles. His principal area of interest is analytic metaphysics as it plays out in the intersection between contemporary analytic philosophy and classical Indian and Buddhist philosophy.

GALEN STRAWSON taught philosophy at the University of Oxford for twenty years before moving to Reading University in 2001. He has held visiting positions at NYU (1997) and Rutgers University (2000). Between 2004 and 2007 he was Distinguished Professor of Philosophy at the City University of New York Gradu- ate Center. He is the author of *Freedom and Belief* (OUP 1986), *The Secret Connexion: Realism, Causation and David Hume* (OUP 1989), *Mental Reality* (MIT Press 1994), *Selves: An Essay in Revisionary Metaphysics* (OUP 2009), and the principal author of *Consciousness and its Place in Nature* (Imprint Academic 2006). A selection of his philosophical papers, *Real Materialism and Other Essays,* was published in 2008 (OUP).

EVAN THOMPSON is Professor of Philosophy at the University of Toronto. He received his BA in Asian studies from Amherst College, and his PhD. in philosophy from the University of Toronto. He is the author of *Mind in Life: Biology, Phenomenology, and the Sciences of Mind* (Harvard University Press 2007), and a co-editor (with P. Zelazo and M. Moscovitch) of *The Cambridge Handbook of Consciousness* (Cambridge University Press 2007). He is also a co-author, with

F. J. Varela and E. Rosch, of *The Embodied Mind: Cognitive Science and Human Experience* (MIT Press 1991), and the author of *Color Vision: A Study in Cognitive Science and the Philosophy of Perception* (Routledge Press 1995). He is currently working on a new book, titled *Waking, Dreaming, Being: New Revelations about the Self from Neuroscience and Meditation*. Thompson held a Canada Research Chair at York University (2002–2005), and has also taught at Boston University. He has held visiting positions at the Centre de Récherche en Epistémologie Appliqué (CREA) at the Ecole Polytechnique in Paris, and at the University of Colorado at Boulder. He is a member of the Mind and Life Institute's Program and Research Committee.

DAN ZAHAVI is Professor of Philosophy and Director of the Danish National Research Foundation's Center for Subjectivity Research at the University of Copenhagen. He obtained his PhD. from Katholieke Universiteit Leuven in 1994 and his Dr.phil. (Habilitation) from University of Copenhagen in 1999. He was elected member of the Institut International de Philosophie in 2001 and of the Royal Danish Academy of Sciences and Letters in 2007. He served as president of the Nordic Society for Phenomenology from 2001 to 2007, and is currently co-editor in chief of the journal *Phenomenology and the Cognitive Sciences*. In his systematic work, Zahavi has mainly been investigating the nature of selfhood, self-consciousness, and intersubjectivity. His most important publications include *Husserl und die transzendentale Intersubjektivität* (Kluwer 1996), *Self-awareness and Alterity* (Northwestern University Press 1999), *Husserl's Phenomenology* (Stanford University Press 2003), *Subjectivity and Selfhood* (MIT Press 2005), and, together with Shaun Gallagher, *The Phenomenological Mind* (Routledge 2008).

Introduction

MARK SIDERITS, EVAN THOMPSON, DAN ZAHAVI

When I see a bright blue sky and hear the wind stirring the leaves, there is awareness of the blue color and the rattling sound. Is there also the awareness of my seeing the blue and hearing the sound? Does being conscious necessarily involve being self-conscious in some sense? And if it does, would this count as evidence for the existence of a self? These are the sorts of questions that the papers in this volume are meant to explore. The explorations embarked on here employ tools and techniques drawn from a number of distinct philosophical traditions: phenomenology, analytic philosophy of mind, and classical Indian and Buddhist philosophy. While these traditions have all investigated the questions of the self and the reflexive nature of awareness, they have for the most part done so independently of one another. So it might be best to begin by attempting to develop a common framework within which to locate the different approaches they employ.

To ask whether, when I am aware of blue I am also aware of my awareness of blue, is to ask whether consciousness is necessarily reflexive or self-intimating. To use the latter expression is to do two things: to suggest that being conscious is a matter of being intimate or 'in touch', of bringing the object into proximity with the self understood as what is 'within', and to invite the question whether the reflexivity at issue involves anything that might properly be called my self. To start with the second point: it might be said that consciousness' being reflexive would be no different than a statement's being self-referential. The statement 'This sentence contains five words' can be described as reflexive just in the sense that in assessing its truth we need look at nothing else besides the very statement itself. In this case the reflexivity of the reference relation is nothing more than this binary relation's involving not the normal two relata but just one. If the thesis that consciousness is reflexive or self-intimating were understood this way, there would be no suggestion that the thesis is at all connected to the claim that there is a self. To think it is would be to conflate the quite distinct expressions 'myself' and 'my self'.

Some will welcome such a diagnosis, since it would mean that we can investigate the reflexivity thesis without having to enter into the murky question of the self's existence and nature. Among them will be those who deny the existence of a self on other grounds. But some will find this dismissal all too quick. They will claim that what we find when we carefully scrutinize the self-intimating nature of our states of awareness is quite different from the simple self-linking exhibited by self-referential statements and the like. If it is true that consciousness is aware of itself not just in bouts of introspective reflection but always, then perhaps this serves as a clue to the nature of subjectivity and hence of the subject. The idea is that a careful investigation of the self-intimating nature of consciousness will bring into clearer focus the phenomenal character of experience, thereby allowing us to discern an otherwise elusive common element in all our conscious states. It is widely held that what is distinctive about experiential states is their 'what-it-is-like-ness' or phenomenal character: there is something it is like to be in the state of seeing that blue color, and it is the presence of this phenomenal character that marks the difference between a sentient being and a mere color-detection mechanism. The present suggestion is that the reflexivity of consciousness is at least partly constitutive of what-it-is-like-ness, and that this in turn tells us something important about that for which it is so like, the subject of phenomenal states.

Critics may still have their doubts. The suggestion just mooted involves what can be described as a move from subjectivity to subject, and one might question the legitimacy of such a move. One might agree that what is distinctive about consciousness is precisely its subjective or phenomenal character, its 'what-it-is-like-ness', yet wonder why this should require us to supply something to serve as the subject to which the seemings are presented. Even if it is granted that 'what-it-is-like' demands completion with a dative—'what-it-is-like-for'—it might still be said that the reflexive nature of consciousness allows us to fill that slot without invoking anything that could be called a self. For, such a critic would insist, the consciousness whose self-intimation is at least partly constitutive of the experience of seeing blue, can play that role for that experience, while another consciousness fills a similar role for the experience of hearing the rattling of the leaves. These being distinct episodes of consciousness, the move to a self as unifying subject of distinct experiences is illegitimate.

This little debate brings out something that might have seemed obvious all along: that before we can investigate a possible linkage between the thesis that consciousness is reflexive and the question of the existence of a self, we must enter the murky waters and clarify just what a self might be. The parties to the above debate hold what are sometimes called egological and non-egological views of consciousness respectively. But what is this 'ego' or self about whose possible involvement in and disclosure through consciousness and self-consciousness they are debating? It is generally agreed that each of us has a sense of self: the (perhaps somewhat elusive) feeling of being the particular person one is. It might seem that the best way to answer the present question would be by exploring this sense and trying to find its underlying structure. And much of the Western philosophical discussion of the issue has followed this path. But the Indian tradition suggests otherwise. Indian philosophical investigations of the self begin with the suspicion that the sense of self that everyone seems to have might be importantly mistaken—indeed that this might be the cause of our being bound to the wheel of saṃsāra or beginningless rebirth. So while our commonly acknowledged sense of self might be worth investigating, we should not assume that doing so will lead directly to an understanding of what the self is.

A word might be in order at this point concerning the soteriological concerns that stand behind much of the Indian philosophical tradition. In this tradition it is often claimed that one should study philosophy in order to overcome the ignorance that results in bondage to a cycle of potentially never-ending rebirths: philosophy will help us find whatever truth lies behind our possibly mistaken views about our identity. Since very few philosophers today subscribe to the view that we are trapped on a wheel of saṃsāra, this fact about the Indian context might make it seem implausible that there could be much fruitful dialogue between the Indian and Western traditions on the topic of the self. But this response might be over-hasty. For it might be that at least some of the concerns that motivate discussions of the self in the Western tradition are, at bottom, similar in nature. To look for the self is to look for what might be thought of as the essence of the person. And essences are often thought to determine what something is good for. Knowledge of the self is sometimes sought because of the promise that such knowledge might help resolve concerns about the meaningfulness of the lives of persons. Now, such concerns might be thought to stem from the realization of human finitude. And those Indian philosophers who see persons as subject to a process of rebirth that is without beginning and possibly without end seem to be denying human finitude. But this overlooks two points: rebirth also means re-death, and endless repetition can drain things of all meaning. While the ethical dimension is often left out of current discussions of the self, it might be an unacknowledged presence that helps shape the debate all the same. That Indian philosophers explicitly thematized this dimension might actually give their deliberations added value.

Initially we might classify views about the self as falling into three broad types: substantialist, non-substantialist and non-self theories. While non-self theorists deny the existence of a self, substantialist and non-substantialist self theorists affirm its existence but disagree about its nature. A substantialist view is one that takes the self to be a substance or property-bearer, the substrate in which different properties are all located at one time or, for substances thought to persist, at different times. Taking as a model the common-sense idea of a thing as an entity that bears a variety of qualities, substantialist theorists see the self as at least minimally the subject of experience, that entity to which conscious states are given. It may then be asked whether the self ever occurs devoid of the property of being conscious. Descartes is generally understood to have claimed not, thereby committing to the view that we are conscious even in dreamless sleep and when comatose. Others hold instead that consciousness is but one of a variety of properties that the self bears at different times. Among its other properties are typically those that also make the self the agent of actions, and thus a fit object of moral appraisal. But the key point for our present concerns is that, according to one form of substantialist view, consciousness stands to the self as red color does to the pot: as a quality to a substance in which it contingently inheres.

Non-substantialist self theorists hold that the self is not a substance or property-bearer standing in relation to a consciousness that is in some sense distinct from it. (Note that even a substantialist who holds that the self is essentially conscious, while claiming that the self never fails to be conscious, thinks of the self as a substance, with consciousness as its essential nature—hence belonging to a distinct ontological category from that of consciousness.) Instead the non-substantialist sees the self as just consciousness itself.

Non-substantialists disagree over just how many selves there are, with the Indian school of Advaita Vedānta famously claiming that there is just one (and that this is the only thing there is). But they agree that the self is something that is just of the nature of consciousness, and that we are mistaken in attributing agency, or any other property that might involve variation, to the self. The self is just 'the witness', or perhaps better, 'a witnessing'.

It is open to such self theorists (as it also is to substantialists) to claim that the self is momentary, coming into existence with each occurrence of cognition in a mental stream and then going out of existence, ordinarily to be replaced by another. But self theorists have largely avoided anything like Galen Strawson's 'pearl self' view, according to which a self lasts only as long as does an individual state of consciousness. This avoidance stems at least in part from widespread agreement that, in addition to serving as the subject of conscious states, a self should also explain various diachronic unities. These unities might include that of a person across different stages in a life (or even across lives), and that involved in agency for projects that unfold over time. But the central unity involved in these discussions is the unity involved in the ability of an experiencer to place the current content of consciousness alongside past and potential future contents in a single stream. It is of course possible for a non-substantialist self theorist to claim that all such diachronic unities can be accounted for without supposing the self to persist. In doing so, however, they would be moving closer to the non-self view.

While the non-self view is hardly unknown in the West (where its best known champions are Hume and Parfit), it has been most extensively explored in the Indian Buddhist tradition. In that context it begins with the common concern that our ordinary sense of self is the source of a certain sort of deep-seated suffering. But rather than say that our mistake lies in identifying with the wrong thing (e.g. the body), or the wrong kind of thing (e.g. a substance), it locates the error in identification as such. Buddhist monastic practice is generally aimed at eradication of all identification or 'appropriation' (*upadāna*). Buddhist philosophical practice contributes to this by attempting to prove that there is no entity that might serve as the referent of 'I', and to explain how the belief that there is such an entity might have arisen. Various strategies are used in different schools, but one common element is an attempt to show that nothing persists in the way that a self would presumably have to. Like Hume, Buddhist philosophers typically point to the fleeting nature of all we find when we carefully observe the inner states of the person. That we should nonetheless believe there to be a persisting subject of those states is explained by the example of the row of ants: what from a distance seems to be a single enduring thing turns out on closer examination to be a large collection of distinct things each of which is replaced by a new member at the next moment. The claim is that the 'I' is posited to explain the felt unity among the inner states, when that feeling of unity can instead be explained by appeal to our cognitive limitations: there seems to us to be a single thing, the row of ants, only when we look from afar.

This kind of approach to defending the non-self view might be criticized in a variety of different ways. One might, for instance, challenge the assumption that the self must persist, or one might argue that wholes such as the row of ants do exist as persisting things even as their parts are replaced. Perhaps more fundamentally, one might ask whether the search for the self should be construed as the search for an entity of any kind. There is an activity that is commonly called 'seeking one's self', and this is not the search for some entity, but for some core set of convictions and other dispositions that gives structure and unity to one's life-plans and projects. In recent discussions of the self, the concept of a narrative self has figured prominently, and that concept may be useful here. The basic idea is that as agents acting in the world in time, we require some scheme for fitting individual affordances into an overall hierarchy that facilitates prioritizing our responses. This is provided when we view our lives as narratives that we are simultaneously living out and making up. By viewing ourselves as both the author and the central character in the story of our lives, we achieve the ability to formulate long-term plans and projects, work out subordinate goals, and thus avoid paralysis each time we are presented with a new opportunity for action. If this is true of us, it would explain why the question of personal identity is so commonly taken not as the question of the necessary and sufficient conditions for diachronic identity of persons, but instead as the *characterization* question: 'Who am I?' understood as a request for an account of core values and commitments. This leads to the question whether the search for the self should not be understood as just the attempt to answer the characterization question. If so then the non-self theory might be readily dismissed on the grounds that it is simply asking the wrong question.

To this challenge, the non-self theorist will respond that to simply acquiesce in the characterization question is to leave untouched its underlying presupposition: that there is an entity that is both the author and the central character in one's life-story. It is this presupposition that requires proper philosophical scrutiny, using the tools of metaphysical inquiry. Is there a core self that might fill the role marked out for it by the characterization question? Indeed, it is not just the non-self view that is threatened by a narrative self-constitution approach to the self. Non-substantialist self theories are as well. While such theories affirm the existence of a self, the self they affirm is just a witness and not an agent, and hence not the sort of thing that could be an author or play its assigned role in a proper narrative. Only substantialist self theories supply the kind of self that could serve to flesh out this presupposition of the narrativity approach. Both non-self theorists and non-substantialist self theorists attack substantialism on precisely this point. In their eyes the narrativity approach reflects commitment to a certain set of values and a certain social structure. The idea is that we learn to see our lives as narratives because this turns out to be an efficient way to promote such goals as rational autonomy and harmonious social interaction. Seen in this light, the notion of the self as author and central character of a narrative begins to look like it might be no more than a useful fiction, something we take to exist only because its posit is required in order to make coherent a certain way of life.

In the Indian context, the upshot of all this is that the debate over the existence and nature of the self was fought out on straightforwardly metaphysical grounds. For instance, both non-self theorists and non-substantialists argued, along familiar lines, that the general concept of a substance as property-bearer is incoherent. And of course substantialists had things to say in reply to such objections. There were, likewise, pitched battles over the problem of the one and the many: does the whole exist over and above its many parts, whether as identical with, or distinct from, those parts? One might wonder whether such debates do not inevitably end in deadlock, so that there is reason to question the assumptions that generate them. The relevant assumption here is that our practice of construing our lives as self-authored narratives requires the existence of a self that might serve as author and the bearer of other properties. Why not simply acquiesce in that practice and put our philosophical tools to work trying to clarify the characterization question? If we are to do metaphysics at all, why not just do descriptive metaphysics, metaphysics that disallows significant revisions in our conception of ourselves and our place in the cosmos? On this construal, the narrativity approach reflects a deep-seated disillusionment with the classical philosophical project. It sees the search for the self understood as an entity as hopelessly confused: given the failure of that search to reach any agreed-upon solution, we should instead think of the self as an ongoing process of self-constitution.

Here is one point where the soteriological/ethical dimension to the Indian debate over the self becomes relevant. The parties to that debate refused to rule out a priori the possibility that our ordinary sense of self might be based on an error. One thing this brings out is the fact that some of the intuitions at work in the debate over the self might derive from unexamined value commitments. In choosing to carry out the debate as a purely metaphysical one, in not acquiescing in the pure narrativity approach, the Indian philosophers expressed the hope that philosophical rationality might enable us to settle the dispute on objective grounds. Perhaps one can justifiably dismiss such hope as naive. But even so it is still important that one be aware that one is doing so, and on precisely what grounds.

There are, then, four general types of answer one might give to the question, what is the self: substantialist, non-substantialist, non-self, and pure narrativity. In the case of the reflexivity thesis things are a little simpler. Either one affirms that in being conscious one is always in some sense aware of being so, or else one denies this. Indeed, if we confine our attention to recent discussions, it might seem as if there is really just the affirmative view, and all the action is in trying to work out how such self-cognizing occurs. The reflexivity thesis has many distinguished proponents in the Western tradition (beginning, according to some, with Aristotle), and although controversial currently enjoys widespread acceptance. This may stem from a certain conception of what makes a mental state a conscious state. If, for instance, one defines consciousness in terms of representation, this seems to let in too much: there are states of an organism that we might say represent its environment for that organism, yet we are reluctant to call such states conscious, since they seem to lack the right sort of interiority or subjectivity, of what-it-is-like-ness. The firing of the right neurons in the frog's fly-detection mechanism could be said to represent to the frog the presence of a fly in its visual field, yet we might be unwilling to say there is something it is like for the frog to see the fly. Hence the attractiveness of high-order theories, according to which conscious states are those mental states that are the objects of higher-order monitoring. What is debated is whether such monitoring is best thought of as perception-like in its directness, or as mediated by thought in some fashion. The difficulty for this approach is that the concept of higher-order monitoring suggests that it is in relation to a distinct state that a given state is a conscious state. This conflicts with the widely held intuition that consciousness is an intrinsic property. If it is also held that all conscious states involve what-it-is-likeness, whatever cognition achieves the awareness of the conscious mental state must be somehow intrinsic to that very state itself. Hence the attraction of self-representation theories, according to which a conscious state is one that represents itself in the right way. (It should be noted that this approach has both higher-order and single-order formulations.) It is of course true that sometimes in states of introspective reflection we take our mental states as objects. (To use the current terminology, an introspective state is 'thetically' aware of its target mental state.) Such introspective reflection might be thought of as involving two distinct mental states, one as target and the other as what achieves the awareness of the target. The claim of the reflexivity thesis is different. It is the claim that every cognition has, as part of its very structure, an at least tacit or non-thetic awareness of itself as cognizing its object. It is this thesis—that consciousness is self-intimating—that is widely accepted in current discussions.

The reflexivity thesis was actively debated in the Indian philosophical tradition. It was generally agreed that we are sometimes aware of our own conscious mental states, for example in introspective reflection. The question was how this is possible. The two possible answers are: by other-illumination, and by self-illumination. The view of other-illumination theorists is that when there is such reflective awareness of a cognition, it is achieved by a distinct monitoring cognition. While any cognition may be cognized, not every cognition actually is: it is only in states of introspective reflection that one is aware of one's conscious states themselves, as opposed to the objects of those states. Self-illumination theorists agree that the typical case of introspective reflection involves two distinct cognitions. But they hold that this sort of explicit (thetic) awareness of one's own cognitions is only possible because every cognition is tacitly or non-thetically conscious of itself in being thetically aware of its object. Cognitions are necessarily reflexively aware.

Various arguments were given in support of each side of this debate. Other–illumination theorists appealed to a widespread anti–reflexivity intuition, to the effect that an entity cannot perform an operation on itself: a knife cannot cut itself, a fingertip cannot touch itself, and even the most skilled acrobat cannot stand on their own shoulders. Self-illumination theorists argued that cognizing a past cognition involves memory, and one cannot remember what one did not experience, so in order to avoid an infinite regress one must suppose that the past cognition was cognizant of itself at the time of its occurrence. The operative metaphor of cognition as illumination itself fed the debate. Self-illumination theorists pointed out that the lamp that illuminates the objects in the room is itself illuminated. Other-illumination theorists responded that it makes no sense to say that light is illuminated: to be the sort of thing that might be illuminated, something must also be such that it can exist in the dark, and light cannot exist in the dark. But the use of the illumination metaphor suggests an answer to a different question: why did this debate take place in the Indian tradition while the issue has not been much discussed in modern Western philosophy? One suggestion is that this has to do with the status of representationalist theories of perception in the two traditions. More specifically, the suggestion is that when representationalist theories of perception come to be widely accepted, they bring with them a view of consciousness that may make the reflexivity thesis appear self-evident.

The conceptual resources available to us to explain just what consciousness is are extremely limited. To be conscious, we may say, is to be aware, to be awake, to cognize, but these are all just near-synonyms. In these circumstances, a widely used metaphor may play an important role in guiding our thought along certain lines. When we think of consciousness in terms of the notions of disclosure or intimation, we may be thinking of it as what brings the outside world within. The metaphor of illumination suggests something different. Illumination is something that takes place outside. When I turn on the light in the room, the illuminated objects stay where they are, apart from me. But now that they are illuminated I can see where they are, and what they are, and can put that information to use. Illumination makes them available to me as items of use. This metaphor would be perfectly acceptable to someone who held a direct realist theory of perception. It would fit in with a conception of perceiving according to which consciousness goes out in the world by way of the sense organs and grasps objects as they themselves are. Of course the metaphor is also acceptable to someone who thinks of perception along representationalist lines: consciousness is then what illuminates the inner theater of the mind, thereby making visible the image of the object that has been fashioned by the sense organs and brought into the theater. While direct realist theories of perception do have their supporters, they do not enjoy the broadest support today; the representationalist picture is thought by many to better cohere with what we now know about perceptual processing and the properties of physical objects that are involved in that processing. But classical Indian philosophers engaged in a spirited debate over direct realism and its rivals (representationalism and subjective idealism). And to a direct realist it is not obvious that all conscious states have a subjective character. For them, to be conscious is just to have a state that represents the object.

If this is right, it will come as no surprise that among the Indian self theorists, it was the substantialists who held the other-illumination view. Substantialists see the self as ontologically distinct from consciousness. If what consciousness does is represent the object, then it may no longer seem mandatory to hold that conscious states have a subjective character. If that to which conscious states represent the object is a self, then given that the self is distinct from those states, it seems possible that the self might be informed about the object without being informed about the state whereby it came to have that information. Of course Descartes was a substantialist, and is widely taken to have held the self-illumination view. But Descartes also held that the self is essentially conscious. This, together with his embrace of a representationalist theory of perception, push him in the direction of the metaphor of intimacy or presencing, whereby one cannot fail to be conscious of what is closest and most immediately present. Other substantialists, by making consciousness a contingent property of the self, leave the door open to holding that the self is only occasionally aware of its cognitive activity (just as it is only occasionally aware of its activity of adjusting the posture of the body).

Non-substantialism quite naturally lines up with the self-illumination view. The case of the non-self view is more complicated. Hume seems to have held the reflexivity thesis (see *Treatise* I.iv.2.37, 137), but most Buddhist schools are other-illuminationist. The exceptions are two schools that affirm

representationalist and subjective idealist accounts of perception respectively.
This could be taken as additional evidence concerning the role of indirect
theories of perception in suggesting a model of consciousness that is supportive
of the reflexivity thesis. More important to our present purposes, however, is
the question how these self-illuminationist non-self theorists distinguish their
view from that of a non-substantialist self-illumination theorist who holds that
the self is momentary. Buddhist self-illuminationists are of course concerned to
maintain the Buddhist orthodoxy that there is no self, but if every occurrence
of consciousness grasps itself in grasping its object, why does that not make
such an occurrence a plausible candidate for the role of referent of 'I'?
Buddhists generally insist that our concept of the self is that of a persisting
entity, but why not suppose that it is this belief, and not the belief in a self, that
is in error? The Buddhist self-illuminationist's answer is interesting. They
claim that the concept of the self is necessarily the concept of a subject of
experience. But, they maintain, the distinction between subject and object
of experience, while necessary for thought, is nonetheless a conceptual
superimposition that distorts the nature of reality. When it is correct to say
'It is raining', it would be a mistake to suppose that the state of affairs that
makes this sentence true includes an agent that performs the activity of
raining. The 'it', we say, is supplied just to meet the demands of syntax. In
reality there is just the single event of raining, which our grammar then
represents in terms of a two-component model. The claim is that the
demand for a distinct subject and object in experience is similar. If this is
right, then it is the non-substantialist theory that collapses into the non-self
view, and not the other way around.

   Indian theorists were careful to keep separate the questions how cognition is cognized and how the self is known to exist. While Descartes'
Second Meditation would have it that in thetic awareness of our own
awareness we are directly acquainted with the self, other views are possible.
A substantialist might hold that, in general, in perceiving a quality of a
substance one perceives that substance, or they might instead hold that, at
least in certain cases, some further cognitive operation is required in order to
cognize the substance that bears that quality. So a self-illuminationist substantialist could hold that, while we are always directly aware of our cognitions, the self is cognized only through introspection, or by inference or
abduction. Similar complexities attend the non-self view: one might, for
instance, hold that a cognition cognizes itself, yet still insist that further

inquiry is needed to ascertain that the occurrence of cognition is not evidence for the existence of a self. Only in the case of self-illuminationist non-substantialism does there seem to be a particularly tight connection between the answers to the two questions. If one takes the self to be nothing but cognition, then one will naturally think of reflexive awareness as cognition of the self. But since reflexive awareness could not by itself tell us whether the cognition being cognized endures, if the self is thought to be persisting, then once again additional evidence is needed to make the identification go through. The *cogito* was not, for instance, unknown to Indian philosophers. But unlike Descartes, Indian self-theorists did not take it to make their case for them. Their suspicions concerning the ubiquitous I-sense held them back.

One way of trying to circumvent some of these difficulties might be to shift from the straightforwardly metaphysical question of the self's existence and nature to the epistemological question of how one comes to have knowledge of oneself and one's states. There has been much recent discussion of the phenomenon commonly called immunity from error through misidentification. We are of course prone to all sorts of errors in our self-ascriptions. I may, for instance, think of myself as kind and gentle when in fact I'm a miserable wretch. Carefully constructed experiments demonstrate that it is even possible, at least in laboratory settings, to induce mistakes about how one is moving one's own hand. It is claimed, however, that one cannot be mistaken in attributing a given conscious state to oneself. If I have the feeling as of its being cold in the room, then I cannot be mistaken as to whether this is how I represent the room as being. If the reflexivity thesis is true, this might go some way toward accounting for such immunity from error. To say of a cognition that it is self-intimating would seem to be to say precisely that its presentation of its content is something about which there could be no mistake. If this guarantee could then be extended to also cover the sense that the current presenting is in some way unified with other presentings, the way might be open to justifying some sort of self theory, while avoiding the murky metaphysical depths. This approach will meet resistance, though, from those who reject the claim that phenomenal character is the hallmark of consciousness. For those who do not already accept the notion that there is necessarily something it is like to be in a conscious state, the so-called immunity from error will be no more informative than the sign that announces 'You are here', unaccompanied by a map or any other source of information about one's location. And, it will be claimed, if the reflexivity thesis is uninformative it can do no work in settling the dispute over the existence and nature of the self.

At this point we can glimpse the convergence of several lines of support for a pure narrativity approach, one that eschews recourse to strictly metaphysical considerations in defending a self. One line of support derives from the sense that the metaphysical approach leads nowhere: such questions as whether the whole exists over and above the parts—so that a self might be the emergent product of a dynamically interactive aggregate—appear to be irresolvable. This might be taken to suggest that some other approach is necessary. Another line of support stems from the fact that the notion of a narrative self seems to capture much that is important in the sense of self most people possess. In particular, it brings to the fore the link between self and well-being: living well is thought to require that one's life be seen as having a trajectory, a narrative arc. Metaphysical approaches, even those that affirm a self, can at best be only half-hearted in their defense of this requirement; often they are downright dismissive, calling the narrative self a mere useful fiction. Yet another line of support derives from the fact that the reflexivity thesis, with its affirmation of interiority, makes possible the sort of rich inner life at the heart of the narrativity approach. The thought here is that even if the reflexivity thesis fails to deliver convincing evidence that the self exists, it does secure an inner dimension to human existence, and with it the possibility of richly meaningful lives. The convergence of these lines of support does not constitute a proof that the narrative approach is the right one to pursue. But it may give us a better sense of what a total package might look like at this end of the continuum. And this may in turn clarify what lies at the other end, as well as what the range of intermediary positions could look like.

The papers in this volume reflect a variety of stances on this fundamental question of whether the metaphysical approach is a viable one for philosophy, or one that should be replaced by the (more modest?) project of working from within human experiential reality and trying to limn its structures. Each takes up a position in the continuum of possible views and combinations of views. The first essay in this collection, by Joel Krueger, argues in favor of a non-self theory that accepts the reflexivity thesis. The argument begins with a survey of rival views that will serve as a useful introduction to themes explored by many other papers in this volume. To be rejected, Krueger claims, are views that deny the reflexivity thesis, since these are unable to account adequately for the phenomenal character of consciousness. But this leaves in place a variety of rival views, all charging that subjectivity requires a subject—that there must be a self for which things seem a certain way—and thus that a non-self theory is to be rejected. Krueger chooses the egological view of Dan Zahavi as his chief target. Krueger uses an investigation of the notion of narrative selfhood to show how one might plausibly arrive at Zahavi's idea of the minimal self as the form of self-theory that is best supported by careful consideration of phenomenality. Narrative approaches, Krueger argues, can answer the characterization question, but not the identity question; they cannot supply the sort of self that seems required if we are to at all explain our ability to look for a story in our lives. What the careful consideration of phenomenal character can support is a minimal self, the subject whose existence is allegedly disclosed in and through the reflexive nature of consciousness. The difficulty is that if we are to avoid going beyond the evidence of that disclosure, we could at best say that in each of my experiences I am aware of a self; to call them all my self is to go beyond the evidence by identifying each as part of a persisting stream. Krueger suggests, in other words, that the evidence of phenomenal character could only support a non-substantialist view, and that such a view lacks the resources to establish the needed permanence and stability that would keep it from collapsing into a non-self position.

The problem for the self-theorist might be put as one of supplying a self that is both transcendent and contentful. Substantialist views are good at supplying the transcendence. Substances as property-possessors necessarily transcend their properties. They thereby make it possible to understand diachronic identity over change in those properties. The problem with seeing the self as a substance comes when we try to specify the evidence for diachronic identity. The appeal of narrativity approaches stems in large part from the fact that they suggest where to look for an answer: the owner of the present experience is the same substance as the owner of those past experiences because these characteristics are related in the right way to those characteristics. The difficulty lies in saying how any relation between the characteristics had by one thing at one time and those of another thing at another time could establish that the two things are identical. Krueger's objection to Zahavi's minimal self theory is that in trying to avoid the well-known difficulties that attend the transcendence of the substantialist view, it loses its grip on identity.

Dan Zahavi's paper is his response to this sort of challenge, one that has been leveled by a number of critics. What he calls the experiential core self is, he claims, something of which one is immediately aware in the self-givenness that characterizes all conscious states. His fundamental challenge to his critics is to explain how there could be subjectivity without a subject. His specific interlocutors in this essay are Miri Albahari and Georges Dreyfus. Both share Zahavi's endorsement of the reflexivity thesis, but reject his notion of an experiential or core self, albeit on slightly different grounds. For Albahari, Zahavi's core self is too thin to count as a self, since it lacks the crucial features of being unconstructed but bounded: of being something that can serve as author of narrative constructions, and that accounts for one's sense of distinctness from other persons. Zahavi responds that what is actually disclosed in experience is not something existing distinct from all experiential content, but instead just a uniform structure that is common to all my experiences: their being given as *mine*. To disqualify this as a self is to impose the demand that a self be something that transcends all experience; it overlooks the possibility that the self might actually be given in experience, just not in the way in which the object is given. He also points out that Albahari's own view, which she calls a non-self view, actually looks rather like the sort of non-substantialist self theory that affirms an enduring witness consciousness. And he wonders how a non-self theorist could maintain that while the self does not exist, it appears to the uninformed as though it does: how can things seem a certain way without there being someone for whom they so seem?

While Albahari could say that her witness consciousness allows her to answer this question, Dreyfus might be somewhat more hard pressed, since his credentials as a non-self theorist seem unimpeachable. If he agrees that phenomenal character is inextricably bound up with the self-givenness of consciousness, how can he refuse the label 'self' to this feature of subjectivity? Dreyfus might respond that the reflexivity that characterizes all conscious-ness only pertains to individual conscious states, which are impermanent. Zahavi has several replies. First, phenomenological investigation discloses a temporal dimension to individual conscious states, so that present-moment awareness inevitably involves awareness of past and future. Second, the concept of the self is multifaceted and multidimensional, and the concept of the core self is meant to capture just one key aspect. His warnings against trying to impose a univocal definition of self suggest that he shares some of the narrativity approach's impatience with the demands of the metaphysician.

In her contribution to this volume, Miri Albahari describes her position as a non-self theory that affirms the reflexivity thesis. But, given its affinities with the Advaita Vedānta position, it is not entirely clear whether her view might not better be thought of as a kind of non-substantialist self theory. She is, in any event, quite explicit in her rejection of any bundle-theoretic version of non-self. Bundle theorists maintain that our sense of self is illusory insofar as it represents as a unified entity what is, in fact, merely a bundle of discrete things. Bundle theorists thus maintain that the self that we routinely take ourselves to be is constructed out of elements found in experience, yet would also have to exist prior to such construction, and hence is non-existent. Albahari agrees that our ordinary sense of self is illusory, and she shares with the bundle theorist the need to explain how we could come to have such a sense if it is in important respects erroneous. But she denies that the bundle theorist's approach could succeed in showing both that the self is constructed and that it is illusory. She distinguishes between two forms of bundle-theoretical non-self view: the non-reflexive variety, that denies the reflexivity thesis, and the reflexive variety that affirms that thesis. The argument against both presupposes that the illusion of the self could be dissolved through direct introspection, without reliance on philosophical argument or any other form of inference. Given this stricture, the bundle theorist must hold it possible to directly confirm in one's experience that the self is constructed, namely by apprehending the impermanence of the cognitions that on their view constitute the bundle. Albahari's claim is that, regardless of whether or not one takes consciousness to be reflexive, this turns out to be impossible: no cognition could decisively undermine the sense that, while the present cognition differs from other cognitions in its intentional object, it does not differ in terms of perspectival ownership—that there is a mere witnessing that is common to all my experiential states.

This sketch raises the question how Albahari's view differs from Zahavi's. Zahavi, it will be recalled, affirms the existence of a minimal or experiential core self. Albahari positions herself on the side of non-self theories. Yet both see in the self-givenness of consciousness important evidence for an enduring perspectival owner of conscious states. The difference lies in what they take 'self' to mean. While Zahavi rejects any attempt at giving a univocal definition of a concept that he takes to be multifaceted and multidimensional, Albahari claims to give an analysis of the self that we ordinarily take ourselves to be. Since Zahavi's experiential self lacks many of the features revealed by that analysis, she considers it too thin to count as a self. The witness consciousness that is revealed in the self-givenness of perspectival ownership lacks the crucial feature of boundedness, and thus cannot play the role of core self for the narrativity project. It is just a witnessing, and thus cannot ground the sense of agency and separateness at the heart of the ordinary conception of the 'I'. This is the reality that underlies the illusion of the self but is not to be thought of as a self. This move allows Albahari to avoid the difficulties that attend any version of bundle theory, while apparently also escaping troubling questions about a permanent self's relation to changing empirical content. In this as well, her approach resembles that of Advaita Vedānta; the interested reader would do well to consult the papers on this topic by Fasching and Ram-Prasad. The question one might pose for Albahari is whether she is willing to pay the price that Advaita accepts for an enduring witness: that all diversity in content (or for that matter anything else) turns out to be illusory.

The paper by Georges Dreyfus takes up the problem of defending from a Buddhist perspective the claim that consciousness is reflexive but ownerless—that there is subjectivity but no subject. As Dreyfus makes clear, not all Buddhist non-self theorists accept the reflexivity thesis. But the non-self thesis is sometimes taken to mean that persons are utterly lacking in interiority or subjectivity, and Dreyfus is concerned to make clear that this is not true for at least one part of the Buddhist tradition, namely the school that affirms the reflexivity thesis. A self-theorist like Zahavi will then want to know how one can affirm a dimension of subjectivity while denying that there is a self that serves as subject of experiential states. Dreyfus' response resembles that of Albahari. The self at issue for Buddhists is one that ordinary people have a sense of being, hence something that might be at least intimated in ordinary experience: the self whose existence Buddhists reject is thus not a purely structural requirement.

Like Albahari as well, Dreyfus locates the core of the illusion of self in the presence in each conscious moment of reflexive awareness. Dreyfus,

though, would not be willing to call this 'witness consciousness', since for
the view he defends, the distinction between the content of a cognition and
a cognition's grasping of that content is a mere conceptual superimposition.
This move would allow Dreyfus to answer Albahari's basic objection to all
forms of bundle theory: that they cannot solve the binding problem and
thus account for the felt sense of diachronic unity in our experience. The
view Dreyfus defends is a kind of bundle theory, since it claims that while a
certain basic form of consciousness is present at each moment in the life of a
person, the basic consciousness is constantly renewed. The appeal to the
ultimate non-duality of consciousness and content is not, though, the
answer Dreyfus actually gives to the question how we are to know that
the reflexive awareness occurring in any one cognition is not identical with
the reflexive awareness occurring at other times in the same mental stream
(and thus something distinct from the content of any particular cognition).
To give that answer he would have to reject a doctrine he embraces, that in
certain meditative states there occurs consciousness that is devoid of all
content and merely discloses itself. To the extent that this is taken to be a
'purified' form of consciousness, the implication is that there are no grounds
on the basis of which one might distinguish between the consciousness
occurring at any one moment and that occurring at other moments. One
would then be back to Albahari's enduring witness consciousness. What this
difficulty might suggest is that it is not as easy as one might hope to settle the
issues at play here through appeal to the data of experience alone. Dreyfus
claims that he is doing phenomenology without ontology, but it is not clear
that the view he favors can be defended without appeal to the sorts of
mereological considerations that non-self theorists of a more metaphysical
stamp typically bring up. For a rather different take on the same part of the
Buddhist tradition that Dreyfus explores, the interested reader will want to
look at the contribution by Jonardon Ganeri.

The contribution of Evan Thompson seeks to show that the proper
defense of the reflexivity thesis poses difficulties for those who hold a strict
form of non-self theory. He begins by examining the memory argument for
self-illumination, which concludes that all cognitions are reflexively aware,
on the grounds that since one does not remember what one did not
experience, one could not remember a past experience unless at the time
one had the experience one was aware not only of its object but also of the
experiencing of the object. The argument has often been criticized as

question-begging, but Thompson responds to these critics by formulating it in such a way that a key premise is grounded in purely phenomenological considerations. The claim is that episodic memory has a phenomenal structure that is best represented as the immediate awareness, not of the past object but of the object as object of a past experiencing. This is then said to be best explained by the reflexivity thesis. One might wonder whether this formulation of the memory argument captures what those Buddhists who accept self-illumination had in mind, but here Thompson is more interested in the truth about subjectivity than in historical-philological questions.

Thompson then explores how this reading of the memory argument would affect the dispute between self theorists like Zahavi and those non-self theorists who accept the reflexivity thesis. His conclusion is that because episodic memory presents the past experience as something lived through by me, a self-illumination theorist cannot defend non-self simply on the grounds that the subjectivity revealed in an individual cognition is not thereby revealed to be something that endures. If the grounds for affirming the reflexivity thesis are those given in the memory argument, and that argument is best construed phenomenologically, then considerable pressure will be put on the non-self theorist to grant the force of evidence that is often construed as revealing an enduring 'I'. Thompson hastens to add that this need not be seen as the total defeat of the non-self view, since the revised memory argument does not establish the existence of a separately existing self. Given the ethical concerns that motivate most formulations of non-self view, however, it is not clear that this will be at all consoling. Their project has typically been to show that our sense of an 'I' that endures rests on a mistake, but if we must take the phenomenological account of episodic memory at face value, it becomes more difficult for them to claim (as they generally do) that our intuitions in these matters are not to be trusted. They would then be in a position similar to that of the bundle theorist who also accepts Albahari's stricture that a self-illusion must be dissolvable through direct introspection: they would be constrained to accept a body of evidence that they would prefer to reject on philosophical grounds. But for additional discussion of the sort of view Thompson defends, the interested reader will want to consult the paper by Matt MacKenzie.

Jonardon Ganeri's paper for this volume takes up the views of the same school of Buddhist philosophy (Yogācāra) that figured in Georges Dreyfus' essay. Ganeri, though, looks at the earliest phase in the development of Yogācāra philosophy, specifically at the initial formulation of the idea that there is a distinctive form of consciousness involved in the fabrication of a self. (The views that Dreyfus develops come largely from later Tibetan sources.) Already in this phase, Ganeri claims, there was recognition that consciousness is pre-reflectively, reflexively aware. This then became the basis for a new account of the source of false belief in a self, one that Ganeri sets out to reconstruct and evaluate. The puzzle revolves around the fact that, while reflexivity means one is always in some sense aware of being in the mental state one is in at the time, the non-self theorist claims it is a mistake to go on to assert that one is in that state. A self theorist denies that there is a mistake here: to say 'I am seeing blue' is just to articulate the self-awareness that is implicit in every experience. Ganeri begins by raising an issue for Zahavi's defense of the self: what Zahavi calls the core or experiential self fails to individuate thinkers, insofar as the *ipseity* present in any given stream at any particular moment is qualitatively identical with that in any other stream. But that would still leave us without a reason to think there is a mistake involved in this transition.

Instead of pursuing this question through phenomenological investigation, Ganeri chooses to examine our use of the first-person pronoun 'I'. This methodological choice has strong precedent in the Buddhist tradition, which early on claimed that belief in a self stemmed from a mistaken semantic theory. The question is whether such an approach will serve the interests of the non-self theorist once reflexivity has been acknowledged. Now, as Ganeri points out, when Buddhist non-self theorists claim that the seemingly referring expression 'I' actually fails to refer, further metaphysical argument is then required to sustain the denial of a referent. What Ganeri wonders is whether this route can be avoided just by questioning the assumption that 'I' is in the referring line of work at all. The key to doing this lies in the so-called immunity to error through misidentification that first-person reports generally share. While this is often taken to reflect a certain sort of privileged access that the self has to its own states, Ganeri sees clues in the work of Wittgenstein, Anscombe and Candrakīrti that such immunity might instead signal that 'I' is not being used to refer at all. The question can be asked whether pursuit of this strategy will lead in the end to the denial of subjectivity.

The paper by Wolfgang Fasching that is included here claims that there is much we can learn about the Advaita Vedānta view of the self if we approach it from a phenomenological perspective. His paper begins with a brief discussion of the soteriological concerns common to Advaita and Buddhism, and explores how these concerns lead to a common rejection of any substantialist self-theory. This leaves the alternatives of non-self and non-substantialism. Fasching claims that the non-self view must embrace the self-illumination theory in order to give a phenomenologically adequate account of subjectivity. By adopting the strategy of impermanence the non-self theorist tries to keep the adoption of self-illumination theory from leading to the countenancing of a subject: a self-illuminating cognition is not a self because it does not endure. Fasching thinks this strategy must fail, since it does not acknowledge an all-important aspect of all cognitions: that they include the sense of being experienced by *me*. That this witnessing endures can be argued for on the basis of the diachronic unity of appercep-tion. But Fasching is cognizant of the danger for a non-substantialist in such an appeal—that it suggests the self is a separately existing entity. He believes that the Advaitin can avoid this trap by refusing to separate the presencing that is the mode of being of each experience and the content of the experience. He takes this to be the point of the Advaitin insistence that the self is neither an object of experience nor the subject of experience, but somehow transcends both. Careful phenomenological investigation of the mode of givenness of experience can, he thinks, help us make sense of this. What this leaves unanswered, however, is why we should not distinguish between the presencing that is constitutive of the currently occurring experience, and the presencing that was constitutive of a past experience, given that the two experiences have different contents. The Buddhist self-illuminationist will appeal to this difference in content in deploying their impermanence strategy. It is at this point that Advaitins have typically invoked their claim that all difference is illusory, that ultimately there is only the one Self that is not to be distinguished from pure Being (Brahman). It is recourse to this radical non-dualism (*a-dvaita-vāda*) that they have relied on to answer the charge that a non-substantial witnessing must be just as variable as its contents, and so must be impermanent. Fasching wishes to avoid what to many has seemed like a desperate metaphysics, and so confines his account to the phenomenology that he takes to underlie the Advaita position. The question that might be asked, however, is how one is to prevent a metaphysical stand-off over the status of the mental stream. The non-self theorist holds that the stream is conceptually constructed out of individual consciousness-events; the non-substantialist holds it to be a single enduring thing. The soteriological concerns that motivated the Indian debate suggest that an answer is required.

Chakravarthi Ram-Prasad, in his paper for this volume, takes this Advaitin bull by its (non-dual) horn: he makes explicit the role of non-dualism in Advaita's account of the self as pure luminosity. He starts with a discussion of the rejection of a substantial self that is common to Buddhism and Advaita. In this they are united in their opposition to those who wish to salvage as much as possible of the common-sense view that the first-person pronoun 'I' refers to the self. Where they part company is over the correct analysis of 'I'. Buddhist non-self theorists typically claim that 'I' is just a useful way to refer to a large collection of suitably arranged psychophysical elements, none of which is a self; on this analysis our mistake lies in taking there to be one thing when there are really only the many. Advaitins, instead, think our mistake lies in taking there to be a many when strictly speaking there is just the one. This is what lies behind their insistence that 'I' does not refer to the self. Their self, as pure luminosity or presencing, is real but does not individuate, whereas 'I' must individuate. On this view, 'I' refers to the organ involved in the presentation to consciousness of the object. The common error of taking it to refer to the self is explicable, given its close association with the self and the apparent utility of such identification. But if the self is of the nature of consciousness, and is for that reason not to be construed as a substance, then it can be neither object nor subject, in which case individuation is always an error. This yields a ready answer to the question of self-luminous consciousness' identity over time: if diversity of content is mere appearance, then the impermanence of consciousness may be safely ruled out. But this will probably be of little comfort to most non-substantialists, who think of the self as inherently perspectival in nature.

Matt MacKenzie claims, in his paper, that the self might be described (putting it in Buddhist terms) as 'dependently originated and empty, but nevertheless real'. To say of something that it is empty is to say that it lacks intrinsic nature, a thing's intrinsic nature being the way that it is, independently of how other things are. To say of something that it is dependently originated is to say that it arises in dependence on causes and conditions. For most Buddhists, anything that lacks intrinsic nature is not ultimately real: if all a thing's properties are relational, if it has a determinate nature only through its relations to other things, then it must be conceptually

constructed. Some Buddhists also claim that anything dependently originated is empty. All Buddhists would agree that the self is dependently
originated and empty. The surprise comes in the claim that the self is real
all the same. The question is how something that is conceptually constructed could nonetheless be real.

For MacKenzie the answer lies in a form of emergentism. He claims that
the behavior of certain sorts of dynamic processes eludes reductive explanation, in that the behavior of the system as a whole cannot be accounted for
just in terms of facts about its constituents. The person is just such a system,
with the first-person perspective and phenomenality one characteristic
result of this emergent process. The idea seems to be that when psycho-
physical elements are organized in the right way, their interaction results in a
sense of mine-ness without which episodic memory is inexplicable, so that a
minimal core self must be acknowledged as real, despite its being wholly
constituted by completely impersonal entities. Emergentisms are a common
response to the sorts of difficulties one encounters when complex systems
resist reductive causal explanation. But the general strategy has its problems
as well. One difficulty lies in explaining the relation between the system and
its constituents in such a way as to avoid the absolute idealist conclusion that
the only real is the one grand system. Another problem is that it can be
difficult to say when we are entitled to conclude that the behavior of a
complex system will forever resist reductive causal explanation. Perhaps the
key question to ask here, however, is how the ethical concerns behind the
Buddhist non-self project can be reconciled with the claim that an emergent
self is empty but real.

Galen Strawson's views on the self are well known. In his paper for this
volume, he extends those views to the question whether the self is aware of
itself. Like most other contributors, he accepts the reflexivity thesis. And
since his self is just the 'thin subject' or present-moment cognizing, it
follows from the reflexivity thesis that the self is aware of itself. But the
awareness being attributed here is non-thetic. What Strawson is interested
in challenging is the almost universally accepted claim that the self cannot be
present-moment directly and thetically aware of itself. A substantialist who
accepts the reflexivity thesis, but thinks of cognition as a mode of the self,
could say that in reflective consciousness the self is thetically aware of itself.
But this thetic awareness would not be direct, going as it does through
direct awareness of the cognition to indirect awareness of the self as subject

of the cognition. Strawson's subject is the cognition itself. Yet he claims that in certain meditative states there is fully thetic awareness of the cognizing subject. Is it after all possible that the fingertip can touch itself?

Strawson answers the last question in the negative, but he takes the case of self-awareness to be different. This may be because he takes the distinction between subject and object of cognition to be a conceptual superimposition on something intrinsically non-dual. If so, he then faces the same challenge that confronts the Buddhist non-self self-illumination theorist who takes this tack: resolving the paradox of inexpressibility that results when one claims that the true non-dual nature of cognition is inexpressible. If, on the other hand, he wants to join Dreyfus in rejecting the claim that cognition is non-dual, on the grounds that objectless cognition is possible, then like Dreyfus he will need some way of answering Albahari's charge that his subject is just her enduring witness and not anything transitory at all.

Our last paper, by Mark Siderits, is the only one to explore the option of rejecting the reflexivity thesis. He begins with the standard Buddhist formulation of non-self, and considers the objection that a reductionist strategy can show that some putative entity is not ultimately real only if there is that to which it might appear that the entity is real. On this objection, any attempt to show that the self just consists in purely impersonal entities must be self-defeating, in that it requires that there be that to which it appears that the self is real. Self-illumination theory is one way in which non-self theorists have attempted to answer this objection. Siderits claims, though, that the arguments for the reflexivity thesis are not sufficiently compelling to overcome its strongly counter-intuitive character, so that it might be worth exploring what the alternative is for the non-self theorist. Since none of the many Buddhist schools that were other-illuminationist developed detailed accounts of how cognition might be cognized, the answer Siderits develops is speculative, based as it is on the views of non-Buddhist Indian other-illuminationists. The resulting theory has it that cognitions are never directly cognized, and are cognized only through an abductive inference from the global availability—availability to such systems as the faculties of speech, memory, and action-guidance—of information about the object. Since it then follows that mental states have the property of being conscious only extrinsically, through their relations to other states, consciousness itself turns out to be reducible: cognitions are not among the ultimate constituents of which persons are composed.

This strategy would certainly answer the objection. If its seeming to us as if we are conscious is just a useful way for a certain sort of information-processing system to manage the flow of information, then there need not be a self to explain the fact that the system self-represents. Consistent application of reductionist metaphysics would preserve the ethical aims behind the non-self view. The question that must be asked here, though, is whether this is not, as with Advaita, a desperate metaphysics. At the end of his paper, Siderits explores the image of fully enlightened beings that one finds in some Buddhist devotional literature. These beings are depicted as so skilled at exercising compassion that they act in the world on full auto-pilot, never actually cognizing the beings they help. When this image is read in the light of a reductive approach to consciousness, the suggestion would be that the soteriological aim behind non-self is to overcome the illusion that we are not zombies. To say that most readers will find this implausible is probably not an overstatement.

1

The Who and the How
of Experience

JOEL W. KRUEGER

1. Introduction

Does consciousness require a self?[1] In what follows, I argue that it does not.
I concede at the outset that this is a counterintuitive thesis. For, a central
feature of conscious states is that their mode of appearance (i.e. how they are
given) exhibits an irreducibly first-personal nature. My experiences are
distinctly my own, given to me and only me. This first-personal 'how' of
consciousness is what secures its phenomenal character. And it seems natural
to assume that this how points back to a 'who': a stable, enduring, conscious
subject at the receiving end of phenomenal states. But is the assumption that
a how requires a who warranted? I will argue below that, just because the
subjective character of consciousness gives rise to a *sense* of self—that is, the
felt sense of being a stable who, or owner of conscious episodes—it does not
follow that this who really exists in any autonomous or enduring sense.

First, I do some background work, briefly discussing the phenomenological notion of the 'minimal self' before then looking at a Buddhist conception of selfless subjectivity. Next, I examine the minimal self more carefully,
along with what is sometimes termed the 'narrative self', and argue for the
experiential primacy of the former. I then argue that the phenomenal
character of consciousness, which the minimal self-model is supposed to

[1] I am grateful for conversations with the participants of the 'Self-No-Self' workshop in Copenhagen, Denmark, April 15–16, 2009, which greatly assisted my thinking about the issues discussed in this
paper. I am also especially grateful to Mark Siderits for his critical comments on an earlier version of this
paper, as well as the very helpful comments from two anonymous reviewers.

capture, does not require the existence of a stable, permanent, or unconditioned self (or 'who'). At best, minimal self theorists (e.g. Zahavi 2005), who
look to identify the self with the phenomenal character of consciousness,
ought to speak instead of transient minimal phenomenal *selves*. An enduring
who is thus neither necessary nor sufficient for a how.

2. Preliminaries: The Philosophical Importance of the Minimal Self

Why focus on the minimal self? There are three reasons. First, as developed
(often implicitly) in phenomenologists such as Husserl, Sartre, and Merleau-
Ponty—and given robust articulation in the work of neo-phenomenologists
such as Shaun Gallagher and Dan Zahavi—the notion has direct bearing on
how we understand the very nature of consciousness *qua* consciousness:
namely, the phenomenal or subjective character of conscious experience.
The phenomenal character of experience refers to the 'what it's like' quality
of different conscious episodes that gives them their particular phenomenology: for example, what it's like to sip a single malt Scotch, view a vivid
yellow tulip, blush at the memory of a youthful indiscretion, or feel the
smoothness of an oak table. The phenomenological notion of the minimal
self, and the particular structural analysis of consciousness that the minimal
self is a crucial part of (discussed below), are thus concerned with laying bare
the defining feature of consciousness.

The second reason to focus on the minimal self in this context is that,
according to its defenders, it links intimately, not just to the ontology of
consciousness, but to the most basic form of self-experience: the experience
of being a *subject* of conscious states, a *thinker* of thoughts, a *feeler* of feelings,
an *initiator* of actions, etc. In other words, the minimal self captures the
feeling of phenomenal interiority that is perhaps the central aspect of
selfhood—the feeling that I, and only I, have this particular first-hand
mode of access to the goings-on in my head at this very moment.[2] The

---

[2] As Galen Strawson notes, the realization that one enjoys privileged access to one's interiority 'comes
to every normal human being, in some form, in childhood. The early realization of the fact that one's
thoughts are unobservable by others, the experience of the profound sense in which one is alone in one's
head—these are among the very deepest facts about the character of human life' (Strawson 1999a: 2). But
developmentally speaking, the experience of phenomenal interiority is probably even more basic than

minimal self looks to offer a characterization of this primitive form of phenomenal self-acquaintance.

The third reason for focusing on the minimal self is that, due to its subtlety and ubiquity—it is claimed to be an invariant structural feature of consciousness, meaning that every conscious entity is, or has, a minimal self—it is potentially an especially difficult self for Buddhism to get rid of. Philosophical discussions of the minimal self offer a subtle brand of realism about the self. Due to its place within a defensible characterization of phenomenal consciousness, the phenomenological notion of the minimal self presents a unique challenge to the Buddhist deflationary project of denying the ultimate reality of the self. Moreover, since Buddhist philosophy is deeply preoccupied with questions about the nature of self and subjectivity, the notion of the minimal self resonates organically with Buddhist philosophical concerns. It offers a fruitful point of contact for thinkers working from within the tradition of Western phenomenology and philosophy of mind to engage with Buddhist philosophy. Now, having clarified the reasons for focusing on the minimal self in this context, I want to examine next the notions of subjectivity and no-self as developed in Buddhist philosophy.

3. Self, Subjectivity, and No-Self in Buddhist Philosophy

Buddhism famously denies the existence of a fixed, permanent, or enduring self.[3] According to the Buddhist tradition, both physical and mental phenomena arise, exist, and pass away within a vast, interrelated network of causes and conditions. This continual process of arising, existing, and passing away is the process of dependent origination (*pratītya-samutpāda*), one of the core notions of Buddhist thought. Buddhism argues further that

---

Strawson concedes. Research on neonate imitation (discussed in more detail in section 4) suggests that newborn infants have an immediate sense of their own interiority, and there are reasons to attribute this primitive self-awareness to some nonhuman animals. One thus needn't possess the concept of interiority (which is generally thought to be an aspect of possessing a 'theory of mind') to have the experiential sense of one's interiority, of being the sort of thing (i.e. a self) with an inner experiential dimension unique to oneself.

³ I am indebted to both Georges Dreyfus (1997) and Matt Mackenzie (2008) for the discussion in this section.

all entities, events, and processes have no substantial reality outside of this dynamic matrix of dependent origination. So, things like chariots, pots, and persons are ultimately empty (*śūnya*) of fixed or intrinsic nature (*svabhāva*).[4] Since the psychophysical complex of the person (or self) is subject to the same causes and conditions as everything else, it, too, is ultimately empty of intrinsic nature. This is the other core doctrine of no-self (*anātman*), the most well-known and controversial aspect of Buddhist thought. What is perhaps less well known, however, is that some Buddhist thinkers argue that the denial of the self does not necessarily go hand-in-hand with a denial of subjectivity. These thinkers offer a model of consciousness that preserves its phenomenal character while nevertheless denying that the phenomenal character of consciousness is dependent upon the existence of a fixed, enduring, or unconditioned subject. This is not the place to survey the vast Buddhist literature on this topic. Instead, we can focus on two specific forms of self-awareness discussed in the literature, one broad and one narrow, and look at how they relate to an analysis of (no-)self and phenomenal consciousness.

The first of these notions is the broader form of self-awareness captured by the term *ahaṃkāra*, which denotes 'I-maker' awareness, the sense of oneself as a single entity enduring throughout time. This is the sense of being an autonomous self, distinct from the flux and flow of ever-changing experiences. Additionally, the term also captures the egocentric structure of human existence—our tendency to act and make decisions which reflect our own self-interests (Mackenzie 2008: 247). The term *svasaṃvedana*, on the other hand, is a narrower form of self-awareness. It refers to the immediate acquaintance we have with both the *content* of our conscious states (i.e. the intentional object that an experience is an experience of, such as a perception of a tree, a memory of a childhood experience, or the image of a unicorn), as well as the *character* of our conscious states (i.e. the first-person phenomenal mode of access to the intentional content, such as the act of perceiving a tree, remembering a childhood experience, or imagining a unicorn). Put differently, *svasaṃvedana* refers to the 'self-illuminating' (*svaprakāśa*) character of conscious states. When I have an experience of, for example, the sound of a car roaring by on the street

---

[4] A central debate within Buddhist philosophy concerns whether all things are empty of intrinsic nature, or whether there are some things (e.g. *dharmas*, or momentary, individual atoms or tropes) which have intrinsic nature. See Siderits (2007) for a clear introduction to this debate (and others) within the Buddhist philosophical tradition.

outside, I am simultaneously aware, in that single experience, of both the
object-as-given (i.e. the sound of the car roaring by) as well as *my experience of the
object-as-given* (i.e. the auditory experience of the car roaring by as *my* auditory
experience). Every consciousness episode thus has a dual-aspect, Janus-faced
structure. It involves, at the same time, a world-directed objective aspect
(*grāhyākāra*) as well as an implicit,[5] self-reflexive subjective aspect (*grāhakākāra*)
(Dreyfus 1997: 345–53). But these two forms of self-awareness, *ahaṃkāra* and
svasaṃvedana, are connected (i.e. they dependently condition one another), in
that '*svasaṃvedana* yields mental states with at least implicit first-person contents—e.g. "I am aware of a cup", "I am in pain", etc.—which reinforces the
ahaṃkāra' (Mackenzie 2008: 247). Yet *svasaṃvedana* is the more phenomenologically primitive feature of experience. It can be present without necessarily
invoking *ahaṃkāra*. However, the converse is not the case.

The seventh-century Indian Buddhist thinker Dharmakīrti makes much
of this distinction in developing his reflexivist view of self-awareness.[6]
Dharmakīrti claims that, 'If cognition were not itself perceived, perception
of an object is never possible' (quoted in Mokṣākaragupta 1985: 51). Consciousness must thus be immanently self-reflexive, Dharmakīrti insists, since
without the simultaneous awareness that one is aware, a given conscious state
can't rightly be called *conscious*, as opposed to an unconscious state or subpersonal process. According to Dharmakīrti, a phenomenally conscious state
is a state that the subject is aware of. So, unless mental state M is in some sense
self-conscious, there is nothing that it is like to be in M, and M is thus not a
phenomenally conscious state. Dharmakīrti argues that, therefore, self-
awareness is a necessary feature of consciousness: it is a constitutive feature
of its phenomenal character as conscious.[7] But how do we account for this
primitive form of self-awareness? What is its phenomenological structure?

Anticipating Sartre (1943/1956) as well as other more recent discussions
(e.g. Kriegel 2003), one argument Dharmakīrti gives is the infinite regress
argument.[8] According to Dharmakīrti, the reflexive self-awareness central

---

[5] This form of self-awareness is implicit in that it is not the result of a voluntary act of introspection or
reflection. I will also characterize this form of self-awareness as 'immanent' to phenomenally conscious
states.

[6] Dreyfus (1997) offers extensive analysis. Dunne (2004) is an excellent introduction to Dharmakīrti's
thought as a whole.

[7] He writes, 'The [mind] understands by itself its own nature' (quoted in Dreyfus 1997: 340).

[8] One also finds versions of this argument in Aristotle, Descartes, Locke, Leibniz, Kant, and
Brentano, among others. See Kriegel (2003).

to consciousness cannot be the product of some sort of internal monitoring, such as a second-order reflective act or separate act of introspection or perception that takes the original state as its object.[9] Rather, on pain of infinite regress, reflexive self-awareness must be a first-order feature of conscious states. For, if an occurrent mental state M is only conscious (i.e. self-aware) when it is taken as an object by a numerically distinct second-order mental state, M*, a regress threatens. In order for the second-order mental state M* to be conscious, it would have to be taken as an object by a numerically distinct third-order mental state, M**, and so on ad infinitum. Therefore, to avoid this regress, it must be that, when a subject S is consciously aware, A, of an object, O—and is, moreover, self-aware, A*, of being consciously aware of O—the self-awareness (A*) *that one is aware of O* is built into the very structure of that experience. More simply, A* is an intrinsic or tacit form of 'self-reference without identification' (Shoemaker 1968) that does not rely on a second-order, meta-act of reflection or perception for its phenomenal character. Put yet another way, this form of immanent self-awareness is *nondyadic*. It does not have an intentional (i.e. act-object, or dual) structure, but is instead a pre-reflective self-consciousness, a nondyadic mode of awareness of one's conscious acts and the way that different objects are given first-personally through those acts (Sartre 1943/1956: 119–126). According to Dharmakīrti, then, the immanent self-reflexivity of conscious states is what secures their phenomenal character. It is a form of givenness that gives conscious states their first-personal character as well as their 'seeming' quality, such as how the taste of a single-malt Scotch, or the warm associations summoned by a childhood memory, seem to the subject who has these states.

This is not the place to assess the strength of these and other arguments Dharmakīrti gives in support of his conception of *svasaṃvedana*.[10] Rather,

---

[9] Contemporary versions of these views, respectively, are defended by higher-order perception (or 'HOP') theorists such as Armstrong (1968) and Lycan (1997), and higher-order thought (or 'HOT') theorists such as Rosenthal (1993).

[10] Dharmakīrti offers another argument for *svasaṃvedana*, which we might term the 'feeling-tone' argument. For Dharmakīrti, all intentional objects are given through an affective valence or feeling-tone—positive, neutral, negative—that colors how we experience these objects. But since this feeling-tone is an experiential property (i.e. a property of the subject, not the object), and since, moreover, the feeling-tone is always given simultaneously with the object, it follows that in every experience the subject simultaneously apprehends both the object *and* herself (i.e. via the presence of a subject-referring feeling-tone). We can thus conceptually distinguish two aspects of each mental state: its world-presenting objective aspect (*grāhyākāra*) and its subject-referring subjective aspect (*grāhakākāra*). However,

the point of this discussion is to indicate that within the Buddhist tradition there is room for a view that admits the reality of subjectivity, while nevertheless denying the ultimate existence of an enduring self. Dharmakīrti insists that conceding the subjective or self-reflexive character of consciousness is compatible with the core Buddhist notion of *anātman*. This is so, he urges, because *svasaṃvedana* is the phenomenally continuous, first-person perspective one has on the stream of one's own experience. But this first-person perspective or experiential dimension at the heart of consciousness is not itself a self. It is a feature of the *stream* of experience, and not a self standing *behind* the experience. As such, it is dynamic, relational, and perpetually in flux, dependently conditioned by the continually changing interplay of successive contents (i.e. the intentional objects of experiences) and acts (i.e. the first-personal phenomenal modes of access *to* successively changing contents). But again, there is nothing fixed, permanent, or unconditioned standing behind, or distinct from, this stream. There is simply the first-personal stream itself.

Thus, while Dharmakīrti argues that consciousness is intrinsically personal, that is, it manifests in a first-personal *how*, or mode of givenness, it doesn't follow, he further insists, that there is a single, stable *who* serving as the recipient of this stream. Dharmakīrti's discussion of the self is in this way a deflationary realism. The sense of self at the core of phenomenal consciousness (*svasaṃvedana*) is indeed very real. This quality, for Dharmakīrti, is subjectivity: it is what makes consciousness the unique phenomenon that it is. And each act of cognition thus has this aspect of subjectivity. Additionally, the sense of being a self with a temporally extended, historically constituted identity (*ahaṃkāra*) is also real. But to infer that subjectivity (*svasaṃvedana*) entails the real existence of a stable phenomenal self, or to infer that *ahaṃkāra* refers to a permanent, stable historical self, is a mistake. This mistake arises, Dharmakīrti argues, from our tendency to reify the sense of self central to the phenomenal character of consciousness. That is, we reify either, on one hand, the self-reflexive, first-personal character of conscious states—falsely assuming that the mineness of experience picks out a permanent, substantial *me*—or, on the other hand, the broader form of 'I-maker' self-awareness that emerges over time, and which is fed by the

phenomenologically and ontologically, these aspects are nondyadically conjoined within the unified structure of each state. See Dreyfus 1997: 400–403.

first-person perspective of *svasaṃvedana*. To reiterate, we reify the *sense* of self intrinsic to consciousness (which is indeed very real) and mistakenly posit from this an enduring *substantial* self (which is not real). In the end, however, both *svasaṃvedana* and *ahaṃkāra* are impermanent phenomena. Neither picks out the ultimate reality of a stable enduring self, since each ultimately rests on a continuum of transient states.

Having briefly sketched a Buddhist conception of subjectivity *sans* the self, I next want to look at two contemporary philosophical models of self: the narrative self-model, which is the focus of the next section, and the minimal self, which will be introduced in the section thereafter.

4. Self as Story: Narrative Self-Models

There is no unequivocal use of the term 'self'. Ulrich Neisser famously delineates five types of self: the ecological, interpersonal, extended, private, and conceptual self (Neisser 1988: 35). More recently, Galen Strawson (1999b) has distinguished twenty-one concepts of self! Surely there are even more. While this sort of conceptual proliferation might be warranted, given that the self is a multidimensional notion incapable of being reduced to a few restrictive categories relative to a particular disciplinary inquiry, some simplification can assist our discussion. Recent philosophical debates have focused on two notions of self that have particular relevance for understanding the nature of consciousness since they capture both the phenomenal character of experience as well as its temporal (i.e. synchronic and diachronic) unity and social situatedness. These notions are the 'minimal self' (Gallagher 2000; Zahavi 2005) and the 'narrative self' (Dennett 1991; Schechtman 1996; Damasio 1999; Hutto 2008).

A significant portion of our self-understanding as reflective creatures is structured by the symbolic mediation of narratives. Narratives help us organize and interpret our own experiential histories, share these histories with others, and meaningfully participate in the lives and experiences of others by entering into their ongoing narratives. One of our most distinctive traits is that we don't just reason—we tell stories about how we reason (Hutto 2007: 1; MacIntyre 1981: 201). However, according to some theorists, narratives do more than lend dramatic texture to our lives. The narratives we tell—narratives that we cannot *help* but tell, given the way our brains are hardwired (Dennett 1991)—play a significant role in shaping and even constituting the self. The self is thus a narrative construction.[11] Daniel Dennett famously writes: 'Our tales are spun, but for the most part we don't spin them; they spin us. Our human consciousness, and our narrative selfhood, is their product, not their source' (Dennett 1991: 418).

What counts as a narrative remains a contentious issue within the current literature; I have no aspirations of settling the debate here. However, although a precise definition is unnecessary for present concerns, a glance at possible candidates will be helpful both for establishing the general contours of narrative approaches to the self as well as clarifying precisely how narrative accounts of self sit next to minimal accounts of self. To begin simply: narratives are constructed, and not merely discovered. Narratives are thus a uniquely human enterprise. Moreover, narratives are distinct from mere chronicles of temporally indexed events, such as the timeline of a person's life (Danto 1965). What is constructed in narrative must be a relation between at least two events and/or states of affairs united by some relatively loose, non-logical relation (Lamarque 2004: 394). But this thin characterization of narrative says little of the temporal structure of narratives and nothing of their social character. Nor does it say anything about their role in constructing the self.

Alasdair MacIntyre (1981) offers an alternative. Although he fails to define 'narrative' explicitly in *After Virtue*, MacIntyre nevertheless develops a rendering that brings out the temporal, social, and self-constituting character of narratives. He writes:

The story of my life is always embedded in the story of those communities from which I derive my identity. I am born with a past; and to try to cut myself off from that past, in the individualist mode, is to deform my present relationships . . . What I am, therefore, is a key part of what I inherit, a specific past that is present to some degree in my present.

(MacIntyre 1981: 205–206)

---

[11] Defenders of narrative accounts of self include both philosophers (e.g. Alasdair MacIntyre 1981, Charles Taylor 1989, Daniel Dennett 1991, Paul Ricoeur 1992, Marya Schechtman 1996, Shaun Gallagher 2003, David Velleman 2006, Daniel Hutto 2008, and Anthony Rudd 2009) and psychologists (e.g. Donald Spence 1982, Jerome Bruner 1986, and Mark Freeman 1993).

As MacIntyre notes, the self is always embedded in a network of pre-existent socio-cultural narratives. These narratives have their own history, independent of my existence. But my own present self-understanding is very much a product of these narratives—and in this sense, the present self that I understand myself to be is shaped by stories others have told prior to my existence. Part of my narrative self-identity thus predates my existence. Additionally, I am not the sole author of the narratives through which I understand myself. My self-understanding is largely shaped by the narratives of other authors: '[W]e are never more (and sometimes less) than the co-authors of our own narratives . . . In life, as both Aristotle and Engels noted, we are always under certain constraints. We enter upon a stage which we did not design and we find ourselves part of an action that was not of our making' (MacIntyre 1981: 213). With the nod towards Aristotle and Engels, MacIntyre is emphasizing the point that the narrative self is a product, not simply of other story-telling individuals, but additionally of the unique time, place, and linguistic culture that constrain the sort of stories the narrative self hears and tells (Turner 1991: 184). Processes of self-understanding are in this way irreducibly social, culturally embedded affairs. And the self, as narrative construction, is thus dialectically linked with otherness.[12]

To focus the discussion somewhat, I would now like to differentiate two possible ways of parsing narrative accounts of self: what I will term, respectively, (1) the narrative enhancement account (NEA), and (2) the narrative constitution account (NCA). NEA is the less ambitious. It simply claims that some, but indeed not all, aspects or parts of the self are at least potentially enhanced or explicated by narratives. This weaker account accepts that, while some aspects of the self (e.g. cultural and ethnic identifications, gender representations, etc.) only emerge through the self's participation within different narratives, other more primitive features of the self (e.g. its neurobiological basis, core set of psychological characteristics or traits, its experiential status as a first-person perspective on the world, etc.) are fixed independently of any sort of self-narrative. Formulated this way, NEA does not claim that the self as a whole is constituted by the various narratives it spins. NEA allows for the prior existence of some sort of pre-narrative self capable of being narratively explicated or enhanced in the first

---

[12] Paul Ricoeur insists that 'the selfhood of oneself implies otherness to such an intimate degree that one cannot be thought without the other' (Ricoeur 1992: 3).

place. MacIntyre, for example, seems to endorse NEA when he insists that, 'It is important to notice that I am not arguing that the concepts of narrative or of intelligibility or of accountability are *more* fundamental than that of personal identity' (MacIntyre 1981: 203).[13] Again, the salient point is that, for NEA, the narrative self is a derivative notion dependent upon a more basic pre-narrative self.

On the other hand, the stronger account of narrative selfhood offers a constitution claim: namely, that the self is literally constituted by narratives. The self is ultimately nothing but a dense constellation of interwoven narratives, an emergent entity that gradually unfurls from (and is thus constituted by) the stories we tell and have told about us. As we've already seen, Dennett (1989, 1991) seems to hold this view. Again, recall his insistence that 'like spider webs, our tales are spun by us; our human consciousness, and our narrative selfhood, is their product, not their source' (Dennett 1991: 418). Drawing inspiration from Dennett (among others), Marya Schechtman similarly characterizes her own 'self-constitution' view as the claim that 'a person exists in the convergence of subjective and objective features. An individual constitutes herself as a person by coming to organize her experiences in a narrative self-conception of the appropriate form' (Schechtman 1996: 134).

This brief characterization of narrative-self models hints at their theoretical richness for understanding the dynamic, relational, and situated nature of the self. However, our discussion in the previous section has already suggested a difficulty for NCA. Exploring this difficulty is the work of the next section.

5. Pre-Narrative Selfhood

There is a difficulty with NCA that doesn't plague NEA. It is this: the NCA 'self as story' story seems to weave an incomplete story of the self. Put differently, in order to be a narrative-telling creature—in order to cast oneself as the protagonist in one's own narrative—one must already be the possessor of, in addition to the linguistic capacities needed to construct a

---

[13] Actually, MacIntyre's view here isn't entirely clear. See Williams (2009) for discussion and criticism.

narrative, a more primitive pre-narrative, embodied first-person perspective on the world. Narrative selves must always already be conscious subjects, since a creature that lacks subjectivity cannot simultaneously be a creature that produces narratives *about* that subjectivity. But the converse isn't true. We can be conscious—again, we can be the possessor of an embodied first-person point of view on the world, including a pre-reflective sense of being an embodied first-person perspective—without simultaneously being a subject who produces narratives *about* this first-person point of view. Narratives are thus not essential to basic forms of subjectivity or minimal phenomenal selfhood in the way that embodied first-person perspectives are. And NCA is therefore pitched at too high an explanatory level, as variations of this approach overlook the minimal forms of phenomenal selfhood that pre-exist narrative selfhood. Indeed, narratives play a central role in practical reasoning, deliberation, and self-reflection, and in generating our sense of being a culturally situated social self with a unique experiential history. But the narrative self is not an essential phenomenal feature of our first-person perspective on the world. Rather, these two things dissociate both conceptually and experientially. The first-person perspective, or the subject to whom the world is given in a first-personal mode of presentation, is thus phenomenologically and ontologically prior to the narrative self. According to Shaun Gallagher, this minimal self is

[p]henomenologically, that is, in terms of how one experiences it, a consciousness of oneself as an immediate subject of experience, unextended in time. The minimal self almost certainly depends on brain processes and an ecologically embedded body, but one does not have to know or be aware of this to have an experience that still counts as a [minimal, or pre-narrative] self-experience.

(Gallagher 2000: 15)

This minimal self is the subject of experiences which provide pre-narrative fodder for later narratives (Menary 2008: 73). But again, the subject or minimal self that has these experiences pre-exists the narratives it later constructs.

It might help to mark a conceptual distinction between the notions of 'self' (i.e. the immediate, moment-to-moment experience of being a first-person perspective on the world) and 'person' (i.e. the broader experience of being an entity that endures through time). As we've already seen, we find a similar distinction made from within the classical Indian Buddhist tradition[14] which, to reiterate, recognizes two central forms of self-experience: (1) *svasaṃvedana*, or the immanently self-reflexive awareness consciousness has of itself, and (2) *ahaṃkāra*, or 'I-maker' self-awareness, which is the temporally extended sense of oneself as a single, enduring entity, ontologically distinct from the stream of experience.[15] While the former is the more phenomenologically primitive form of self-experience, the latter is arguably the notion of self we think of when someone asks the question, 'Who are you?'. When we consider ourselves as individuals with unique hopes, aspirations, and intentions—as singular individuals importantly distinct from others, and with a moral and existential status uniquely our own—we are thinking of ourselves as narrative *persons*, in an encompassing mode of 'I-maker' awareness.[16]

However, if we accept that this self/person distinction is a coherent conceptual distinction, it seems that, in order to be a person, one must already be a self, since one cannot have a holistic 'I-maker' experience of personhood (including the elements of one's narratives, such as character, personality traits, memories, convictions, motivations, and the sense of a unified existential history spread out over time) unless one is already a subject of experience in some minimal sense. The minimal phenomenal self thus has persistence conditions distinct from those of narrative persons. Narrative self-models, in both their weaker enhancement form as well as their stronger constitution form, are more accurately understood to be models, not of selves, but of *persons* (Zahavi 2005: 129).

To underscore this distinction between self and person, and to reinforce the experiential primacy of some sort of minimal phenomenal self, we can look to a number of empirical studies. Consider first Antonio Damasio's

---

[14] For the sake of historical precision, it should be noted that not *all* schools of Indian Buddhism hold that cognition is self-reflexive (e.g. Mādhyamika thinkers such as Candrakīrti (ca. 600–650) and Śāntideva (fl. 8th century)).

[15] To be clear, while Buddhism acknowledges a phenomenological distinction between the two forms of self-experience I am here distinguishing, the terms 'person' and 'self' are used somewhat differently within Buddhist philosophy. A person (*pudgala*) is simply a causally continuous, psychophysical complex of different aggregates (*skandhas*) arranged in the right sort of way. And with the exception of the Pudgalavāda tradition of early Buddhism, most Buddhists believe that the person is ultimately reducible to this psychophysical complex, that is, the person has no independent existence over and above it. The self (*ātman*), as an experiential feature, is thus an aspect of this causal series, and is as impermanent as is every other aspect.

[16] See also Albahari (this volume) for more on ordinary, and ultimately delusive, forms of self-experience.

(1999) discussion of David, a 46-year-old patient suffering from an unusually drastic form of memory loss brought on by a severe case of encephalitis. In the span of a few weeks, David's encephalitis caused major damage to his left and right temporal lobes. The result of this damage was that David lost both the ability to retain any new facts in memory, as well as the ability to recall 'virtually any thing, individual, or event, from his entire life'—meaning that 'his memory loss goes almost all the way to the cradle' (Damasio 1999: 115). David lives in an ever-shifting window of short-term memory: about forty-five seconds (Damasio 1999: 118). In virtue of his radical memory loss, David has lost the ability to construct any sort of narrative unity to his life and actions; he is incapable of forming a narrative self, or what Damasio terms an 'autobiographical self', which according to Damasio emerges from the 'extended consciousness' stretching across the whole of a person's life (Damasio 1999: 17).

Nevertheless, David retains a minimal self. David presents rich phenomenal consciousness. He 'fares perfectly well on the core consciousness checklist' (Damasio 1999: 116).[17] David exhibits attentive wakefulness; his experiences are colored by various background emotions, and he articulates preferences; he acts purposively within the situations he enters into. In short, David has preserved an experiential self, and he is immediately aware of himself *as* an experiential self, aware that the content of his moment-to-moment experience is his. Yet David has completely lost the sense of himself as a historically extended, narratively structured person— precisely because, with the catastrophic erosion of his memory, he no longer has the ability to explicate himself as such.

Work on neonatal imitation also lends support to the self/person distinction as well as to the experiential primacy of the minimal self. Multiple studies indicate that neonates come into the world with a proprioceptive self: a minimal form of self-awareness emerging from very basic experiences of themselves as embodied and situated creatures. This minimal self-awareness enables neonates less than an hour old to imitate a range of facial, vocal, and gestural expressions (Meltzoff and Moore 1977, 1983, 1997; Kugiumutzakis 1985, 1999). These imitative episodes appear to be intentional, in that they are not merely reflexive but rather indicate a capacity to learn to match

---

[17] 'Core consciousness' is Damasio's expression for our moment-to-moment sense of being an awake and experiencing subject (i.e. a minimal self) (Damasio 1999: 16).

the presented gesture (Meltzoff and Moore 1983). Neonate imitation presupposes three significant pre-narrative capacities, all of which themselves presuppose an experienced sense of minimal phenomenal selfhood: (1) the capacity for experientially distinguishing self and other; (2) the capacity for locating and using body parts proprioceptively, that is, without vision (since neonates haven't yet seen their bodies); (3) the capacity to recognize the presented face as of the same kind as its own face (neonates don't imitate non-human objects). As Shaun Gallagher notes, 'One possible interpretation of this finding is that these three capacities present in neonates constitute a primitive self-consciousness, and that the human infant is already equipped with a minimal self that is embodied, enactive, and ecologically attuned' (Gallagher 2000: 17). Of course, since neonates lack the linguistic capacities needed to construct and comprehend narratives, they have no sense of themselves as a narrative entity, that is, as a person. Nevertheless, neonate imitation research indicates that a minimal sort of self-experience, the sense of being a unified, embodied perspective on the world, is present from birth.

At this point, there are several potential responses that defenders of NCA might offer. Schechtman, for example, concedes a conceptual distinction between self and person but argues that narratives are nonetheless central to both categories (Schechtman 2007: 171). In order to constitute oneself as a narrative *person*, 'one must recognize oneself as continuing, see past actions and experiences as having implications for one's current rights and responsibilities, and recognize a future that will be impacted by the past and present' (Schechtman 2007: 170). A narrative *self*, Schechtman continues, is constituted by assimilating temporally remote actions and experiences into my present self-experience in such as way that these events 'condition the quality of present experience in the strongest sense, unifying consciousness over time through affective connections and identification' (Schechtman 2007: 171).

But the problem with Schechtmans's distinction here is that, again, it is pitched at too high a level of explanation, passing over features of phenomenal consciousness and forms of self-experience that seem to be independent of narrative. It is also a strikingly disembodied account of self-constitution. Which of these two forms of narrative constitution, for instance, as defined by Schechtman, apply to Damasio's David? Certainly not the first, since David lacks a robust sense of having a created history that constrains his present actions and decisions. Similarly, while David's consciousness seems to present a unified character, it's not clear that this phenomenal unity is the result of any kind of narratively structured process of 'affective connection and identification'. David's capacity for memory is simply too impoverished to speak this way: the unity of his phenomenal experience must thus be due to a different mechanism. Schechtman might respond by urging that, even within a short forty-five second window, David can still construct 'micro-narratives' that unify his experiences and allow him to make affective connections with temporally remote actions and events (e.g. the door he opened ten seconds ago while walking into the room, or the initiation of his reach to grasp a light bulb that needs changing). But this is an awfully strained way of using the term 'narrative', since the temporal extension and social character of these sorts of micro-narratives is exceedingly limited. Moreover, it's not at all clear that we need appeal to narrative to explain certain fundamental forms of embodied self-experience and skillfulness.

This becomes clear by returning to the neonatal imitation studies mentioned previously. Again, it's difficult to discern how Schechtman's distinction would be neatly applied to these cases. Far from a 'blooming and buzzing' model of experience, it now appears that even very young infants present a surprisingly rich form of self-awareness rooted in an ecological experience of their body and their body's practical relation to the world. They seem to grasp implicitly that they have a body, and they feel that this body can be made to do things, including imitate the expressions and gestures of others—despite neither having seen their body nor possessing any sort of linguistic or narrative understanding of it. This capacity points towards a range of embodied self-experience and skills (e.g. neonatal imitation, reaching for and grasping a cup, driving a car, responding to an opponent's volley while playing tennis) that operate without narrative intervention. Additionally, our ability to enact pre-narrative embodied skills so efficiently suggests that there exists a primitive form of bodily self-experience that is independent of narrative articulation. The young infant is immediately acquainted with its body and the things its body can do; the skilled driver and tennis player enact dynamically coherent, context-sensitive sequences of complicated motor actions that unfold without the explicit guidance of narrative scripts. This immediate acquaintance with oneself as an embodied perspective on the world is a phenomenologically minimal form of self-experience.

Schechtman might respond by arguing that some narratives operate un-consciously, that is, some narratives are *implicit* narratives that guide action and determine the appropriate responses in a given context, but that they do so without ever reaching the level of phenomenal awareness. In fact, she has done just this (Schechtman 1996: 115–117). But like the micro-narrative rejoinder, this, too, is a problematic move. For, pushing narratives down to the murky levels of subpersonal representation compromises their fundamen-tally public or social character, and transforms them into computational processes hidden away inside the brain (Menary 2008: 71). Additionally, it makes it more difficult to see why implicit narratives, if they have a subpersonal character, ought to be explanatorily prioritized over other kinds of subpersonal processes when it comes to understanding the constitu-tion of the self. This is not to deny that Schechtman's rich narrative account of self has significant explanatory value. Again, the point is simply that there exist more basic pre-narrative forms of self-experience that Schechtman's account, and indeed NCA accounts more generally, can't satisfactorily account for.

The take-away lesson is that personhood is a more articulated, but ultimately derivative notion, phenomenologically and ontologically depen-dent upon the experiential primacy of a minimal phenomenal self. The minimal self is therefore a condition of possibility for developing more articulated forms of narrative personhood: pre-narrative experiences give structure to, and provide content for, narratives (Menary 2008: 79). But narrativity is not essential to phenomenal consciousness the way that some minimal form of self-experience is. Now, having spent some time discussing aspects of the narrative self and arguing for the experiential primacy of the minimal phenomenal self, I want to investigate next the structure of the minimal self more carefully before then questioning whether it is warranted to speak of this form of self-experience as a substantial *self*.

6. First-Personal Givenness and the Minimal Self

As should by now be clear, the concept of the minimal self is motivated by the intuition that 'even if all of the unessential features of self are stripped away . . . there is still some basic, immediate, or primitive "something" that we are willing to call a self' (Gallagher 2000: 15). Unlike the narrative account of self, this intuition brackets considerations of the self's historicity and sociality, and looks instead to excavate a more fundamental dimension of phenomenal consciousness.[18] According to its defenders, the minimal self is something I can fail to articulate (i.e. give narrative expression to), but something that I cannot fail to be (Zahavi 2005: 116). Every moment that I am conscious is another moment that I am, or have, a minimal self. This is a thoroughly phenomenological conception of the self, casting the self as an experiential dimension, central to the very structure of consciousness. Since Dan Zahavi is the most ardent current defender of this view, in what follows I will focus critically on his characterization of the minimal self.

There are a number of ways of arguing for the existence of the minimal self. One line of argument follows the discussion of the previous section: namely, the idea that narrative accounts of self (as well as other forms of self-experience similarly dependent upon having the appropriate reflective, linguistic, and/or conceptual capacities) are pitched at too high an explanatory level. These approaches pass over more subtle, but no less significant, pre-narrative forms of self-experience central to the phenomenal nature of consciousness *qua* consciousness. Damasio's discussion of David, as well as research on infant imitation, both indicate a minimal phenomenal self-experience present prior to, or in the absence of, narrative constructs. This is because 'every conscious state, be it a perception, an emotion, a recollection, or an abstract belief, has a certain subjective character, a certain phenomenal quality of "what it is like" to live through, or undergo, that state. This is what makes the mental state in question *conscious*' (Zahavi 2005: 119). The phenomenality of a conscious state, the argument goes, is independent of its narrative structure. Furthermore, it discloses a primitive kind of self. Any organism capable of phenomenal consciousness thus has a minimal self.

Two key ideas are central to understanding Zahavi's formulation of the minimal self: 'first-personal givenness' and 'mineness'. I will look at these ideas in turn. Zahavi contends that we need to make a conceptual distinction between, on one hand, what the *object* is like for the subject, and on the other, what the *experience of the object* is like for the subject (Zahavi 2005: 121). Importantly, this is merely a conceptual distinction allowing us to grasp the world-directed structure of consciousness. For, within each conscious state, these aspects are unified parts of a coherent experience. Echoing Dharma-

---

[18] Sartre argues that, 'pre-reflective consciousness is self-consciousness. It is this same notion of *self* which must be studied, for it defines the very being of consciousness' (Sartre 1943/1956: 123).

kīrti's assertion discussed above, Zahavi argues that, when I have an experience of an object, such as visually perceiving a tomato on a table, part of my subjective experience is constituted by properties of the object (i.e. redness, smoothness, roundness, etc.). These properties play a central role in fixing the phenomenal character of a given state. But these properties, in fact, do not exhaust the phenomenal character. There is another, more subtle, phenomenological aspect present: namely, the phenomenal property of *experiencing myself experiencing*. Put differently, I experience these features of the object in a mode of first-personal givenness, a mode of disclosure that is a phenomenologically basic form of reflexive self-experience. Zahavi writes:

This first-personal givenness of experiential phenomena is not something incidental to their being, a mere varnish that the experiences could lack without ceasing to be experiences. On the contrary, this first-personal givenness makes the experience *subjective*. To put it another way, their first-personal givenness entails a built-in self-reference, a primitive experiential self-referentiality . . . the experiential dimension does not have to do with the existence of ineffable qualia; it has to do with the dimension of first-personal experiencing.

(Zahavi 2005: 122–23)

Therefore, what makes a particular conscious state subjective is that it is always given in a first-personal mode of presentation: it involves a first-person perspective that is implicated within the very manner of how experiential content is manifest to the subject. This first-person perspective provides the structure through which the world presents itself within a given state. Again Zahavi:

Phenomenology pays attention to the givenness of the object, but it does not simply focus on the object exactly as it is given; it also focuses on the subjective side of consciousness, thereby illuminating our subjective accomplishments and the intentionality that is at play in order for the object to appear as it does.

(Zahavi 2005: 123)

Echoing Dharmakīrti once more, Zahavi insists that the dimension of first-personal experiencing does not involve any sort of higher-order act of reflection or perception.[19] Rather, the minimal self is what originally

---

[19] Zahavi is critical of higher-order (both HOT and HOP) theories of consciousness (Zahavi 2005: 17–20).

makes possible higher-order acts of self-reflection and objectifying thema-tization in the first place. Self-reflection necessarily presupposes a more phenomenologically primitive perspective (i.e. that of a minimal self), capable of initiating higher-order objectifying acts of self-reflection.[20] The first-person givenness of conscious states is thus immanently self-reflexive, that is, it is 'an intrinsic feature of the primary experience' (Zahavi 2005: 17). This is simply another way of saying that '[w]hen we investigate appearing objects, we also disclose ourselves as datives of manifestation, as those to whom objects appear' (Zahavi 2005: 123). What is disclosed is the minimal phenomenal self.

What about 'mineness'? According to Zahavi, mineness is a quality of the various modes of first-personal givenness (e.g. perceptual, imaginative, recollective, etc.) through which intentional content is given. Mineness reveals a conscious state's being owned, that is, a state's being immediately recognized as given to, or for, a particular subject (or minimal self). For '[w]hen I (in nonpathological standard cases) am aware of an occurrent pain, perception, or thought from the first-person perspective, the experi-ence in question is given immediately, noninferentially, and noncriterially as *mine*' (Zahavi 2005: 124). Once more, however, mineness is an invariant structural feature of consciousness. It is a 'subtle background presence' pervading various modes of first-personal givenness, and is not the product of an explicit act of self-reflection or self-perception (Zahavi 2005: 124). To clarify further: mineness is a qualitative feature of consciousness itself (i.e. an experiential property), independent of the properties (e.g. the redness or smoothness of a tomato on a table) that intentional objects are presented as having. Taken together, Zahavi argues that the twin notions of first-personal givenness and mineness offer us a minimal, but phenome-nologically significant, rendering of the self that 'is not something that stands opposed to the stream of consciousness, but is, rather, immersed in conscious life; it is an integral part of its structure' (Zahavi 2005: 125).

Before turning to critical analysis, we can note that there is much to recommend Zahavi's view. First, it is of immense historical-philosophical

---

[20] Consciousness, Mark Rowlands observes, is essentially a 'hybrid entity' that can be both *object* and *act* of experience (Rowlands 2001: 122). Zahavi insists that the modality of the former is dependent upon the modality of the latter—and thus that consciousness-as-act (of which the minimal self is an essential part) is phenomenologically primitive.

interest, unifying and deepening a common thread in the work of a number of prominent phenomenologists. More substantially, it helps us get a grip on a particularly elusive feature of experience that is difficult to pin down. Zahavi challenges the widely held view that phenomenal consciousness is genuinely diaphanous. For, if we are pre-reflectively aware of an occurrent phenomenal state as ours—if conscious states are immanently self-reflexive, in other words, as Zahavi (and, indeed, Dharmakīrti) argues that they are—consciousness thus contains more than simply the representational content of its intentional object(s). Each state harbors a pre-reflective self-awareness of the minimal self to whom the state is given. The phenomenal character of consciousness is thus not exhausted by the items that conscious states are conscious of: there is more to experience than its content. And any theory of consciousness worth its salt has to account for this subtle, but essential, feature of experience.

However, to put the objection simply (and this is really the heart of this paper): has Zahavi successfully shown that the minimal self is a *self*? Is his truly an egological conception of consciousness? Zahavi answers both questions in the affirmative. The minimal self, according to Zahavi, is an invariant structural feature of consciousness that remains constant throughout the life of the subject: 'Whereas we live through a number of different experiences, the dimension of first-personal experiencing remains the same . . . it may be described as an *invariant* dimension of first-personal givenness throughout the multitude of changing experiences' (Zahavi 2005: 132). On the face of it, this is an intuitive claim that seems to square with the sense that we are, in fact, the same self throughout the course of our respective lives. (Dharmakīrti, recall, also concedes the intuitive force of this sense of being a single stable self.) But, given his phenomenological characterization of the minimal self, is Zahavi justified in making this claim? I suggest he is not. Specifically, I want to challenge the idea that the minimal self is indeed a self—that is, if we take the self to be *invariant* (i.e. a singularly unified, enduring, and unconditioned thing that stays the same through the life of the conscious subject). In the remainder of this paper, I will argue that Zahavi is, at best, warranted in speaking of minimal *selves*, not a minimal *self*. In this sense, his account is actually compatible with the no-self view developed by Dharmakīrti.

7. Minimal Self as Stream, Structure, or Something Else?

To begin, the Buddhist would likely offer the following question to Zahavi: what aspect of our experience is *invariant*, exactly? What precisely stays the same? Zahavi's response is: the first-personal 'experiential dimension' within which phenomena are given. And this answer, Zahavi would continue, is enough to qualify his view as an egological theory of consciousness. There seem to be at least two ways of cashing out this idea, however, and Zahavi's discussion of the minimal self seems at times to conflate these two options. Yet I want to suggest that they need to be kept conceptually distinct—and moreover, that neither is adequate for establishing the invariant 'selfness' of the minimal self. For the sake of simplicity, I will speak of the minimal self characterized (1) as *stream*, versus the minimal self characterized (2) as *structure*.

Like Dharmakīrti, Zahavi insists that the minimal self is distinct from the intentional object. It is on the act side of the consciousness-object relation. But the minimal self is not then distinct from our conscious acts themselves. Rather, Zahavi further insists that the minimal self is part of the very stream of our world-directed conscious activity. Just as it is not reducible to the narratives that develop subsequent to our experiences, the minimal self is also neither an ego-pole nor a distinct principle of identity standing behind, or apart from, the phenomenal stream (Zahavi 2005: 106). Again, it is located *within* the stream as 'an integral part of its structure' (Zahavi 2005: 125), that is, as 'a feature or function of its givenness' (Zahavi 2005: 106). The minimal 'stream self' therefore exhibits a relational dynamism as part of its character. It is constituted immanently within the activity of the mind's encounter with the world. This situatedness within the stream of consciousness is what allows the minimal self to account for the unity of experience, and is what leads us to ascribe past, present, and future experiences to a single, enduring subject.

But note carefully some of Zahavi's other descriptions. Of egological views (which he insists that his view is), Zahavi writes:

An egological theory would claim that that when I watch a movie by Bergman, I am not only intentionally directed at the *movie*, nor merely aware of the movie being *watched*, I am also aware that it is being watched by *me*, that is, that *I* am *watching* the *movie*. In short, there is an object of experience (the watching), and there is a subject of experience, myself.

(Zahavi 2005: 99)

And in characterizing the non-egological, or no-self view, Zahavi continues:

In contrast, a *non-egological* theory . . . would deny that every experience is for a subject. It would, in other words, omit any reference to a subject of experience and simply say that there is an awareness of the watching of the movie . . . minimal self-awareness should, consequently, be understood as the acquaintance that consciousness has with *itself* and *not* as an awareness of the experiencing *self*.

(Zahavi 2005: 100)

Yet there is a tension here. Recall Zahavi's earlier claim that the minimal self is simply a 'feature or function' of the first-personal givenness or 'self-luminosity' (Zahavi 2005: 62) of the phenomenal stream. In fact, at one point Zahavi urges that, in order to understand his insistence that the minimal self be identified with the first-personal character of phenomenal consciousness, we ought to 'replace the traditional phrase "subject of experience" with the phrase "subjectivity of experience"' (Zahavi 2005: 126). This is because the former seems to imply an autonomous, stream-independent ego—which Zahavi denies—whereas the latter adequately captures the sort of immanent stream self Zahavi endorses. The minimal self thus is, simply, *the subjectivity of experience* (which includes the various features that Zahavi carefully analyzes). But if this is all that the minimal self is, it seems that Zahavi is really endorsing the sort of non-egological view he claims to be opposing! Nothing in this characterization of the self-luminosity of the phenomenal stream is in conflict with Dharmakīrti's view—except for the final step Zahavi wants to make in reifying the stream self into something permanent and invariant.[21]

To the question, 'Where is the minimal self?', Zahavi clearly answers, 'In the stream of consciousness itself'. But if we now return to our earlier

---

[21] To be fair, Zahavi himself notes that the simple distinction between egological and non-egological views of consciousness (e.g. Gurwitsch 1941) is far too crude, and therefore that more subtle ways of characterizing the relation between consciousness and self-consciousness are needed (Zahavi 2005: 146). However, Zahavi's stated desire to pinpoint various 'invariant' structures of experience (e.g. the *ipseity* of the 1st person experiential dimension)—coupled with, moreover, his argument that these structures qualify as a minimal form of selfhood—would seem to indicate that Zahavi sees himself as aligned with the egological camp, even if his particular approach is more nuanced than traditional egological views (see Zahavi 2005: 99).

question, 'What aspect of experience (i.e. the stream self) is invariant?', it is not clear that Zahavi has a ready-to-hand answer. For, if the minimal-self-as-stream-self is composed of the same aspects of the phenomenal stream, it is every bit as impermanent, that is, empty (*śūnya*) of fixed or intrinsic self-nature (*svabhāva*) as is the dynamically flowing, relationally constituted stream itself. Put otherwise, the stream exhibits a dependently conditioned (*pratītya-samutpanna*) nature, dynamically constituted by the ongoing interplay of successive acts and contents. The minimal self, as the phenomenal stream, simply refers to the dynamic coherence of the phe-nomenal stream *in the first-personal givenness of its flowing*. But there is nothing fixed, stable, or enduring about this stream (or indeed, the stream self)— save for its fundamental impermanence. It seems, then, that the Buddhist could charge Zahavi with what Thomas Metzinger has called the 'error of phenomenological reification' (Metzinger 2003: 22): mistaking the mine-ness, or immanently self-reflexive character of experience, for a stable or permanent me. Likewise, Dharmakīrti would invoke the image of a candle, asserting that it is a similar mistake to infer the sameness of the candle flame at each moment from the enduring presence of illumination. Though the self-reflexive character of individual conscious states provides a persistent source of illumination, the self-reflexivity behind this illumination is, in fact, the property of distinct, impermanent, ever-flowing states.[22]

A presupposition of Zahavi's resistance to non-egological views seems to be the assumption that such views must eject subjectivity from their char-acterizations of consciousness to render them truly 'selfless'. And Zahavi rightly resists any model of consciousness that looks to jettison its phenom-enal character (e.g. Dennett 1979, 1991). But as should now be clear, this presupposition is not warranted. Dharmakīrti, who certainly argues for a no-self view of consciousness, is quite insistent that subjectivity nevertheless needs to be at the center of any model of consciousness. He simply resists Zahavi's final, reifying move of identifying subjectivity with a permanent self. For Dharmakīrti, the self-reflexive character of occurrent phenomenal states does, indeed, refer back to a phenomenal self: a subject or first-person perspective to whom the content of these states is phenomenally manifest. But again, this phenomenal self is dependently conditioned by, or arises from, the dynamic interplay of successive acts and objects, which means that

---

[22] But see Fasching (this volume) for a response to this objection.

it has no intrinsic self-nature. It isn't some *thing* distinct from this interplay. It is the interplay itself. As such, it is fundamentally impermanent, arising and passing away within the continual stream of ever-new acts and contents. Thus, Dharmakīrti would likely be content to speak of numerically distinct minimal selves: dependently conditioned, temporary subjects that arise, exist, and pass away within the span of an occurrent episode of consciousness. And if this analysis of Zahavi's view of the minimal self is correct, it seems that Zahavi, too, is warranted only in speaking of a plurality of numerically distinct, minimal phenomenal selves.[23] For the first-personal givenness of experience, according to Zahavi, is phenomenally conditioned by experiential phenomena (i.e. objects of experience)—and vice versa. Experiential phenomena are never given anonymously, but always first-personally. Thus, first-personal givenness and experiential phenomena are necessarily co-given. But since experience is always in flux, an ever-flowing stream of (first-personal) acts and first-personally given experiential phenomena (i.e. objects)—and since, moreover, the minimal phenomenal self is identical with its experiences, as Zahavi argues—it follows that the stream self is constantly changing. In other words, there is no numerically identical minimal phenomenal self. Rather, there is simply a phenomenal continuum of minimal selves, each ensuring that experiential phenomena are manifest in a mode of first-personal givenness.

But this is not the end of the matter. For at times Zahavi also seems to characterize the minimal self, not in terms of its stream character, but rather its structural character, that is, the minimal self understood purely as a *formal structure* of consciousness. For instance, he writes that, 'As long as we focus on the first-personal mode of givenness of the stream of consciousness, we are dealing with a kind of pure, formal, and *empty individuality* which the subject shares with all other subjects' (Zahavi 1999: 165). But if the minimal self is merely an empty structural feature of consciousness, how is the phenomenal character of experience individuated? How does subjectivity become *my* subjectivity? For a purely formal feature of consciousness—whether it be minimal selfhood, intentionality, its field-like structure, or something else—cannot in itself exhibit phenomenal character. Formal features are conditions of possibility for consciousness to occur the particular

---

[23] This would also bring Zahavi closer to Galen Strawson who, as Strawson himself notes, shares some affinities with the Buddhist view of the self (Strawson 1999a: 18).

way that it does; they cannot be given *to* consciousness, much the same way that an eye cannot see itself. These features need to be phenomenally 'filled in' via the dynamic interplay of acts and contents.

Zahavi recognizes this objection. He says that, as a formal feature of consciousness, the minimal self's phenomenal character

> only manifests itself on the personal level, in its individual history, in its moral and intellectual convictions. It is through these acts that I define myself; they have character-shaping effect. I remain the same as long as I adhere to my convictions. When they change, *I* change. Since these convictions and endorsed values are intrinsically social, we are once more confronted with the idea that the ego in its full scope and concretion cannot be thought or understood in isolation from the Other. The ego is only fully individualized when personalized, and this happens only intersubjectively.
>
> (Zahavi 1999: 166)

But the problem with this reply is that it seems to appeal to a narrative conception of self to explain how the unique particularities of my identity are constituted. And this is fine, except that narratives, too, are by definition impermanent. They are the result of multiple authors, and are constantly being retold and revised. Moreover, I am rarely the sole author of my own self-narrative, and thus my identity is, to a very large degree, dependently conditioned by others. My narrative self thus constantly develops and changes, taking on new elements while abandoning other outmoded or forgotten elements. As Zahavi puts it, 'Therefore, I, we, and world belong together' (Zahavi 1999: 166). The narrative self depends on others for its existence: it is relationally constituted. Put otherwise, it lacks intrinsic self-nature, as the Buddhist would argue, and is thus empty of fixed or permanent character. Additionally, appealing to narrative self-models to explain how subjectivity is individuated still encounters the challenge discussed earlier: namely, a failure to explain pre-narrative forms of phenomenal self-experience. So, a story of the pre-narrative minimal stream self is still needed to explain how the structural self is individuated, phenomenally speaking. But as I have just argued, this way of characterizing the self cannot establish the self's fundamental invariance, either. So it seems that, by appealing to either narrative or minimal self-models (including the latter understood either as stream or as structure), we've yet to pinpoint the resting place for a stable, permanent, or enduring self.

8. Concluding Thoughts

In this paper, I have attempted to show that Buddhist philosophy offers a characterization of consciousness that (1) foregrounds its phenomenal character, but which (2) denies that this phenomenal character entails the existence of a fixed, enduring, or unconditioned self. I then examined two contemporary self-models: the narrative self and the minimal self, and summoned empirical research in support of my claim that the latter is dissociable from, and, indeed, experientially prior to, the former. Finally, I've looked more closely at Dan Zahavi's lucid defense of the minimal self, and offered reasons for thinking that, while his discussion rightly explicates several core features of phenomenal consciousness, it nevertheless fails to establish the necessary existence of a stable, fixed, or enduring self that stays the same throughout the life of the conscious subject. Buddhism claims that we are fundamentally empty persons—despite strong and persistent forms of self-experience that seem to suggest the contrary. It remains to be seen, of course, if this claim is ultimately true. But if the above analysis is correct, it's a view at least worth taking seriously.

References

Armstrong, D. (1968), *A Materialist Theory of Mind* (London: Routledge & Kegan Paul).

Bruner, J. (1986), *Actual Minds, Possible Worlds* (Cambridge, MA: Harvard University Press).

Damasio, A. (1999), *The Feeling of What Happens* (San Diego, CA: Harcourt).

Danto, A. (1965), *Analytical Philosophy of History* (Cambridge: Cambridge University Press).

Dennett, D. (1979), 'On the Absence of Phenomenology', in Donald F. Gustafson and Bangs L. Tapscottt (eds.), *Body, Mind, and Method* (Dordrecht: Kluwer).

——(1991), *Consciousness Explained* (Boston : Little Brown and Company).

Dreyfus, G. (1997), *Recognizing Reality: Dharmakīrti's Philosophy and its Tibetan Interpretations* (Albany: SUNY Press).

Dunne, J. (2004), *Foundations of Dharmakīrti's Philosophy* (Boston: Wisdom Publications).

Freeman, M. (1993), *Rewriting the Self: History, Memory, and Narrative* (London: Routledge).

Gallagher, S. (2000), 'Philosophical Conceptions of the Self: Implications for Cognitive Science', *Trends in Cognitive Sciences* 4: 14–21.

——(2003), 'Self-Narrative, Embodied Action, and Social Context', in Andrzej Wiercinski (ed.), *Between Suspicion and Sympathy: Paul Ricoeur's Unstable Equilibrium (Festschrift for Paul Ricoeur)* (Toronto: The Hermeneutic Press).

Gurwitsch, A. (1941), 'A Non-Egological Conception of Consciousness', *Philosophy and Phenomenological Research* 1: 325–338.

Hutto, D., ed. (2007), *Narrative and Understanding Persons* (Cambridge: Cambridge University Press).

——(2008), *Folk Psychological Narratives: The Sociocultural Basis of Understanding Reasons* (Cambridge, MA: MIT Press).

Kriegel, U. (2003), 'Consciousness as Intransitive Self-consciousness: Two Views and an Argument', *Canadian Journal of Philosophy* 33: 103–132.

Kugiumutzakis, G. (1985), *The Origin, Development and Function of Early Infant Imitation*, PhD thesis, psychology, Uppsala University, Sweden.

——(1999), 'Genesis and Development of Early Infant Mimesis to Facial and Vocal Models', in Jacqueline Nadel and George Butterworth (eds.), *Imitation in Infancy* (Cambridge: Cambridge University Press).

Lamarque, P. (2004), 'On Not Expecting Too Much from Narrative', *Mind and Language* 19: 393–408.

Lycan, W. (1997), 'Consciousness as Internal Monitoring', in Ned Block, Owen Flanagan, and Güven Güzeldere (eds.), *The Nature of Consciousness* (Cambridge, MA: MIT Press).

MacIntyre, A. (1981), *After Virtue: A Study in Moral Theory* (Notre Dame, IN: University of Notre Dame Press).

MacKenzie, M. (2008), 'Self-Awareness without a Self: Buddhism and the Reflexivity of Awareness', *Asian Philosophy* 18: 245–266.

Meltzoff, A. and K. Moore (1977), 'Imitation of Facial and Manual Gestures by Human Neonates', *Science* 198: 75–78.

——(1983), 'Newborn Infants Imitate Adult Facial Gestures', *Child Development* 54: 702–709.

——(1997), 'Explaining Facial Imitation: A Theoretical Model', *Early Development and Parenting* 6: 179–192.

Menary, R. (2008), 'Embodied Narratives', *Journal of Consciousness Studies* 15: 63–84.

Metzinger, T. (2003), *Being No One: The Self-model Theory of Subjectivity* (Cambridge, MA: MIT Press).

Mokṣākaragupta (1985), *Bauddha-tarkabhāṣā*, edited by Badri Nath Singh (Varanasi: Asha Prakashan).

Neisser, U. (1988), 'Five Kinds of Self-knowledge', *Philosophical Psychology* 1: 35–59.

Ricoeur, P. (1992), *Oneself as Another*, translated by Kathleen Blamey (Chicago: University of Chicago Press).

Rosenthal, D. (1993), 'Higher-order Thoughts and the Appendage Theory of Consciousness', *Philosophical Psychology* 6: 155–166.

Rowlands, M. (2001), *The Nature of Consciousness* (Cambridge: Cambridge University Press).

Rudd, A. (2009), 'In Defence of Narrative', *European Journal of Philosophy* 17: 60–75.

Sartre, J. (1943/1956), *Being and Nothingness*, translated by Hazel E. Barnes (New York: Washington Square Press).

Schechtman, M. (1996), *The Constitution of Selves* (Ithaca, NY: Cornell University Press).

——(2007), 'Stories, Lives, and Basic Survival: A Refinement and Defense of the Narrative View', in Daniel D. Hutto (ed.), *Narrative and Understanding Persons* (Cambridge: Cambridge University Press).

Shoemaker, D. (1968), 'Self-reference and Self-awareness', *Journal of Philosophy* LXV: 556–579.

Siderits, M. (2007), *Buddhism as Philosophy: An Introduction* (Indianapolis: Hackett Publishing Co.).

Spence, D. (1982), *Narrative Truth and Historical Truth* (New York: W.W. Norton).

Strawson, G. (1999a), 'The Self', in Shaun Gallagher and Jonathan Shear (eds.), *Models of the Self* (Exeter: Imprint Academic).

——(1999b), 'The Self and the SESMET', in Shaun Gallagher and Jonathan Shear (eds.), *Models of the Self* (Exeter: Imprint Academic).

——(2005), 'Introduction', in Strawson (ed.), *The Self?* (Oxford: Blackwell Publishing).

Taylor, C. (1989), *Sources of the Self: The Making of the Modern Identity* (Cambridge, MA: Harvard University Press).

Turner, J. (1991), 'To Tell a Good Tale: Kierkegaardian Reflections on Moral Narrative and Moral Truth', *Man and World* 24: 181–198.

Velleman, J. D. (2006), *Self to Self: Selected Essays* (New York: Cambridge University Press).

Williams, B. (2009), 'Life as Narrative', *European Journal of Philosophy* 17: 305–314.

Zahavi, D. (1999), *Self-Awareness and Alterity: A Phenomenological Investigation* (Evanston, IL: Northwestern University Press).

——(2005), *Subjectivity and Selfhood: Investigating the First-Person Perspective* (Cambridge, MA: MIT Press).

2

The Experiential Self: Objections and Clarifications

DAN ZAHAVI

1. Introduction

Let me start with three quotes from Sartre's *L'être et le néant*—three quotes that conjointly articulate a view of consciousness that I think is widespread among phenomenologists, and which I personally endorse.

It is not reflection which reveals the consciousness reflected-on to itself. Quite the contrary, it is the non-reflective consciousness which renders the reflection possible; there is a pre-reflective *cogito* which is the condition of the Cartesian *cogito*.

(Sartre 2003: 9)

This self-consciousness we ought to consider not as a new consciousness, but as the *only mode of existence which is possible for a consciousness of something.*

(Sartre 2003: 10)

[P]re-reflective consciousness is self-consciousness. It is this same notion of *self* which must be studied, for it defines the very being of consciousness.

(Sartre 2003: 100)

What is Sartre saying here? First of all, on Sartre's view, an experience does not simply exist, it exists in such a way that it is implicitly self-given, or as Sartre puts it, it is 'for itself'. This self-givenness of experience is not simply a quality added to the experience, a mere varnish: rather for Sartre the very *mode of being* of intentional consciousness is to be *for-itself* (*pour-soi*), that is, self-conscious (Sartre 1967, 2003: 10). Sartre is, moreover, quite explicit in emphasizing that the self-consciousness in question is *not* a new consciousness. It is not something added to the experience, an additional mental state, but rather an intrinsic feature of the experience.[1] When speaking of self-consciousness as a permanent feature of consciousness, Sartre is, consequently, not referring to what we might call reflective self-consciousness. Reflection (or higher-order representation) is the process whereby consciousness directs its intentional aim at itself, thereby taking itself as its own object. According to Sartre, however, this type of self-consciousness is derived; it involves a subject–object split, and the attempt to account for *self*-consciousness in such terms is, for Sartre, bound to fail. It either generates an infinite regress or accepts a non-conscious starting point, and he considers both options unacceptable (Sartre 2003: 8).

According to Sartre, the right alternative is to accept the existence of a pre-reflective and non-objectifying form of self-consciousness. To put it differently, on his account, consciousness has two different modes of givenness, a pre-reflective and a reflective. The first has priority since it can prevail independently of the latter, whereas reflective self-consciousness always presupposes pre-reflective self-consciousness. So to repeat, for Sartre pre-reflective self-consciousness is not an addendum to, but a constitutive moment of the original intentional experience.

In a subsequent move, Sartre then argues that consciousness, far from being impersonal and anonymous, is characterized by a fundamental selfness or selfhood precisely because of this pervasive self-givenness, self-intimation, or reflexivity. To quote the central passage from Sartre once again: 'pre-reflective consciousness is self-consciousness. It is this same notion of *self* which must be studied, for it defines the very being of consciousness.'

2. The Experiential Self

One way to interpret Sartre's final claim is as follows. Sartre (along with other phenomenologists) is drawing attention to a specific aspect of our experiential life, one that is so close to us, so taken for granted, that we tend

---

[1] Let me emphasize that the choice of the term 'intrinsic' is precisely meant to emphasize the difference from a higher-order or reflection-based account of self-consciousness, where self-consciousness is conceived in terms of a relation between two mental states. The term is not meant to indicate that we are dealing with a feature that our experiences possess in complete independence of everything else. To put it differently, to talk of self-consciousness as an intrinsic feature of experience is not to deny that the (self-conscious) experience in question is also intentional and world-directed.

to overlook it. As illustration, consider the following example. Imagine a situation where you first see a green apple and then see a yellow lemon. Then imagine that your visual perception of the yellow lemon is succeeded by a recollection of the yellow lemon. How should we describe the phenomenal complexity? One rather natural way to do so (which leaves out the fact and added complication that the whole scenario is played out in the imagination) is as follows: First, we have an intentional act of a specific type (a perception) which is directed at a specific object (an apple). Then we retain the intentional act-type (the perception), but replace the apple with another object (a lemon). In a final step, we replace the perception with another act-type (a recollection) while retaining the second object. By going through these variations, we succeed in establishing that an investigation of our experiential life shouldn't merely focus on the various intentional objects we can be directed at, but that it also has to consider the different intentional types or attitudes we can adopt. This is all trivial. But then consider the following question. If we compare the initial situation where we perceived a green apple with the final situation where we recollected a yellow lemon, there has been a change of both the object and the intentional type. Does such a change leave nothing unchanged in the experiential flow? Is the difference between the first experience and the last experience as radical as the difference between my current experience and the current experience of someone else? We should deny this. Whatever their type, whatever their object, there is something that the different experiences have in common. Not only is the first experience retained by the last experience, but the different experiences are all characterized by the same fundamental first-personal character. They are all characterized by what might be called a dimension of *for-me-ness* or *mineness* (Sartre uses the term *ipseity*—selfhood—from the Latin, *ipse*). It is, however, important to point to the special nature of this mineness. It is not meant to suggest that I own the experiences in a way that is even remotely similar to the way I possess external objects of various sorts (a car, my trousers, or a house in Sweden). Nor should it be seen primarily as a contrastive determination. When young children start to use the possessive pronoun, it frequently means 'not yours'. But as Husserl observes in one of his manuscripts, when it comes to the peculiar mineness (*Meinheit*) characterizing experiential life, this can and should be understood without any contrasting others (Husserl 1973b: 351), although it may form the basis of the self-other discrimination.

Some might object that there is no property common to all my experiences, no stamp or label that clearly identifies them as mine. But this objection is misplaced in that it looks for the commonality in the wrong place. The for-me-ness or mineness in question is not a quality like scarlet, sour, or soft. It doesn't refer to a specific experiential content, to a specific *what*, nor does it refer to the diachronic or synchronic sum of such content, or to some other relation that might obtain between the contents in question. Rather, it refers to the distinct givenness or *how* of experience. It refers to the first-personal presence of experience. It refers to the fact that the experiences I am living through are given differently (but not necessarily better) to me than to anybody else. It could consequently be claimed that anybody who denies the for-me-ness or mineness of experience simply fails to recognize an essential constitutive aspect of experience. Such a denial would be tantamount to a denial of the first-person perspective. It would entail the view that my own mind is either not given to me at all—I would be mind- or self-blind—or present to me in exactly the same way as the minds of others.

Sartre's basic move, which is to link the notion of self to pre-reflective self-consciousness, is nicely captured in a formulation by another French phenomenologist, Michel Henry, who writes that the most basic form of selfhood is the one constituted by the very self-manifestation of experience (Henry 1963: 581, 1965: 53). But who or what is this self that has, or lives through, the experiences? The phenomenological account I favor can be seen as occupying a kind of middle position between two opposing views. According to the first view, the self is some kind of unchanging soul substance that is distinct from, and ontologically independent of, the mental experiences and worldly objects it is the subject of. According to the second view, there is nothing to consciousness apart from a manifold of interrelated changing experiences. We might, to adopt some traditional labels, speak of the self as the owner of experiences, and the self as the bundle of experiences, respectively. By contrast, the self currently under consideration—and let us call it the experiential core self—is not a separately existing entity, but neither is it simply reducible to a specific experience or (sub-)set of experiences. If I compare two experiences, say the perception of a green apple and the recollection of a yellow lemon, I can focus on the difference between the two, namely the respective object and mode of presentation, but I can also attend to that which remains the same, namely the first-personal self-givenness of both experiences. To put it differently, we can distinguish a multitude of changing experiences from a *ubiquitous* dimension of first-personal self-givenness, and the proposal is that we identify the latter with the experiential core self. So on this view, the self is defined as the very subjectivity of experience, and is not taken to be something that exists independently of, or in separation from, the experiential flow.

When talking of first-personal self-givenness, one shouldn't think of self-reference by means of the first-person pronoun; in fact, one shouldn't think of a linguistically conditioned self-reference at all. Nor should one have an explicit or thematic kind of self-knowledge in mind, one where one is aware of oneself as a distinct individual, different from other individuals. No, first-personal self-givenness is meant to pinpoint the fact that (intransitively) conscious mental states are given in a distinct manner, with a distinct subjective presence, to the subject whose mental states they are, a way that in principle is unavailable to others. When saying 'distinct', the claim is not that the subject of the experience is explicitly aware of their distinct character: the point is not that the subject is necessarily attending to the distinctness in any way. But the first-personal self-givenness is distinctive even before, say, a child becomes explicitly aware of it, just as it is unavailable to others even prior to a child recognizing this.

Now, there are obviously various ways one might both elaborate on, as well as challenge this account. Does it fall victim to what Block has called the refrigerator illusion? Is our ordinary waking life characterized by an absorbed mindless coping, rather than by pre-reflective self-awareness? Is first-personal self-givenness and mineness a post hoc fabrication, something imputed to experience by subsequent mentalizing and theorizing? I don't have time to respond to these worries on this occasion (but see Zahavi 1999, 2005, 2009). Rather, I want to press ahead and directly engage with some of the criticisms that have been raised by defenders of a no-self doctrine. I will, more specifically, look at various objections recently made by Albahari and Dreyfus.

3. The Illusory Self

In her book *Analytical Buddhism: The Two-Tiered Illusion of Self*, Albahari's basic aim is to argue that the self is an illusion. What notion of self is she out to deny? She initially provides the following definition: The self should be understood as a unified, happiness-seeking, unbrokenly persisting, ontologically distinct conscious subject who is the owner of experiences, the thinker of thoughts, and the agent of actions. What is interesting about Albahari's proposal is that, whereas many advocates of a no-self doctrine have denied that consciousness is characterized by unity, unbrokenness, and invariability, and taken the denial of these features to amount to a denial of the reality of the self, Albahari considers all three to be real features of consciousness, but she nevertheless considers the self to be illusory (Albahari 2006: 3).

To get clearer on why she thinks this is the case let us look more closely at a distinction she introduces among different forms of ownership, namely *possessive ownership*, *perspectival ownership*, and *personal ownership*. We can ignore possessive ownership, which in this context is of less interest, since it merely denotes the fact that certain objects (a car, a pair of trousers, etc.) can be regarded as mine by right of social convention. But what is the difference between personal ownership and perspectival ownership? Personal ownership is a question of identifying oneself as the personal owner of an experience, thought, action: it is a question of appropriating certain experiences, actions, thoughts, etc. as one's own, that is, a question of either thinking of them as being *mine* or apprehending them as being part of *me* (and this is something that can occur either pre-reflectively or reflectively). By contrast, for a subject to own something in a perspectival sense is simply for the experience, thought, or action in question to present itself in a distinctive manner to the subject whose experience, thought or action it is. So the reason I can be said to perspectivally own my thoughts or perceptions—if one will excuse this slightly awkward way of talking—is because they appear to me in a manner that is different from how they can appear to anybody else. When it comes to objects external to the subject, what will be perspectivally owned isn't the object, but the specific manner through which the object appears to the subject (Albahari 2006: 53).

Albahari argues that there is a close link between having a sense of personal ownership and having a sense of self. When the subject identifies certain items as being itself or being part of itself, it will harbor a sense of personal ownership towards the items in question. But this very process of identification generates the sense of a self-other distinction. It constitutes a felt boundary between what belongs to self and what doesn't. Thereby the self is cast as a unified and ontologically distinct entity—one that stands apart from other things (Albahari 2006: 73, 90). In this way, the subject understood as a mere point of view is turned into a substantial personalized entity (Albahari 2006: 94). To put it differently, for Albahari, there is more to being a self than being a point of view, than having perspectival ownership.

One way to bring out the difference between perspectival and personal ownership is to point to possible dissociations between the two. Pathology seems to provide some examples. In cases of depersonalization, we can come across thoughts, feelings, etc. which are perspectivally owned, that is, which continue to present themselves in a unique manner to the subject, without however being felt as the subject's own (Albahari 2006: 55). Thus on Albahari's reading, the process of identification fails in depersonalization, and as a consequence, no sense of personal ownership regarding the experience in question will be generated (Albahari 2006: 61).

Let us now consider Albahari's self-skepticism. What does it mean for the self to lack reality? What does it mean for the self to be illusory? On Albahari's account, an illusion involves a conflict between appearance and reality. X is illusory if x does not have any appearance-independent reality, but nevertheless purports to have such reality, that is, we are dealing with an illusion if x purports through its appearance to exist in a particular manner without really doing so (Albahari 2006: 122). One obvious problem, however, with such a definition is whether it at all makes sense to apply it to the self. Does the self really purport to exist outside of its own appearance, or is the reality of the self rather subjective or experiential? This consideration leads Albahari to redefine the notion of illusion slightly. If the self purports to be what she calls unconstructed, that is, independent from the experiences and objects it is the subject of, and if it should turn out that it in reality depends, even if only partially, on perspectivally ownable objects (including various experiential episodes), then the self must be regarded as being illusory (Albahari 2006: 130).

Albahari also emphasizes the need for a distinction between self and sense of self. To have a sense of x, doesn't necessarily entail that x exists. Indeed, whereas Albahari takes the sense of self to exist and be real, she considers the self itself to be illusory (Albahari 2006: 17). Contrary to expectations, our sense of self is not underpinned by an actually existing ontologically independent self-entity. Rather, all that really exists is the manifold of thoughts, emotions, perceptions, etc. as well as a pure locus of apprehension, which Albahari terms *witness-consciousness*. It is the experiential flow in conjunction with this locus of apprehension that generates the sense of self. But if this is so, the self lacks an essential property of selfhood, namely ontological independence (Albahari 2006: 72). In short, the illusory status of the self is due to the fact that the self does not have the ontological status it purports to have. Thoughts appear to be owned and initiated by an independently existing unified self, but rather than preceding the experiences, rather than thinking the thoughts, it is in reality the other way around. It is not the self that unifies our thoughts and experiences, they do so themselves with some help from the accompanying witness-consciousness (Albahari 2006: 130–132). To repeat, although it might seem to the subject as if there is a pre-existing self which identifies with various intentional states, the reality of the matter is that the self is created and constructed through these repeated acts of identification (Albahari 2006: 58).

As I mentioned at the beginning, an interesting aspect of Albahari's proposal is that she considers many of the features traditionally ascribed to the self to be real, it is just that they—in her view—become distorted and illusory if taken to be features of the self (Albahari 2006: 74). For instance, Albahari takes our conscious life to be characterized by an intrinsic, but elusive, sense of subjective presence, one that is common to all modalities of awareness, that is, one that is common to seeing, hearing, thinking, feeling, introspecting, etc. (Albahari 2006: 112, 144, 156). What does this subjective presence amount to? It includes the experience of being the perspectival owner of various experiences. It also includes diachronic and synchronic unity. Although we experience various objects, and although the objects we experience might change from one moment to the next, there still appears to be an unbroken consciousness that observes the change without itself changing (Albahari 2006: 155). Indeed, while from a first-person perspective it certainly makes sense to say that I have various experiences, we automatically feel them to belong to one and the same consciousness. For Albahari, all these features are properly ascribed to the witness-consciousness, and she is adamant that we have to distinguish witness-consciousness from self. Whereas the latter on her definition involves felt boundaries between self and non-self, the former doesn't.

Let me recapitulate. For Albahari, one can be aware without being presented to oneself as an ontologically unique subject with personalized boundaries that distinguishes a *me* from the rest of the world. One can be aware without being aware of oneself as a personal owner, a thinker of thoughts, an agent of actions. Examples that come to mind are cases of pathology. Albahari asks us to consider both the real life case of epileptic automatism and the hypothetical case of global depersonalization. In both cases, the person or patient would be awake and responsive to the environment, so there would be awareness present. But there would be no sense of a bounded individual self; there would be a complete lack of personal ownership; there would be no sense of me or mine (Albahari 2006: 171, 177). Albahari suggests that such a state of mind might not only be encountered in pathologies, but also in newborn infants, and in primitive organisms. And as she then points out in the conclusion of her book, and this is of course where her Buddhist orientation becomes evident, if we were to attain enlightenment, we would move from consciousness-plus-self-illusion to consciousness-*sans*-self-illusion, and the latter condition, although strictly speaking not identical with global depersonalization—after all, it correlates with highly advanced cognitive capacities—might nevertheless be compared to it (Albahari 2006: 161, 207).

4. Self vs No-Self

The debate between advocates of self and no-self accounts is complicated by the fact that there is rather little consensus about what precisely a self amounts to, just as there is little agreement on what a no-self doctrine entails. Albahari's account in *Analytical Buddhism* constitutes a neat example of this. As we have just seen, Albahari basically denies the reality of the self and argues that it is illusory. To that extent, she should obviously count as a defender of a no-self account. At the same time, however, Albahari ascribes a number of features to what she calls witness-consciousness—features including invariance, unconstructedness, and ontological independence, features that many defenders of a traditional notion of self would consider essential and defining features of self. In fact, whereas I would suggest that we replace the traditional notion of a 'subject of experience' with the notion of a 'subjectivity of experience'—the first phrasing might suggest that the self is something that exists apart from, or above, the experience and, for that reason, something that might be encountered in separation from the experience, or even something the experience may occasionally lack, the second phrasing, however, excludes these types of misunderstanding—Albahari wants to retain the former notion, since she considers the subject ontologically distinct from the experiences. Some might consequently claim that Albahari, despite her official allegiance to the no-self doctrine, is actually committed to a more robust notion of self than many contemporary defenders of the self, myself included.[2] But of course, one might also make the reverse move. I defend the reality of self, but according to Albahari, the notion of self that I operate with is so thin, and ultimately so revisionary in nature, that she in a recent article has claimed that my position ends up being very similar to that of the no-self theorists I am criticizing (Albahari 2009: 80). When I first encountered this criticism, I was somewhat puzzled, but I have subsequently come to realize that there is an obvious sense in which Albahari is right. It all comes down to what precisely a no-self doctrine amounts to. As Ganeri has recently pointed out, there is no simple answer to the question of whether the aim of the no-self doctrine—insofar as one can at all speak of it in the singular—is to identify and reject a mistaken understanding of self—one that perpetuates suffering—or whether the point is rather to reject and dispel all notions of self (Ganeri 2007: 185–186).[3]

In his paper in this volume, Dreyfus has explicitly defended the view that, although the no-self view does entail a denial of a self-entity, it shouldn't be read as entailing a denial of subjectivity. There is on his view no enduring experiencing subject, no inner controller or homunculus. Rather what we find is an ever-changing stream of consciousness. This stream is, however, to be conceived of as a process of self-awareness. Dreyfus consequently argues that consciousness is characterized by pervasive reflexivity, by a basic

---

[2] Consider that although Albahari denies unconstructedness of self, she ascribes it to witness-consciousness. As she puts it at one point, 'awareness must be shown to exist in the manner it purports to exist. Awareness purports to exist as a witnessing presence that is unified, unbroken and yet elusive to direct observation. As something whose phenomenology purports to be unborrowed from objects of consciousness, awareness, if it exists, must exist as *completely unconstructed* by the content of any perspectivally ownable objects such as thoughts, emotions or perceptions. If *apparent* awareness... turned out to owe its existence to such object-content rather than to (unconstructed) *awareness itself,* then that would render awareness constructed and illusory and hence lacking in independent reality' (Albahari 2006: 162). This seems to commit one to viewing awareness as an ontologically independent region. It is not clear to me why one would want to uphold such a view of consciousness in the first place.

[3] Needless to say there is also a rather significant difference between claiming that experience is fundamentally selfless and claiming that a dissolution or annihilation of self is an ultimate state we can (and should) seek to attain.

self-presencing that is part and parcel of our experiential life, and not to be conceived of as an additional or separate act of cognition. In opposition to some of the bundle theorists, Dreyfus consequently denies that experiences are fundamentally impersonal, as if the attribution of first-personal self-givenness to our experiential life is a post hoc fabrication. Rather, our experiences are from the very start intrinsically self-specified (Dreyfus, this volume, p. 120). But although Dreyfus, by implication, is prepared to accept the reality of subjectivity, he insists that distortion arises the moment we interpret this subjectivity as a bounded, unified self (Dreyfus, this volume, p. 123). In short, the undeniable presence of a transient flow of self-aware experiences doesn't entail the existence of an enduring self-entity, rather the latter is on Dreyfus' view an illusory reification (Dreyfus, this volume, p. 31). More specifically, whereas Dreyfus wants to retain perspectival ownership and synchronic unity—and claims that both features are guaranteed by subjectivity—he argues that there is no diachronically unified self. There is no enduring entity that stays the same from childhood to adulthood.

Let me divide my critical rejoinder into three parts.

1. First of all, I reject the univocal definition of self provided by Dreyfus and Albahari. Both are very confident in spelling out what a self is, and after having defined it, they then proceed to deny its existence. In my view, however, the definition they provide is overly simplistic. There is no doubt that some people have defended the notion of self that Albahari and Dreyfus operate with, but I would dispute the claim that their notion is *the default notion*, that is, that it is either a particularly classical notion of self or that it is a particularly commonsensical notion, that is, one that is part of our folk psychology. Consider again the claim that the self—if it exists—is some kind of ontologically independent invariant *principle of identity* that stands apart from, and above, the stream of changing experiences; something that remains unchanging from birth to death; something that remains entirely unaffected by language acquisition, social relationships, major life events, personal commitments, projects, and values, something that cannot develop or flourish nor be disturbed or shattered. Frankly, I don't see such a notion as being very much in line with our pre-philosophical, everyday understanding of who we are. As for the claim that the definition captures *the* (rather than *a*) traditional philosophical understanding of self, this is also something I would dispute. Just consider, to take some (not entirely)

randomly chosen examples: the accounts we find in Aristotle or Montaigne (for informative historical overviews, cf. Sorabji 2006, Seigel 2005). In any case, when comparing the definition of self provided by Albahari and Dreyfus to the definitions found in contemporary discussions of self, it will immediately be evident that the latter discussions are far more complex, and far more equivocal, and that there are far more notions of self at play, including notions of ecological, experiential, dialogical, narrative, relational, embodied, and socially constructed selves. This complexity is ignored by Albahari and Dreyfus, and they thereby fail to realize that many of the contemporary notions of self—including those employed by most empirical researchers currently interested in the development, structure, function, and pathology of self—are quite different from the concept they criticize. To mention just one discipline that can exemplify this, consider developmental psychology and the work of developmental psychologists such as Stern (1985), Neisser (1988), Rochat (2001), Hobson (2002), or Reddy (2008). Thus, rather than saying that the self does not exist, I think self-skeptics should settle for a far more modest claim. They should qualify their statement and instead deny the existence of a special kind of self.

2. Albahari and Dreyfus both insist on distinguishing subjectivity and selfhood. Although Dreyfus doesn't say so explicitly, he would presumably agree with Albahari when she claims that my own notion of self is too thin and minimal, too deflationary and revisionary. In reply, let me right away concede that my thin notion of self is unable to accommodate or capture all ordinary senses of the term 'self'. In fact, it has some clear limitations, which I will return to in a moment. But although it certainly doesn't provide an exhaustive understanding of what it means to be a self, I think the very fact that we employ notions like *first-person* perspective, for-*me*-ness and *mineness* in order to describe our experiential life, the fact that the latter is characterized by a basic and pervasive immanent reflexivity, by *self*-specificity and pre-reflective *self*-awareness, is sufficient to warrant the use of the term 'self'. When arguing that an account of our experiential life that fails to include a reference to self is misleading and inadequate, I am to a large extent motivated by my opposition to the impersonality thesis, the no-ownership view, the strong anonymity claim (or whatever we want to call the position in question). I wish to insist on the basic (and quite formal) individuation of experiential life as well as on the irreducible difference

between one stream of consciousness and another stream of consciousness. Indeed, rather than obstructing or impeding a satisfactory account of inter-subjectivity, an emphasis on the inherent and essential individuation of experiential life is a prerequisite for getting the relation and difference between self and other right. I consequently fail to see how a radical denial of the reality of self will ever be able to respect the otherness of the other. To put it differently, I don't think the question of whether there is one or two streams is a matter of convention. The fact that we frequently share the same opinions, thoughts, beliefs, and values doesn't change this. As Wilde put it, 'Most people are other people. Their thoughts are some one else's opinions, their lives a mimicry, their passions a quotation' (Wilde 1969: 97). But again, this observation targets a different issue.

Of course, some might maintain that first-personal givenness is just too formal to act as individuating principle. After all, all experiences, not only mine but everybody's, are characterized by first-personal givenness, so how could such givenness serve to pinpoint and define me? This objection is wrongheaded, however, in that it precisely fails to take the first-person perspective seriously. Consider two clones that are qualitatively identical when it comes to physical and mental characteristics. From a third-person perspective, it would indeed be hard to distinguish the two (except in terms of spatial location), and the presence of first-personal givenness would be useless as a criterion of individuation, since both of their experiential streams would possess it. Indeed, from a third-person perspective there would be no significant difference at all between the first-person givenness characterizing the experiential stream of clone A, and the first-person givenness character-izing the experiential stream of clone B. But compare, then, what happens if we instead adopt the first-person perspective. Let us assume that I am one of the clones. Although my mental and physical characteristics are qualitatively identical to those of my 'twin', there will still remain a critical and all-decisive difference between me and him, a difference that would prevent any confusion between the two of us. What might that difference consist in? It obviously has to do with the fact that only my experiences are given in a first-personal mode of presentation to me, whereas the qualitatively identi-cal experiences of my clone are not given first-personally to me at all, and are therefore not part of my experiential life. As mentioned earlier, it is the particular first-personal *how* rather than some specific content which most fundamentally distinguishes my experiences from the experiences had by others. This is why I wish to insist that the subjectivity of experience, its first-personal character, although quite formal, does individuate experiential life. This is also why it can function as placeholder for features traditionally associated with the self.

Importantly, this emphasis on the first-personal character of experience does not entail an endorsement of the view that the self is unconstructed or unconditioned, in the sense of being ontologically independent of the experiences or the surrounding world, nor does it entail the view that the self is bounded in the sense of involving a strict division between self and world.[4] As a case in point, consider and compare Neisser's and Heidegger's notions of self. According to Neisser's notion of ecological self, all perception involves a kind of self-sensitivity: all perception involves a co-perception of self and of environment (Neisser 1988). As for Heidegger, he explicitly argues that we should look at our intentional experiences if we wish to study the self. On his account, our experiential life is world-related, and there is a presence of self when we are engaged with the world, that is, self-experience is the self-experience of a world-immersed self (Heidegger 1993: 34, 250). But to deny that there is a strict boundary between self and world, to concede that self and world cannot be understood independently of each other and that the boundary between the two might be plastic and shifting, is not to question the reality of the difference between the two. To take an everyday example, consider the ever-shifting boundary between the sea and the beach. That the boundary keeps shifting is no reason to deny the difference between the two. To put it differently, contrary to the views of Albahari and Dreyfus, I would dispute that unconstructedness and bound-edness are essential features of self, features that any viable notion of self must include. This is also why I reject the attempt to distinguish subjectivity and selfhood. As I see it, to reject the existence of self while endorsing the reality of subjectivity is to miss out on what subjectivity really amounts

---

[4] Though, as already pointed out, I am committed to the view that there is indeed a firm boundary between self and other—as long as our concern is limited to the experiential notion of self. To quote James, 'Absolute insulation, irreducible pluralism, is the law. It seems as if the elementary psychic fact were not *thought* or *this thought* or *that thought*, but *my thought*, every thought being *owned*. Neither contemporaneity, nor proximity in space, nor similarity of quality and content are able to fuse thoughts together which are sundered by this barrier of belonging to different personal minds. The breaches between such thoughts are the most absolute breaches in nature' (James 1890: 226).

to—it is to pay lip service to the idea that we should take the first-person perspective serious.

3. My third comment concerns the metaphysical framework we are operating within. In recent years, quite a number of people have stressed the existence of convergent ideas in Western phenomenology and Buddhism. It has been claimed that both traditions represent serious efforts to nurture a disciplined first-person approach to consciousness (cf. Varela and Shear 1999), and some have even started to speak of Buddhist phenomenology (cf. Lusthaus 2002). I am not denying the truth of this, but when appraising Buddhist views of the nature and status of self, one should not overlook the fact that they are also driven and motivated by strong metaphysical and soteriological concerns, and that this occasionally leads to claims and conclusions that are quite far removed from phenomenology. As an example, consider the Abhidharmic view that billions of distinct mind-moments occur in the span of a blink of the eye (cf. Bodhi 1993: 156).

Dennett (1992) and Metzinger (2003) both deny the reality of the self, and part of their reason for doing this, part of the reason why they think the self is fictitious, is that a truly fundamental account of reality on their view can dispense with self. Some Buddhist metaphysicians would share this view (cf. Siderits' and MacKenzie's contributions to this volume). Although I have sympathy with the idea that we shouldn't multiply entities beyond necessity, I think the view in question is far too austere. It is hard to see why one shouldn't declare social reality fictitious on the same account. If there is no self, there can hardly be a *you* or a *we* either. In fact, it is hard to see why we shouldn't also declare the world we live in and know and care about (including everyday objects and events like chairs, playing cards, operas, or marriage ceremonies) illusory. Again, such a view is quite different from the phenomenological attempt to rehabilitate our life-world.

In the preceding, I have discussed a thin experiential notion of self, and have tried to present and defend this view. Ultimately, however, I favor what might be called a multidimensional account of self. I think the self is so multifaceted a phenomenon that various complementary accounts must be integrated if we are to do justice to its complexity. I consequently don't think that the thin notion I have defended above is sufficient. It must be supplemented by thicker notions that capture and do justice to other important aspects of self. More specifically, I think our account of human reality is inadequate if we don't also consider the self that forms plans, makes promises, and accepts responsibilities, the self that is defined and shaped by its values, ideals, goals, convictions, and decisions. Consider as a case in point the issue of emotional investment: consider that we respond emotionally to that which matters to us, to that which we care about, to that towards which we are not indifferent. In that sense, one might argue that emotions involve appraisals of what has importance, significance, value, and relevance to oneself. Consider the extent to which emotions like shame, guilt, pride, hope, and repentance help constitute our sense of self. Consider in this context also the role of boundaries and limits. Your limits express the norms and rules you abide by; they express what you can accept and what you cannot accept. They constitute your integrity. To ask others to respect your boundaries is to ask them to take you seriously as a person. A violation of, or infringement upon, these boundaries is felt as invasive, and in some cases as humiliating. To put it differently, when it comes to these facets of self, I think boundaries, values, and emotions are extremely important, but I don't think an emphasis on boundaries has much to do with the endorsement of an enduring soul-substance that remains the same from birth to death. And I don't see why opposition to the latter should necessitate a rejection of the former as well. We are dealing with a culturally, socially, and linguistically embedded self that is under constant construction. But is this fact a reason for declaring the self in question illusory? I don't see why, unless, that is, one's prior metaphysical commitments dictate it.

5. Diachronic Unity and the Self

Let me end with a question that I quite on purpose have saved for last. It concerns the relation between self and diachronic unity. Is persistence and temporal endurance a defining feature of self?

We all have a direct experience of change and persistence. We can hear an enduring tone or a melody, just as we can see the flight of a bird. This phenomenological finding must be accounted for, and as a distinguished line of thinkers—including James, Bergson, Husserl, and more recently, Dainton—have argued, a mere succession of synchronically unified but isolated momentary points of experience cannot explain and account for our experience of duration. To actually perceive an object as enduring over time, the successive phases of consciousness must somehow be united experientially, and the decisive challenge is to account for this temporal binding without giving rise to an infinite regress, that is, without having to posit yet another temporally extended consciousness whose task is to unify the first-order consciousness, and so forth ad infinitum. To account for the diachronic unity of consciousness, there is, however, no need for an appeal to some undivided, invariable, unchanging, trans-temporal entity. In order to understand the unity in question, we do not need to search for anything above, beyond, or external to the stream itself. Rather, following Husserl, I would propose that the unity of the stream of consciousness is constituted by inner time-consciousness, by the interplay between what Husserl calls primal impression, retention, and protention. Rather than being pre-given, it is a unity that is established or woven. This is not the right place to delve into the intricacies of Husserl's complex account (see, however, Zahavi 2003, 2004, 2007a), but on his account, even the analysis of something as synchronic as the conscious givenness of a present experience would have to include a consideration of temporality. For the very same reason, I would reject Dreyfus's attempt to make a sharp distinction between synchronic unity which he accepts, and diachronic unity which he rejects. You cannot have synchronic unity without some amount of diachronic unity (if ever so short-lived). To claim otherwise is to miss the fundamental temporal character of consciousness. Now, perhaps it could be objected that our experience of diachronic unity is after all 'merely' phenomenological and consequently devoid of any metaphysical impact. But to think that one can counter the phenomenological experience of unity over time with the claim that this unity is illusory and that it doesn't reveal anything about the true metaphysical nature of consciousness is to make use of the appearance-reality distinction outside its proper domain of application. This is especially so, given that the reality in question, rather than being defined in terms of some spurious mind-independence, should be understood in terms of experiential reality. For comparison, consider the case of pain. Who would deny that pain experience is sufficient for the reality of pain? To put it differently, if one wants to dispute the reality of the diachronic unity of consciousness, one should do so by means of more convincing phenomenological descriptions. To argue that the diachronic unity of consciousness is illusory because it doesn't match any unity on the subpersonal level is to misunderstand the task at hand.

Very well, the skeptic might retort, but accepting that our experiential life has a certain temporal density and extension is hardly the same as accepting the existence of a persisting self from birth to death. Quite right, I would reply, but even the former might be sufficient if you want to defend the existence of transient short-term selves, as Galen Strawson has consistently done (Strawson 2000), and I don't think Dreyfus has provided arguments against that specific notion of self.[5] But more importantly, although Dreyfus denies that in his own case there is an entity that has endured from his childhood in Switzerland to his being a grown-up adult in the US, he does concede that we, in the case of episodic memory, do not have two absolutely different persons, the person remembering and the person remembered. In fact, on his account, we do have to keep first-personal self-givenness in mind, and although the remembering person is in some sense different from the one being remembered, the difference is certainly not as great as the one that separates me from other people (Dreyfus, this volume, p. 132). My present act of remembering and the past act that is being remembered both share similar first-personal self-givenness. They consequently have something in common that distinguishes them from the experiences of others. As Dreyfus continues, when I remember a past experience, I don't just recall its content, I also remember it as being given to me. Now on his account, there is something distorting about this, insofar as the past experience is remembered as mine (thereby suggesting the existence of an enduring self), but as he continues, this isn't a complete distortion either (Dreyfus, this volume, p. 132).

On my account, there is no experiential self, no self as defined from the first-person perspective, when we are non-conscious.[6] But this does not

---

[5] In his defense of a no-self account, Krueger claims that a Who is neither necessary nor sufficient for a How. In arguing for this view, Krueger repeatedly concedes that it might be legitimate to speak of minimal selves (rather than of a minimal self) (Krueger, this volume, p. 47). However, I find it quite hard to understand how the existence of a plurality of selves is compatible with, or might even count in favor of, a no-self theory, unless, of course, one stacks the deck by presupposing a quite particular definition of self.

[6] This is also why I don't think the notion of experiential self will allow us to solve all relevant questions regarding personal identity and persistence over time. Consider, for instance, the case of a man who early in life makes a decision that proves formative for his subsequent life and career. The episode in question is, however, subsequently forgotten by the person. He no longer enjoys first-person access to it. If we restrict ourselves to what can be accounted for by means of the experiential core self, we cannot speak of the decision as being his, as being one he made. Or take the case where we might wish to ascribe responsibility for past actions to an individual who no longer remembers them. By doing that we postulate an identity between the past offender and the present subject, but the identity in question is

necessarily imply that the diachronic unity of self is threatened by alleged interruptions of the stream of consciousness (such as dreamless sleep, coma, etc.), since the identity of the self is defined in terms of givenness rather than in terms of temporal continuity. To put it differently, experiences that I live through from a first-person perspective are by definition mine, regardless of their content and temporal location. Thus, I don't think there is any mistake or distortion involved in remembering the past experiences as mine. Obviously this is not to say that episodic memory is infallible—I might have false beliefs about myself—I am only claiming that it is not subject to the error of misidentification (cf. Campbell 1994: 98–99). But does that mean that I take the first-personal self-givenness of the experiences as evidence for the persistence of an underlying enduring self? No, I don't, since the self I have been discussing in this paper is the experiential self, the self as defined from the first-person perspective—neither more nor less. I think this self is real and that it possesses real diachronicity, but as already mentioned I don't think its reality—its phenomenological reality—depends on its ability to mirror or match or represent some non-experiential enduring ego-substance. Having said this, let me just add that, although I don't think there is distortion involved in remembering a past experience as mine, there is admittedly and importantly more than just pure and simple identity. Episodic memory does involve some kind of doubling or fission; it does involve some degree of self-division, self-absence, and self-alienation. Episodic memory constitutes a kind of self-experience that involves identity as well as difference. At least this is pretty much phenomenological orthodoxy. As Husserl already insisted, recollection entails a self-displacement, and he went on to argue that there is a structural similarity between recollection and empathy (Husserl 1954: 189, 1966: 309, 1973a: 318, 1973b: 416). A related idea is also to be found in Merleau-Ponty, who wrote that our temporal existence is both a condition for, and an obstacle to,

again not one that can be accounted for in terms of the experiential core self. But given my commitment to a multidimensional account of self, I would precisely urge us to adopt a multilayered account of self. We are more than experiential core selves, we are, for instance, also narratively configured and socially constructed persons (cf. Zahavi 2007b). We shouldn't forget that our life-stories are multi-authored. Who we are is not something we exclusively determine ourselves. It is also a question of how we are seen by others. Even if there is no experiential self (no self as defined from the first-person perspective) when we are non-conscious, there are various other aspects of self that remain, and which make it perfectly legitimate to say that *we* are non-conscious, that is, that we can persist even when non-conscious. For a recent, very elaborate, and rather metaphysical discussion of these questions, cf. Dainton (2008).

our self-comprehension. Temporality contains an internal fracture that permits us to return to our past experiences in order to investigate them reflectively, yet this very fracture also prevents us from fully coinciding with ourselves (Merleau-Ponty 2002: 402).

But again, to some this answer might be dissatisfactory and evade the real issue: Is there or is there not an identical self from birth through childhood, adolescence, adulthood, and old age. Ultimately, I think this question is overly simplistic, since it presupposes that the self is one thing, and that there is a simple yes or no answer to the question. I disagree, and think the answer will depend on what notion of self we are talking about. But let me forego this complication and stick to the problem of whether or not the experiential self, the self as defined in terms of subjectivity, remains invariant across large time stretches. To put it differently, when remembering—from the first-person perspective—an episode that took place fifteen years ago, when remembering that past experience as mine, are we then confronted with a case where the experiential self has remained the same? Is the experiential self that originally lived through the experience 15 years ago, and the experiential self that today recalls the past experience, one and the same numerically identical self, or are we merely dealing with a relationship between two qualitatively similar selves, where the current self might stand, say, in a unique causal relationship to the former self?

I must confess my initial hesitancy when faced with these kinds of metaphysical questions: a hesitancy that probably stems from the fact that this simply isn't the way the self has traditionally been discussed in phenomenology. But here is my, perhaps surprising, reply. I find the idea that a stream of consciousness might start off as mine and end up being somebody else's radically counter-intuitive (cf. Dainton 2008, 18). Moreover, the moment one insists that the stream of consciousness is made up of a plurality of ontologically distinct (but qualitatively similar) short-term selves, one is inevitably confronted with the question regarding their relationship. I don't see any real alternative to the following proposal: their relationship is akin to the relationship between my self and the self of somebody else. And I find this proposal absurd.

But even if similarity doesn't amount to identity, surely—some might object—we need to distinguish an account claiming that the stream of consciousness involves some form of experiential *continuity* from an account claiming that it somehow involves diachronic *identity*. My response will be to question the relevance and significance of that distinction in the present context. To put it differently, in my view the continuity provided by the stream of consciousness, the unity provided by shared first-personal self-givenness, is sufficient for the kind of experiential self-identity that I am eager to preserve. If you find this insufficient, I think you are looking for the wrong kind of identity.[7]

References

Albahari, M. (2006), *Analytical Buddhism: The Two-Tiered Illusion of Self* (New York: Palgrave Macmillan).

——(2009), 'Witness-Consciousness: Its Definition, Appearance and Reality', *Journal of Consciousness Studies* 16/1: 62–84.

Bodhi, Bhikkhu, (ed.) (1993), *A Comprehensive Manual of Abhidharma* (Seattle, WA: Buddhist Publication Society).

Campbell, J. (1994), *Past, Space, and Self* (Cambridge, MA: MIT Press).

Dainton, B. (2008), *The Phenomenal Self* (Oxford: Oxford University Press).

Dennett, D. (1992), 'The Self as the Center of Narrative Gravity', in Frank S. Kessel, Pamela M. Cole, and Dale L. Johnson (eds.), *Self and Consciousness: Multiple Perspectives* (Hillsdale, NJ: Erlbaum).

Ganeri, J. (2007), *The Concealed Art of the Soul: Theories of Self and Practices of Truth in Indian Ethics and Epistemology* (Oxford: Oxford University Press).

Heidegger, M. (1993), *Grundprobleme der Phänomenologie (1919/1920)*. Gesamtausgabe Band 58 (Frankfurt am Main: Vittorio Klostermann).

Henry, M. (1963), *L'essence de la manifestation* (Paris: PUF).

——(1965), *Philosophie et phénoménologie du corps* (Paris: PUF).

Hobson, R. P. (2002), *The Cradle of Thought* (London: Macmillan).

---

[7] One might here mention Ricoeur's careful distinction between two concepts of identity: Identity as sameness (*mêmeté*) and identity as selfhood (*ipséité*) (Ricoeur 1990). The first concept of identity, the identity of the same (Latin: *idem*), conceives of the identical as that which can be re-identified again and again, as that which resists change. The identity in question is that of an unchangeable substance, or substrate, that remains the same over time. By contrast, the second concept of identity, the identity of the self (Latin: *ipse*), has on Ricoeur's account very little to do with the persistence of some unchanging personality core. Whereas questions regarding the first concept of identity take the form of What questions, questions regarding the second concept take the form of Who questions, and must be approached from the first-person perspective.

Husserl, E. (1954), *Die Krisis der europäischen Wissenschaften und die transzendentale Phänomenologie: Eine Einleitung in die phänomenologische Philosophie*, Husserliana 6 (Den Haag: Martinus Nijhoff).

——(1966), *Analysen zur passiven Synthesis: Aus Vorlesungs- und Forschungsmanu-skripten 1918–1926*, Husserliana 11 (Den Haag: Martinus Nijhoff).

——(1973a), *Zur Phänomenologie der Intersubjektivität: Texte aus dem Nachlass. Erster Teil: 1905–1920*, Husserliana 13 (Den Haag: Martinus Nijhoff).

——(1973b), *Zur Phänomenologie der Intersubjektivität: Texte aus dem Nachlass. Dritter Teil: 1929–1935*, Husserliana 15 (Den Haag: Martinus Nijhoff).

James, W. (1890), *The Principles of Psychology I* (London: Macmillan and Co.).

Lusthaus, D. (2002), *Buddhist Phenomenology: A Philosophical Investigation of Yogacara Buddhism and the Ch'eng Wei-shih Lun* (London: Routledge).

Merleau-Ponty, M. (2002), *Phenomenology of Perception* (London: Routledge).

Metzinger, T. (2003), *Being No One* (Cambridge, MA: MIT Press).

Neisser, U. (1988), 'Five Kinds of Self-knowledge', *Philosophical Psychology* 1/1: 35–59.

Reddy, V. (2008), *How Infants Know Minds* (Cambridge, MA.: Harvard University Press).

Ricoeur, P. (1990), *Soi-même comme un autre* (Paris: Seuil).

Rochat, P. (2001), *The Infant's World* (Cambridge, MA: Harvard University Press).

Sartre, J. (1967), 'Consciousness of Self and Knowledge of Self', in N. Lawrence and D. O'Connor (eds.), *Readings in Existential Phenomenology* (Englewood Cliffs, N.J.: Prentice-Hall).

——(2003), *Being and Nothingness* (London: Routledge).

Seigel, J. (2005), *The Idea of the Self: Thought and Experience in Western Europe Since the Seventeenth Century* (Cambridge: Cambridge University Press).

Sorabji, R. (2006), *Self: Ancient and Modern Insights about Individuality, Life and Death* (Oxford: Clarendon Press).

Stern, D. N. (1985), *The Interpersonal World of the Infant* (New York: Basic Books).

Strawson, G. (2000), 'The phenomenology and ontology of the self', in D. Zahavi (ed.), *Exploring the Self* (Amsterdam: John Benjamins).

Varela, F. and Shear, J. (eds.) (1999), *The View from Within: First-Person Approaches to the Study of Consciousness* (Thorverton: Imprint academic).

Wilde, O. (1969), *De Profundis* (London: Dawsons).

Zahavi, D. (1999), *Self-Awareness and Alterity: A Phenomenological Investigation* (Evanston, IL: Northwestern University Press).

——(2003), 'Inner Time-Consciousness and Pre-reflective Self-Awareness', in D. Welton (ed.), *The New Husserl: A Critical Reader* (Bloomington, IN: Indiana University Press).

Zahavi, D. (2004), 'Time and Consciousness in the Bernau Manuscripts', *Husserl Studies* 20/2: 99–118.

——(2005), *Subjectivity and Selfhood: Investigating the First-Person Perspective* (Cambridge, MA: MIT Press).

——(2007a), 'Perception of Duration Presupposes Duration of Perception—or Does it? Husserl and Dainton on Time', *International Journal of Philosophical Studies* 15/3: 453–471.

——(2007b), 'Self and Other: The Limits of Narrative Understanding', in D. D. Hutto (ed.), *Narrative and Understanding Persons* (Cambridge: Cambridge University Press).

——(2009), 'Is the Self a Social Construct?' *Inquiry* 52/6: 551–573.

3

Nirvana and Ownerless Consciousness

MIRI ALBAHARI

1. Introduction

A Buddhist friend remarked recently: 'Perhaps one or two *arahants* exist in the world'. 'Arahant' (or *arhat*) is a Buddhist term for someone who has attained the *summum bonum* of Buddhist practice. Such a state is known as 'enlightenment' or *nirvāna*. While Buddhist traditions will differ in their exact depictions of nirvana, most would agree that a sense of the self, with its attendant feelings of 'me' and 'mine', is extinguished. With it is extinguished the capacity to suffer mentally. There is a radical shift in motivational structure: no longer do such persons seek gratification from any state of affairs. Losing family or suffering illness fails to dent their equanimity. The arahant operates from a different basis: no more identifying with the 'I' of such situations than most of us would identify with burning leaves on a fire. Yet they still act fluently in the world—with great joy and spontaneity and compassion.

The 'perhaps' of my Buddhist friend was meant to indicate the extreme rarity of such people. Buddhist tradition holds the pull of craving and attachment, needed to sustain the illusion of self, to be so strong that it would take lifetimes of dedicated practice to vanquish. As a philosopher, I am interested in taking the 'perhaps' another way: not as an indication of rarity, but of *modality*. Is it really psychologically possible for an arahant to exist, human brains and minds being what they are? Can people really become so free from the sense of self that they no longer identify with their bodies or minds, and yet still act fluently and without suffering in the world? Or is such an idea, which has inspired thousands to be ordained as monks or nuns, likely to be steeped in religious fantasy? Serious investigation into the possibility of nirvana has not yet entered mainstream analytic philosophy, even though its implications for the metaphysics of mind, if it *were* possible, could well be significant. Western philosophy has tended to zero in on the structure of the ordinary person's mind, the extraordinary being confined to pathological impairment. If nirvana was shown to be possible, then I contend that much of value could be learnt from analyzing the mind's extraordinary capacities.

To the extent that nirvana can be described (itself a matter of contention), it is so multifaceted that no investigation could do justice to all aspects within a single work. This is compounded by the fact that Buddhist traditions diverge on how nirvana is to be exactly understood. My own interpretation focuses particularly on the relation between nirvana and no-self, and is based upon a philosophical reconstruction from discourses (sutras) of the Pali Canon (which I call 'Pali Buddhism' for short). We will see that this challenges an orthodoxy considered by many to be classically 'Buddhist'.

I mentioned that most Buddhist traditions agree that nirvana entails insight into the truth of no-self, such that certain feelings of 'me' and 'mine' are vanquished (however these key notions are to be understood). So when investigating the possibility of nirvana, it is worth asking of a chosen Buddhist tradition: What is the most likely relationship between the sense of self and the ubiquitous feeling of ownership (or 'mineness') had towards one's thoughts and experiences? Could any form of consciousness survive the possible destruction of these ownership-feelings? Could ownerless consciousness be an underlying feature of the everyday mind? The goal of this paper is to draw together the most salient points about consciousness, ownership, and no-self that arose from my initial foray into Pali Buddhism, and to further develop some of the arguments in relation to later work on the subject.[1] I hope it will transpire that even a preliminary investigation into the psychological possibility of nirvana can be a valuable

---

[1] Many of the concepts and arguments in this paper originated in my book *Analytical Buddhism* (2006) and in my (2009) paper, some of which are developed here further, sometimes from a different angle. Other arguments (such as that supporting my interpretation of no-self in Pali Buddhism) are entirely new. (A detailed canonical defense of my interpretation of nirvana and no-self can be found in chapters 2–3 of Albahari 2006).

exercise in drawing distinctions that may help to illuminate the architecture of the *everyday* mind.

The paper has three parts. In Part One, I outline in some detail the notion of self that I contend is most central to Pali Buddhism: the self that is purported to have illusory status. It is not an abstract or ethereal concept (such as a non-physical soul), but a notion that describes the very thing that most of us unquestioningly take ourselves to be. If this were indeed not the case, then there would be little relevance to the possibility of *losing* the sense of a self in the process of attaining nirvana.

In Part Two, I argue that the process of attaining nirvana (as construed in Pali Buddhism) would place important constraints on the structure of the self-illusion, setting it apart from standard Western accounts of no-self. It is fairly uncontentious that each person seems somewhat aware of a stream of various objects, including thoughts and perceptions, and that these objects seem presented, in our conscious awareness, to a point of view. This point of view appears to be unified, both synchronically and, from moment to waking moment, diachronically. (I term this point of view a 'perspectival owner'.) But does the perspectival owner really exist? On most Western theories of no-self (pioneered by Hume), this unified conscious perspective lies at the heart of the self-illusion. All the conscious mind is really furnished with, it is claimed, are bundles of evanescent mental phenomena: thoughts and perceptions (etc.) that interact with mental mechanisms to create the illusion of a unified perspective that observes them. Of crucial relevance here is that the Buddhist theory of no-self is typically depicted by Buddhist scholars of different traditions as a type of bundle theory. While I have argued elsewhere that a bundle theory of no-self is not supported by specific sutras in the Pali Canon, the purposes of this paper are chiefly philosophical. To this end I offer a new argument against interpreting Buddhist sutras as bundle-theory reductionism—whether the reductionism is non-reflexive (discussed in this volume by Mark Siderits) or reflexive (discussed in this volume by Georges Dreyfus, Evan Thompson, Matthew MacKenzie, and Joel Krueger). I argue that if we take seriously the soteriological Buddhist injunction that the truth of no-self in nirvana is to be known experientially (e.g. through meditation) rather than just inferentially (e.g. through philo-sophical analysis), then a bundled mind will not be the sort of thing that can be known in the right way. The heart of the self-illusion will instead, I contend, lie in the personalized *identity* that seems to place a boundary around the (real) unified perspective, turning it into what I call a 'personal owner'. I contend that this boundary, underpinning the sense of 'who I am' versus 'what I am not', is the true target of early Buddhist practices that seek to eliminate the sense of a self. What remains after the sense of self has dissolved is a unified perspectival 'witness–consciousness' that, insofar as it lacks the illusion of a personal self, is intrinsically ownerless.

If nirvana is possible, and my arguments are accepted, then it has implications for how the everyday mind is structured. The personal-owner-self will be an illusion, while the unified witness–consciousness, which comes through in the ordinary sense of self, will be real. The mind will therefore exemplify a 'two-tiered' rather than 'bundled' illusion of self. In Part Three, I offer some independent reasons for supposing that the two-tiered illusion of self is exemplified in the everyday mind.

2. The Central Notion of Self

If nirvana is the seeing-through of the self-illusion, then investigation into its possibility must be clear on the kind of self that is supposedly seen through. This is especially important if, as Dan Zahavi and Joel Krueger claim, definitions of the self abound (Zahavi, this volume, p. 66, Krueger, this volume, p. 34). It is also important that the 'self' in this case depicts something central, something that most of us have a sense of being. Should it turn out, for instance, that the 'self' of Buddhist sutras refers primarily to an immortal soul, the prospect of seeing through the illusion of self would be irrelevant to most people, who do not presuppose its existence.[2] Else-where, I spend some time extracting from early Buddhist sutras the relevant notion of the self, and then arguing that this notion of the self, which closely matches that alluded to by many Western philosophers (such as Hume, James, and Dennett), is presupposed in our modes of thinking and living.[3] For reasons of space I will not recite the arguments here, although I will insist, *contra* Zahavi, that it is very much a notion 'in line with our

---

[2] This is not to deny that the Buddha did caution Brahmanical thinkers against becoming enamoured with more theoretical elaborations of the self, involving eternal, non-physical impartite entities serving as the vehicle of rebirth.

[3] See Albahari (2006, chs. 2–4).

pre-philosophical, everyday understanding of who we are' (Zahavi, this volume, p. 66). The purpose of this section is, thus, to elucidate what I take to be the central features of this assumed self, drawing in particular on a distinction that I make between perspectival and personal ownership. As already hinted, the distinction will figure centrally in my account of how the self is illusory and what survives its destruction. In essence, then this commonly assumed self is a unified, unbrokenly persisting subject of experience with personalized boundaries and a perspective on the world. It is a thinker, owner, and agent that stands behind, and is somewhat in charge of, the stream of thoughts and experiences, as opposed to being constructed by them.

First and foremost, the self (that we have a sense of being) is a *subject*, as opposed to *object* of experience. 'The subject' describes that aspect of the ordinary self which is the inner locus of the first-person perspective: the conscious embodied viewpoint from which the world is apprehended. The subject's modus operandi is simply to observe or *witness* objects through a variety of perceptual and cognitive modalities. I hence use the term 'witness-consciousness' to describe the purely observational component that is common to all modes of conscious apprehension, perceptual or cognitive.[4] While this term has sometimes been used by scholars of Advaita Vēdanta with additional metaphysical commitment (e.g. Bina Gupta 1998), or to convey a relation of dependence with experiential objects (e.g. Wolfgang Fasching, this volume), my use of the term is intended to be neutral on this front. That said, my usage is quite congruent with Fasching's, insofar as he writes that witness-consciousness is 'nothing but seeing itself' (as opposed to a thing that 'sees') and is experientially present to our conscious life (Fasching, this volume, p. 194). (Later I will argue, in agreement with Fasching, that witness-consciousness is unified and to some extent unbroken, but importantly, this is not built into my definition of the term).

I use the term 'object' to describe anything that can possibly be attended to by a (witnessing) subject: thoughts, perceptions, trees, bodies, actions, or events. Any conscious creature is uniquely positioned to observe (via witness-consciousness) an array of such objects as pains, thoughts, or its

---

[4] For a full definition and defense of the reality of witness-consciousness, see Albahari (2009). In Albahari (2006), I specifically relate the notion of witness-consciousness to that of the consciousness aggregate (Pali: *khandhā*; Sanskrit: *skandha*)—one of the five conditioned elements that Pali Buddhism claims to constitute a person.

own body, from a perspective to which no other creature has direct access. Insofar as various objects appear to a subject's perspective, in this direct first-personal way, the subject can be termed a *perspectival owner* of the objects. While the perspectival owner or minimal subject is built into the self, it does not, as it stands, amount to a self: it is rather a mere locus for the first-person perspective. The relation that perspectivally owned objects bear to the subject *qua* perspectival owner matches what Dan Zahavi calls the 'first-personal givenness' or 'for-me-ness' of experience, and it is at play whenever one speaks of 'my headache', 'my body', or 'my actions'. I don't concur with Zahavi, however, in holding that for-me-ness *is* a minimal self or subject, as for-me-ness is a dimension of the stream of experiences rather than the subject experiencing the stream. (This will become relevant later in the discussion).[5]

Of note is that the subject (and the wider self) cannot appear directly to itself in the focal manner of a perspectivally owned object, so although seeming to have a subtle phenomenal character (and hence a *sense* of itself), which can be enhanced during meditational practice, the subject is perpetually elusive to its own focally attentive purview. *Elusiveness* is thus a key attribute of the minimal subject, *contra* Strawson (this volume) who insists that a subject can be attentively (or 'thetically') aware of itself as it is in the present moment.

The self, as I've indicated, is more than just an elusive subject *qua* perspective on the world: it is a subject assimilated with several other roles. First and foremost is the role of *personal owner*. A personal owner, a *me*, is a subject with an *identity* (or 'who-I-am-ness') as opposed to a merely impersonal point of view. In relation to this identity as personal owner, the existing ownership of various items, whether perspectival (such as thoughts or feelings) or possessive (such as houses or cars), also takes on a personal 'mineness' dimension. In relation to one's felt identity as a Michael Jackson fan, for example, an autographed record by the artist is felt to be personally, not just possessively owned. In this manner such items become warmly infused with a sense of mineness that goes beyond a rational recognition of one's legal status as owner of the object. Conversely, the sense of personal ownership or mineness towards an object will seem to reveal a facet of one's

---

[5] See, for example, Zahavi (2005a; 9–10) and Zahavi (2005b: 122–123). The distinction between witness-consciousness and for-me-ness is discussed further in Albahari (2009: 67–68).

fixed self-identity as its personal owner, enhancing the sense of *me-ness*. A felt identity is made perspicuous through *identification*, where certain ideas (such as gender, race, character traits, basic roles) are appropriated to a subject's perspective, such that the world seems approached through their filter. As J. David Velleman puts it, identification occurs when a part of the personality 'presents a reflexive aspect to [one's] thought' such that it becomes one's 'mental standpoint' (Velleman 2002: 114). The most basic and pervasive role to be identified with is simply that of the perspectival owner. In this manner, the subject does not merely approach the world and its objects from an impersonal psycho-physical point of view (through whatever sense modality); it deeply *identifies* with that viewpoint as a concrete place where *I, the self*, am coming from. In tandem with perspectival ownership, then, the sense of personal ownership is almost always in operation whenever one alludes to such things as 'my thoughts', 'my headache', 'my body', or 'my actions'.

While feelings of desire and attachment are possibly the most salient phenomenal indicators of a sense of personal ownership (and hence identity as a personal owner), these feelings need not be present for the sense of such ownership to exist. This is particularly true in cases of profuse and mundane phenomena such as thoughts, sensations, and one's body. The sheer ubiquity with which such items are presented as personally 'mine' makes it quite impossible, in normal cases, to discern the distinct phenomenal quality of such 'mineness'. For, as it happens, most people do not know what it is like to lack it. It is mainly pathological impairments, where the sense of personal ownership seems lost or compromised, that draw attention to the fact that there is this other major type (or sense) of ownership alongside the perspectival and possessive varieties. Subjects of anosognosia, for instance, may feel that a paralysed limb 'does not belong' to them, while subjects of depersonalization commonly sense a disconnection in ownership from many of their thoughts.[6] While in cases of depersonalization the lack of personal-ownership feelings tends not to be global (e.g. they still identify as the subject of the dreadful condition that has befallen *them*), there is nevertheless a notable

---

[6] A level of disconnection in the sense of personal ownership may sometimes occur via the mode of agency, such that one feels that someone else has authored a particular line of thought, such as during 'thought insertion' in schizophrenia. As I consider the sense of agency to be grounded in a sense of personal ownership, the general point remains: a compromise in identification as author of the thought is a compromise in some level of identification as its personal owner.

lack of identification with the perspectival owner of those thoughts from which they do feel disconnected. With reference to any object, then, a lack of personal mineness goes in tandem with a lack of personal me-ness. (Note that a possible suspension in the sense of personal ownership does not by itself prove such ownership to lack independent reality, any more than its suspension during deep sleep would prove its lack of reality. This point will be returned to later).

Subsumed under the role 'personal owner' are other frequent modes of identity that further delineate the type of self we take ourselves to be. Two closely related such modes are *agent* and *thinker*. 'The agent' is the owner-subject in its capacity of initiating actions. Taking pride or being ashamed of perspectivally owned actions is an obvious way of identifying with the perspectival owner *qua* agent, such that one deeply feels 'I am the initiator of this action' (think of the proud winner of an Olympic medal). Such emotions also provide evidence of regarding oneself to have special causal powers that enable the active choice of one course of action over another, as opposed to a passive determination by the flow of events. To feel guilty, for instance, implies an assumption that one should not have acted in a particular way—and hence, arguably, an assumption that one could have acted differently. Intentional actions originate in thought, so the *thinker* is a closely related mode of identity. Importantly, we take ourselves to be the originator, controller, or observer of the thoughts, rather than to be, in essence, the content of thought. Put in terms of an attribute, the assumed self is something that is *unconstructed*—that is, not constructed from the content of thoughts and perceptions, etc.—some underlying thing that is their precedent rather than their product.

Any sense of identity, whether with a general role such as owner or agent, or a specific idea about who one is (for example, a female ice-dancing champion), evokes the elusive feeling of being bounded by that identity. Faced with the world and its objects, the subject thus reflexively presents not merely as a point of view, but as a *unique and bounded thing* with a point of view. This attribute of *boundedness* is absolutely central to the assumed self: it turns the perspectival into a personal owner. The bounded self seems, moreover, to be perfectly *unified*, in that its differing and shifting roles and identities (such as personal owner/actor/thinker, female/skater/champion) appear seamlessly integrated within the very same subject. A feeling of excitement at the upcoming ceremony may simultaneously trigger all the different roles, but it does not feel to the subject as if each role or identity corresponds to a numerically distinct self, or even to different compartments within a single self. Importantly, the field of unity seems to extend beyond the roles of the subject to share in the set of objects perspectivally and personally owned by it. Perceptions, thoughts, and experiences, felt as belonging to the subject, present as belonging to the subject's very same field of consciousness, such that it seems natural to say: 'I, the self, am simultaneously aware of the white ice and the cheering crowd', or 'The very same self that a few minutes ago saw the white ice heard the cheering crowd'. While the unity of consciousness is a philosophical topic unto itself, the point here is simply that *unity* is a feature central to the commonly assumed self at stake in this discussion.

Unity is not only synchronic but diachronic. *Unbrokenness* describes that aspect whereby unity of the self is diachronically extended, and it is useful to divide this into (i) the specious present (temporally ordered over a very short interval), (ii) the span from one specious present to the next, and (iii) the longer term, whether awakening from deep sleep or persisting over a lifetime. *Invariability* captures the phenomenal side to this assumed identity—the elusive feel of it being the very same underlying 'me' that belies all kind of change to body and personality. So in addition to the flux of experience, famously noted by Hume, there is the sense of a background unbroken *me* that observes the experiences, and that typically persists beyond the scope of a waking episode. For example one may, upon awakening from deep slumber, flinchingly recall an embarrassing venture from the night before—or perhaps four years before—indicating a strong implicit identification with the perspectival owner of the regrettable action. Or one may awaken with a brilliant plan for the future. Such identification as the 'longitudinal' self helps solidify the sense of being a personal owner, such that the self takes on what Antonio Damasio (1999) calls an 'autobiographical' dimension (although this feature does not seem *essential* to the self).[7]

I have mentioned *unconstructedness* in the context whereby the self is tacitly but deeply assumed to be that which underlies and originates the thoughts, rather than that which is constructed by them: their precedent

---

[7] Galen Strawson defines an 'Episodic' person as such: 'one doesn't figure oneself, the self or person one now experiences oneself to be, as something that was there in the (further) past and will be there in the (further) future' (Strawson 2008: 210). He contrasts this with 'Diachronic' persons who do have a sense of identity with their earlier and future selves.

rather than their product. This assumed feature actually underpins the entire self. For as the self *qua* thinker presents implicitly as that elusive, unbroken, bounded subject which is *unified* with the roles of agent, owner, experiencer, and observer, the feature of unconstructedness will extend naturally to each and every role and attribute of the self. So if the self truly exists, as per its manner of presentation, then every one of its features will be unconstructed—the precedent, not the product of the stream of objects (thoughts, experiences, perceptions) to which it tacitly seems opposed.

3. How Nirvana, as Construed in Pali Buddhism, Structures the Illusion of Self

How, in general terms, might this self turn out to be illusory? Could it be illusory in more than one way? These questions are addressed in this section, where I propose that the standard Western 'bundle theory' of no-self differs markedly from how no-self ought to be understood if nirvana, as depicted in Pali Buddhism, is possible. As already mentioned, this will involve a major challenge to the typical forms of Buddhist reductionism that cast no-self in Buddhism as a type of bundle theory.

What does it take, in general terms, for something to be illusory? Illusions (including delusions and hallucinations) essentially involve a mismatch between appearance and reality, such that something appears to be a particular way, when, in reality, it is not actually that way. Typical cases include the Muller Lyer Illusion (two lines appearing to be of unequal lengths when they are actually of equal length), a hallucination of the pink elephant, the sense of being watched by extra-terrestrials. In all these instances, the world does not veridically underpin the way the world appears to be, whether the medium of appearance is perceptual or cognitive. If the self is illusory, then the world (which includes the world of subjectivity) must similarly fail to deliver at least one of its defining characteristics as presented via the self's characteristic mode of appearance.

Given that the self purports to be something that is entirely unconstructed in all its defining features, a straightforward route to casting the self as illusory suggests itself: argue that at least one of these features is constructed from the content of those thoughts, experiences, and perceptions to which the self seems opposed. In this way, the self will not be what it fundamentally appears to be—it will be (at least in part) the product, rather than the precedent, of thoughts and experiences. Put another way, the *sense* of self, which presents as being thoroughly grounded in (and actually identical to) the (unconstructed) self, will be grounded in factors other than this self.

A word about the sense of self is in order here, since 'self' and 'sense of self' are sometimes confused. The sense of self is the *appearance* of a self, pertaining to the reflexive feeling or conscious impression of being a self. Throughout the discussion, I have been supposing that this feeling, although elusive to attentive purview, is real enough. What is in question is the veracity of its content: the self. Indeed, philosophers who deny the existence of the self do not generally deny the sense of self, any more than those who deny the existence of libertarian free will would deny the common feeling of such free will. In fact, as libertarian free will is sometimes (although not always) ascribed to the self in its capacity of being an agent, it can, because of the history of debate on the subject, provide a useful illustration of just how it is that a feature of the self (that we assume we are) may fail to reflect reality: how the sense of self, in other words, may fail to be grounded in a self.

Suppose, then, that determinism is correct, leaving no ontological room for an entity that could genuinely originate one course of action over another (the past being what it is). Suppose also that we (most humans) have a sense of being a self with this controversial sort of agency (a feeling that may be evidenced through such emotions as guilt). The feeling of free will will reflexively convey the cognitive content of being an entity that really does exercise such agency—not just of appearing to exercise it. So if determinism is to rule out the reality of such agency, then the sense of being a self *qua* libertarian agent will not be grounded in an actual agent-self, as it appears to be, but (at least partially) in the *content* of thoughts and feelings to which the self seems ontologically opposed. The thoughts and feelings will, in other words, be helping to create the conscious impression of there being a source of agency that is able to exercise libertarian control over the thoughts and feelings and actions—when, in reality, there is no such source of agency. The self, *qua* libertarian agent, will thus be an illusion created by the content of thought (etc.). It will fail to exist in the essential manner that it purports to exist, as something that stands entirely behind the thoughts, authoring the intentional actions.

To recapitulate: if the self exists, then it is an entity with a conjunction of unconstructed essential roles and features. Should at least one of these roles or features (such as agency) turn out to be mentally constructed, then the self, so defined, will not exist. The usual (but unacknowledged) strategy at the heart of most attempts to deny the existence of self is thus to argue that at least one essential feature of the self is a mental construct. Seeing this strategy at work will help to determine more exactly how the typical Western construal of no-self could differ from the way in which the self would fail to exist if nirvana were possible. I first examine some standard Western accounts of no-self before comparing this analysis to the case at hand.

David Hume is commonly considered to have pioneered the Western philosophical position on no-self, his work sometimes compared by scholars to the Buddhist no-self doctrine. He argues that, instead of there being an unbroken, underlying entity which unites the varying perceptions and accounts for their identity, as there appears to be, there is merely:

a bundle or collection of different perceptions, which succeed each other with an inconceivable rapidity, and are in a perpetual flux and movement....There is properly no simplicity [unity] in it [the mind] at any one time, nor *identity* in different, whatever natural propension we may have to imagine that simplicity and identity.

(Hume 1739: I, IV, vi)

As for what accounts for the *sense* of identity:

The identity which we ascribe to the mind of man is only a fictitious [viz., constructed] one, and of a like kind with that which we ascribe to vegetables and animal bodies. It cannot therefore have a different origin, but must proceed from a like operation in the imagination upon like objects.... identity [and simplicity] is nothing really belonging to these different perceptions, and uniting them together, but is merely a quality which we attribute to them, because of the union of their ideas in the imagination when we reflect upon them.

(Hume 1739: I, IV, vi)

Hume regards the appearance of the self's unity and identity to be under-pinned, not by factors that include *actual unconstructed* unity ('simplicity') and unbroken, unchanging identity ('uninterruptedness' and 'invariability'), but by mental factors such as 'the union of their ideas in the imagination when we reflect upon them'. The self, in other words, is a mental construct *by virtue of* the fact that unity and (short and long-term) identity have constructed status.

The illusion is hence that of an unconstructed entity, a self, whose features of unity and unbroken identity objectively underpin our *sense* of unity and identity. In reality, there are no such principles of unity or identity that actually underpin this impression, either in the self or in the mind. There is only a diversity of rapidly fleeting perceptions that, when acted upon by the memory and imagination, create the impression of an entity with unity and identity.

Casting unity and unbroken persistence as central to the self's constructed, and hence, illusory status turns out to be a strategy common to virtually all Western accounts of no-self. For instance, William James makes it clear that the unity and unbrokenness we commonly ascribe to the self are unconstructed:

common-sense insists that the unity of all the selves is not a mere appearance of similarity or continuity, ascertained after the fact. She is sure that it involves a real belonging to a real Owner [a source of unity], to a pure spiritual entity of some kind. Relation to this entity is what makes the self's constituents stick together as they do for thought.

(James 1890: 337)

On James's position, the self's supposed unity and unbrokenness is, as Owen Flanagan puts it, 'an after-the-fact construction, not a before-the-fact condition for the possibility of experience' (Flanagan 1992: 177, 178). Flanagan's own defense of the no-self doctrine follows James' insofar as he bestows illusory status to the self principally via the features of unity and unbrokenness (with other features such as agency riding on this):

The illusion is that there are two things: on one side, a self, an ego, an 'I', that organizes experience, originates action, and accounts for our unchanging identity as persons and, on the other side, the stream of experience. If this view is misleading, what is the better view? The better view is that what there is, and all there is, is the stream of experience. 'Preposterous! What then does the thinking?' comes the response. The answer is that 'the thoughts themselves are the thinkers' (James, 1892, 83)[8] . . . We are egoless.

(Flanagan 1992: 178)

On a similar theme, Daniel Dennett writes:

---

[8] Flanagan cites William James (1892), *Psychology: The Briefer Course*, G. Allport (ed)., New York: Harper and Row, 1961.

Each normal individual of this species makes a *self*. Out of its brain it spins a web of words and deeds and, like other creatures, it doesn't have to know what it's doing; it just does it . . . Our tales are spun, but for the most part we don't spin them; they spin us. Our human consciousness, and our narrative selfhood, is their product, not their source . . . These strings or streams of narrative issue forth *as if* from a single source . . . their effect on any audience is to encourage them to (try to) posit a unified agent whose words they are, about whom they are: in short, to posit a *center of narrative gravity*.

(Dennett 1991: 418)

These thinkers typify the way in which the self is denied in Western philosophy, by giving constructed and thereby illusory status to the central unified subject, where the unity is understood to be both synchronic and diachronic. While the accounts differ in their details of how exactly the impression of unity and unbrokenness is constructed—such as which mental faculties contribute to the illusion—all of them deny the existence of self principally via this avenue. The impression of unity and unbrokenness, as it qualifies a minimal subject (or perspectival owner) standing opposed to the stream of experience, must be entirely fabricated from the bundle of discrete mental phenomena to which it seems opposed. Essentially, they are what are known as *bundle theories* of the self.

I now ask: is this way of understanding the self as illusory—as a bundle theory that denies unconstructed reality to unity and unbrokenness to the self *qua* minimal subject—in line with how we should understand the status of 'no-self' if nirvana, as depicted in the Pali sutras, is to be possible? As I noted in the Introduction, this is exactly how Buddhist philosophical tradition has typically understood the doctrine of no-self. To this end, there are different versions of the bundle theory. The more extreme version (a non-reflexive reductionism inspired by Abhidharma tradition), has it that all impressions of unity—synchronic and diachronic—are illusory constructs from an ontology of momentary, causally connected aggregates. A less extreme version of bundle theory (which I call 'reflexive reductionism', inspired mainly by Yogācāra-Sautrāntika tradition) allows a measure of synchronic unity to exist through each conscious experience being reflexively aware of itself (perhaps for the length of a specious present).[9] Such temporal unity, however,

---

[9] My use of the term 'reflexive reductionism' is intended to depict the allegiance to bundle-theory, rather than reflect how its advocates would label their position (they would probably not, in their own context of use, call it 'reductionist').

does not extend beyond the specious present, and it belongs not to any subject, but to the discrete experiences that form the changing stream of consciousness. All variants of bundle theory within the gamut of Buddhist tradition thus uphold the unreality or illusory status of an unbroken and unified witness-consciousness which, as modus operandi of the (minimal) subject, stands apart from and observes the stream of experience. (Note that while Dreyfus (this volume) does not regard reflexive reductionism as a bundle theory, it counts as a bundle theory for the purposes of this discussion). Now I am well aware that the argument about to be offered, which defends nirvana (in the sutras) as entailing the unbroken unity of observational witness-consciousness (at least during the scope of waking life), flies in the face of many Buddhist philosophical traditions—and so will in that sense be denied by many to be truly 'Buddhist'. So be it. What I do contend is that my position offers a more coherent philosophical reconstruction of the early Buddhist sutras than the bundle theory, and that the position, although not stated explicitly in the sutras, is quite consistent with them.

Before commencing with the argument, I need to say more about how reflexive and non-reflexive varieties of reductionism are to be distinguished. According to reflexive reductionism (discussed in various forms by Dreyfus, Thompson, MacKenzie, and Krueger in this volume) 'consciousness cognizes itself in cognizing its object' (Siderits, this volume, p. 318), so there is nothing more to consciousness than the cognizing experiences themselves. Put another way, the immediate object of a cognition is not the object out there in the world (such as the blueberry): it is the phenomenal experience of cognizing the object and 'the experience of seeing blue is just the occurrence of a cognition that has blue color as its form' (Siderits, this volume, p. 317). A stream of different consciousnesses thus amounts to a stream of multi-modal experiences: there is no separate cognizing subject. According to non-reflexive reductionism (discussed by Siderits in this volume), consciousness is not self-intimating in this way: it is an object-directed awareness that arises in conjunction with the various sensory or mental objects (including experiences) that form its intentional content. I address each version in turn, beginning with the latter.

On Buddhist non-reflexive reductionism 'consciousness arises in dependence on contact between sense faculty and sensible object. . . . the consciousness that takes the color of the flower as object must be distinct from that which takes its smell as object a moment later' (Siderits, this volume,

p. 313). Each momentary consciousness imparts information to the next moment: there is no temporal gap between each moment. Each composite moment of object-directed consciousness (if it is, *contra* reflexive reductionism, more than just the occurrence of the target mental or sensory object) will presumably have built into it an invariant observational component, by virtue of which it is labeled 'conscious', and by virtue of which the illusion of unbroken observational consciousness, central to the illusion of self, is generated (just as the illusion of a continuous unified circle of fire in a whirling firebrand is generated by the invariant fiery nature of each distinct occurrence of the fire). Now I think that despite their differences, Buddhist traditions would converge in supposing that nirvana involves a transformative insight into the nature of mental reality that is based primarily upon first-person experiential observation, rather than intellectual puzzle-solving. One cannot get enlightened simply by studying philosophy or calculating laboratory results. On the Buddhist (non-reflexive) reductionist picture, then, the 'person' who has attained nirvana will directly 'see through' the illusion of self by viewing the nature of persons to be nothing but a fleeting causally connected bundle of discrete aggregates—including the very cognition that discerns it to be so. Our previous deep-seated assumption of being an unbroken, unified conscious self that witnesses the flow of phenomena will be dramatically overturned, as that consciousness itself becomes discerned as part of the very flow. Burmese meditation master Venerable Mahāsi Sayādaw describes the keen level of discernment in a way that lends support to the reductionist picture:

And the dissolution of consciousness noticing those bodily processes is apparent to him along with the dissolution of the bodily processes. Also while he is noticing other bodily and mental processes, their dissolution, too, will be apparent to him in the same manner. Consequently, the knowledge will come to him that whatever part of the whole body is noticed, that object ceases first, and after it the consciousness engaged in noticing that object follows in its wake. From that the meditator will understand very clearly in the case of each successive pair the dissolution of any object whatsoever and the dissolution of the consciousness noticing that very object. (It should be borne in mind that this refers only to understanding arrived at through direct experience by one engaged in noticing only; it is not an opinion derived from mere reasoning).

(Sayādaw, 1994: 23)

Given that nirvana must entail, as Venerable Sayādaw intimates, 'an under-standing arrived at through direct experience' as opposed to 'an opinion derived from mere reasoning', I think that there is something incoherent about a picture which, when taken literally, has the meditator experientially aware that their discerning consciousness is impermanent. I contend that the best way to make sense of such a passage is to suppose that the meditator is actually aware of different *directions* that are being taken by consciousness (in virtue of the objects)—a picture that does not entail Buddhist reductionism. So when the Pali sutras speak of consciousness as being impermanent, I take this to mean that the intentional content of consciousness—that to which consciousness is directed—is constantly changing. One moment there is consciousness of green and round, and the next, consciousness of crunching and apple-taste. But this is not the same as saying that the observational component that is directed towards these objects is itself arising and passing away. So what is my argument against this interpretation of Pali Buddhism?

Let me first be clear on what I am not arguing. I am not arguing that the impression of unified unbroken consciousness is impossible under reducti-vist ontology. My argument is instead based upon an epistemic aspect that grows out of the idea that the primary mode for understanding the mind, in nirvana, is experiential. Nirvana is often depicted as 'ultimate' in the Pali sutras, not only in an axiological but an epistemic sense. Statements made from the nirvanic perspective are taken to be authoritative: there is never the idea that they could be usurped by philosophical or scientific discovery. For example, there is never any intimation in the Pali sutras that the Buddha or arahant could be mistaken in saying such things as 'conditioned phenom-ena are impermanent, conducive to suffering and without a self'. I call this the 'Experience Condition':

Experience Condition: The primary mode of knowledge/wisdom/insight, in the nirvanic state, is based on first-person experience and the first-person perspective has authority over the third-person theoretical perspective. In cases of a conflict between first-personal nirvanic perspective and third-person theoretical perspec-tive, regarding the nature of the conscious mind, the first-person nirvanic perspec-tive trumps the theoretical.[10]

---

[10] Note that I am not defending the Experience Condition as a stand-alone condition in this paper, although towards the end of the paper it re-emerges as a suggested way to save the appearances. In relation to the concept of nirvana across Buddhist traditions, however, the Experience Condition may

I will argue that the Experience Condition entails (on the nirvanic hypothesis) that the aspect of consciousness which cognizes the impermanence of phenomena is neither discrete, nor reducible to the changing stream—at least during wakefulness. I begin by asking: how would the cognizance of an impermanent consciousness (by an impermanent consciousness) work on a reductivist account? It could not be that each moment of consciousness reflexively observes its own coming and going. For regardless of whether or not we are dealing with reflexive consciousness, it would entail the contradictory state of a conscious moment being present to its own coming and going. The impermanence (or diachronic disunity) of the discerning cognitions must therefore, on any reductivist account, be experienced retrospectively.[11] So let us suppose that a discerning cognition at t_3 is a momentary member in a causal chain of conscious moments t_1- t_n and that it retrospectively (whether via memory or retention) discerns the impermanence of prior members of the chain. As this cannot include itself (t_3), it will have to discern, say, the numerical transition from moments t_1 and t_2, before itself becoming retrospectively discerned as impermanent by a later cognition, say t_5. And here is where I see the problem for *non-reflexive* reductionism, for the only way that t_3 can experientially distinguish the transition from t_1 to t_2

need further defense. For example, Siderits (this volume) points out that in Yogācāra subjective idealism, consciousness is regarded as ultimately non-dual in nature. Nirvanic realization will involve a complete dissolution of the idea that there is an external world with its objects—and hence, according to Siderits, a dissolution in the feeling of subjective interiority which must depend upon the subject/object split. Thus 'Yogācāra subjective idealism involves an explicit disavowal of the perspectival self argued for by Albahari' (this volume p. 318). So if the ideal nirvanic state involves no sense of interiority or first-person perspective, then how can nirvanic authority be indexed to a first-person perspective? Here we must tread carefully; 'first-person perspective' or 'interiority' is ambiguous. If it means 'experience confined to a dualistic subject/object structure' then I would agree that ultimate non-dual consciousness must lack this structure, and so the first-person perspective must lack ultimate authority. But if it means that 'there is something it is like to experience non-dual consciousness'—and elsewhere (2006) I attempt to convey in some detail what this could mean—then 'first-person perspective' would not be disavowed by non-dual consciousness. (I suspect that it lies behind many of the intimations that nirvana is experienced, not inferred). Be that as it may, I would insist that so long as objects *are* experienced, the dualistic (subject/object) first-person perspective, with its perspectival subject, is unavoidable. And so long as the domain of judgment from the nirvanic perspective is about subjective experience in its relation to its objects, then the Experience Condition, even if construed narrowly, remains intact. If it cannot but seem as if objects are being witnessed by (a subject's) unbroken conscious awareness, then (if nirvana is possible) this will indeed be how things are, even if the unbroken awareness, in its intrinsic nature, is not confined to the perspective of a subject.

[11] I put aside any problem that might arise with elusiveness of the discerning cognition, as it is not clear that non-reflexive reductionists would accept this aspect, and I want to engage in the debate on their terms.

is by discerning the changing *content* of t_1 to t_2—the *object* towards which each consciousness is directed. But this does not tell us that at each moment, the observational component is in fact numerically discrete—it just tells us that the objects are. There is in fact no way to phenomenologically tell whether the underlying 'objective' scenario (if there is a further truth to the matter) is that of a contiguous chain of numerically discrete discerning consciousnesses, generating the illusion of unbroken consciousness taking different objects, or that of an unbroken discerning consciousness cognizing an array of different objects—in line with how things seem. That is because the observational component, which renders each moment of non-reflexive consciousness to be *conscious*, is qualitatively invariant, leaving no marker by which the contiguous numerical transition could be experientially discerned (it's not as if there will be a little jolt at each transition). The observational component to each conscious moment will thus seem, from the first person experiential perspective, to be unbroken—regardless of the underlying ontology. To use Thomas Metzinger's (2003) phrase, the mind will be 'phenomenally transparent' to the extent that any underlying ontology, regarding the impermanence of the discerning cognition, will be inaccessible to subjective experience. This is a problem for non-reflexive reductionism. We should expect the nirvanic insight into impermanence and no-self to be experientially and cognitively dramatic, invoking a shift from the incorrect to the correct perspective. But how could this happen, if there is no way to phenomenologically discern the incorrect (unbroken) from the correct (discrete) state?

At this point, the non-reflexive reductivist may reply: if the nature of the discerning cognition cannot be determined one way or the other, then we cannot conclude that the discerning cognition is *unbroken*, any more than we can conclude that it is discrete. Here is where the Experience Condition comes in. If it is accepted that the nirvanic first-person perspective is authoritative on the nature of our mental life, and that from the nirvanic perspective it cannot but seem as if there is unbroken observational consciousness from one moment to the next (sustained throughout waking life), then there won't *be* a hidden ontology at variance with the appearance. Things will be as they seem: appearance and reality will converge. Inferring the discerning consciousness to be discrete (as Siderits does) involves, *contra* the Experience Condition, taking the third-person perspective, with its method of philosophical inference, to be authoritative. In Venerable

Sayādaw's terms, it is putting 'an opinion derived from mere reasoning' ahead of 'understanding arrived at through direct experience'. If the discerning consciousness does turn out to be discrete, it cannot therefore match the model of non-reflexive reductionism.

Does reflexive reductionism fare any better? The problem with non-reflexive reductionism arose because the invariant observational component within each moment of consciousness made it impossible to discern its numerical transition from one conscious moment to the next. Reflexive reductionism does not appear to succumb to this problem, for any impression of unbroken and invariant conscious observation must crumble under sharper scrutiny. Why? Because there is no more to consciousness than simply the stream of experience itself (e.g. visual, auditory, proprioceptive)—there is no separate observational component that takes each experience as an object. Each experience is reflexively aware of itself, which is what makes it a *conscious* experience. And as each conscious experience is qualitatively different, it will be quite possible to retrospectively tell (say at t_3) when a moment of consciousness (say t_1) has ceased and another (t_2) has begun. Hence each reflexive moment of consciousness will be experientially discernible as impermanent, such that it does not fall prey to the Experience Condition. The findings from this first-person perspective of authority will trump any theory that insists, in line with the self-illusion, that there really is a minimal unified subject that unbrokenly observes the changing phenomena. Any impression of a separate invariant subject of experience will be generated through cognitive processes (and theoretical accretions) that have us paying insufficient attention to the degree of change in our conscious life. Nirvana will thus entail insight into the real fact that the degree of change, being far more dramatic than we'd assumed, does not support an unbroken self (or indeed subject) that observes the stream.

It may be tempting to object that while non-reflexive reductionism goes *beyond* the scope of experience, by attributing numerical discreteness to an invariant observational component of consciousness, reflexive reductionism *under-describes* the scope of experience, by failing to acknowledge that there is more to conscious experience than just the manifold. For does not the very idea of a nirvanic *first-person perspective* convey that there is more to our conscious life than *just* the manifold of experience, and might this dimension not point to an invariant observing subject? If reflexive reductionism fails to describe the phenomenology of conscious experience properly, by leaving out the first-person perspective, then it will, at the very least, not satisfy the Experience Condition.

This objection, as it turns out, misconstrues reflexive reductionism—or at least the versions that have been portrayed in certain schools of Indian, Chinese, and Tibetan Buddhist philosophy (see Thompson, Dreyfus, Siderits, MacKenzie, and Krueger, this volume, for a discussion of these positions). If we look more closely at the kind of phenomenal considerations advanced in favor of reflexive reductionism, we will see that the first-person perspective is not ignored. For instance, in his discussion of the position (this volume), Dreyfus speaks of the 'first-person self-givenness' of experience. The notion of first-person givenness has been articulated at some length by Zahavi (2005, this volume), whose phenomenologically inspired position shares with reflexive reductionism the central tenet of bestowing reality to only the stream of experience, rather than to a witnessing subject of the stream (his insistence on diachronic unity between specious presents within the stream differentiates him from the full-fledged reflexive reductionist). Of first-person givenness, Zahavi maintains that our conscious experience is not deeply impersonal or anonymous but is structured by a fundamental self-givenness in such a way that 'the experiences I am living through are given differently (but not necessarily better) to me than to anybody else' (Zahavi, this volume, p. 59). Hence no matter how similar my experience of the green apple is to Miguel's, there is a perspectival belongingness between my experiences that make them cohere together as 'mine' in a way that they do not with any of Miguel's experiences. Zahavi continues: '... anyone who denies the for-me-ness or mineness of experience simply fails to recognize an essential constitutive aspect of experience. Such a denial would be tantamount to denial of the first-person perspective' (Zahavi, this volume, p. 59). Or as Evan Thompson puts it, the experience (if from memory) 'is given from within as an experience formerly lived through first-personally, that is, by me' (Thompson, this volume, p. 173). In other words, all our experiences are presented through a perspective and this perspectival for-me-ness reflexively had by each one of our experiences constitutes our first-person perspective (as the experiences seem to be *for* the same *me*), lending our experiential life the *impression* of unity across time.

But while this may now correctly describe our experience, the type of problem that plagued non-reflexive reductionism threatens to re-emerge. For how can we phenomenally tell whether the situation is that of numerically discrete and contiguous (qualitatively invariant) for-me-nesses, or just one unbroken for-me-ness, which may well point to an invariant observer? The reflexive reductionist will again respond that this misunderstands their position—we *can* tell. Just as the identical sheen belonging to each colored bead on a string doesn't prevent us discerning the different beads by their color and shape, the identical reflexive for-me-ness belonging to each conscious experience doesn't prevent us from discerning the different experiences by their varying qualities. For remember: on reflexive reductionism, a qualitative change within experience amounts to a numerical switch in consciousness; diachronic unity (at least beyond the scope of the specious present), along with the subject as locus for synchronic unity, is fundamentally an illusion.

But we may now wonder where this leaves the commonly asserted idea of an invariant and separate subject standing apart from and observing the stream of experiences. Are philosophers such as Hume, James, and Dennett uniformly mistaken in their description of the phenomenology of our experience—and indeed, of the very sense of self enumerated earlier in this piece? Is the minimal observant subject no more than a careless theoretical reification that evaporates under careful phenomenal scrutiny? It would appear so, according to its proponents. Reflexive reductionists are generally adamant that a separate perspectival observer (or observational component) is not to be introduced into either the phenomenology or the ontology of conscious life. In keeping with this aspect of the position, Zahavi goes so far as to redefine 'the self' as the subjectivity of experience: 'the self is defined as the very [invariant] subjectivity of experience and is not to be taken to be something that exists independently of or in separation from the experiential flow' (Zahavi, this volume, p. 60).

The crucial issue at this stage is not that of whether there really *is* an invariant observational component (or perspectival owner) that is intrinsic to our conscious life, but whether there *seems* to be—or more accurately, whether there *must* seem to be (such that it survives phenomenal scrutiny). While I agree that for-me-ness characterizes our experience, I contend that it structures our conscious life far more dramatically than as just a reflexive sheen on the bead of each experience. It necessarily *bifurcates* our experience into subject and object. For so long as our diverse experiences seem to be *for* me—and for the very same me over time, no less—there is no escaping that there will seem to be a perspectival 'me' that the experiences are for. Or to put it more simply: so long as objects are experienced as being given to a subject there must seem to be *a subject* to which they are given. (Galen Strawson, this volume, p. 275, argues for a logical corollary of this position, claiming that so long as there is subjectivity, there must, as a matter of logical fact, be a minimal subject—although I am not going so far as to claim yet that the subject is *real*.) This strongly suggests that the phenomenology of experience contains more than simply the flow with its first-personal givenness. As a matter of phenomenal necessity, there will seem to be a perspectival owner that stands apart from the stream, such that it cognizes the experiences that are first-personally 'given' to it.[12]

Suppose the reflexive reductionists re-assess their phenomenological stance, agreeing that the ascription of first-person givenness entails the (elusive) appearance of a subject to which the experiences are given. They are still free to defend the *ontological* side of their position by insisting that, despite appearances, there is no separate subject of experience. If they are correct in this assessment, then the witnessing subject will be a mere illusion projected forth by the invariant dimension of an otherwise diverse stream of experiences. If a subject-realist is correct in their ontological assessment, then the appearance of the observing subject will reflect how things actually are. And here is where reflexive reductionism *does* get into trouble. Just as the dispute over whether the observational component is unbroken cannot be resolved without going beyond the first-personal appearance and appealing to philosophical analysis, the dispute over whether the minimal observing subject (to whom experiences are given) is chimerical cannot be settled without going beyond how things must appear. So if reflexive reductionists are correct in supposing the subject of experience to be chimerical rather than real, then nirvanic insight into this fact will have to be purely intellectual, rather than experientially based. With no experiential avenue through which to characterize the potential shift from incorrect to correct perspective, the dramatic nirvanic insight into no-self will be left unaccounted for.

But as mentioned earlier, the Pali sutras do not leave such matters unsettled: matters are arbitrated by the Experience Condition, which privileges the first-person perspective of nirvana. If it must seem, from the nirvanic perspective, that there is a minimal subject of our changing experience, then this will not be a mere appearance that can be usurped by

---

[12] I develop this line of argument from another angle in Albahari (2009).

theoretical inference. The limits of nirvanic appearance will dictate the scope of mental reality. So if nirvana (as depicted in the Pali sutras) is possible, reflexive reductionism does no better than the non-reflexive version at eliminating the invariant and unbrokenly observing subject of experience. The cognitive transformation of nirvana, I conclude, cannot be an insight into the fact that our mental life lacks such a perspectival owner and entirely comprises fleeting cognitions.

This leaves us with the question: in virtue of what features should we say that the self is constructed (hence illusory), if nirvana, as depicted in Pali Buddhism, is to be possible? How do we construe the cognitive transformation whereby the constructed status of the self is seen through? I contend that personal ownership and boundedness (and agency to the extent that it requires identity as a personal owner of the actions) are the most likely features of the self to be constructed. To reiterate: a personal owner is a perspectival owner that has identified with a variety of roles (including the basic role of perspectival owner), such that the bare witnessing perspective is cemented into a definitive thing with an identity (a 'me'). It is a subject with personalized *boundaries*, which personally (not just perspectivally) owns its thoughts, perceptions, feelings, experiences, and possessions. Given that there are known pathologies which compromise the usually ubiquitous sense of bounded identity, it is quite possible to conceive of a state, akin to global depersonalization, where all sense of bounded identity is lost. This opens up the distinct cognitive potential for a transformative experiential insight into the reality of no-self, although by all accounts it will not be pathological.

On this hypothesis, the illusion of self will arise through the mechanism of identification. Identification (to reiterate) is the appropriation of mental content to the subject's perspective, such that the content seems to qualify (and hence filter) the very outlook through which the world is approached. To the untrained perspective, it will appear as if identification is not constructing, but revealing various aspects of the self's permanent, prior existence. But the bounded self will in fact, on this hypothesis, be constructed through the process of identification. On the face of it, this sounds rather similar to how MacKenzie describes the process of 'self-appropriation' (MacKenzie, this volume p. 264). There is a crucial difference, however. On MacKenzie's construal of Buddhism (a version of reflexive reductionism), the minimal unbroken subject *emerges* from the act of appropriation, giving it a constructed status (à la bundle theory), whereas on my construal of Buddhism, the minimal unbroken subject is the unconstructed locus of appropriation. With each act of identification, the perspectival owner imports its unconstructed, unified and unbroken witness-consciousness into the illusion of self, such that it appears that the bounded self is the originator of these qualities. And with each act of identification, the discrete mental content (identified with by the minimal subject) colors the perspectival outlook of the subject, such that the unconstructed subject appears as a bounded personal owner. (The dual constructed/unconstructed contribution is the reason I call it the *two-tiered* illusion of self). To the extent that unity and unbrokenness are ascribed to a subject that seems personally bounded, the unconstructed features will themselves undergo a measure of distortion. Hence: thoughts, feelings, perceptions, and experiences will seem presented to a personal unified owner insofar as there is the sense of being a *someone* with a personal boundary that operates from, and is in charge of, the unified perspective. The personal unified owner/agent/thinker will assume a thicker diachronic identity as the natural (moment-to-moment) *unbrokenness* of witness-consciousness becomes folded into the impression of a bounded self with a life-history and anticipated future that plans, remembers, deliberates, and wishes.

In view of this analysis, I propose that nirvana, as a deep and transformative insight into no-self, be understood as the culmination of a process whereby the trained use of witness-consciousness, through meditation, brings about a full de-identification from all mental and physical phenomena.[13] The result will be the undoing of the self illusion. How exactly the process of de-identification could work is a topic for further research, but the general idea, I contend, is as follows. Identification is the appropriation of highly impermanent mental content (objects) to a subject's first-person perspective. So long as the objects remain appropriated to the subject's perspective, as part of the self's 'unconstructed' identity, their status as impermanent objects will be effectively rendered invisible, such that the subject is change-blind to their coming and going. The process of meditation will train the subject's attention to become increasingly percipient of

---

[13] The general strategy of attaining nirvana, through de-identifying from all phenomena, has support from the famous *Anattā-lakkhana Sutta* in the Pali Canon. In this, the Buddha urges his disciples to lose the sense of personal ownership and identification towards all categories of object (mental and physical), such that there is the discernment: 'This is not mine. This is not my self. This is not what I am'.

the degree to which mental phenomena do change. So long as objects are being viewed for what they really are—as changeable objects—they cannot be simultaneously appropriated to the subject's perspective. By extrapolation, a full observation of all perspectival objects in their true state of transience, from moment to conscious moment, will imply a complete lack of identification with any of them. I anticipate that the process of de-identification would gain extra momentum as the subject repeatedly observes, with increasing clarity, the mechanism by which identification works (via its undoing). Just as uncovering a magician's trick makes it impossible to keep on being fooled by it, lifting the veil of identification will make it impossible to remain fooled by its content of self-identity. Viewing the real nature of consciousness as unbounded by ties of identification is, I hold, what nirvanic insight actually entails. It may be tempting to hold that in view of such a realization, the arahant now believes 'I am not a bounded self—I am witness-consciousness'. This is misguided, for such a belief would incur further identification and hence a new binding identity. Nevertheless, I contend that nirvana involves a direct realization that consciousness, in the impersonal sense, is ownerless, in the personal sense.

4. Implications for the Everyday Mind

At the outset, I intimated that investigation into the psychological possibility of nirvana could have important implications for how we are to understand the architecture of the everyday mind. I have defended a position on how to best interpret the doctrine of no-self if nirvana, as portrayed in Pali Buddhism, is indeed possible. So if nirvana *is* psychologically possible, it will place significant constraints upon the structure of the everyday mind, such that at the very least it (a) harbors an illusion of self that is (b) constructed in the prescribed 'two-tiered' manner (with the constructed and unconstructed contributors). (Conversely, should it turn out that there is a self, or that the bundle theory of no-self is correct, then nirvana, as I've depicted it, will not be psychologically possible). In this section, I sketch some independent reasons to suppose that the self is a two-tiered illusion. While this will not, of course, suffice to prove the psychological possibility of such nirvana, it will strengthen the case for supposing that it is possible.

I approach this task in two parts: first, through gesturing at some empirical evidence that suggests the mind to have a structure *compatible* with a two-tiered illusion of self, and second, via an argument which suggests the structure to be indeed *best explained* by the two-tiered illusion of self (with constructed and unconstructed contributors).

Is there reason to suppose that the mind could be structured in a way that is compatible with the two-tiered illusion of self? What sort of empirical evidence might count towards such a hypothesis? I contend that the right sort of evidence would involve established cases, in neuropsychological literature, where there appears to be the presence of perspectival ownership (and hence witness-consciousness) without any sense of personal ownership. For this combination, after all, is what survives in the 'ownerless' consciousness of nirvana. The potential absence of personal-ownership feelings would provide some evidence that personal ownership is not essential to conscious life, increasing the likelihood of it being constructed (and hence, amenable to deconstruction). Conversely, the perpetual persistence of perspectival ownership to conscious life would increase the likelihood that it is an essential, unconstructed feature of the mind (that can perhaps be utilized in an attempt to undermine the sense of personal ownership).

It is perhaps ironic, then, that the clearest evidence (outside the Buddhist domain) for perspectival ownership sans personal ownership lies in that of pathological brainstates—quite opposite to exalted nirvana. Earlier in the paper, I alluded to the pathologies of depersonalization and anosognosia, where the impairment appeared to compromise a degree of personal but not perspectival ownership over one's thoughts, feelings, and body. For example, in episodes of depersonalization, there is often a reported sense of disconnection from streams of perspectivally owned thought, such that it is not uncommon to hear phrases like 'the thoughts that cross my mind do not belong to me'. In these cases, it seems that there is little doubt that the type of ownership compromised is personal and not perspectival. However, the very fact that such subjects commonly report being distressed about their condition would suggest they still identify as the subject of the distressing symptoms and hence, as a personal owner that takes itself to be bounded by its predicament. What is needed is evidence of perspectival ownership coupled with a *complete* lack of personal owner-ship feelings.[14]

Such evidence, I contend, may well be found in the pathological impair-ments of epileptic automatism, akinetic mutism, and the advanced onset of Alzheimer's disease (Damasio 1999: 98), as well as in infants or perhaps people awakening from general anaesthetic. In an episode of epileptic or absence automatism, which can be brought on by a brain seizure, patients will suddenly freeze whatever they are doing, and after a few seconds of suspended animation, perform simple actions (such as walking about) with a completely blank expression. Upon recovering from the episode, the be-wildered patient will have no memory of what just occurred. Damasio, who had such patients in his care, writes:

[The patient] would have remained awake and attentive enough to process the object that came next into his perceptual purview, but inasmuch as we can deduce from the situation, that is all that would go on in the mind. There would have been no plan, no forethought, no sense of an individual organism wishing, wanting, considering, believing. There would have been no sense of self, no identifiable person with a past and an anticipated future—specifically, no core self and no autobiographical self.

(Damasio 1999: 98).

This passage, I believe, provides good evidence to suppose that, through suspension of the 'core self' (corresponding closely to the *sense of self* that has been described in this paper), the feeling of personal ownership—with its trappings of identification and emotional concern—can be entirely absent, while bare perspectival ownership remains through the patient's simply being awake enough to respond minimally to his environment.[15] (The 'autobiographical self' is an extension of the core self, by which the idea of one's personal history and anticipated future becomes integrated with one's assumed identity).

---

[14] It may be suggested that creative absorption and highly attentive 'flow states' provide better examples of states where [the sense of] personal ownership has dropped away while perspectival ownership is present. Perhaps this is true. But, it is not apparent to me whether such states, short of being had by someone who is an arahant (hence presupposing the psychological possibility of nirvana), provide clear-cut documented evidence of cases where there is *no* remnant [sense] of personal ownership.

[15] Damasio (1999) himself seems to rule out linguistically the possibility of residual conscious awareness by routinely defining 'consciousness' as 'consciousness with a sense of self'. For obvious reasons, I resist this move.

This case (and others) demonstrates the real possibility of a mindscape that is quite compatible with the model of the two-tiered self-illusion. But it does not in itself show the two-tiered model to *best explain* the phenomenon. There are at least two rival explanations that need ruling out. First, it could be that the self really does exist as an unconstructed feature of the mind, and that what has happened in such cases is that the *sense* of self has become suspended, while the self has persisted, holus bolus, all along. Not even the most ardent self-realists would wish to deny that the *sense* of self gets suspended during episodes of deep sleep. They would claim that during these unconscious phases, the self unbrokenly persists, such that upon awakening one *rightly* assumes it to have been the very same self that went to sleep. So why couldn't the self persist during the epileptic automatisms? Second, even if the self is an illusion, could it not be the case that both personal *and* perspectival ownership are constructed? A bundle theorist need not have any quibbles with Damasio's way of explaining the constructed nature of personal ownership. It is just that they would also add unity and unbrokenness to the mental construction of self, as indeed, Damasio himself does. There are no constraining assumptions about nirvana to rule out this possibility. Eliminating each of these rival explanations will thus be necessary in order to defend the two-tiered illusion of self, such that: (a) personal ownership is constructed/illusory and (b) perspectival ownership is not.

First, consider the specter of realism about the self. Is there reason to favor the hypothesis that the self *qua* personal owner is constructed and illusory rather than, as it purports to be, unconstructed? The advantage of the unconstructed-self hypothesis is that it does preserve the appearances. All things being equal, it is better to preserve appearances than not to: one has to tell less of a complicated story of how the appearances have the features that they do. But are all things equal here? Often what lurks behind claims that reject the veracity of appearance in favor of an illusion hypothesis are metaphysical assumptions about what items are to be allowed in one's favored ontology (consider the austerity of the Churchlands' eliminative materialism), or scientific theories about the workings of the world and its subjects (consider theories about color-illusion). In the case of the self, both factors are at play. Damasio, for instance, offers a scientifically motivated account about how the bounded aspect of self arises (and how it can disappear in pathology), which leads me to be optimistic that an entirely adequate (even if in part speculative) explanation for this aspect can be found, without recourse to a self at all.[16] My metaphysical assumption is that if science can adequately explain the phenomena, using known properties and mechanisms, then it is better to avoid appealing to metaphysically extravagant alternatives to explain the data, which would multiply entities beyond what is necessary. Compared to the scientifically viable components that are needed to explain the mechanism of identification, the unconstructed self is a metaphysically extravagant entity.

Now to the second worry. Accepting that the *personal owner* (as a whole) is constructed, is there reason to suppose that the *perspectival owner* (a component of the personal owner) is not? I have only argued, so far, that the appearance of the perspectival owner is real—that there must seem to be a unified subject to which the stream is given. But it might turn out that the perspectival owner, even if operating as the locus of identification, is itself a mental construct, rather than unconstructed as it purports to be. In such a case it seems conceivable that its mental construction could occur through some avenue other than identification, perhaps through the innate action of memory and the imagination, as Hume claims. In such a case, the constructed synthesis of unity and unbrokenness (as it applies to witnessing perspective) could occur below the threshold of what we could ever be aware of, ruling out any hope of cutting through the illusion of self in the manner that Buddhist practice thinks possible. The advantage of such a hypothesis parallels that of the previous argument. It seems more scientifically parsimonious to favor a theory that appeals to relatively known quantities, such as thoughts, perceptions, memory, imagination, and the brain, than to quantities that are metaphysically mysterious. The presence of an intrinsically unified, invariant and unbroken witness-consciousness that qualifies the perspectival owner does, by comparison, seem to be more mysterious, not only because it resists reduction to the more familiar psychological components, but because, unlike thoughts and perceptions, it is elusive to attentive observation, making it more resistant to both scientific and introspective methods.

---

[16] More specifically, Damasio (1999) regards the feelings of desire-driven emotion, which fuel personal ownership and identification, to be essential in constructing the bounded sense of self. Evidence for this hypothesis is that all signs of such emotion are entirely absent during episodes of epileptic automatism and suchlike. I've argued elsewhere (Albahari 2006: ch. 8), that the close ontological relation between desire-driven emotions and the sense of self is remarkably congruent with the teachings of Buddhism (to let go emotional investment in desire-satisfaction (Pāli *taṇhā*, Sanskrit *tṛṣṇā*).

I've argued elsewhere (e.g. Albahari 2009) that the unified perspectival subject cannot be illusory (as conditions for the possibility of an illusion taking hold require there to be a perspectival subject). I now wish to present a different but related argument for the reality of such a (unified) subject, which focuses on conditions for the possibility of a stream of experience. Putting aside versions of eliminative materialism (that altogether deny reality to subjective life)[17], advocates of a bundle theory will insist that any impression of a unified perspectival subject (should they agree to such an impression) is an illusory projection from the stream of discrete, causally connected, multi-modal experiences. Why illusory? Being a causal projection from the stream, the subject will not be unconstructed by the stream, as it purports to be. But what, then, can it mean for the stream to cause the subject (or its appearance thereof)? For A to cause B, A has to in some way exist independently of B (even if A cannot occur without B occurring at the same time). The stream of diverse experience must thus in some way exist independently of the 'perspective' to which it 'appears'—a position I find untenable. Reflexive reductionists are right here to insist that such experiences, by their very nature, are subjective phenomena, first-personally given. But they stop short of admitting a real 'first person' (the perspectival owner) to which the experiences are given: the experiences must exist *in and of themselves* as first-personally given. Now, while I granted this possibility in the previous section, it on closer inspection borders on contradictory. For what could 'first-personal givenness' mean, other than 'given to a (real) first-personal perspective'? (It cannot mean 'given to an illusory perspective'!) 'First-personal givenness' is in this respect a success term: the givenness of an experience to a perspective from which it is observed entails the reality of the observational perspective to which it is given. Hence the stream of diverse experience, if first-personally given, cannot ontologically precede (and hence cause the appearance of) the perspectival owner.

But must such experiences (in order to be experiences) appear to a synchronically unified perspective? Well, if we consider any object-experience at a given time, down to the simplest sensation, it will always be possible to parse it into dimensions of which one is simultaneously aware (for example, seeing a stretch of sky entails being simultaneously aware of

---

[17] I discuss an eliminative materialist brand of no-self in Albahari (2006: 165–167).

different locations of color). The dimensions of the experience must thus be synchronically present to the single perspective that observes it. Must the experiences appear to a diachronically unified perspective? Despite Abhidharma scholars, I cannot comprehend how an experience could present as *literally* momentary, disappearing the very moment it arises, for how then could it be said to exist at all? On this point I agree with Zahavi in his critique of Dreyfus (this volume): no matter how brief, a lived experience must have some duration, otherwise it is akin to a mathematical point, a mere abstraction. So for any stream of experience to occur, it has to occur to a point of view, and for its content to recognizably exist at all, it must be unified to that point of view for at least the specious present. In short, there can no more be a stream of experiences that ontologically precede (and give rise to) the unified minimal subject(s) to which it appears, than there can be physical objects that ontologically precede (and give rise to) the space in which they appear. A unified minimal subject (à la perspectival owner) cannot be caused by the stream of experience: it is integral to the conscious episode itself.

Does the argument immunize longer-term diachronic unity from illusory status, where the perspectival owner seems, via witness-consciousness, to persist unbrokenly and invariantly from one specious present to the next (and hence, for the duration of each waking episode)? It does not. It is conceptually possible for there to be a stream of discrete, invariant perspectival owners, each conditioning the next, such that there appears to be only one unbroken invariant witness of the stream. Since the situation cannot be resolved by appealing directly to phenomenology, the most promising strategy may well be to defend a version of the Experience Condition, which privileges the first-person perspective. On this principle, clashes between theory and experience will be resolved in favor of the latter— provided the disputed domain of reality is restricted to the experiential. In a very interesting passage (which defends diachronic unity of—and be-tween—the specious presents), Zahavi appeals to exactly such a principle:

Now, perhaps it could be objected that our experience of diachronic unity is after all 'merely' phenomenological and consequently devoid of any metaphysical impact. But to think that one can counter the phenomenological experience of unity over time with the claim that this unity is illusory and that it doesn't reveal anything about the true metaphysical nature of consciousness is to make use of the appearance-reality distinction outside its proper domain of application. This is especially so, given that the reality in question, rather than being defined in terms of some spurious mind-independence, should be understood in terms of experiential reality. For comparison, consider the case of pain. Who would deny that pain experience is sufficient for the reality of pain? To put it differently, if one wants to dispute the reality of the diachronic unity of consciousness, one should do so by means of more convincing phenomenological descriptions. To argue that the diachronic unity of consciousness is illusory because it doesn't match any unity on the subpersonal level is to misunderstand the task at hand.

(Zahavi, this volume, p. 72)[18]

While this version of the Experience Condition needs further defense and elaboration (it should not easily allow for the existence of libertarian free will or the self, for instance), it goes some way towards establishing that moment-to-moment, unbroken, invariant witness-consciousness is real. This in turn goes some way towards establishing that the bundle theory, which bestows constructed status to such witness-consciousness, is false.

The possibility of nirvana, I argued earlier, implies a two-tiered illusion of self. In this section, I have argued that (a) the architecture of the mind is empirically compatible with a model of two-tiered self-illusion, in that it allows the absence of a sense of personal ownership to be coupled with the presence of what would seem to be perspectival ownership and (b) the best explanation for this empirical data is one that supports a two-tiered illusion of self (as opposed to self-realism or the bundle theory). This provides the possibility of nirvana with an independent measure of support.

5. Conclusion: The Challenge Ahead

Nirvana is the undoing of the self-illusion, and on the account offered, it will be a process by which the perspectival owner de-identifies with any idea held about 'who one is'. The sense of being a bounded personal owner will be gradually eroded, freeing the (personally) ownerless consciousness intrinsic to nirvana. Having established the architecture of mind as potentially suitable for such de-identification, one might suppose that an easy task

---

[18] Zahavi would insist that the phenomenology does not support a diachronically unified *witness-consciousness*. I hope to have shown why it *is* the correct phenomenological description.

lies ahead in proving the psychological possibility of nirvana. This is far from true. A major obstacle pertains to the very case studies that served to buttress my earlier arguments. In all the cases where Damasio alludes to a sense of personal ownership being notably absent, the pathology is so severe that the patient is unable to function in the world. Ownerless consciousness has been malfunctioning consciousness. These sorts of considerations lead Damasio to conclude that 'a state of consciousness which encompasses a sense of self as conceptualized in this book is indispensable for survival' (Damasio 1999: 203 204).

A major challenge for those defending the psychological possibility of nirvana is thus to show how it could be possible for the sense of self to be eroded in ways that avoid debilitating pathology. A clue may well lie in the quality of attention that is cultivated during meditation. In all the cases enlisted by Damasio, where the sense of personal ownership is entirely suspended, the quality of attention has been abnormally low (e.g. in epileptic automatism, Alzheimer's disease and akinetic mutism). The high quality of attention that is cultivated in the meditative states may thus offset the pathological side-effects, especially as Damasio notes higher-quality attention to be a reliable indicator of mental acuity (Damasio 1999; 182–183). With the mounting studies outlining the neuropsychological benefits of meditation, a measure of empirical support may well, already, be forthcoming.[19]

References

Albahari, M. (2006), *Analytical Buddhism: The Two-Tiered Illusion of Self* (Houndmills: Palgrave Macmillan).

——(2009), 'Witness-Consciousness: Its Definition, Appearance and Reality', *Journal of Consciousness Studies* 16, 1: 62–84.

Damasio, A. (1999), *The Feeling of What Happens: Body and Emotion in the Making of Consciousness* (London: William Heinemann).

Dennett, D. C. (1991), *Consciousness Explained* (London: Penguin Books).

Flanagan, O. (1992), *Consciousness Reconsidered* (Cambridge, MA: MIT Press).

[19] My thanks to Mark Siderits, Evan Thompson, Dan Zahavi and the anonymous reviewers for their critical feedback on earlier drafts. My thanks to the philosophy department at the University of Calgary for providing a venue from which to take on the critical feedback during my sabbatical leave.

Gupta, B. (1998), *The Disinterested Witness: A Fragment of Advaita Vedānta Phenomenology* (Evanston, IL: Northwestern University Press).

Hume, D. (1739–40/1978), *A Treatise of Human Nature*, ed. L. A. Selby-Bigge and P. H. Nidditch (Oxford: Oxford University Press).

James, W. (1890/1981), *The Principles of Psychology: Vol. 1*. The Principles of Psychology (Cambridge, MA: Harvard University Press).

Metzinger, T. (2003), *Being No One* (Cambridge, MA: MIT Press).

Sayādaw, Mahāsi The Venerable (1994), *The Progress of Insight: A Treatise on Satipaṭṭhāna Meditation*, translated from the Pāli with notes by Nyānaponika Thera (Kandy, Sri Lanka: Buddhist Publication Society).

Strawson, Galen (2008), 'Episodic Ethics', in *Real Materialism and Other Essays* (Oxford: Clarendon Press).

Velleman, J. D. (2002), 'Identification and Identity', in Sarah Buss (ed.), *Contours of Agency: Essays on Themes from Harry Frankfurt* (Cambridge MA: MIT Press).

Zahavi, D. (2005a), 'Commentary on: Metzinger. T. *Being No-one: The Self-Model Theory of Subjectivity*', *Psyche* 11, 5.

——(2005b), *Subjectivity and Selfhood: Investigating the First-Person Perspective* (Cambridge, MA: MIT Press).

4

Self and Subjectivity: A Middle Way Approach

GEORGES DREYFUS

1. Introduction

In recent years, the topic of consciousness has drawn increasing attention among philosophers and cognitive scientists. This renewed interest, at times described as a 'consciousness boom', has come in the wake of a new willingness to include in the discussion of the mind sciences the subjective dimensions of mental phenomena, despite the fact that they may be difficult to conceptualize within the framework of current scientific approaches. Such willingness has at times been rather nervous and timid, but it has also been genuine, allowing the field of the mind sciences to consider views of the mind and practices that had been previously neglected. This is true of meditation, which is gradually being considered as a respectable object of study rather than a mysterious phenomenon to be either dismissed or put on a pedestal. This newly found openness has also started to include Asian views of the mind, particularly Indian ones.[1]

This inclusion is obviously welcome but not without difficulties. Indian views are often couched in a language that makes them not readily accessible to non-specialists. They also often address questions that are not always easy to integrate within the context of contemporary discussions. Hence, the inclusion of traditional Indian views about the mind within the new mind sciences is not an easy or immediate task. It requires a complex process of translation of the relevant aspects of the Indian tradition on the part of scholars of that

---

[1] For an excellent discussion of the scientific study of meditation, see Lutz, Dunne, and Davidson (2007: 499–554).

tradition, a process that involves not just the philological exploration of new sources, but also the development of the philosophical concepts necessary to connect this old tradition to contemporary concerns. This process has started recently[2] but has still some way to go before we can say with confidence that the Indian views about the mind and consciousness have been well understood and integrated into the contemporary discussions.

The goal of this essay[3] is to contribute to this process by attempting to relate some of the Buddhist views to contemporary discussions concerning consciousness. It should be clear, however, that in dealing with this topic I have no pretension to provide 'the Buddhist view of consciousness'. Buddhism is a plural tradition that has evolved over centuries to include a large variety of views about the mind. Hence, there is no one view that can ever hope to qualify as 'the Buddhist view of consciousness'. Moreover, the exploration of a difficult concept such as consciousness should not be thought of as a matter that can be completed easily. Buddhist traditions contain a wealth of material relevant to the mental, but such wealth is not always obvious. Hence, the inclusion of Buddhist views of consciousness should be thought of as an ongoing process of translation in which the richness of the Buddhist tradition is gradually connected to contemporary discussions rather than as a finished product.

In discussing consciousness within the Buddhist context, it is difficult to avoid broaching another very large topic, that of the self. Buddhism is often presented in the contemporary philosophical literature as advocating a thorough denial of the reality of the self akin to the bundle theory of the person attributed to Locke, Hume, and Parfit. This no-self view of the person is also at times understood to entail not just the thorough denial of the reality of any self-entity, but also to enable us to dispense with notions such as consciousness, experience, and subjectivity. In this essay, I argue that, although the bundle theory of the person has support within the Buddhist tradition, it is not as universally admitted as is often assumed, and certainly does not represent 'the Buddhist view of the person'. For

---

[2] See, for example, Waldron (2002) and Dreyfus and Thompson (2007).

[3] I would like to thank all the people who have helped me in sorting these difficult ideas. I cannot mention all of them, but particular thanks are due to Joseph Cruz, Evan Thompson, Mark Siderits, John Dunne, Miri Albahari, Jeffrey Hopkins, Gerald Hess, Jay Garfield, Robert Roeser, and many others, for their useful comments and feedback.

one, a significant minority of Buddhist Indian thinkers reject altogether the no-self view, advocating a position according to which the self exists as a process based on, but not reducible to, the body–mind complex (Priestly, nd.). But even among the majority of thinkers who rally to the dominant no-self standpoint, there are substantial differences about the ways in which the person is conceptualized within a no-self paradigm. This seems particularly true of the Yogācāra tradition, which offers an account of the person as being selfless and yet centered around the notion of reflexive subjectivity, a view that goes well beyond the bundle theory of the person and stands in stark contrast with the elimination of notions such as consciousness and experience, as I show here.

In arguing for what I believe is a more defensible Buddhist view of consciousness and the person than is often presented in the secondary literature, I offer a philosophical reconstruction, rather than an historically accurate rendering of what the original texts actually said. Hence, I feel free to mine Indian and Tibetan sources without being bound to adopt all the views that these texts advocate. For example, I often rely on the Abhidharma, particularly its Yogācāra version, and its Tibetan offshoots, which I believe contain a wealth of psychological and philosophical insights relevant to contemporary concerns but not yet fully exploited. But in arguing for a Yogācāra-inspired view of the person and consciousness I do not feel compelled to take a stance on the often debated question of whether the Yogācāra view entails a form of idealism or not.[4] My concerns here are quite different, being limited to cognitive and phenomenological considerations, which are not always usefully connected to metaphysical or ontological questions.

In the following pages, I discuss the nature of the person in Buddhist philosophy within a phenomenologically informed perspective that examines the sense that we have of ourselves rather than focusing on purely ontological considerations. I rest my analysis on the distinction between self and subjectivity, arguing that we need a Buddhist account of the latter, not as an objective self-entity, but as a process of self-awareness. In making my case, I address the phenomenological tradition and its views of subjectivity, particularly through the work of Dan Zahavi, who has shown the

---

[4] This topic has been the focus of an enormous literature that cannot be listed here. For two interesting recent contributions, see Lusthaus (2002) and Hopkins (2002).

contributions that phenomenology can make to an account of consciousness within the context of contemporary cognitive science and analytical philosophy. I also examine Miri Albahari's important delineation of a principled distinction between subjectivity and self as a basis for the elaboration of an account of subjectivity within a no-self paradigm. Like Zahavi and Albahari, I do not limit my discussion to purely philosophical or doctrinal considerations, but attempt to connect my presentation to some of the contemporary neuroscientific discussions of the self, particularly those of Antonio Damasio. In the second part of my presentation, I explore some of the resources that the Buddhist tradition, particularly the Yogācāra Abhidharma, offers for the conceptualization of subjectivity. There I show the contributions that often misunderstood Yogācāra doctrines, such as that of the basic consciousness, can make to our understanding of subjectivity. In the process I take issue with Albahari's view of a transcendent subject, arguing that we need to find ways to explain subjectivity as a feature of ordinary cognitive processes, rather than as a supramundane *nibbānic* consciousness. I also show how this Yogācāra view of a basic consciousness relates to contemporary questions concerning the holistic nature of consciousness, questions addressed by thinkers such as John Searle and others. In this way, I show how a Buddhist view informed by contemporary phenomenology can steer a middle course between the reductionist rejection of subjectivity and the reificatory acceptance of a self-entity. I conclude with a few remarks on the centrality of the notion of experience in a Buddhist account of consciousness and the person, arguing that its repudiation by Dennett-inspired scholars such as Sharf is an obstacle to our understanding of the full range of Buddhist views.

2. A Yogācāra-Inspired View of Consciousness

The basics of the Buddhist conception of the mind I defend here derive from the Abhidharma tradition. Briefly, the object of the Abhidharma is to analyze the realm of sentient experience and the world given in such experience, in a language that undermines the postulation of an enduring unified subject. The Abhidharma analyzes experience into its basic elements (*dharmas*), listing and grouping them into the appropriate categories. In this project, the Abhidharma is following the central tenets of Buddhist philosophy, the twin ideas of non-substantiality and dependent origination. On this view, the phenomena given in experiences are not unitary and stable substances, but complex and ephemeral formations of basic events arising within complex causal nexuses. This is particularly true of the person, who is not a substantial self but a construct that comes to be only in dependence on complex configurations of multiple mental and material events (the aggregates).

This no-self view has important consequences for understanding the cognitive process, which unfolds not through the control of a cognitive executive, but on the basis of the interaction of competing factors, whose strength varies according to circumstances.[5] There is no enduring experiencing subject, inner controller, or homunculus that manages or observes the cognitive process. Rather, the moments of awareness exercise all the functions necessary to cognition and constitute it. Each moment of awareness comes to be in dependence on various conditions (preceding moments of awareness, object, sensory basis, etc.). Having arisen, it performs its function and dissolves, giving rise to the next moment of awareness, thus forming a stream of consciousness or continuum (santāna, rgyud) not unlike James' stream of thought or Husserl's mental flux. Hence, for the Abhidharma, the mind is not an entity or a substance. It is not a thing, a kind of mechanism that produces thoughts, memories, or perceptions, but a constantly changing process, a continuum of rising and ceasing complex and multi-layered mental events, which are, at least indirectly, phenomenologically available.[6]

This way of thinking about the mental is relevant to contemporary discussions about the ontology of the mind. Although Buddhism is often presented (and rightly so) as advocating a kind of event dualism,[7] which supports a worldview in which we undergo a multiplicity of lives, it should be noted that the Abhidharma view of the mind can be taken in

---

[5] This point is well made by Bodhi (2000: 158, 165). It should be clear that this denial of the existence of a central unit concerns the phenomenology of consciousness, not its ontological basis (sub-personal brain states), about which Buddhist analysis of consciousness has little to say.

[6] As will become clear below, we need to distinguish between what is phenomenologically available and what is introspectable. Many cognitive processes such as what is happening in deep sleep are below the threshold of ordinary consciousness and hence unavailable to introspection, but inasmuch as they mark our experiences they are phenomenologically available, albeit indirectly.

[7] For a presentation of a form of Buddhist dualism, see Jackson (1993). It should be clear, however, that Buddhist dualism differs from Cartesian dualism in that it holds that there are two types of events, not two types of substance. Hence, it may be more amenable to being naturalized.

an ontologically neutral way, compatible with a number of contemporary views of the mind. This is so because the central concern of the Abhidharma analysis of the mental is a description of the complexity of the components of mental processes as they are phenomenologically available, not an analysis of the ontological basis of mental processes, a basis that is not readily available to the kind of analysis central to its project.

I will defend a view of the mind that embraces this perspective, limiting myself to the discovery of the phenomenology of mental states and leaving ontological questions to the side. It is in this context that I understand the distinction that most Ābhidharmikas draw between the real components of the mind–body complex and the fictional, or illusory, self. Whereas traditional Ābhidharmikas hold this distinction to have some ontological implications and to provide the basis for an event dualism, I limit its purview to the phenomenological domain. The cognitive processes taken here to be real are so taken because they are irreducible to more basic phenomenologically available components, not because they are taken to be the ultimate building blocks of the universe, for if we were to consider their ontology we would have to face the difficult question of their relation to the domain of sub-personal brain states.[8]

For the Abhidharma, the mind is composed, we said, of a series of mental states. Each state can be conceptualized as being a moment of awareness (*citta, sems*) endowed with various characteristics, the mental factors (*caitesika, sems byung*). Awareness, which is also described as consciousness (*vijñāna, rnam shes*), is primary, in that it is aware of the object and cognizes it, whereas mental factors qualify this awareness and determine it as being pleasant or unpleasant, focused or unfocused, calm or agitated, positive or negative, etc. Vasubandhu describes consciousness (i.e. awareness) as the 'apprehension of each object'.[9] Similarly, a basic Theravāda Abhidharma manual defines it as 'nothing other than the process of cognizing the object' (Bodhi, 2000:27). Most Buddhist thinkers, both inside and outside of the Abhidharma tradition, agree on this description of the mental as consisting of moments of awareness with various characteristics. What they disagree about is the analysis of the way in which consciousness cognizes its object.

---

[8] For a brilliant, but inconclusive, take on this topic, see Kim (1998).
[9] Poussin (1971: I. 30). Translation from the French is mine.

Many Abhidharma thinkers (belonging to various schools such as Vaib-hāṣika, Theravāda, etc.) argue that consciousness simply consists of a naked encounter with reality in which the mind grasps the object itself. These thinkers do not posit any appearance as an intentional object or cognitive mediator over and above the object itself. Others, at times described as belonging to the Sautrāntika or the Yogācāra traditions, have argued that this idea of a bare encounter with reality does not explain the nature of cognition.[10] For what does it mean for the mind to apprehend an object? Either apprehension is just a metaphor (that of physical grasping) for a process in need of further clarification, or it is a hopelessly naive view deprived of explanatory power. According to these thinkers, consciousness does not grasp its object directly, but through the disclosure of its appearance. The object does not appear directly or nakedly to consciousness but through the phenomenal form (*ākāra, rnam pa,* literally 'aspect') it gives rise to in the cognitive process, its manifestation within the field of consciousness.[11] Awareness of the object is then the beholding by consciousness itself of the phenomenal form of the object. The implication of this view is that consciousness is intrinsically self-aware.

Dignāga articulated this view of consciousness through the doctrine of self-cognition (*svasaṃvedana*). Dharmakīrti developed this view, presenting self-cognition as a kind of apperception, the sense that we have of being able to register our mental states as being our own.[12] This self-awareness is neither introspective nor reflective, for it does not take inner mental states as its objects. Rather, it is the self-specifying function of every mental episode that brings about a non-thematic awareness of mental states as our own so that the person automatically knows whose experiences he or she is experiencing. This self-awareness is pre-reflective, providing the basis for introspection, the paying attention to some of our mental states. Hence, the

---

[10] These two ways of understanding consciousness as being first and foremost object-directed or reflexive represent two distinct ways of conceptualizing consciousness in Indian philosophy. The Nyāya school of brahmanical realism, for example, argues that consciousness first and foremost illuminates another object, and that self-awareness is necessarily reflective, whereas the idealist Vedānta holds that consciousness is self-luminous (*svayamprakāśa*), in that it is directly aware of itself and only indirectly aware of the object. See Ram-Prasad (2007), as well as this volume.

[11] Chim Jampeyang (1989: 126–127). A similar view is found in Sazang Mati Penchen (n.d), 32–33. This discussion follows Tibetan doxographical categories. For a modern scholarly examination of these categories, see Mimaki (1979). For a critique of these categories, see Cabezon (1990: 7–26).

[12] For a discussion of this important doctrine, see Dreyfus (1997: chs. 19 and 25). For a discussion of earlier views on self-cognition, see Yao (2005).

reflexivity that is at play here does not require a separate cognition but is the necessary consequence of the analysis of consciousness as the beholding of a phenomenal form within the field of consciousness.[13]

This explanation of consciousness as the experiencing of the form of the object within the field of consciousness may not provide, however, the final word in the Yogācāra tradition, for it already presupposes a basic duality between consciousness as the experienced object (*grāhyākāra*, i.e. apprehended aspect), and consciousness as the experiencing (*grāhakākāra*, i.e. apprehending aspect) of that object. This duality is the basis for the ordinary ways in which we conceptualize our experience of external objects as being directly available to us, while being radically separated from our awareness. But this view is mistaken, for consciousness is neither cut off from reality nor is it in immediate contact with it. Rather, consciousness proceeds by constructing the object that it perceives. We have no access to reality outside of our mental constructions, and any reality that seems given to us immediately as clearly distinct from our mental life is in fact irremediably entangled with this mental life, its predispositions, expectations, distortions, etc.[14]

Several Buddhist meditative traditions refer to the experience of a non-dual mode of cognition in which consciousness appears as a luminous self-presencing background against which ephemeral cognitive episodes take place, much like clouds drifting away against the blue sky. The Tibetan Nyingma tradition of the Great Perfection (*rdzogs chen*), for example, presents a view of awareness as being limpid and luminous while self-aware. Awareness is described as shining through in between thoughts, much like the sky appears in between clouds. A description of how the practitioner is introduced to such deep states explains:

When it [awareness] stares at itself, with this observation there is a vividness in which nothing is seen. This awareness is direct, naked, vivid, unestablished, empty, limpid luminosity, unique, non-dual clarity and emptiness. It is not permanent, but

---

[13] There are here obvious parallels with the phenomenological view of consciousness as involving a pre-reflective self-awareness as articulated by Husserl and Sartre. For an excellent discussion of these views within a perspective informed by contemporary cognitive sciences and analytic philosophy of mind, see Zahavi (2005).

[14] This is not unlike Husserl's description of the natural attitude in which we assume that the world of ordinary objects is given immediately to us and exists simply out there for us, at hand. See Welton (1999: 60).

unestablished. It is not nihilistic but radiantly vivid. It is not one, but manifoldly aware and clear. It is not manifold but indivisibly of one taste. It is none other than this very self-awareness.[15]

These meditative instructions offer the glimpse of an experience of awareness as being clear and without content, while being self-aware. This is also described as 'awareness as such' (sems nyid), the state in which awareness experiences itself without the distortions imposed by the dualistic structure through which we usually deal with reality. In this state, consciousness appears as empty since it is free from any content, but it is not nothing either since it is luminous, having a basic self-presencing or reflexivity that is irreducible to the usual subject-object structures of our ordinary conception of experience. This non-dual state seems to correspond, at least partly, to how many Yogācārins understand consciousness at its deepest level, that is, as being free from dualistic distortions and experiencing itself directly. Although we think of experience as having a dual structure, in reality the duality is more a result of how we interpret experience than an accurate reflection of its nature. In its most basic state, consciousness does not exist apart from its object. Both subject and object forms are superimposed on a consciousness that is but a single field of awareness.

This description of a non-dual awareness is important to understanding the view of subjectivity delineated here, but it also creates a challenge for philosophical analysis. In this view, consciousness is non-dual, and hence beyond the reach of conceptualization. It may be experienced directly or evoked indirectly by helpful metaphors and instructions on how to reach such a state, but it cannot be described. Hence, we may find it difficult to articulate a view of subjectivity based solely on this level of analysis. To do so, we may want to move a notch down to a level of analysis at which non-dual awareness appears in its dualistic manifestations. This is the level of analysis at which consciousness is understood to disclose its phenomenal form by assuming the form of the object. In doing so, awareness also reveals itself in its apprehending aspect.[16] This subject-object duality helps us

---

[15] Karma Chagme (1998: 108). A critical study of the Nyingma views of the mind, with a view of its connection to the Yogācāra tradition, seems to be of obvious interest and yet remains to be written. There are also interesting parallels within the Theravāda tradition. See Collins (1982: 246–47).

[16] In Dharmakīrti's tradition, these two levels of analysis are at times referred to as False Aspectarian (alīkārāvāda, mam dzun pa) and True Aspectarian (satyakārāvāda, mam bden pa). In the first perspective, consciousness is conceived as being non-dual in its nature, the phenomenal form or aspect being merely

understand the nature of subjectivity, and to distinguish it from the further and coarser distortion of conceiving of ourselves as enduring self-entities. Hence, in the following pages, I will assume this level of analysis of ordinary subjectivity as consisting of the experiencing of an object as given to awareness, and argue that we can distinguish it from a coarser level of distortion at which we reify subjectivity as being a bounded self.

The upshot of this discussion is that, for the Yogācāra, consciousness is not merely intentional (the fact that it is about something) but phenomenal and hence reflexive. Consciousness is not just the apprehension of an object, it is also the disclosing of the mode of appearance of that object to a subjectivity that experiences that object in particular ways, while being pre-reflectively aware of its experience. Hence, consciousness is best thought of as a continuum of self-aware experiences of various phenomenal qualities (a feeling of pain, a visual impression, thoughts, wants, etc.), so that it makes sense, in Thomas Nagel's words, to talk about what it is like for the subject to undergo this or that experience when he or she apprehends an object (Nagel 1974).

Some contemporary philosophers of mind describe these phenomenal qualities as *qualia,* the experiential qualities of the apprehension of objects.[17] Insofar as this term refers to the phenomenological data intrinsic to consciousness, its use does not raise any special problem. There is, however, a great danger of reifying consciousness and making it into the introspection of a succession of private, ineffable, and transparent entities that parade within the Cartesian theater of our mind and can be known with clarity and certainty by a witness.[18] This understanding of the mind and of the nature of *qualia* is deeply alien to the account suggested here. For one thing, the theater metaphor suggests that our mental life is composed of a succession of clearly delineated experiential states, such as images or feelings of pain in the same way that a show consists of a series of scenes. But clearly

superimposed on a purely reflexive awareness. In the second perspective, the phenomenal form is also taken to be a distortion of a non-dual awareness, but this distortion is understood to have some basis in the nature of consciousness. Here I will be following the second perspective, although I am also suggesting that both can be seen as complementary, providing different levels of analysis, rather than antagonistic views. For a discussion of these two views, see Dreyfus (1997: ch. 27).

[17] For a reader on the various contemporary views within the philosophy of mind, see Chalmers (2002).

[18] This colorful expression is due to Dennett (1991).

delineated states hardly exhaust the range of phenomenological data.[19] There are numerous aspects of our mental life, such as diffuse feelings, inchoate emotions, vague recognitions, etc., that do not conform to such a model and that are nevertheless elements of consciousness. Moreover, the theater metaphor suggests that consciousness is a succession of clearly delineated states grasped by introspection. But this cannot be right. The phenomenal aspect of consciousness cannot be reduced to what is appre-hended by introspection, for we are able to introspect only a fraction of what we experience pre-reflectively. The assertion of the phenomenal nature of consciousness entails that consciousness is reflexive, but not that its content can be reduced to introspectable mental states. Consciousness is a constantly changing, multi-layered, deep and extraordinarily complex flux, which can be penetrated only gradually and partially, as will become clear below. Finally and more importantly, the theater metaphor is wrong-headed in that it is inherently dualist, positing a distinction between the observer and the observed, a view profoundly antithetical to the no-self position central to my account. Consciousness is not a feature dualistically and retrospectively attributed to mental states by a witness, but is an inherent feature of mental states inasmuch as they are self-specified.

The difference between the view argued for here and the Cartesian view of consciousness as a transparent self that has privileged access to its own content becomes clear when we realize that, in this view, our ordinary sense of what it is to be conscious is to a very large extent a grand illusion.[20] At one level, it distorts reality by creating an illusion of stability in a constantly changing world, as suggested by various phenomena such as change blind-ness, attentional blink, etc. (Palmer 1999: 537–539). The illusion of stability does not just concern the objects of our experience but the ways in which we conceive of ourselves as stable self-entities appropriating these objects, as we will see shortly. It also concerns the very subject–object structure that serves as the basis of our ordinary experience, the sense that we have of an immediately given and yet fully separated objective reality. It is on this basis that we conceive of a world in which we are stable selves, who encounter other stable entities.

---

[19] This point is made forcefully and cogently by Petitot, Varela, Pachoud, and Roy (1999: 11).

[20] I am using *Cartesianism* as defined by O. Flanagan, that is, as the view that 'each person is in an epistemically privileged position with respect to the content of his or her mind . . .' (1999: 66). Whether this actually corresponds to Descartes' own position is a different matter.

It should also be clear, however, that this view of conscious experience as non-dual and distorted is quite different from the view of those who seek the elimination of any subjective notion, holding that consciousness is completely illusory, being fully reducible to the subject's beliefs about his or her experiences, as I take Dennett to argue for.[21] From the Buddhist perspective articulated here, our mistake is not to think that things appear to us, but to assent to the ways things appear to us and thus take for real our own mental creations. The view articulated here aims for a middle ground that steers clear of two extreme positions. By denying the transparency of consciousness, I seek to avoid the extreme of reification, here the Cartesian assertion of a transparent subject able to know with certainty ideas, feelings, and emotions. By asserting that there is a phenomenological asymmetry between first- and third-person perspectives and by taking seriously the fact of being appeared to, I seek to escape from the other extreme, the complete elimination of any notion of subjective experience. Both extremes short-change the cognitive process and provide overly simplistic models of consciousness that fail to account for its complexities, as will become clear below.[22]

This view of consciousness as reflexive is not, however, without important questions concerning the doctrine of no-self. For if consciousness entails self-awareness, does it not follow that there is a unified subject, and hence a self that is not just a convenient label used to designate a bunch of aggregates? And if this is so, doesn't this contradict the cornerstone of most Buddhist philosophy, the unambiguous repudiation of the self? In the following pages I respond to these questions by making an important distinction between subjectivity and self. I argue that this distinction can provide a strong basis for a defense of the no-self position, while giving ordinary subjectivity its due place within the Buddhist philosophy of the person.

---

[21] For thoughtful discussions of Dennett's views on experience, see the special issue of *Phenomenology and Cognitive Sciences* 6 (2007). For a view of the controversy surrounding the issue of whether our sense that experiences, particularly visual ones, have a rich phenomenological content is a grand illusion or not, see the special issue of the *Journal of Consciousness Studies* 9.5–6 (2002).

[22] It should be said, however, that the kind of rich phenomenological discussions of meditative experiences that one would expect in a tradition like Buddhism, where meditation is supposed to play a central role, have yet to be produced, or if they exist, analyzed by Western scholars at great length. There are here and there interesting suggestions, but as far as I know, the range of descriptive accounts available is still very limited.

3. Consciousness, Subjectivity and the Self

This question of the connection between the notions of consciousness and self is obviously important for Buddhist philosophy, both in its classical formulations and in the attempts that some of us are engaged in to address contemporary discussions from a Buddhist perspective. It also parallels important discussions within the Western philosophical tradition where in the last few years the topic of the self has received renewed attention. A number of thinkers, such as Parfit, Dennett, Strawson, Metzinger, etc., have argued for a radical rejection of the self, sometimes with explicit reference to Buddhist views. Within the phenomenological tradition, Sartre, in his wonderful *La Transcendence de l'ego,* holds a similar perspective, arguing that the ego is reflectively constructed on the basis of the self-aware flow of consciousness.

Other thinkers have rejected this no-self perspective. Dan Zahavi, for example, argues in his excellent *Selfhood and Subjectivity* that the phenomenological view of consciousness as implying a pre-reflective awareness makes it impossible to do without some notion of self. For Zahavi, if I understand him correctly, the self is based on a real structure of invariance that provides the act-transcendent and moment-transcendent identity-pole necessary to a coherent account of subjectivity. Subjectivity entails first-person self-givenness, the fact that when the subject has an experience, there is no doubt about who is having the experience. There may be vast uncertainties concerning the modalities and content of my experience (Was my experience pleasant or neutral? Did I really see or did I merely imagine? Did I taste chocolate or artificial flavoring, etc.), but there is no room to doubt whether it is I or somebody else who had the experience. As Zahavi puts it, 'When I undergo an experience, I cannot be in doubt about who the subject of that experience is' (Zahavi 2005: 124). But for Zahavi first-person self-givenness is not sufficient for subjective experience, which requires a pole of invariance in relation to which I can decide that the experience is mine. Zahavi explains:

The self-givenness of a single experience is a necessary, but not a sufficient, condition for this type of self-awareness to occur. The latter entails more than a simple and immediate self-awareness; it also entails a difference or a distance that is bridged, that is, it involves a synthesis. This is so because the self cannot be given as an act-transcendent identity in a single experience. It is only by comparing several experiences that we encounter something that retains its identity through changing circumstances.

(Zahavi 2005: 131)

For Zahavi, subjectivity implies unity. I am not just conscious of various experiences causally connected. Rather, I am conscious of experiences as happening to a single self. This singularity is not just synchronic (something to which I will come back), but diachronic as well. As a subject of experience, I am aware of myself as having experiences across temporal distance. Hence, when I recall an experience, I am not just projecting unity over the past and the present subjects but I am becoming aware of what I, the unified self, experienced earlier.

This phenomenological defense of the self represents an important challenge for the kind of Buddhist view of consciousness articulated here, and zeroes in on what I take to be the central issue in the debate between proponents of the self and their adversaries, namely, the question of diachronic unity. For if consciousness is pre-reflectively self-aware, that is, if (ordinary) experiences are given as having an intrinsic mineness, does it not follow that there must be an *I* in relation to whom experiences can be said to be mine? And if this is so, does this not show that there exists a self that transcends the present moment? This challenge also represents a welcome opportunity to elaborate a richer Buddhist view of the person, a view that accounts, not just for the ontological rejection of a self entity, but also includes within the purview of the Buddhist philosophy of the person the experiential dimensions that are fundamental to a number of practices, and without which sense cannot be made of many aspects of the Buddhist tradition.

To respond to Zahavi's arguments it may be useful to include in the conversation Miri Albahari's recent contribution to the Buddhist philosophy of the person. In her insightful and important work, Albahari (2006) argues, if I understand her correctly, that an adequate view of the person within the context of Buddhist philosophy requires a crucial distinction between the self and the subject. Whereas the former is an illusion to be deconstructed, the latter is quite real. For Albahari, the subject is characterized by its ability to witness. She says:

The *modus operandi* of a subject seems, to put the point broadly, to be its realized capacity to observe, know, witness and be consciously aware. I shall use the term 'witnessing' (or 'witnessing consciousness') to cover all these modes of apprehension, but when I do so I am to be taken as talking only about the phenomenal cases of such apprehension. By 'phenomenal' I mean that there is something it is like to be undergoing the apprehension . . . Minimally construed, witnessing can be described as the broadest mode of phenomenal apprehending, subsuming all species of conscious experiencing, perceiving, thinking and introspecting, whether these apprehendings are attentive or inattentive, human or non-human.

(Albahari 2006: 7–8)

Albahari's arguments seem to dovetail with the phenomenological view of consciousness sketched above. When I undergo an experience, this experience is not just an element in a complex impersonal flux. Rather, it is given as mine immediately, and without any possibility of mistake. This self-givenness seems to correspond to what Albahari means by the notion of subject and its ability to witness all species of conscious experiences. Consciousness is the ability to be aware of one's experiences immediately.

For Albahari, the subject is to be distinguished sharply from the self, which is a result of the mistaken assumption that the subject is a self.[23] Such illusion is based on a mechanism of identification through which the subject is identified with the aggregates. For example, when I feel really healthy, I identify with the body. It is as if the subject becomes fused with the body felt as healthy. At other times I identify with my mind, deluding myself into thinking 'I am really smart'. In this way, the subject is identified as being more than a mere witness, as being a bounded entity that endures over time through the appropriation of various parts of the body–mind complex. Albahari gives this definition of the self:

A self is defined as a bounded, happiness-seeking/*duḥkha*-avoiding (witnessing) subject that is a personal owner and controlling agent, and which is unified and

---

[23] Albahari (2006: 51) states: 'On the Buddhist position, we are to understand that the witnessing subject makes the (deeply mistaken) assumption of *being* a self through its very act of assuming various *khandās*.' I think that this formulation, which seems to imply that the witnessing consciousness mistakes itself for a self, is problematic. It seems that if the subject is unconditioned and unbroken in its presence, as Alabhari argues, it cannot be mistaken and hence cannot make wrong assumptions. Rather, it seems that what needs to be said is that other mental states (desire, ignorance) take the subject to be a self. This is in fact the Yogācāra view, as I will show below.

unconstructed, with unbroken and invariable presence from one moment to the next, as well as with longer-term endurance and invariability.

(Albahari 2006: 73)

For Albahari, the self is conceived by attributing to the subject character-istics that it does not have, particularly those of being bounded, being a personal owner and a controlling agent. The self arises out of an identifica-tion of the subject as being the personal owner of a particular aspect of the body–mind complex. In our example of feeling healthy, it is the body that provides a reflexive lens through which the subject is seen. By identifying the subject in this way, this filter creates a sense of boundedness. I am not just a subject witnessing the health of the body, I am defined and delimited by this healthy body. This sense of boundedness creates a boundary between what is thus identified and everything else. In this way a fundamental bifurcation is created within my cognitive universe between what is on the side of the self and of the other, that is, everything else. This boundary is in reality quite fluid. At various times I identify with different aspects of the body–mind complex. I may even identify with my favorite sports team. But I am usually not aware of this fluidity, for when I identify with this or that aspect of my personality, I conceive of myself as a self-evident and rigidly delineated entity, firmly separated from the rest of the world. This rigid sense of separation also entails a quality of specialness. The separation that is made between *I* and the rest of the world is loaded with extremely powerful emotions. I am not just different from the rest of the world but I am first and foremost extremely special, the one and only one who is more important than anything or anybody else. Finally, I am also the autonomous agent who is in charge of the mind–body complex and its actions. I am the seat of free will, the entity that freely decides and initiates all my movements. I am the author of what I do, in control of my actions. (Albahari 2006: 73)

I think that Albahari's discussion is extremely insightful and makes a significant contribution to Buddhist philosophy by delineating more pre-cisely what it is that most Buddhist philosophers reject when they deny the self. This is important, for as several Tibetan Buddhist thinkers have argued,[24]

---

[24] Tsongkhapa is one of the most famous Buddhist thinkers to have argued that identifying the self to be refuted is an important step in the process of insight. In fact, his whole approach to the no-self doctrine is based on the drawing of an explicit distinction between the self that is to be refuted and the self that exists conventionally. See Tsongkhapa (2002: III.126).

it is hard to understand the no-self standpoint without identifying what the self is that is being rejected. I believe that the self that is the target of many traditional Buddhist arguments corresponds quite closely to Albahari's description. For example, the seventeenth-century Geluk thinker Jamyang Zhaypa explicitly compares the relation of the self to the aggregates, to that between head merchant and the merchants whom he leads.[25] Like the head merchant who commands the other merchants but is also one of them, the self is misconceived as being in charge of the aggregates, though it does not appear separately from them. This metaphor of the self as the boss in charge of the mind-body complex, which is meant to illustrate how we ordinarily misconceive of the self (not how the self exists), corresponds to the sense of self that is rejected in a number of canonical sources. For example, the Buddha is presented as offering this argument in the *Samyutta Nikāya* (iii.66–67):

Body is not a self. If body were a self then it might be that it would not lead to sickness; then it might be possible to say, 'Let my body be like this, let my body not be like this'. But since body is not a self, so it leads to sickness, and it is not possible to say, 'Let my body be like this, let my body not be like this'.

(Gethin 1998: 136)

This argument from the lack of control, as well as the others that cannot be examined here,[26] quite clearly points to a sense of the self as defined by its being in control of the aggregates, being an agent in charge of acting, as well as being an enduring entity clearly separated from the rest of the world and worthy of special concern. It is this sense of bounded self closely connected to our sense of agency that is the target of Buddhist arguments, which seek to expose its illusory nature.

Thus, it seems that we have here the basis for a Buddhist response to Zahavi's challenge. This response rests on the distinction between two senses of who we are: the subject, or, rather subjectivity, that is, the continuum of momentary mental states with their first-personal self-givenness, which are central to being a person (more on this shortly), and the self,

---

[25] For Jamyang Zhaypa, this example illustrates the self rejected by most Buddhist schools (what he calls the coarse object of refutation), not the most subtle form of self-delusion. Like Tsongkhapa, Jamyang Zhayba believes that there is a more subtle level of misconception of the self that is the special target of Prāsaṅgika reasonings. See Hopkins (2003: 651, fn. B); Lopez (2006: 170).

[26] The Pali Canon presents two other arguments. The first argues against a permanent self, whereas the second argues against the self from mereological considerations. See Collins (1982: 97–103).

which is an illusory reification of subjectivity as being a bounded agent enduring through time, rather than a complex flow of fleeting self-specified experiences. Hence, the perceptions, thoughts, and memories that arise within the continuum of my mind are not impersonal. They are clearly mine in the sense of there being no possible doubt about who is the subject of these experiences. But this does not entail that there is an act-transcendent pole of identity, an entity that endures before and after the moment of experience, in relation to which I can establish that these experiences are mine, for all that there is a succession of self-aware subjective states.

We may wonder, however, about the situation in which I recall past memories. When I remember my being a schoolboy in Switzerland, it seems that I, the remembering person, am the same person as the one who is being remembered. Is this an illusion? Or is Zahavi right to argue that the only possible way to make sense of this experience is to posit a moment-transcendent structure in relation to which the identity of the remembering person and remembered person can be established? The answer of the proponents of the no-self position is, I believe, quite clear. The sense of diachronic unity of the self is at the heart of the illusion of the self, which in many respects arises from blindness to change. There is no entity that endures from my childhood in Switzerland to my being a grown-up in North America. Does this mean that we can say that the person who is remembering is different from the one who is being remembered? Buddhist thinkers have often balked at this last point, asserting that the remembering and the remembered persons are neither different nor the same.[27] What do they mean by this rather enigmatic statement? Should we not bite the bullet and state quite clearly that the remembering and the remembered persons are different?

This is where I think it is important to keep in mind the importance of the first person self-givenness at the heart of the Buddhist notion of person articulated here. Although in some sense the remembering person is different from the one who is being remembered, this difference is not the same as the

---

[27] For example, Candrakīrti states that 'because Maitreya and Upagupta are different people, their constituent factors cannot be included in the same continuum' (Huntington 1989: 164). Classically, the Buddhist view that the remembered and the remembering persons are neither different nor the same is interpreted as deriving from the negation of the self. Since there is no self, it makes no sense, except in a strictly conventional way, to ask whether the remembering person is the same as the remembered one. Here I argue that, although right, this interpretation may not provide the full story, and that a discussion of the self-givenness of remembered experiences adds to our understanding of the assertion that the remembered and the remembering persons are neither different nor the same.

one that separates me from other people. When I remember being a child in Switzerland, I am not just recalling the circumstances in which I used to live, but I am also remembering these circumstances as being given to me in the first person mode. To put it slightly differently, when I remember my childhood in Switzerland, I am not just remembering the object of my past experience, but also the subjective states that underwent this past experience. Although these mental states are not the same as the states that remember, they both share a similar first-person self-givenness, a commonality that is not being shared with anybody else. The sense of unity that underlies my memory arises out of the fact that when I remember my past experiences I do not just recall their content, but I also remember them as being given to me. It is true that the *I* who underwent the experience is not the same as the one remembering. Hence, when I recall these experiences as being mine, this memory involves a partial distortion. But inasmuch as I remember these memories in a first person mode, this remembering is not completely illusory either, and captures something that separates these memories from those of everybody else. Hence, Buddhist thinkers are not wrong to assert that the remembering and the remembered persons are not identical but that they are also not completely different either, since they share in the ways in which experiences are given to them.

Moreover, the proponents of no-self are also not without justification in raising doubts about Zahavi's assumption that the unity of our subjective life requires an act-transcendent pole of identity enduring through the multiplicity of experiences. For, what is the nature of this act-transcendent pole of self-identity? Zahavi answers that the self is constituted by the invariant structure of first-person self-givenness shared by the various experiences. This structure supports the process of temporalization that is necessary to experience. That is, we do not just have one experience after another, but rather we perceive them to stand in a temporal order. This process of temporalization is based on the retentive and protentive abilities of consciousness to keep track of past experiences and to anticipate new ones.[28] If I

---

[28] I am here rapidly glossing over the complex topic of time consciousness, one of Husserl's greatest insights. I take it that the view of consciousness as being retentive of past moments and protentive toward future ones is far from being incompatible with Buddhist anti-substantialism, and may even offer important resources to further its philosophical project. For a remarkably clear presentation of this difficult subject, see Zahavi (2005: 49–72). For a discussion in relation to the neurosciences, see Thompson (2007: ch. 11).

understand him correctly, Zahavi holds that the self is this structure, which
stands unchanged through the temporalized experiences, much like James'
rainbow appearing on a waterfall (Zahavi 2005: 67). But the very use of this
metaphor seems to raise doubts about the reality of the self rather than prove
its existence. For what is real here? Is it the rainbow, or is it the waterfall, its
water, and the sunlight? Is it not the case that the structure that is conceived
to be the unified self is an abstract structure superimposed on the passing of
experiences, much like the rainbow is a visual illusion created by sunlight
and the drops of water?

From the nominalist perspective that is at the heart of most Buddhist
traditions, the unity of this self-givenness is conceptually constructed on the
basis of the passing of the causally related temporalized experiences. What is
real for the Abhidharma tradition whose standpoint is reflected here are
the causally effective elements that make up reality (the *dharmas*): here the
various transient experiences that we undergo in temporal order, and the
memories we have of them. The diachronic unity that we conceive them to
share is just a construct created by memory on the basis of the fact that each
experience is given in a first-person mode and inscribed within a temporal
order. Hence, although the unity that is conceived to encompass various
experiences is not completely divorced from reality, it is not fully real either.
It is a fiction that conceptually stands for the complex causal connections
that exist in reality. It is a convenient way to understand reality, what
Buddhists call a conventional truth, not a causally effective part of the fabric
of reality.

Does it follow then that the person is just a convenient fiction imposed
on a group of impersonal elements? And if this is so, are we not back to the
bundle theory of the person that we sought to reject in the first place? The
conclusions that we can draw from this discussion are, I believe, quite clear.
The view of the person argued for here differs from the bundle theory in the
understanding of the basis necessary for the attribution of the concept of
person. The bundle theorist argues that the person is conceptually constructed to account for the complexity and continuity of impersonal and
anonymous elements, and that the personal character attributed to these
components arises only through a post hoc fabrication. The view I am
arguing for agrees that the person is a conceptual fiction, but holds that there
is, at the phenomenological level, a minimal self-consciousness present in
any experience necessary to the attribution of this concept. When we

attribute to ourselves personhood, we do so, not just through a retrospective imputation on the impersonal elements of our mind–body complex, but on the basis of the self-givenness of our experiences, which are not given in a neutral mode and then retrospectively made into our own, but, rather, arise as belonging to a minimal *I* (the constantly changing stream of pre-reflective self-aware experiences, not the reified self). Hence, the experiences on the basis of which we understand ourselves as persons are not impersonal but intrinsically self-specified, and this is why they are immune to any possible doubt as to whom the subject of the experience is.[29]

From this perspective, the Buddhist doctrine of no-self is not just an ontological or a metaphysical take on the question of personal identity, it is also a phenomenological inquiry into the various senses that we ordinarily have of ourselves, inquiry that seeks to distinguish the distorted from the more realistic sense of self. It is from this perspective that our discussion has focused on at least two ways in which we conceive ourselves: as a transient flow of subjective experiences (more on this later), and as a bounded enduring self-entity endowed with a sense of agency. The Buddhist project of self-transformation is based on the separation of these two senses of who we are, to undermine the latter, which some Tibetan Buddhist thinkers describe as the *innate apprehension of self* (*bdag 'dzin lhan skyes*) (Hopkins 1983: 96–109), about which more will be said below. Hence, from this perspective, if the self exists, it must correspond to this innate sense of self.[30]

This claim raises at least two questions. First, are these Buddhists right to assert that there is an innate sense of self in ordinary beings, and that its content is as they have described it, namely a boss in charge of the mind–body complex? Second, are these Buddhists right to claim that, if the self exists, it must correspond to the sense of self that we ordinarily have? I believe that Albahari's phenomenology of the self goes some way toward answering positively the first question. I also believe that some of the contemporary cognitive science discussions concerning the self (more on this shortly) bring us some degree of confidence that the Buddhist description of the self is not without some basis in reality, though only further research will enable us to reach firmer conclusions. As for the second query,

---

[29] For a thoughtful discussion of this process of self-specification, both at the experiential and the pre-personal levels, see Legrand (2007).

[30] This is obviously ignoring the deeper level at which the subject–object structure disappears.

it raises large metaphysical questions that cannot be addressed here, but I think that Galen Strawson is on the right track when he states:

Here I think there is a fundamental dependence: metaphysical investigation of the nature of the self is subordinate to phenomenological investigation of the sense of self. There is a strong phenomenological constraint on any acceptable answer to the metaphysical question which can be expressed by saying that the factual question 'Is there such a thing as a mental self?' is equivalent to the question 'Is any (genuine) sense of self an accurate representation of anything that exists?'

(Strawson 1997: 409)

For Strawson, the inquiry into the nature of the self needs to relate to the ways in which we actually conceive of ourselves. This requirement that metaphysical considerations be constrained by phenomenology is very germane to the Buddhist approach, for the goal of the no-self doctrine is to support a program of meditative training aimed at freeing us from the negative habits (such as attachment and aversion) created by our sense of self. Hence, to be effective, such a doctrine needs to address the ways in which we actually conceive of ourselves, not just some abstract features considered from a third-person perspective. Obviously such an assumption can be challenged, but it would be hard to deny that it is at the heart of the Buddhist approach. Moreover, like Strawson, I think that it makes a great deal of sense.

This primacy of the first-personal dimension in the inquiry about the self may also help us understand how the Buddhist position articulated here differs from Zahavi's view, according to which the self is based on an invariant structure that provides the condition of the possibility of temporal experience. From the Buddhist perspective articulated here, the putative self is not just the object of an ontological inquiry but has to match, if it exists, the ways in which we ordinarily conceive of ourselves. There are several ways in which we can do this, as shown here. We can conceive of ourselves as a changing subjectivity or as an enduring entity in charge of the body-mind complex, but neither of these ways corresponds to the view of the self as an invariant structure. The idea of such an abstract structure is part of a transcendental analysis, and as such is quite different from the empirical phenomenology pursued here.[31] This transcendental approach may or may

---

[31] It should be clear that I am using here the term 'empirical' rather loosely. In particular, it is not meant to indicate any connection to a scientific approach, but just to signal that the Abhidharma view delineated here differs in important ways from Husserl's transcendental approach.

not be a fruitful way to think about the conditions of the possibility of personhood, but it does not match our ordinary ways of conceiving of ourselves, and hence fails the requirement that metaphysical inquiry into the self be based on an examination of our ordinary sense of self.

4. Various Senses of Self and Cognitive Sciences

This discussion of the nature of the person has intriguing parallels in recent discussions in cognitive science about the self, particularly Damasio's distinction between the proto-self, the core self, and the autobiographical self. The starting point of Damasio's explanation of selfhood is the feeling that whatever action I do, I always have the sense that it is I, rather than somebody else, who is doing the action. Thus, there is a quiet presence of a sense of self in my conscious life, a presence that never falters as long as I am actively engaged.[32] This sense of self corresponds to the core self, which remains stable across the life of the organism. It is not exclusively human, does not depend on conventional memory, language, or reasoning. It is not, however, continuous, but arises transiently, being constantly re-generated anew for every activity in which we are engaged. It is also remarkably stable, being constantly recreated in essentially the same fashion. This core self is based on a proto-self, which is the neural system of coordination of the functions necessary to keeping the organism alive, being in charge of maintaining homeostatic regulation within the organism's physical boundaries. As such, it is not conscious, and becomes so only when it is represented as the core self. Finally, the core self is extended through its being represented by memory and language. This extended self is not punctual but covers the whole of our life. This sense of self is narratively constructed, being born out of our interactions with others. Hence, as Macintyre (1985) puts it, it is not our exclusive creation, for 'we are never more (and sometimes less) than the co-authors of our own narratives'.[33]

This presentation of three levels of selfhood seems to be quite germane to our distinction between self and subjectivity, and our description of the sense of

---

[32] Damasio (1999). This discussion of Damasio also relies on the useful summaries presented by Zahavi (2005: 138–139), and Albahari (2006: 182–188).

[33] A. MacIntyre (1985: 213). Quoted by Zahavi (2005: 109).

self as the boss in charge of leading the mind-body complex, a sense that is to be undermined by Buddhist arguments and practices. The idea of a core self seems to match quite closely the Buddhist description of the (mistaken) sense of self as based on a basic level of agency. In the simple actions in which we engage in daily life (grabbing a chair, holding a pot, going to a place, etc.) we feel that we are in command. We freely decide to act and initiate the action, which we try to bring to a successful conclusion. Obviously the result of our action is not in our control, but the action itself is, or so we think. This basic sense of agency, the sense that I have of being an active entity in charge of directing the mind-body complex, corresponds quite well to Damasio's core self.

But our sense of self is not just a way to create unity and coordinate the mind–body complex. It is also a way to mobilize emotional resources for the actions necessary to maintain the integrity of our organism. We do not just protect ourselves by planning and acting in response to painful or pleasant stimuli, but our actions are guided and enhanced by emotional responses that allow for quick decisions and the mobilization of energy. These emotions do not just push us to act mechanically, like a reflex would, but, rather, influence us cognitively.[34] They inform us of the nature of the situation we are facing, telling us whether we are in danger (fear), in a favorable setting (joy), or about to encounter a rival (jealousy). The effectiveness of emotions is that they provide compelling information leading to immediate appraisals of the situation, and thus prepare us for action. But this effectiveness is greatly enhanced by the fact that they address our core sense of who we are. It is because it is I who is in danger that I feel particularly afraid. Obviously, I can be afraid for others, but we all know the difference between the fear that I have for myself and the fear that I have for utter strangers. It is this overriding and asymmetrical concern that I have for myself that accounts for the strength of emotions. This concern is a result of the bounded nature of the self, which is not just separate from the rest of the world, but also invested of a sense of specialness. This is what accounts for its being, in the words of James, the 'home of interest',[35] and gives particular effectiveness to the emotions.

---

[34] Whether emotions are necessarily cognitive in the full sense of the word is a complex question. Prinz (2004) offers an interesting analysis according to which emotions do not need to be cognitive and can be what he calls embodied appraisals. Even then, however, they do influence us cognitively.

[35] James (1983: 285). For a similar argument about the evolutionary advantages that a sense of self brings about, see Humphrey (2006).

This core sense of self is not a realistic representation of the organism. Rather, it is a kind of phantom that the organism conjures for the sake of acting effectively and thus maintaining its integrity. In this perspective, the self is a construction that the organism creates for the sake of homeostatic boundary preservation, presumably with some evolutionary advantages. In humans, this sense of self emerges gradually and matures through a long process of interaction with caretakers and the world. It starts in the first few weeks of life when, after a first period of innately pre-attuned responses to the solicitations of the environment, newborns start to be able to recognize their caregiver by forming more integrated cognitive models. At this stage, babies have a restricted range of actions within a very limited sense of the world as being formed by small discrete islands of sensory-affective coherence. They also do not have any explicit sense of themselves, but inasmuch as they are able to alter their sensory experiences in limited ways, they do seem to have a nascent sense of self. This core sense of self develops dramatically during the later stages (particularly, but not only, during the sensorimotor stage) when babies become capable of differentiating and coordinating the landscapes that were previously experienced as discrete. This enables them to interact with people through full sequences of actions rather than just rudimentary actions. Babies start to initiate conversations through loud vocalization in the context of visual contact with the caretaker. They also start to play with their caretaker, initiating actions of reaching, grabbing, etc. Those are the early signs of the emergence of a full-blown sense of agency that is experienced in a more continuous fashion, and hence extends beyond the spatial and temporal boundaries of individual situations. It is also the period in which the first seeds of reflective self-representation are planted, when babies start to look at their own bodies and form models of their own capacities. These cognitive and affective capacities concerning the self further develop through various stages that are well outside of the purview of this essay.[36]

The core sense of self that emerges through this developmental process is central to how we act at the most basic level. It starts at a very early age and

[36] My discussion is based on Case (1991). It should be clear that the few points made here have no pretension at discussing adequately the early developmental process (a complex topic well beyond my competence) but are just meant to illustrate the ways in which some of the Buddhist discussions of the self intersect with some of the contemporary concerns. I must thank here R. Roeser for drawing my attention to this interesting article.

gradually matures in ways that allow the person to become autonomous with all the cognitive and affective capacities associated with human agency. This development relies on the symbolic capacities that allow us to conceive of ourselves as extending through long periods of time, rather than being limited to the immediacy of the present. But the existence of this extended sense of self should not obscure the fact that, although our core sense of self is greatly extended by our acquisition of language, it is not created by language, for it exists prior to the development of symbolic capacities. Hence, contrary to the extended self, it exists in any animals that can act in a coordinated fashion, even in the absence of any symbolic capacity.

This core sense of self seems to correspond to the Tibetan Buddhist descriptions introduced earlier, the idea of an *innate apprehension of the self* (*bdag 'dzin lhan skyes*), the sense that we have of being the CEO of the mind–body complex (see above). Tibetan thinkers distinguish this core sense of self from the acquired apprehension of the self (*bdag 'dzin kun gtags*), the extended sense of self that develops on the basis of symbolic capacities, however rudimentary they may be. From a Buddhist perspective, however, the presence of this core sense of self and its extension through symbolic systems do not have only evolutionary or developmental advantages, but also bind us into a condition of suffering (what Buddhists call *duḥkha*, i.e. suffering, dis-ease, dissatisfaction, restless struggle, etc.). It leads to our being bound by afflictive states such as attachment and anger, states that are based on the illusory sense of the self. For without such a sense of self, we would still experience emotions, but they would not be invested with the extremely compelling power they ordinarily have. We would then have a capacity to act more freely, that is, without being compelled by our usual self-centered reactive patterns and negative habits, but would still be able to tap into the source of energy that emotions provide.

The idea that one can be free from the sense of bounded self is quite radical and raises many questions, particularly concerning the nature of action.[37] For if the deconstruction of the self entails the removal, or at least the radical transformation, of our sense of agency, how is such a liberated person (the *Arhat*) to act? This question concerns not only the intention that may push such a person to act but also the kind of unity

---

[37] For a series of extremely interesting discussions about agency and its relation to notions of self, see Roessler and Eilan (2003).

necessary for action. How can a person without a self feel involved and act?
What is the phenomenology of such a sense of agency as distinguished from
our ordinary self-based sense of agency? These are obviously important
questions that cannot be treated in such a short essay.[38] One thing that
should be clear, however, is that from a Buddhist perspective, the deconstruction of the self does not affect the person as subjectively conscious.
This point is not without some importance, for in many contemporary
discussions there is often a tacit identification of consciousness and self.
For example, Damasio often uses the two notions interchangeably, speaking
of *core consciousness* as synonymous with *core self* (Damasio 1999: 7, 10, 27).
This conflation may make some sense, given that for ordinary beings the
two often go together. Nevertheless, from a Buddhist perspective, even in
ordinary beings the two are not identical. Stressing such a difference seems
to be one of the contributions that Buddhist philosophy can make to the
contemporary discussion about the self.

   To clarify this point, we need to go back to our Abhidharmic discussions
and examine the nature of the subject as it is articulated by the Yogācāra
tradition. This will be the occasion to examine further Albahari's contribution to the Buddhist philosophy of the person and argue for an alternative
to her depiction of the subject as a transcendent witnessing consciousness.
This will also allow us to strengthen the case for our distinction between
subjectivity and self, and show its relevance to modern discussions of this
topic within the cognitive sciences.

5. The Nature of Subjectivity

For Albahari, the subject is to be sharply distinguished from the self.
Contrary to the latter, the subject cannot be found as such in our ordinary
states of mind, but only in what she calls 'nibbānic consciousness'. This
consciousness is the state of mind that a fully liberated person, an *Arhat*,
experiences. It is unconditioned, and hence beyond the limitations of time,
space, quality, and relation. It involves immeasurable peace and happiness,
being untainted by any suffering or human limitation. Its mode of operation

---

[38] For some insightful thoughts on this question, see Siderits (2003: ch. 5).

is witnessing and hence it suffuses ordinary states of mind, though it remains unavailable as such to the ordinary beings mired in ignorance (Albahari 2006: 29).

This view of the subject is somewhat surprising, and seems at times to have more in common with Vedānta than with Buddhist sources. This is not to say that there are no Buddhist sources that would support such a position. Albahari provides a number of quotations from the Pali canon that at least partly support her position, but I must confess that I remain unconvinced. For one thing, Albahari presents her view as 'the Buddhist position', a pretension that cannot be sustained in view of the diversity of views within any Buddhist tradition, as argued above. Her view certainly qualifies as a Buddhist view, and would be well supported by some of the views found in the Mahāyāna tradition, where the idea of an enlightened state of mind existing in ordinary sentient beings (the *tathāgatagarbha*) is well known,[39] though far from being universally accepted. But more importantly, I find this description of subjectivity as a transcendent and static presence not terribly helpful, for it seems to fly in the face of the constantly changing nature of subjectivity. For although we have a sense of a constant presence in our psychic life, this constancy seems to be better accounted for as a constantly changing but always renewed background of awareness, rather than an unchanging presence. This does not mean that we should entirely reject Albahari's analysis, but we need to avoid speaking of 'the subject' as some kind of transcendent entity, and instead find more grounded ways to articulate the nature of subjectivity by focusing more particularly on the relation between consciousness and embodiment. To do so, we turn to the Yogācāra sources and their discussion of the eight types of consciousness.

In most Abhidharma systems, there are six types of consciousness: five born from the five physical senses (sight, hearing, smell, taste, and touch) and mental cognition. Each type of sensory cognition is produced in dependence on a sensory basis, one of the five physical senses, and an object. This awareness arises momentarily and ceases immediately, to be replaced by another moment of awareness. The sixth type of consciousness is mental. It is considered by the Abhidharma as a sense-consciousness, like the five types of physical sense-consciousness, though there are disagreements about its basis.[40]

[39] For an explanation of this concept, see Ruegg (1969 and 1989).
[40] For an extended discussion of the nature of this sixth consciousness, see Guenther (1976: 20–30).

Some Abhidharma thinkers, such as Asaṅga, argue that these six types of consciousness do not exhaust all the possible forms of awareness. To this list, they add two types of awareness: the basic consciousness (*ālaya-vijñāna, kun gzhi rnam shes*) and the ego consciousness (*kliśṭa-manas, nyon yid,* lit., afflictive mentation).[41] The idea of a basic consciousness, a constant, neutral, and subliminal baseline consciousness, has evoked various reactions among Buddhist scholars, both traditional and modern. Conze is perhaps the most outspoken critic of this idea, which he described as 'a conceptual monstrosity' (Conze 1973: 133). The reason for his objection is that the idea of a basic consciousness seems to reintroduce the continuity of a self, within a tradition that emphasizes change and discontinuity as being at the core of the person.

Classically, the doctrine of the basic consciousness is meant to answer the objection that if there is no self and the mind is just a succession of mental states, how can there be any continuity in our mental life? How are propensities and habits transmitted if mind merely consists in a succession of fleeting mental states? And more importantly, how can Buddhists explain, within such an unstable configuration, the doctrine of karma, which presupposes continuity over many lifetimes? Asaṅga's answer is that there is a more constant form of neutral consciousness, which is still momentary, but created anew at every moment in a similarly subliminal form. This basic consciousness is to be distinguished from the six types of consciousness mentioned above which are described as manifest consciousness (*pravṛtti-vijñāna, 'jug shes*). Being subliminal (lit., unclear), the basic consciousness usually goes unnoticed. It is only in special circumstances, such as fainting or deep sleep, that its presence can be noticed or at least inferred. Being neutral, this consciousness can serve as the repository of all basic habits, tendencies, propensities, and karmic latencies (the *vāsanā*) accumulated by the individual, thus providing some degree of continuity. Hence, it is called 'basic consciousness'.[42]

---

[41] Rahula (1980: 17). Although the Theravāda Abhidharma does not recognize a distinct basic consciousness, its concept of *bhavanga citta,* the life constituent consciousness, is quite similar. For a view of the complexities of the *bhavanga,* see Waldron (2003: 81–87).

[42] The word *ālaya* is often glossed as home, store, basis, etc., and is often translated as 'store consciousness', but I have preferred the more meaningful 'basic consciousness,' which corresponds to the Tibetan *kun gzhi.*

The assertion that there is such a basic consciousness raises difficult questions, which I wish to examine here briefly to provide a philosophical defense of a doctrine that has often been neglected by those interested in Buddhist philosophy. It should be clear, however, that in doing so I will feel free to provide a philosophical interpretation of this doctrine, rather than a literal rendering of Yogācāra sources. The first question that needs to be confronted is raised by the assertion of the existence of a subliminal form of consciousness. For if it is not manifest, how can it be said to be a form of consciousness? We must remember that, in the perspective articulated here, consciousness is not a substance but continuously changing mental states that are directly or indirectly phenomenologically relevant. There are a number of mental processes that are outside of our field of ordinary awareness. For example, the brain is constantly engaged in regulating the vital functions. It is also constantly monitoring the body, which is bombarded by external stimuli, most of them well below the threshold of awareness. But most of these processes are usually not included within the purview of consciousness since we are not aware of them. Hence, it would then seem that the processes that Yogācārins include within the purview of the basic consciousness are quite real, but lie outside of the field of awareness, and hence do not warrant the use of the term 'consciousness'. In fact, they correspond to Damasio's proto-self, the non-conscious level of the homeostatic control processes through which biological identity is maintained.

The Yogācāra response is that the mental processes included within the scope of the basic consciousness may be outside of ordinary forms of awareness, but are not in principle removed from phenomenological inquiry. Hence, they can be thought of as being forms of awareness, rather than totally unconscious. This view of a 'non-conscious' awareness may seem surprising but has been defended by some contemporary thinkers. Robert Hanna and Michelle Maiese, for example, have argued that the connection between information processing and subjectivity is deep and intrinsic (what they call 'the Deep Consciousness thesis', Hanna and Maiese 2009: 28–57). For them, all the cognitive processes that take place below the threshold of ordinary awareness are nevertheless conscious in some minimal sense. This is so because consciousness and embodiment have an intrinsic and mutual relation that goes, so to speak, all the way down. As long as we are alive, the body itself has a subjective feel to it that is connected to the many cognitive processes that take place below the threshold of ordinary awareness. Hence, these processes are not entirely outside of the purview of phenomenological inquiry. Even deep sleep, often cited as the paradigm of a non-conscious state, has a certain phenomenological feel to it. It is part of the constantly changing flow of experiences that we undergo, and is retained as such. When we wake up from deep sleep, we do not feel that there was nothing before, but, rather, we feel that we are emerging from a particular mode of experience that is different, for example, from a comatose state.[43]

This idea of a basic consciousness functioning at a level deeper than ordinary awareness dovetails with Damasio's idea of a non-conscious proto-self at the same time that it challenges its clear demarcation between the conscious and the non-conscious. In opposition to Damasio's non-conscious proto-self, Yogācāra sources argue that there is a basic level of awareness not usually identified as consciousness but not completely non-conscious either. In this perspective, the separation between the conscious and the non-conscious becomes a matter of degree. The basic consciousness is the baseline of consciousness, the passive level out of which more active and manifest forms of awareness arise in accordance with the implicit preferential patterns that structure emotionally and cognitively this most basic level of awareness. Hence, consciousness is a multi-layered process that ranges from the inchoate level of subliminal awareness to the clearest states of mindfulness in which I seem to be fully present to the present moment. As such, it cannot be captured by a simple either/or distinction.

The basic consciousness is also presented by Yogācāra sources as connected to our sense of embodiment, being described as pervading the body and accounting for the difference between a living body and a corpse (Lamotte 1973: 58). This form of consciousness seems to correspond to the implicit sense of the body and its relation to its surroundings alluded to above. This sense of the body is passive and inchoate, but provides the cognitive background out of which more salient elements make sense. For example, I am walking on a path. Suddenly, the path on which I was walking gives out and I lose my balance. At this point, I am explicitly aware of my body as falling. But it is not the case that before this event I was totally unaware of my body. Rather, I had a subliminal awareness that

---

[43] It should be noted that, for the Yogācārins, consciousness exists in its basic form even in coma, as we will see shortly.

encompassed my whole body, a sense of its aliveness, its occupation of a certain space, its movements, its relation to its immediate environment, etc. It is out of this dim, and yet patterned, space of awareness that my falling is apprehended. I am surprised because I had a sense that my body was on firm ground and yet I am suddenly falling. This is when my sense of the body emerges from a subliminal level of awareness in sharp focus. This background awareness, which is described by some phenomenologists as *operative orientation,* seems to be not unlike the Yogācāra idea of a basic consciousness, a subliminal and yet structured space of awareness that contains all the predispositions, and provides the cognitive backdrop to more manifest forms of awareness.[44]

Basic consciousness also provides an articulation of the person that goes beyond the bundle theory mentioned above. According to the Yogācāra perspective, the basic consciousness is at the core of the idea of the person. It is on its basis that the person understands himself or herself as a person. For whether the person identifies himself or herself with the mind or the body, it is always against the background of the basic consciousness that this identification takes place. This is why several Yogācāra texts describe the basic consciousness as the person. For example, the *Sūtra of the Heavily Adorned* describes the basic consciousness as the 'self of effects, the self of causes, and also the internal self, dependent on the body of the embodied' (Hopkins 2003: 439). I take this rather surprising characterization of the basic consciousness as a self to refer to its being a process of constantly changing moments of self-aware experience on the basis of which the person self-identifies. This is how the Yogācārins understand the basic consciousness, that is, as the basis mistaken by the ego consciousness as being a self. In this way, the core sense of self is constructed out of the misapprehension of the basic consciousness as being an entity that is bounded, in control of our actions, and enduring through time. Hence, it should be clear that although the basic consciousness has a close connection to the notion of the person, it is not a self in the sense delineated here, since it is neither enduring (moment-transcendent), nor is it bounded or endowed with a sense of agency.

---

[44] For an insightful discussion of this notion, see Steinbock (2005). It should be clear that my identification of the basic consciousness with operative orientation is a rather free interpretation of the basic consciousness doctrine.

The close connection between the person and the basic consciousness appears quite clearly in the arguments given by Yogācārins to support their views. The first among eight arguments infers the existence of the basic consciousness from its close link to the person within the context of the process of taking birth. This is the central argument among the eight, for it goes to the heart of the traditional Indian Buddhist conception of the person as being part of a continuity that extends over multiple past and future lifetimes.[45] This continuity, popularly misdescribed as *reincarnation,* is not to be understood as entailing the existence of a continuous entity that undergoes multiple lives but, rather, as being based on a constantly changing and yet always renewed process of awareness, much like consciousness in this lifetime is not an enduring entity but a series of changing and yet connected mental states given in the first-person mode. The doctrine of the basic consciousness is, in large part, an attempt to show how the continuity of multiple lives is possible within an event ontology in which there is no enduring substance.[46]

The Yogācāra argument for the basic consciousness is that, without such a consciousness, the process of dying and taking birth cannot be satisfactorily explained. This is so because the six consciousnesses operate only intermittently, being produced only when suitable objects are encountered.[47] At the times of death and birth, all the coarse states of mind have ceased, and the person is plunged in a comatose subliminal state. In such a state the manifest forms of awareness cannot arise. And yet, from the traditional Buddhist perspective, there is the need for consciousness to be present, otherwise there would be no dying and no birth. For the Yogācāra, the stream of consciousness that undergoes the process of dying and being born is the basic consciousness, which is constantly recreated anew as a subliminal state of mind. As long as we are alive, there is an element of subjectivity that is present, a minimal feel of how it is for the person to undergo this process. For the Yogācārins, being a person entails more than being a mere body

---

[45] My discussion of the arguments for the basic consciousness is based on a work written by Tsongkhapa during his youth. See Sparham (1993: 123–142).

[46] For a detailed study of the tension within the Buddhist view of consciousness between the synchronic analysis of consciousness as a stream of momentary mental states and the diachronic necessity to posit some kind of continuity to explain the multiplicity of lives, see Waldron (2003).

[47] The ego consciousness is also not suitable as a candidate for the consciousness of death and rebirth in the absence of the basic consciousness. This is so because the ego consciousness takes the basic consciousness as its object and hence presupposes this consciousness. Sparham (1993: 126).

where a series of ongoing vegetative processes take place. Rather, it implies being a subject of experience, that is, having a sense of ownership of one's body. I can exist only when I own my body, that is, when I feel my body as undergoing an experience, however inchoate such experience may be. Such sense of ownership implies a phenomenal mineness that comes in degrees. I am not aware of my body in the same way when I am asleep or when I am awake. But for the Yogācārins, as long as the person is alive, there is always an ongoing sense of experiencing one's body from the inside, however minimal it may be.

This sense of experiencing the body from the inside, which Albahari aptly describes as perspectival ownership,[48] is what characterizes subjectivity, and hence also the person. This sense of ownership may be extremely minimal, but for the Yogācāra it is necessary. It is to be distinguished from the sense of agency, the sense that one is the author of one's thoughts and actions. Such sense may dissolve, as in the case of some schizophrenics who feel that they have no control over their thought processes. It seems reasonable to argue that what is impaired in these unfortunate people is not their sense of ownership but their sense of agency. They appear to be still experiencing their thought processes and their body from the inside, but they have lost any sense of control over their subjectivity and are left helplessly exposed to all its phantasmic creations, an experience that must be all the more terrifying in that it is felt to be one's own.[49]

Another important dimension of subjectivity is suggested by the second and fifth arguments for the existence of the basic consciousness. These two arguments deduce the existence of the basic consciousness from the possibility of multi-sensory experience. Suppose that I am marching along a narrow path, watching quite carefully where I am stepping. At the same time, I am also aware of the feeling of my feet touching the ground, as well as of my thinking that I need to be careful. This multi-sensory experience would not be possible, argue the Yogācārins, without the basic consciousness. This conclusion may seem far-fetched but points to an important dimension of subjectivity, namely its synchronic unity. That is, I do not feel that it is several 'I's that look, think, and feel, but, rather, that it is a

---

[48] Albahari (2006: 53) distinguishes perspectival ownership, the impression of inhabiting the body from the inside, from personal ownership, the sense of identifying oneself as the owner of one's body.

[49] For a similar point, see Gallagher (2000: 203–239), quoted in Zahavi (2005: 143–144).

single subject who undergoes these multiple experiences at the same time. This subjective synchronic unity is provided in the Yogācāra system by the basic consciousness, which provides the background for the different sensory modalities. Hence, the person has the sense of being a single subject undergoing different experiences at the same time, and in that she is not wrong, since any cognitive activity takes place against the background of the basic consciousness.[50]

This argument from multisensory experience suggests an account of the cognitive process that somewhat differs from the Theravāda view. Like the Yogācāra, the Theravāda views mental processes as starting from the continuum of a subliminal level of awareness (the *bhavanga citta*; Bodhi 2000: 156–165). This continuum is constantly excited by sensory stimuli and hence buzzing with a subliminal perceptual activity. When the conditions are present, an object becomes prominent enough to draw out the continuum, which emerges from its subliminal state to acquire a clear cognition of this object through one of the six sense doors. In this perspective, consciousness can only consider one object at a time. Hence, for the Theravāda, the subliminal awareness is not constantly present but only when there is no focused cognitive activity, contrary to the Yogācāra idea of the basic consciousness. In this perspective, the impression that we have of experiencing simultaneously various sensory objects is not due to a constant cognitive background, but is an illusion created by the tremendous speed of the mind moving from one sensory modality to another. In both views, however, the requirement that experience be synchronically and subjectively unified is maintained, despite the differences in the phenomenological descriptions and the ways in which this subjective unity is conceptualized.

In a recent contribution to the problem of consciousness, Searle has argued for a view of consciousness that is not unlike the one suggested here. Critiquing the building block theory of consciousness, the dominant paradigm in the cognitive sciences, Searle argues for a unified field theory of consciousness, a holistic and yet naturalistic approach to the hard problem of how consciousness is produced by the brain (Searle 2000). For him, the building-block approach faces a number of problems. Mired in an atomistic

---

[50] Sparham (1993: 127–131). This argument from multisensory experience suggests a view of the mind markedly different from the Theravāda Abhidharma position. In this latter perspective, the impression of multisensory experience, and hence the impression of subjective unity, are illusions created by the tremendous speed of the mind moving from one sensory modality to another.

and mechanistic approach that searches for the neurological correlates of consciousness (NCC), it is unable to provide a solution to the binding problem: the question of how to account for the fact that all the various stimuli are united in a single conscious experience. For Searle, the building-block theory cannot solve this problem because its search for the NCC of particular mental states ignores the necessary conscious background that existed before these mental states. Hence, the search for the NCC can never get to consciousness itself. To do so, we need to conceive of consciousness as a unified field, a kind of basal background awareness that goes on as long as we are awake. If I understand Searle correctly, his view is not unlike the Yogācāra doctrine of the basic consciousness, which is also a kind of basal background consciousness. Differing from Searle, however, this consciousness extends beyond the state of wakefulness to include dream and even deep sleep states. But both views strongly emphasize the fact that the synchronic unity of consciousness is an essential feature of subjectivity that must be sharply distinguished from diachronic unity, which is a construction based on memory, and hence to a certain extent illusory.

It is this basic consciousness that provides the subliminal passive backdrop of self-awareness out of which more active and focused mental processes arise. One of these mental processes almost continually present, according to the Yogācāra, is the misconception of subjectivity as being an enduring self. This is what is described as the ego consciousness, which creates the self-phantom, the sense we have of being a bounded and enduring entity in charge of the mind–body complex. One of the peculiarities of the Yogācāra is the description of this sense of the self as a separate type of consciousness. Whereas other Ābhidharmikas consider this sense of self part of the sixth mental consciousness, the Yogācāra tradition insists on its being a distinct seventh type of consciousness, to emphasize the fact that it is constantly regenerated anew in our mental continuum for every activity in which we are engaged, much like Damasio's core sense of self. We may not be directly aware of it, but insofar as we engage in an activity, we are informed by this sense of self that supports our action as well as binds us into our self-centered perspective.

This shows the degree to which consciousness is not a simple phenomenon but has a multiplicity of layers that are revealed only through careful investigation, an analysis that is quite different from the view of consciousness as being 'gappy' presented by Dennett and others (Dennett, 1991).

There may be gaps in the more manifest and superficial forms of consciousness but at a deeper level there is an ever-renewed background of mental presence. This background may be discontinuous in that it is always changing but it is always renewed and hence always there to provide the background of awareness out of which more focused cognitive processes emerge.

I started my analysis of consciousness by stressing the importance of the idea of the non-dual nature of awareness, and arguing that our ordinary sense of a clear separation of the subjective and objective realms is delusive. I also suggested that the non-dual nature of consciousness might be revealed in certain deep meditative states, but that these experiences cannot provide a sufficient articulation of what we ordinarily mean by 'subjectivity'. To do so, we need to analyze the structures of ordinary experience, particularly in its reflexive aspects, as they emerge from the non-dual nature of consciousness. This analysis has brought us to understand how ordinary subjectivity rests on the existence of an ever-renewed background of mental presence which provides a basis for the emergence of more focused forms of cognitive activities. It should be clear, however, that for the Yogācāra this basic consciousness is not the most fundamental level of consciousness. The basic consciousness is part of the dualistic distortion of awareness that I mentioned at the start of my analysis. There is a (phenomenologically speaking) deeper level at which consciousness is aware of itself in a non-dual way. The Yogācāra and other related traditions hold that this form of non-dual awareness can be experienced and actualized through extended meditative practices. In this way, the basic consciousness, which is mere aware clarity unconfined by any cognitive form,[51] is transmuted into a wisdom that is able to undo the cognitive, conative, and affective knots created by duality. How this is done and what this entails are difficult topics that cannot be discussed here, but we need to keep in mind this soteriological dimension if we want to do justice to the depth of the Yogācāra tradition.

---

[51] This is the description given by Ju Mipham, trans. Doctor (2004: 355). Readers who know this author may notice that my approach to the Yogācāra views of the mind bears a certain similarity to those of Śāntarakṣita's views as interpreted by Mipham. It should also be clear, however, that my discussion here is simplified to the point of caricature. In particular I am glossing over a number of extremely complex issues concerning the relation between ordinary and enlightened states of mind. For Mipham's views on this topic, see Hopkins (2006).

6. Conclusion: Are We Still Allowed to Talk About Experience?

Throughout this essay, I have used quite liberally the concept of experience to discuss the topic of consciousness, in defiance of the suspicion that has surrounded this concept within the humanities. This rejection of the notion of experience is all the more unfortunate in that it comes at a time when there is a willingness in some quarters to include the subjective aspects of mental processes within the purview of the mind sciences. Within Buddhist studies, the foremost proponent of this critique of experience has been Robert Sharf, who has brilliantly and provocatively argued against the use of this notion. Reacting to the previous exaggerated emphasis on experience as providing a metaphysical basis for the justification and explanation of Buddhism, Sharf has taken to task those who use the notion of experience as part of a crypto-theological project to create a realm of privacy in which religion can escape the suspicion that has undermined its credibility within the more educated public. As Sharf rightly argues, it is simply not credible to claim that the meaning of texts, rituals, and institutions is to elicit in the mind of the practitioners some inner experience, for this ignores most of what is going on in a religious tradition in order to focus on and distort a few rarefied expressions.

But his provocative and welcome critique of experience goes much further and impugns the very use of this notion, which for Sharf is hope-lessly mired in Cartesian metaphysics. Quoting Dennett with approval, Sharf states his case in this way:

[T]here is a certain tendency to think of experience as a subjective 'mental event' or 'inner process' that eludes public scrutiny. In thinking about experience along these lines, it is difficult to avoid the image of mind as an immaterial substrate or psychic field, a sort of inner space in which the outer material world is reflected or re-presented. Scholars leave the category of experience unexamined precisely because the meaning of experience, like the stuff of experience, would seem to be utterly transparent. Experience is simply given to us in the immediacy of each moment of perception. This picture of the mind has its roots in Descartes and his notion of mind as an 'immaterial substance' (although few would subscribe to Descartes' substance ontology). And following the Cartesian perspective, we assume that insofar as experience is immediately present, experience per se is indubitable and irrefutable.

(Sharf 1998: 94–116)

I cannot address here all the points made by Sharf, but it should be clear that there is a fundamental difference between the target of his Dennettian critique and the phenomenological views that have informed this essay. Sharf assumes in his critique of experience that its use necessarily implies a view of consciousness as being private, transparent, and immune to mistake. I believe that this essay shows that this is simply not the case. It is true that the notion of experience entails a view of the mind as having a subjective side, a side that is often difficult to pin down, but this hardly entails that the mind is enclosed in a private realm, immune to external scrutiny. In fact, phenomenologists such as Husserl, Heidegger, Scheler, and Merleau-Ponty have taken great pains to show that the concern with human experience in no way implies the sealing off of the mind in a realm of transparent absolute privacy. On the contrary, these thinkers have emphasized the opacity of subjectivity and its limitations, and argued that a convincing account of experience cannot isolate what is going on in one's mind, but must consider its inter-subjective dimensions. These dimensions are multiple and complex, ranging from the ways in which bodies interact to the role of empathy and the place of symbolically mediated social interactions.[52] But all these thinkers concur in the same conclusion, that it is only by taking into considerations these dimensions that we can hope to have an adequate sense of what is entailed by the concept of experience.

Hence, it should be clear that although the use of the term 'experience' does signal the importance of subjectivity for a Buddhist account of the person, it does not entail the kind of Cartesian position caricatured by Sharf. I believe that it is time to rehabilitate the notion of experience, and to avoid assuming that its use necessarily leads to a crypto-theological project mired in hopeless metaphysics.[53] I also believe that this rehabilitation is of some importance for the study of Buddhism and its philosophy, importance that goes well beyond the present essay. It will allow the inclusion of the traditions whose views rely more specifically on notions derived from meditative experiences within the purview of Buddhist philosophy. This is perhaps the case of the Yogācāra tradition, whose views are often derived

---

[52] For a brief summary of various views on intersubjectivity, see Zahavi (2005), 147–177. For a thoughtful discussion of the role of empathy, see Thompson (2007), 382–411.

[53] For a response to Sharf and a defense of the place of experience within Tibetan Buddhism, see Gyatso (1999).

from meditative experiences (hence its name), but remain surrounded by some suspicion within Buddhist studies, despite the considerable resources that they offer for the elaboration of Buddhist views of the mind as shown here. This is also true of the tantric tradition, which is often considered as merely practical without much philosophical importance. The neglect of its philosophical content is due to a number of factors that cannot be analyzed here but has had the unfortunate result of removing tantric material from the purview of those who are interested in understanding Buddhist views of consciousness and its relation to the person. Considerable attention has been devoted to the textual material of the tantric tradition, its historical evolution, and its relation to vernacular cultures. Those are all important topics worthy of consideration, but they leave out important areas of inquiry such as the bearing of tantric ideas on our understanding of the person, consciousness, embodiment, etc. To include these views within the purview of Buddhist philosophy, we will need to accept notions that make sense within the context of yogic practices, and hence be open to include within the purview of our conversations the experiential aspects of the tradition. Only then can scholars of Buddhist studies hope to do justice to the full range of Buddhist views of consciousness and the person and, perhaps, be in a position to make significant contributions to our understanding of consciousness.

Bibliography

Albahari, M. (2006), *Analytical Buddhism* (New York: Macmillan).

Bodhi, Bikkhu, ed. (2000), *A Comprehensive Manual of Abhidhamma* (Seattle, WA: BPS Pariyatti Editions).

Cabezon, J. (1990), 'The Canonization of Philosophy and the Rhetoric of *Siddhānta* in Indo-Tibetan Buddhism', in P. Griffiths and J. Keenan (eds.), *Buddha Nature: A Festschrift in Honor of Minoru Kiyota* (San Francisco: Buddhist Books International).

Case, R. (1991), 'Stages of Development of the Young Child's First Sense of Self', *Developmental Review* 11: 210–230.

Chalmers, D. (2002), *Philosophy of Mind* (Oxford: Oxford University Press).

Chim Jampeyang (*mchims 'jam pa'i dbyangs*) (1989), *mDzod 'grel mngon pa'i rgyan* (Xining: China's Tibetan Cultural Press).

Collins, S. (1982), *Selfless Persons* (Cambridge: Cambridge University Press).

Conze, E. (1973), *Buddhist Thought in India* (Ann Arbor, MI: University of Michigan Press).

Damasio, A. (1999), *The Feeling of What Happens* (San Diego: Harcourt).

Dennett, D. (1991), *Consciousness Explained* (Boston: Backbay).

Doctor, T. trans. (2004), *Speech of Delight: Mipham's Commentary on Śāntarakṣita's Middle Way* (Ithaca, NY: Snow Lion).

Dreyfus, G. (1997), *Recognizing Reality: Dharmakīrti's Philosophy and its Tibetan Interpretations* (Albany, NY: SUNY).

Dreyfus, G. and Thompson, E. (2007), 'Indian Theories of Mind', in P. Zelazo, M. Moscovitc, and E. Thompson (eds.), *The Cambridge Handbook of Consciousness* (Cambridge: Cambridge University Press).

Flanagan, O. (1995), *Consciousness Reconsidered* (Cambridge, MA: MIT Press).

——(1999), *The Science of the Mind* (Cambridge, MA: MIT Press).

Gallagher, S. (2000), 'Self-Reference and Schizophrenia', in D. Zahavi (ed.), *Exploring the Self* (Amsterdam: Benjamin).

Gethin, R. (1998), *The Foundations of Buddhism* (Oxford: Oxford University Press).

Guenther, H. (1976), *Philosophy and Psychology in the Abhidharma* (Berkeley, CA: Shambala).

Gyatso, J. (1999), 'Healing Burns with Fire: The Facilitations of Experience in Tibetan Buddhism', *Journal of the American Academy of Religion* 67: 113–147.

Hanna, R. and Maiese, M. (2009), *Embodied Minds in Action* (Oxford: Oxford University Press).

Hopkins, J. (1983), *Meditation on Emptiness* (London: Wisdom).

——(2002), *Reflections on Reality: The Three Natures and Non-Natures in the Mind-Only School* (Berkeley, CA: University of California Press).

——(2003), *Maps of the Profound: Jam-yang-shay-ba's Great Exposition of Buddhist and Non-Buddhist Views on the Nature of Reality* (Ithaca, NY: Snow Lion).

——trans. (2006), *Fundamental Mind: The Nyingma View of the Great Completeness* (Ithaca, NY: Snow Lion).

Humphrey, N. (2006), *Seeing Red: A Study in Consciousness* (Cambridge, MA: Harvard University Press).

Huntington, C. (1989), *The Emptiness of Emptiness* (Honolulu: University of Hawaii Press).

Jackson, R. (1993), *Is Enlightenment Possible?* (Ithaca, NY: Snow Lion).

James, W. (1983), *Principles of Psychology* (Cambridge, MA: Harvard University Press).

Karma Chagme (1998), *A Spacious Path to Freedom*, translated by A. Wallace (Ithaca, NY: Snow Lion).

Kim, J. (1998), *Mind in a Physical World* (Cambridge, MA: MIT Press).

Lamotte, E. (1973), *La Somme du Grand Véhicule d'Asanga* (Louvain: Université de Louvain, Institut orientalist).

Legrand, D. (2007), 'Pre-reflective self-as-subject from experiential and empirical perspectives', *Consciousness and Cognition* 16: 583–599.

Lopez, D. (2006), *The Madman's Middle Way* (Chicago: University of Chicago Press).

Lusthaus, D. (2002), *Buddhist Phenomenology* (New York: Curzon).

Lutz, A., Dunne, J., and Davidson, R. (2007), 'Meditation and the Neuroscience of Consciousness: An Introduction', in P. Zelazo, M. Moscovitc, and E. Thompson (eds.), *The Cambridge Handbook of Consciousness* (Cambridge: Cambridge University Press).

MacIntyre, A. (1985), *After Virtue: A Study in Moral Theory* (London: Duckworth).

Mensch, R. (2001), *Postfoundational Phenomenology* (University Park, PA: University of Pennsylvania Press).

Mimaki, K. (1979), *Le Chapitre du Blo gsal grub mtha' sur les Sautrāntika (Présentation et edition)* (Kyoto: Zinbun Kagaku Kenkyusyo).

Nagel, T. (1974), 'What it is like to be a bat', *Philosophical Review* 83: 435–450.

Palmer, S. (1999), *Vision Science* (Cambridge, MA: MIT Press).

Petitot, J., Varela, F., Pachoud, B., and Roy, J. M. (1999), 'Beyond the Gap: Introduction to *Naturalizing Phenomenology*', in Jean Petitot, Francisco J. Varela, Bernard Pachoud, Jean-Michel Roy (eds.), *Naturalizing Phenomenology* (Palo Alto, CA: Stanford University Press).

Poussin, L de la Vallée (1971), *L'Abhidharmakosha* (Bruxelles: Institut Belge des Hautes Etudes Chinoises).

Priestley, L. (nd.), 'Pudgalavada Buddhist Philosophy', in the Internet Encyclopedia of Philosophy: http://www.iep.utm.edu/p/pudgalav.htm.

Prinz, J. (2004), *Gut Reactions: A Perceptual Theory of Emotions* (Oxford: Oxford University Press).

Rahula, W. (1980), *Le Compendium de la Super-doctrine d'Asanga* (Paris: Ecole Francaise d'Extreme Orient).

Ram-Prasad, C. (2007), *Indian Philosoophy and the Consequences of Knowledge* (Burlington, VT: Ashgate).

Roessler, J. & Eilan, N. (2003), *Agency and Self-Awareness* (Oxford: Oxford University Press).

Ruegg, D.S. (1969), *La Théorie du Tathâgathagarbha et du Gotra* (Paris: Ecole Francaise d'Extreme-Orient).

Ruegg, D.S. (1989), *Buddha-nature, Mind and the Problem of Gradualism in a Comparative Perspective* (London: School of Oriental and African Studies).

Sazang Mati Penchen (*sa bzang ma ti pa chen*) (nd.), *Dam pa'i chos mngon pa kun las btus pa'I 'grel ba shes bya rab rab gsal snang ba* (Beijing: People's Publishing House).

Searle, J. (2000), 'Consciousness', *Annual Review of Neuroscience* 23: 557–578.

Sharf, R. (1998), 'Experience' in M. Taylor, ed., *Critical Terms for Religious Studies* (Chicago: University of Chicago Press).

Siderits, M. (2003), *Personal Identity and Buddhist Philosophy* (Burlington, VT: Ashgate).

Sparham, G. (trans.) (1993), *Ocean of Eloquence: Tsongkhapa's Commentary on the Yogācāra Doctrine of Mind* (Albany, NY: SUNY Press).

Steinbock, A. (2005), 'Affection and Attention', *Continental Philosophy Review* 37 (1): 21–43.

Strawson, G. (1997), 'The Self', *Journal of Consciousness Studies* 4.5–6: 405–428.

Thompson, E. (2007), *Mind in Life* (Cambridge, MA: Harvard University Press).

Tsongkhapa, (2002), *Great Treatise on the Stages of the Path to Enlightenment* (Ithaca: Snow Lion).

Waldron, W. (2002), 'Buddhist Steps to an Ecology of the Mind: Thinking about "Thoughts Without a Thinker"', *Eastern Buddhist* xxxiv 1: 1–51.

——(2003), *The Buddhist Unconscious* (London: Routledge Curzon).

Welton, D. (1999), *The Essential Husserl* (Bloomington: University of Indiana Press).

Yao, Z. (2005), *The Buddhist Theory of Self-Cognition* (London: Routledge).

Zahavi, D. (2005), *Subjectivity and Selfhood* (Cambridge MA: MIT Press).

5

Self-No-Self? Memory and Reflexive Awareness

EVAN THOMPSON

1. Introduction

This paper focuses on two interrelated problems: Does consciousness essentially involve self-awareness? Does self-awareness imply the existence of a self? I will answer yes to both questions, but my yes for the second question will be a qualified one.

I plan to address these two problems by counterpoising two distinct philosophical traditions and debates. The first is the debate over reflexive awareness (*svasaṃvedana*) in Indo-Tibetan Buddhist philosophy. The second is the debate between egological versus nonegological conceptions of consciousness in Western phenomenology.[1]

2. Does Consciousness Essentially Involve Self-Awareness?

2.a The Self-Awareness Thesis

One of the central theses found in the phenomenological tradition is that intentionality (the object-directedness of consciousness) essentially involves

---

[1] A full treatment would require situating these two debates in relation to at least two other broad debates in Western and Indian philosophy—higher-order theories of consciousness versus same-order theories (see the papers collected in Genarro 2004, and Kriegel and Winniford 2006), and reflectionist/other-illumination (*paraprakāśa*) theories of self-awareness (e.g. Nyāya) versus reflexivist/self-illumination (*svaprakāśa*) theories (e.g. Yogācāra). But space demands that I set aside these debates here. See Mackenzie (2007) and Ram-Prasad (2007: 51–99) for further discussion.

self-awareness. Put another way, intentional experience is also necessarily self-experience. The following quotations all express this thesis:

Every experience is 'consciousness', and consciousness is 'consciousness *of*' ... But every experience is *itself experienced* [*erlebt*], and *to that extent* also 'conscious' [*bewußt*].

(Husserl 1991: 291)

[C]onsciousness is consciousness of itself. This is to say that the type of existence of consciousness is to be consciousness of itself. And consciousness is aware of itself *in so far as it is consciousness of a transcendent object.*

(Sartre 1991: 40)

[T]he necessary and sufficient condition for a knowing consciousness to be knowledge of its object, is that it be consciousness of itself as being that knowledge.

(Sartre 1956: liii)

Every consciousness exists as consciousness of existing.

(Sartre 1956: liv)

All thought of something is at the same time self-consciousness, failing which it could have no object.

(Merleau-Ponty 1962: 371)

Exactly what kind of self-consciousness is at issue here? If intentional experience is also necessarily self-experience, what sort of self-experience are we talking about?

2.b Pre-Reflective Self-Awareness

Phenomenologists stand united in rejecting higher-order theories of consciousness (e.g. Rosenthal 2005) and reflectionist/other-illumination (*paraprakāśa*) theories of self-awareness (see MacKenzie 2007; Ram-Prasad 2007: 51–99). According to these theories, self-awareness is the product of a second-order cognitive state taking a distinct, first-order mental state as its intentional object. Phenomenologists from Husserl onwards have, instead, maintained both that intentional experience is pre-reflectively self-aware and that pre-reflective self-awareness is not a kind of transitive (object-directed) consciousness (see Zahavi 2005). In other words, every intentional experience both presents (or re-presents) its intentional object and discloses itself, but this self-disclosure is intransitive. The kind of intransitivity of concern here is not a hidden or suppressed transitivity, in the way 'I sing' is intransitive (where it still makes sense to ask, 'What are you singing'?), but rather an absolute intransitivity, in the way 'I jump' is intransitive (where it makes no sense to ask, 'What are you jumping?') (Legrand 2009). Although the 'what question' can arise for the transitive component of an intentional experience, it cannot arise for the intransitive component of pre-reflective self-awareness. In sum, according to this view, every transitive consciousness of an object is pre-reflectively and intransitively self-conscious. Or as Sartre would say, 'all positional consciousness of an object is necessarily a nonpositional consciousness of itself' (Sartre 1967: 114).[2]

2.c The Argument from Time-Consciousness

In the phenomenological tradition, this conception of intransitive and pre-reflective self-consciousness is closely connected to considerations about time-consciousness and temporality. According to Husserl (1991), the phenomenological structure of time-consciousness entails pre-reflective self-awareness. In our consciousness of temporal phenomena (duration, change, sequence, etc.), three intentional processes work together and cannot operate on their own apart from one another—primal impression, retention, and protention. For example, for each now-phase of a melody, each currently sounding note, there is (i) a corresponding primal impression directed exclusively toward that now-phase, (ii) a retention directed toward the just-elapsed phase of the melody, the just-heard notes, and (iii) a protention of the immediate future phase, the notes of the melody intended as just-about-to-occur. For simplicity, take retention. Any given now-phase of consciousness retains the just-past phases of its intentional object only by retaining the just-past phases of its consciousness of the object: I am aware of the notes of the melody as slipping into the past only through my awareness of the notes as having just been heard by me. Thus, not only is consciousness aware of itself in retention, but it must be retentionally self-aware in order

---

[2] Cf. also these passages: '[T]he object with its characteristic opacity is before consciousness, but consciousness is purely and simply consciousness of being consciousness of that object. This is the law of its existence. We should add that this consciousness of consciousness—except in the case of reflective consciousness . . . is not positional, which is to say that consciousness is not for itself its own object' (Sartre 1991: 40–41). 'We understand now why the first consciousness of consciousness is not positional; it is because it is one with the consciousness of which it is consciousness. At one stroke it determines itself as consciousness of perception and as perception . . . This self-consciousness we ought to consider not as a new consciousness, but as *the only mode of existence which is possible for a consciousness of something*' (Sartre 1956: liv).

to be aware of objects across time. This retentional self-awareness is not a form of transitive consciousness (object-directed intentionality): it is rather an intransitive reflexivity, a passive self-relatedness. In this way, time-consciousness entails pre-reflective self-awareness. More precisely, internal time-consciousness—our implicit awareness of our experiences as flowing in time—is most fundamentally the pre-reflective self-awareness of the stream of consciousness (see Zahavi 2005: ch. 3).

2.d The Reflexive Awareness Thesis

I turn now to Buddhist philosophy. In certain schools of Indian, Chinese, and Tibetan Buddhist philosophy, we also find the view that consciousness or awareness is reflexive (Williams 1998; Yao 2005). The Sanskrit term is *svasaṃvedana*, which has been variously translated as reflexive awareness, self-awareness, and self-cognition. Buddhist philosophical systems that accept this notion explain that it means a cognition's being aware of itself simultaneously with its awareness of an object, and that this kind of self-awareness or reflexive awareness is nondual, that is, it does not involve any subject/object structure (see Sopa and Hopkins 1976: 78). The analogy or simile often used is that of a light, which in its illumination of objects also illuminates itself (see Williams 1998; Yao 2005).

2.e Setting Aside Representationalism

In Buddhist philosophy, the reflexive awareness thesis is associated with what Western philosophers would call representationalism in the theory of perception. According to Dignāga (*c*.480–540 CE) and Dharmakīrti (*c*.600–660 CE), cognition does not apprehend its object nakedly, but rather through an aspect (*ākāra*), which is the phenomenal form of the object left imprinted on cognition. Because the immediate object of cognition is the phenomenal aspect, and the phenomenal aspect is internal to the cognition, every cognition is directed toward a feature of itself, simply in virtue of being directed toward its immediate object. Thus cognition is reflexive, because in the process of revealing external things (by way of the aspect), cognition also reveals itself (see Dreyfus 1997; Dunne 2004).

I mention this traditional connection to representationalism in order to set it aside. From the standpoint of my concerns about self-consciousness in this paper, we can separate the reflexive awareness thesis from representationalism.

It is the reflexive awareness thesis as a phenomenological thesis that is my concern here.[3]

2.f Śāntarakṣita On Reflexive Awareness

I will focus on reflexive awareness as Śāntarakṣita (725–788 CE) understands it (Blumenthal 2004). My reason for choosing Śāntarakṣita is that he maintains that the nature of consciousness is reflexive awareness.[4] Śāntarakṣita states that reflexive awareness is what distinguishes sentience from insentience: The nature of consciousness is reflexive awareness and that which is not reflexively aware is insentient (*The Ornament of the Middle Way* 16, translated by Blumenthal 2004: 237). To the objection that an act cannot be directed toward itself but must be directed toward an object, he replies that reflexive awareness does not have an agent-action-object structure. In other words, the reflexive (self-related) aspect of awareness is intransitive.

2.g The Memory Argument

One of the main arguments for the reflexive awareness thesis is the so-called memory argument, which seems to have originated with Dignāga but is widely discussed by those who advocate the reflexive awareness thesis as well as those who deny it (Williams 1998: 9–10; Yao 2005: 115–117). According to this argument, memory requires previous experience: when one recollects one recalls both the *object* perceived and that *I* have perceived this object, thus no additional higher-order or reflective cognition is required in order to recall the subjective side of the experience (my perceiving), hence reflexive self-awareness or self-cognition belonged to the original experience (i.e. the original experience was not simply one of *perceiving the object*, but also one of *experiencing oneself perceiving the object*).

This classical formulation of the argument is egological because it involves the explicit I-cognition, 'I have perceived this object.' It is also possible, however, to reformulate the argument nonegologically without any explicit I-cognition: Memory requires previous experience: when one

---

[3] The reflexive awareness thesis in Buddhist philosophy is also associated with what Western philosophers would call idealism in metaphysics (the view that there are no extra-mental objects). For further discussion of idealism in Buddhism, see Siderits (2007: 146–179).

[4] By 'nature' Śāntarakṣita means conventional distinguishing characteristic of consciousness, not ultimate intrinsic nature, because as a Mādhyamika philosopher he rejects the view that phenomena, including mental phenomena, have ultimate intrinsic natures.

recollects one recalls both the *object* perceived and the past *seeing* of this object, thus no additional higher-order or reflective cognition is required in order to recall the subjective side of the experience (the seeing), hence reflexive self-awareness or self-cognition belonged to the original experience (i.e. the original experience was not simply one of *perceiving the object* but also one of *experiencing the seeing of the object*).

The nonegological conception is preferable at this stage of our discussion, for we do not wish to prejudge the issue of whether reflexive experience is egological. This issue—egological versus nonegological conceptions of consciousness—will be taken up later in this paper.

It will be useful to have a more formal presentation of the memory argument. Here is my reconstruction of the argument as it is presented by Śāntarakṣita and understood by his Prāsaṅgika Mādhyamika critics (whose criticisms we will shortly examine):[5]

1. When one remembers (say) yesterday's vivid blue sky, one remembers not simply the blue sky, but also seeing the blue sky. In other words, one remembers not just the object seen, but also the visual experience of seeing. Thus the memory comprises both the objective side of the perception (the object seen) and the subjective side of the perception (the seeing). (Phenomenological claim)

2. Thus no additional cognition is necessary in order to recall the subjective side of the original experience. (Phenomenological claim)

3. To remember something one must have experienced it. (Conceptual claim)

4. The causal basis for features of the present memory is corresponding features of the past experience. (Causal claim)

5. So the past visual perception must have included an experience of the seeing, along with the object seen. In other words, the perception must have included an awareness of itself as a visual perception, which is to say that it must have been reflexively self-aware. (Conclusion)

Whether this argument is deductively valid or sound is debatable. I propose, however, to view the argument as an inference to the best explanation.

---

[5] Note that I say 'reconstruction' because I make no claim that my presentation coincides with traditional presentations of the argument by either its advocates or its critics. I do claim, however, that my reconstruction captures the philosophical premises and reasoning that constitute the heart of the argument.

Given the first and second premises as phenomenological evidence, the best explanation for this evidence (so the argument claims) is the hypothesis of reflexive awareness. Understood this way, I find the argument persuasive. To explain why, I turn now to consider criticisms of the memory argument, which I will argue are unsuccessful.

2.h Objections to the Memory Argument

In a recent article, Jay Garfield (2006) presents and endorses two objections to the memory argument made by the Prāsaṅgika Mādhyamika philosophers Candrakīrti (c.600–650 CE), Śāntideva (c.650–750 CE), and Tsong Khapa (1357–1419) (who, as Prāsaṅgika Mādhyamikas, reject reflexive awareness).

First objection: Premise 1 is not proven. The premise assumes that the current memory must be the memory of one's being conscious (being visually aware), rather than simply the memory of that of which one was conscious (the object). But this claim about memory needs to be established.

Second objection: Premise 4 is not proven. It has not been shown that reflexive awareness is ever a cause of memory, or that the only plausible cause of memory is reflexive awareness. Furthermore, an alternative and simpler explanation is available: One sees the blue sky without being reflexively aware of one's seeing; this perception causes a subsequent memory of the blue sky, and on this basis one infers that one was visually aware of the sky. On this view, one infers the subjective side of the original perception; it is not given directly to memory, and hence it was not present reflexively in the original perceptual experience.

Here is Śāntideva's analogy as presented by Garfield: 'A bear is hibernating and is bitten by a rat. He develops an infection at the site of the wound. When he awakes in the spring he experiences the pain of the infected wound and knows on that basis that he experienced a rat bite, even though at the time he was *not aware* that he was experiencing the bite' (Garfield 2006: 210).

To reply to these objections I will draw from Husserl's analyses of memory. Although Williams (1998: 237) states that he is not familiar with the Buddhist memory argument from any Western context, Husserl (1991, 2005) advances similar considerations in his writings on memory and time-consciousness.

2.1 *Reply to the First Objection*

The first premise of the memory argument makes a phenomenological claim about memory: When I remember yesterday's blue sky there is a memory of blue and a memory of seeing blue. The objection is that this claim about memory needs to be established. One way to establish, or at least support, this claim is to ground it on a phenomenological account of memory. Husserl provides what we need in the form of a phenomenological analysis of the intentional structure of episodic memory.

Let me begin with Husserl's distinction between intentional acts of presentation and re-presentation (Marbach 1993: chs. 2 and 3). Perception is presentational; imagination and memory are re-presentational. We can approach this distinction from two sides, the side of the intentional object and the side of the intentional act. In a perceptual experience, such as the perception of a blue pot on the table, the object is experienced as present in its 'bodily being' and thus as directly accessible—one can view it from different vantage points, pick it up and examine it more closely, and so on. In a re-presentational experience, such as the visual memory of the blue pot, the object is not experienced as present and accessible in this way, but as absent. Yet this absence is precisely a *phenomenal absence*, for the experience is of the object *precisely as absent*. This difference on the side of the intentional object between bodily presence and absence corresponds to the difference on the side of the intentional act between presentation and re-presentation. A re-presentational experience intends its object precisely as both phenomenally absent in its bodily being, and as mentally evoked or brought forth. In this way, the object is said to be mentally re-presented, rather than perceptually presented. It is important to note that what makes the experience re-presentational is precisely that its object is mentally evoked or brought forth, while also being phenomenally absent; it is not that the object is mentally evoked or brought forth again. The latter characteristic belongs to memory, but not to creative imagination or free fantasy.

In episodic memory, a situation or event is experienced not as present but as past, and thus absent. Therefore, the past situation or event is necessarily re-presented by the intentional cognition that takes it as its object. The phenomenological question is how this re-presentation subjectively works. According to image theories of memory, in remembering, one apprehends a mental image of something experienced in the past. One problem with these theories is that in memory one does not take oneself to be imagining something that seems like what one remembers (an image or picture of what one remembers): one takes oneself to be remembering the object itself that was once present or the event itself that once occurred. The standard way to deal with this problem is to insist that what one remembers is the past occurrence, not the mental image, but that one remembers the past by way of the mental image. But this move highlights a deeper problem, which is that image theories fail to account for how an image had in the present can yield a memory experience as of something past. Husserl's account of memory as the re-presentation of a past experience aims to overcome this difficulty (Bernet 2002; Marbach 1993: 78–83).

Husserl submits that when one remembers a past occurrence, situation, or event, one also implicitly remembers one's earlier experience of that occurrence, situation, or event. Thus, in memory, one apprehends something (the absent past), not by means of an image—in the sense of a mental picture that exists in the present—but through the mental activity of re-presenting an experience believed to have occurred in the past. Of course, one does not have to entertain this belief explicitly in the episodic memory experience. Rather, in remembering, the re-presented experience is simply subjectively given as having occurred in the past. In memory, one reproduces and relives, as it were, this past experience, but in a modified way, namely, precisely as re-presented, and thus as not occurring now but posited as past. In other words, the past experience is not literally or really reproduced in the present, but is rather reproduced as part of the intentional content of the memory (Marbach 1993: 61). In Husserl's formulation, the present memory does not 'really' contain the past experience, but instead contains it only intentionally and in this way 'intentionally implicates' it (Husserl 1983: 294; Marbach 1993: 34–36, 69–70).[6]

On this view, to remember X is to intend or refer or mentally direct oneself to X by re-presenting an experience of X that is subjectively given as having occurred in the past (or, in a more cognitivist vein, that is believed to

---

[6] It is important to note that such intentional implication is not thought to involve inference. The idea is rather that, in remembering, one relives, as it were, the past experience, which comprises both its intentional object and its pre-reflective and intransitive self-awareness.

have occurred in the past). Notice that the intentional object of the memory is usually the past occurrence (X), not the past experience of it. In other words, it is usually the objective side of the experience (the noema in phenomenological parlance), not the subjective side (the noesis). If the intentional object of the memory is the past experience as such, that is, the subjective side of the experience, then the memory is a reflective memory. Usually, however, the re-presenting of the past experience figures only implicitly and pre-reflectively in one's memory of the past event or situation. In this way, the memory is unreflective.

Husserl maintains that the phenomenal temporal distance between the present and the past is possible only insofar as the present act of remembering evokes both the object and the elapsed consciousness of it. If we suppose that the act of remembering reproduces only the past object, then we cannot explain how this object retains its character of being past or belonging to the past. Yesterday's blue sky is gone, so the only way to reproduce it is in the form of an image. But if yesterday's blue sky appeared only as a mental image apprehended in the present, then how could this image retain the character of pastness? The reason the object recollected in the present retains its character of pastness is that the remembering consciousness comprises two distinct intentional acts—the present act of bringing back the past object, and the past perception of that object. Once again, the present remembering does not really contain the past perception: it contains it only intentionally. The experience of remembering thus involves a kind of doubling of consciousness, for in being the conscious re-presentation of a past object, remembering is also the conscious re-presentation of a previous consciousness. It is precisely this doubling that accounts for the past remaining separated from the present, even though it is remembered in the present (Bernet 2002; Stawarska 2002).

This account of memory clearly grounds the phenomenological claim made in Premise 1 of the memory argument: The memory of yesterday's blue sky intentionally implicates yesterday's experience of seeing the blue sky. Therefore, unless the opponent of the memory argument can provide a superior, or at least equally satisfactory, alternative analysis of the phenomenology of memory, Premise 1 can be taken as an established phenomenological datum about memory in need of explanation. The reflexive awareness thesis—the conclusion of the memory argument—purports to provide that explanation.[7]

2.j Reply to the Second Objection

This objection claims to offer an alternative and better explanation of memory than does the reflexive awareness thesis. On the basis of one's present memory of the past object one knows by inference that one was aware of the object, without that awareness needing to have been self-aware at the time of its occurrence.

The groundwork for replying to this objection has already been laid in the reply to the first objection. The alternative proposal does not account for the phenomenological structure of episodic memory.

According to the proposal, (i) one is subject to an occurrence (a rat bite, a visual cognition of blue); (ii) one lacks any awareness of the occurrence when it happens; (iii) the occurrence causes one later to be aware of some of its effects (pain from the bite, a memory image of blue); and (iv) those effects (as well as others) induce in one a cognitive state directed at the earlier occurrence.

These conditions, however, are not sufficient to account for the experience of memory, specifically for how past experience appears from the first-person perspective in the experience of remembering. To refer mentally to the past (iv) on the basis of the awareness of a mental image in the present (iii) is like reading the date-stamp on a letter and on that basis thinking about the date on which the letter was sent. What is missing here is precisely an experience of the past in the sense of an experience with the phenomenal (intuitional) content of pastness.

According to Husserl, as we have seen, this phenomenal content comes from the past experience being part of the intentional structure of the memory of the object. Memory is not thinking about the past on the basis of present marks (like tree rings or time stamps), it is re-presenting the past by, or through, re-presenting past experience. Thus the reflexive awareness

---

[7] Of course, here I go well beyond anything that Śāntarakṣita explicitly endorses. Indeed, he might not accept the kind of phenomenological reasoning I employ here. My aim, however, is not to offer an account of how Śāntarakṣita might reply to Garfield's objections to the memory argument, but rather to show that Husserlian phenomenology can provide an effective reply to these objections.

thesis (underwritten by Husserl's phenomenology) provides a better account of memory than the alternative.

In the first part of this paper I have defended the memory argument for reflexive awareness against Garfield's (2006) criticisms. The question that now arises—especially given the enlistment of Husserlian phenomenology in support of the memory argument—is whether reflexive awareness implies a self. Or to put the question another way, is reflexive awareness compatible with the doctrinal Buddhist insistence on no-self?

3. Does Self-Awareness Imply the Existence of a Self?

The Buddhist answer to the question of whether self-awareness entails a self is clearly No when 'self' means an enduring entity (one that is wholly present from moment to moment) with an existence separate or somehow distinct from the series of psychophysical events (Dreyfus this volume; MacKenzie 2008). Consciousness alone is the subject of experience. Moreover, according to some views, every conscious experience is momentary and discrete, so strictly speaking there is no persisting subject (no subject that exists for more than one discrete moment). Other views, however, identify the subject with the continuum as a whole, rather than any particular stage of the continuum. In either case, the subject of experience is not equivalent to a self because 'self' is understood to mean a type of subject—one that endures with separate existence. Of course, according to the Buddhist view, it is precisely this type of subject that we mistakenly take ourselves to be as a result of deep-seated cognitive and emotional processes of identification with the psychophysical complex as a self (Albahari 2006).

Certainly, if we subscribe to this distinction between self and subject, then the reflexive awareness thesis and its supporting memory argument do not imply the existence of a self. But is this sharp distinction between self and subject philosophically sustainable? Given that some concept of no-self (*anatta/anātman*) seems to be non-negotiable for the Buddhist, any philosopher who wishes to self-identify (as it were) as a Buddhist would seem to have no option but to account for subjectivity within one or another no-self paradigm (see Albahari 2006; Dreyfus this volume), or perhaps to deny subjectivity as understood here (Siderits this volume). The second option is not one I can consider here. The first one, however, gives rise to a serious tension: The more we enrich the concept of the subject—for example, through considerations about memory and time-consciousness—the more we reduce the conceptual distance between the self and the subject (or subjectivity) of experience.[8]

Let me be more specific. The price to pay for the Husserlian shoring up of the memory argument for reflexive awareness is a robust notion of subjectivity, one that considerably lessens the distance between the notion of a mere subject of experience and a self. In this phenomenological account of memory, the subject (or subjectivity) of experience is precisely the selfhood (*ipseity*) of time-consciousness—the pre-reflective self-awareness of the stream of consciousness as a stream, including the automatic givenness of past experience from within as one's own past experience in retention (primary memory) and remembering (secondary or reproductive memory).

Of course, this phenomenological notion of selfhood is far from the notion of the self as an enduring entity distinct from the flow of mental and physical events. But no phenomenologist would allow that this highly restricted notion of the self should be our touchstone for assessing the phenomenological and metaphysical status of the self (see Zahavi 2005; this volume).[9]

3.a A Nonegological Conception of Consciousness

A challenge now presents itself from within phenomenology in the form of the so-called nonegological conception of consciousness (Gurwitsch 1966). Whereas Husserl thought that phenomenological analysis revealed a transcendental ego abiding through the intentional activities of consciousness, Sartre denied that the stream of consciousness has an ego at its source. Much of the egological versus nonegological debate turns on how to understand the phenomenology of memory, so examining this debate will help to connect the self-no-self issue to our earlier considerations about memory and reflexive awareness.

---

[8] MacKenzie (this volume) provides another option: The self is dependently originated but nonetheless real. I am greatly sympathetic to this approach.

[9] For further criticism of the attempt to distinguish subject and self—criticism that appeals to the importance of the body and embodiment—see Henry and Thompson (in press).

Sartre held that the ego or 'I' is absent from unreflective consciousness. To quote one of his famous examples: 'When I run after a streetcar, when I look at the time, when I am absorbed in contemplating a portrait, there is no I. There is consciousness-of-the-streetcar-having-to-be-overtaken, etc., and non-positional consciousness of consciousness' (Sartre 1991: 48–49). Only when we reflect on such experiences does the ego appear—but always as an object of the reflective act. The ego or 'I' is always an intentional object (hence transcendent) and never a (transcendental) subject: The ego belongs to the content of the reflected experience, whereas both the original unreflected experience and the act of reflection (itself an unreflected experience) lack an ego.

Sartre supports his nonegological position with considerations about memory (Sartre 1991: 43–48). He states that one can recall a past event in two ways: (i) one can focus on the object of the past experience (yesterday's blue sky), or (ii) one can focus on the past experience itself (yesterday's perception of the blue sky). The first kind of recollection, Sartre maintains, is impersonal or nonegological—it does not include an experience of the ego as the subject who perceived the object in the past. The second sort of recollection is reflective and egological—it takes the past act of consciousness as its object and gives rise to the illusion that this act was accompanied by an experience of the 'I' or ego.

How do we know that the past experience was not accompanied by an experience of the ego? Sartre thinks we can revive the past experience in memory, direct our attention to the revived past object without losing sight of the past unreflected experience, yet all the while not turn the memory into a reflective one, and thereby not objectify the past experience. When we, as it were, relive the past experience in this way we see clearly that no experience of the ego figured in its content.

Sartre's conclusion is that the ego does not pre-exist recollection but is a product of recollection. The ego is a kind of retrospective objectification. Objectifying recollection makes it seem as if the ego were there all along, but this appearance is illusory, for the ego is not present in consciousness at the moment when the perception takes place. Consciousness, therefore, at its basic unreflective level, is nonegological.

3.b The Memory Argument Revisited

We can now see why it was important in our earlier discussion of the memory argument not to work with the argument in its classical egological formulation. This formulation invokes reflective memory, that is, memory with an explicit I-cognition and first-person self-reference. Working with this formulation invites confusion because the memory argument at its strongest depends not on an appeal to reflective memory, but rather on an appeal to non-reflective memory—specifically, to the presence of the subjective side of the original experience in the non-reflective memory as showing that there must have been a non-reflective reflexive awareness present in the original experience.

To appreciate this point we can consider three statements of the traditional memory argument. The first comes from Candrakīrti (who then goes on to criticize and reject the argument):

Suppose one argued as follows: One has to maintain that there is reflexive awareness because otherwise, when at a later time, I say, 'I saw . . .' and remember the remembered object, and when I think, 'I saw', there could not be a memory of the awareness of the object of that thought.

(as quoted by Garfield 2006: 203).

The second and third come from Paul Williams, explaining Tsong Khapa's understanding of the argument (Tsong Khapa follows Candrakīrti in rejecting the argument):

Tsong Khapa explains, when we remember, the memory image is seen to be composed of 'formerly this was seen' and 'it was seen *by me*'. Or, as Tsong Khapa expressed it elsewhere, when I remember that I truly saw blue there is a memory of blue and a memory of seeing blue. Thus in the original act there must have been a sensation of blue and also the sensation of seeing blue.

(Williams 1998: 238).

Notice that Candrakīrti's formulation and the first of Williams' glosses of Tsong Khapa's formulation are egological in form. As Williams (1998: 237) observes, the type of memory of concern here is reflective memory. The second gloss of Tsong Khapa's formulation is nonegological.

Here is my reason for belaboring this distinction. If we use the traditional egological formulation, then we run the risk of thinking mistakenly that the memory argument depends specifically on an appeal to reflective memory.

This mistake could lead to the further mistakes of thinking that the memory argument could be countered with Sartre's argument that an ego-experience was not present in the original experience, but rather only retrospectively seems to have been present to the reflective memory, and hence that the original experience was not self-aware. But, of course, this line of thought would miss the whole point of the memory argument. The aim of the argument is not to establish that an ego-experience in Sartre's sense was present in the original experience: on the contrary, it is to establish that the original experience was self-aware—where self-awareness is understood as an intransitive reflexivity. (Of course, this kind of reflexive self-awareness Sartre accepts in the form of his notion of non-positional self-consciousness.) The argument does not depend on any appeal to reflective memory: on the contrary, the argument depends fundamentally on considerations about non-reflective memory: In a non-reflective memory of yesterday's blue sky there is also a non-reflective memory from within of yesterday's seeing of the blue sky. Thus the reason to appeal to non-reflective memory in support of reflexive awareness is that non-reflective memory already automatically recalls the subjective side of the original experience, without needing any additional higher-order cognition or reflective memory.

3.c Memory, Ego, Self

If we use the term 'ego' in Sartrean fashion to refer to the self as an object for reflection, then unreflective experience is egoless. For Sartre, however, this kind of egolessness does not imply that unreflective consciousness lacks selfhood in any sense. On the contrary, as Sartre states: 'it is consciousness in its fundamental *ipseity* which, under certain conditions, allows the appearance of the ego as the transcendent phenomenon of that *ipseity*' (Sartre 1956: 103). As Dan Zahavi (2005: 115) notes, Sartre's fundamental move here is to distinguish between ego-as-object and self-as-subject. Thus, although unreflective consciousness is egoless, it is not selfless.

In certain respects, however, Sartre's treatment of memory and his understanding of selfhood are simplistic compared with Husserl's (see Stawarska 2004). These differences are relevant to the memory argument and the relation between subjectivity and the self.

On the one hand, Sartre emphasizes fresh memory over distant memory in his argument for the nonegological conception of consciousness. He relies on the kind of reproductive remembering that rides on the retention of recent experience, as when you call back a just-elapsed experience and try to relive it.[10] What this emphasis leaves out are the many other kinds of episodic memories from the more remote and distant past.

On the other hand, Sartre juxtaposes remembering an object to reflective memory of an experience. Only the latter, he suggests, presents past experience as my experience. What this juxtaposition leaves out is precisely the Husserlian point that remembering an object already intentionally implicates the past experience of that object. Indeed, the Husserlian insight is that the past experience must be intentionally implicated in the recollection of the object if the object is to retain the phenomenal character of pastness. Although the intentionally implicated past experience need not be given as mine in an objectified egological sense (as the experience of my ego), it is given from within as an experience formerly lived through first-personally, that is, by me.

For Zahavi, this kind of 'first-personal givenness' of consciousness suffices to make consciousness fundamentally egological rather than nonegological (see Zahavi 2005: 99–146). To some extent, however, the issue seems terminological. If 'ego' means self-as-object, as it does for Sartre, then Sartre's nonegological conception seems compatible with Zahavi's insistence that pre-reflective experience is not lived through anonymously, but rather first-personally. After all, to maintain, as Sartre does, that *ipseity* or non-positional self-awareness defines the very being of consciousness would seem to imply that consciousness cannot be fundamentally anonymous, but must be constitutively first-personal.

Of course, we can still ask, what exactly is the status of this 'I' or 'me'? Here it may be possible to reconcile phenomenology and the Buddhist no-self paradigm. From a phenomenological perspective, there is no need to suppose that 'I' or 'me' corresponds to an enduring entity with an existence separate or somehow distinct from the stream of mind–body events. Rather, the 'I' picks out the stream from its own self-individuating phenomenal perspective. To use an Indian turn of phrase, we could say that the stream is fundamentally I-making (*ahaṃkāra*).

---

[10] See Sartre (1991: 46): 'For example, I was absorbed just now in my reading. I am going to try to reconstitute the circumstances of my reading, my attitude, the lines that I was reading. I am thus going to revive not only these external details but a certain depth of unreflected consciousness, since the objects could only have been perceived *by* that consciousness and since they remain relative to it'.

4. Conclusion

In this paper I have defended the memory argument for reflexive awareness, and the reflexive awareness thesis as a phenomenological thesis about the nature of consciousness. At the same time, I have suggested that mounting a proper defence of the memory argument requires a robust account of memory and subjectivity that puts pressure on certain versions of the Buddhist no-self (*anatta/anātman*) doctrine by lessening the distance between the subject and self.

References

Albahari, M. (2006), *Analytical Buddhism: The Two-Tiered Illusion of Self* (Hampshire: Palgrave Macmillan).

Bernet, R. (2002), 'Unconscious Consciousness in Husserl and Freud', *Phenomenology and the Cognitive Sciences* 1: 327–351.

Blumenthal, J. (2004), *The Ornament of the Middle Way: A Study of the Madhyamaka Thought of Śāntarakṣita* (Ithaca, NY: Snow Lion Publications).

Dreyfus, G. (1997), *Recognizing Reality: Dharmakīrti's Philosophy and its Tibetan Interpreters* (Albany, NY: State University of New York Press).

Dunne, J. (2004), *Foundations of Dharmakīrti's Philosophy* (Boston: Wisdom Publications).

Garfield, J. L. (2006), 'The Conventional Status of Reflexive Awareness: What's at Stake in a Tibetan Debate', *Philosophy East and West* 56: 201–228.

Gennaro, R., ed. (2004), *Higher-Order Theories of Consciousness* (Amsterdam: John Benjamins Publishers).

Gurwitsch, A. (1966), 'A Nonegological Conception of Consciousness', in A. Gurwitsch, *Studies in Phenomenology and Psychology* (Evanston, IL: Northwestern University Press).

Henry, A. and Thompson, E. (in press), 'Witnessing from Here: Self-Awareness from a Bodily Versus Embodied Perspective', in S. Gallagher, ed., *The Oxford Handbook of the Self* (Oxford: Oxford University Press).

Husserl, E. (1983), *Ideas Pertaining to a Pure Phenomenology and to a Phenomenological Philosophy, First Book*, trans. F. Kersten (The Hague: Martinus Nijhoff).

——(1991), *On the Phenomenology of the Consciousness of Internal Time (1893–1917)*, trans. J. B. Brough (Dordrecht: Kluwer Academic Publishers).

——(2005), *Phantasy, Image Consciousness, and Memory (1898–1925)*, trans. J. B. Brough (Berlin: Springer).

Kriegel, U. and Williford, K., eds. (2006), *Self-Representational Approaches to Consciousness* (Cambridge, MA: The MIT Press/A Bradford Book).

Legrand, D. (2009), 'Two Senses for "Givenness of Consciousness"', *Phenomenology and the Cognitive Sciences* 8: 89–94.

MacKenzie, M. D. (2007) 'The Illumination of Consciousness: Approaches to Self-Awareness in the Indian and Western Traditions', *Philosophy East and West* 57: 40–62.

——(2008), 'Self-Awareness without a Self: Buddhism and the Reflexivity of Awareness', *Asian Philosophy* 18: 245–266.

Marbach, E. (1993), *Mental Representation and Consciousness: Towards a Phenomenological Theory of Representation and Reference* (Dordrecht: Kluwer Academic Publishers).

Merleau-Ponty, M. (1962), *Phenomenology of Perception*, trans. Colin Smith (London: Routledge Press).

Ram-Prasad, C. (2007), *Indian Philosophy and the Consequences of Knowledge: Themes in Ethics, Metaphysics, and Soteriology* (Aldershot, Hampshire: Ashgate Publishing Limited).

Rosenthal, D. (2005), *Consciousness and Mind* (Oxford: Oxford University Press).

Sartre, J.-P. (1956), *Being and Nothingness*, trans. Hazel Barnes (New York: Philosophical Library).

——(1967), 'Consciousness of Self and Knowledge of Self', in N. Lawrence and D. O'Connor, eds., *Readings in Existential Phenomenology* (Englewood Cliffs, NJ: Prentice Hall).

——(1991), *The Transcendence of the Ego: An Existentialist Theory of Consciousness*, trans. F. Williams and R. Kirkpatrick (New York: Hill and Wang).

Siderits, M. (2007), *Buddhism as Philosophy: An Introduction* (Aldershot: Ashgate Publishing Limited).

Sopa, L. and Hopkins, J. (1976), *Practice and Theory of Tibetan Buddhism* (New York: Grove Press).

Stawarska, B. (2002), 'Memory and Subjectivity: Sartre in Dialogue with Husserl', *Sartre Studies International* 8: 94–111.

Williams, P. (1998), *The Reflexive Nature of Awareness: A Tibetan Madhyamaka Defence* (Delhi: Motitlal Banarsidass).

Yao, Z. (2005), *The Buddhist Theory of Self-Cognition* (London: Routledge Press).

Zahavi, D. (2005), *Subjectivity and Selfhood: Investigating the First-Person Perspective.* (Cambridge, MA: The MIT Press/A Bradford Book).

6

Subjectivity, Selfhood and the Use of the Word 'I'

JONARDON GANERI

I. Asaṅga and Vasubandhu on Self-Consciousness and Conscious Attention to Oneself

A well-known Buddhist philosophy of mind has it that conscious experience is a synthesis of five forms of activity: the processes of registering, appraising, stereotyping, readying, and consciously attending.[1] These philosophers say that the last of these, conscious attention, is relative to a perceptual modality, so that, for example, consciously attending to what is being visually registered is different in kind from consciously attending to what is being registered in touch.[2] They say as well that one can also consciously attend to what is going on in one's mind. This is a mode of conscious reflecting (mano-vijñāna); it is a way of being self-aware, of consciously attending to one's own psychological state.

To these six varieties of conscious attention Asaṅga adds a seventh, which he calls simply manas 'mind'/'consciousness', or else 'defiled mind' (kliṣṭa-manas).[3] It is, he seems to think, a distinct and more basic mode of being

---

[1] The five so-called skandhas or 'ingredients' that combine into individual thoughts or experiences: rūpa, vedanā, samjñā, samskāra, and vijñāna. For details, see Ganeri (forthcoming). This flexible doctrine is transformed in various ways by later Buddhist thinkers, beginning with Asaṅga and Vasubandhu in the c. 4th CE.

[2] Ṣaḍvijñānadhātavaś cakṣurādyāśrayā rūpādyālambanāvijñāptayaḥ (Vasubandhu, Pañcaskandhaka 135).

[3] Thereby adding a new sense for this term, which in its everyday use in Abhidharma is simply synonymous with conscious attention (citta, vijñāna). Kramer (2008) translates kliṣṭa-manas as 'notion of I', and observes that the incorporation of this new concept represents a modification in the traditional system of the five skandhas, a modification that is evident in Sthiramati's commentary on Vasubandhu's Pañcaskandhaka. She says: 'In particular the function of vijñāna-skandha—the original role of which was

self-aware.[4] Asaṅga argues that there must exist a non-perceptual modality of self-consciousness, which is distinctively associated with what is 'mine', as well as being the support of conscious reflection, and something that contributes to the persistence of one's sense of self. Itself ethically neutral, it is nevertheless responsible for the four vices to do with the self:

[Question:] How does one know that *manas* in the sense of 'defiled mind' (*kliṣṭamanas*) exists?

[Answer:] Without it, there could be no uncompounded ignorance, i.e. a basic ignorance not yet associated with all the diverse defilements but standing as their base. Besides, conscious reflecting (*manovijñāna*) must also have a simultaneous support, as do the sensory consciousnesses which have such supports in their material organs. Such a simultaneous support can only be the 'defiled mind'. Also, the very etymology of *manas* has to do with 'mine', which can be explained only by the 'defiled mind'. Also, without it there would be no difference between the non-identifying trance and the cessation trance, for only the latter is free of defiled mind. Also, the sense of an existence of self is always existent in nonsaintly states: there must be some special consciousness to account for the persistence of this sense. The defiled mind is always defiled by the false view of self, pride of self, love of self, and ignorance (about self); but is itself ethically neutral.[5]

Asaṅga's brother Vasubandhu claims that this mode of being self-aware undergoes a 'transformation' into what gets described as a self.[6] He says

---

actual perception—was widened through the inclusion of subliminal forms of mind, like the 'store mind' (*ālaya-vijñāna*) and the "notion of I" (*kliṣṭa-manas*). The strong emphasis placed by Sthiramati on *vijñāna* is evident, for instance, when he states that ordinary people—those who have not perceived reality—regard the *vijñāna* as the self (*ātman*), whereas they view the other four *skandhas* as "mine" (*ātmīya*)' (2008: 155). She adds that '[i]nterestingly, Sthiramati also mentions alternative concepts of the self, for example that of the Sāṃkhya tradition. According to his understanding, the Sāṃkhyas only regard *rūpa-skandha* [matter] as *ātmīya*, and all the other four *skandhas* as *ātman*. He thus claims that for the Sāṃkhyas the self is not only identical to *vijñāna* but also consists of the other factors accompanying the mind (*caitasika*)' (2008: 155). Galloway (1980) translates *kliṣṭa-manas* as 'passional consciousness', and derives interesting information about the notion from Guṇaprabhā's commentary on the *Pañcaskandhaka*. See below. Dreyfus and Thomson (2007: 112) translate *kliṣṭa-manas* as 'afflictive mentation', and comment that '[t]his is the inborn sense of self that arises from the apprehension of the store-consciousness as being a self. From a Buddhist point of view, however, this sense of self is fundamentally mistaken. It is a mental imposition of unity where there is in fact only the arising of a multiplicity of interrelated physical and mental events'.

⁴ See Galloway (1978) for a detailed argument that as a Yogācāra technical term, *manas* should be translated as 'consciousness' rather than neutrally through its cognate in English, 'mind'.

⁵ *Mahāyānasaṃgraha* 1.7; trans. Anacker in Potter (2003) from the extant Chinese and Tibetan translations.

⁶ Galloway (1980: 18) reports from Guṇaprabhā's commentary on Vasubandhu's *Pañcaskandhaka*: [Vasubandhu:] 'In reality, the consciousness (*manas*) has the storehouse perception for its phenomenon.'

that *manas*—'consciousness'—is a way of being aware, associating it with the activity of 'thinking' (*manana*). It takes the store-consciousness (*ālaya-vijñāna*) as its foundation. It undergoes a transformation into something that we metaphorically call a self, but this transformation is the work of cognitive fabrication, and there is in fact no such thing:

The metaphors of 'self' and 'items' which develop in so many ways take place in the transformation of consciousness.

Dependent on [the store-consciousness] there develops a consciousness called *manas*, having that as its basis, and having the nature of 'thinking'.

This transformation of consciousness is a cognitive fabrication, and as it is cognitively fabricated it does not exist.[7]

How are we to make sense of what is going on here? The import of the use of the terms 'conceptual fabrication' (*vikalpa*) and 'metaphorical designation' (*upacāra*), in connection with the self, is that the end-result of the transformation of pre-attentive self-consciousness is the sort of first-person psychological judgment one would express in the words 'I am F'. The transformation has made the self into a conceptual thought-content (*vikalpa*), but the expression of that thought-content uses a word, 'I' for example, in at most a 'metaphorical' sense, or at any rate some usage that is not one of genuine literal reference. (As I will point out below, *upacāra* is not quite metaphor, but nearer to metonymy.)

Let me represent the picture schematically. The claim is that three distinct phenomena are involved in self-consciousness:

1. Conscious attention to one's own states of mind (*manovijñāna*).

This must have a 'support' (*āśraya*). The support is:

2. 'Self-consciousness' (*manas*)—a pre-attentive mode of being self-aware.

[Guṇaprabhā:] This means that it phenomenalizes [sees] the storehouse perception as a self. [Vasubandhu:] 'It is that which is associated with the constant delusion of self (*ātmamoha*), view of self (*ātmadṛṣṭi*), egoism of self (*ātmamāna*), and lust for self (*ātmarāga*), and so on.' [Guṇaprabhā:] It is explained as operating always, and arises as good (*kuśala*), bad (*akuśala*), and indifferent. His saying 'It is of one class' means that it has a passionate (*kliṣṭa*) nature. 'It is continually produced' means that it is momentary.

[7] *Trimśikākārikā*: *ātmadharmopacāro hi vividho ya pravartate | vijñānapariṇāme 'sau ||* Tvk 1a–c *|| tasya vyāvṛtirahatve tadāśritya pravartate | tadālambam manonāma vijñānam mananātmakam ||* Tvk 5 *|| vijñāna-pariṇāmo 'yam vikalpo yadvikalpyate | tena tannāsti ||* Tvk 17a–c *| |*. The translation is from Anacker (1984), slightly modified.

This is subject to 'transformation' (*pariṇāma*). What it is transformed into is:

3. First-person psychological judgment—thinking 'I am F', for some psychological predicate F. The use of the word 'I' here, though, is in some sense not a genuine referring use.

It will help if I begin by stating the conclusions for which I want to argue. I will argue that these claims should be understood as follows. My possession of a first-person perspective, a perspective on my own mental life, has to be underwritten. What underwrites it is the fact that my mental life presents itself to me, in a primitive and pre-attentive way, as being mine. This same primitive mode of being self-aware is rendered in such a way that it seems to justify me in making assertions of the form 'I am F'. In fact, it is never the case that assertions of such a form are true of a self. Uses of 'I' never literally refer to a self. I will argue that this final claim is ambiguous, and distinguish the reading Vasubandhu wishes to give it from another, in my view more promising, idea.

2. Pre-Attentive Consciousness: *manas* and Mineness

The proposal we are examining might be expressed as the conjunction of three propositions:

[1] There is a pre-attentive mode of self-awareness through which my experiences present themselves to me as mine.
[2] First person psychological judgment draws upon additional conceptual resources, ones not available on the basis of [1] alone.
[3] First person psychological judgments do not actually involve genuine reference to a self.

Let me examine these propositions in turn.

The ability, not just to have a world in view, but also to reflect upon the fact that one does, seems to be an essential part of what it means to be conscious. Sidney Shoemaker says that

It is essential for a philosophical understanding of the mental that we appreciate that there is a first person perspective on it, a distinctive way mental states present themselves to the subjects whose states they are, and that an essential part of the philosophical task is to give an account of mind which makes intelligible the perspective mental subjects have on their own mental lives

(Shoemaker 1996: 157).

It is to this task that our Buddhists address themselves when they say that conscious attention to one's own mental life (*mano-vijñāna*) must have a support, which they claim is a pre-attentive mode of being self-aware (*manas*). I think that the point of this argument is easy enough to understand as long as we remember that it is impossible to think about one of one's own mental states, a particular feeling of hope for example, and yet not be sure whose mental state it is. There is no question of having a first person perspective on one's mental life, without that mental life presenting itself to one as one's own. In a much-quoted passage, Peter Strawson says:

It would make no sense to think or say: This inner experience is occurring, but is it occurring to me? (This feeling is anger; but is it I who am feeling it?) Again, it would make no sense to think or say: I distinctively remember that inner experi- ence occurring, but did it occur to me? (I remember that terrible feeling of loss; but was it I who felt it?) There is nothing that one can thus encounter or recall in the field of inner experience such that there can be any question of one's applying criteria of subject-identity to determine whether the encountered or recalled experience belongs to oneself—or to someone else.

(P. F. Strawson 1966: 165)

If I cannot be mistaken about whose inner experience it is that I am experiencing, this is because no identification of a subject, and so no possibility of mis-identification, is involved at all. What I am suggesting, then, is that our Buddhist philosophers explain the 'immunity to error through misidentification' (Shoemaker 1984) of self-ascriptions, by ac- knowledging that when my experience presents itself to me as my own, no representation of myself as a subject takes place. Asaṅga and Vasubandhu postulate, instead, the existence of a primitive mode of self-awareness, a basic awareness of the contents of my inner life (my 'store-consciousness') as mine. And this, in turn, is what makes it possible for me to have a first- person, rather than merely a third-person, perspective on my mental life.

In Sartre's theory of consciousness, I might note in passing, there is a proposal that is in some respects comparable. Sartre speaks of a pre-reflective self-awareness, which 'has no need at all of a reflecting consciousness in order to be conscious of itself. It simply does not posit itself as an object'

(Sartre 1957: 45). Dan Zahavi has redescribed it as 'an immersed non-objectifying self-acquaintance' (Zahavi 2005: 21). Sartre argues that an infinite regress will ensue if such a mode of self-acquaintance is not acknowledged, and it is interesting to observe that we find the infinite regress argument used too by one of Vasubandhu's immediate followers, Diṅnāga, in a defense of reflexivism (Ganeri 1999; see also the contributions by Evan Thompson and Mark Siderits to this volume).

3. First Person Psychological Judgment

Vasubandhu speaks of a 'transformation' of basic self-awareness into explicit self-ascription, a transformation based on conceptual fabrication (*vikalpa*) and justifying only a 'metaphorical' use (*upacāra*) of the language of self. What is difficult is to understand how it can be thought wrong to make the transition from being aware of oneself as being in a certain mental state to explicitly asserting that one is. Vasubandhu's thesis is that this transition demands a new conceptual resource (one which is not in fact available). Is that thesis true?

Zahavi, for one, does not see any difficulty with this transition. He says:

Contrary to what some of the self-sceptics are claiming, one does not need to conceive of the self as something standing apart from or above experiences, nor does one need to conceive of the relation between the self and experience as an external relation of ownership. It is also possible to identify this pre-reflective sense of mineness with a minimal, core, sense of self. . . . In other words, the idea is to link an experiential sense of self to the particular first-personal givenness that characterizes our experiential life; it is this first-personal givenness that constitutes the *mineness* or *ipseity* of experience. Thus, the self is not something that stands opposed to the stream of consciousness, but is, rather, immersed in conscious life.

(Zahavi 2005: 125)

Zahavi's 'minimal self' precisely consists in a 'pre-reflective sense of mineness', and it appears to follow that, to refer to oneself in the first person, nothing more is required than that one's experience be given 'immediately, noninferentially and noncriterially' (2005: 124) as mine. He also says, however, that 'this form of egocentricity must be distinguished from any explicit

I-consciousness. I am not (yet) confronted with a thematic or explicit awareness of the experience as being owned by or belonging to myself. The mineness is not something attended to; it simply figures as a subtle background presence' (2005: 124). So there is, after all, a transition, but it is a transition which involves only *paying attention* to the mineness inherent in my experience, not in the exercise of any new conceptual resource.[8]

I think that Vasubandhu's response would simply be that if someone wants to use the words 'minimal self' as a synonym for the *manas*, then nobody will object to him doing so. On the other hand, if the implication is that the 'minimal self' does what a self is meant to do, then it is too minimal to count. It seems to me that the minimal self does not do one of the things that a respectable concept of self must, and that is to individuate thinkers. It is true of you and me alike that our experience is given to us with an immersed mineness. The property 'being a thought of one's own' is a property like 'being a divisor of itself', which is equally true of every number; the reflexive pronoun is just a place-holder. Zahavi says that 'the particular first-person givenness of the experience makes it mine and distinguishes it for me from whatever experiences others might have' (2005: 124). That choice of words suggests that he thinks that first-person givenness is individuative of individual selves.[9]

François Recanati (Recanati 2007) has an interesting account of the transition we are interested in. He draws a distinction between implicit and explicit *de se* thoughts, a *de se* thought being 'a *de re* thought about oneself, that involves a particular mode of presentation, namely a first person mode of presentation' (2007: 169). He continues:

As Frege wrote in 'The Thought', 'everyone is presented to himself in a particular and primitive way, in which he is presented to no one else'. I call the 'special and

---

[8] Indeed, in Zahavi (1999), Zahavi makes it a 'minimal demand to any proper theory of self-awareness' that it 'be able to explain the peculiar features characterising the subject-use of "I"; that is, no matter how complex or differentiated the structure of self-awareness is ultimately shown to be, if the account given is unable to preserve the difference between the first-person and third-person perspectives, unable to capture its referential uniqueness, it has failed as an explanation of self-awareness' (1999: 13).

[9] Joel Krueger (this volume) seems to share my reservation about the selfhood of the 'minimal self'. To put the point in an Indian vocabulary, the 'minimal self' is somewhat akin to the impersonal Advaitic *ātman*, present equally in all. Zahavi sometimes, however, appeals to an embodiment criterion, rather than to first-person givenness per se, as what individuates distinct minimal selves, and that would certainly adequately distinguish the notion from the Advaita conception.

primitive' mode of presentation which occurs in first person thoughts 'EGO' or rather 'EGO$_x$' where 'x' stands for the name of the person thinking the thought.

(2007: 170).

Explicit *de se* thoughts are *de se* thoughts 'the content of which involves an "identification component" through which the object thought about is identified as oneself'. When a subject looks at themselves in a mirror and thinks 'My legs are crossed', they identify themselves under the concept EGO, and ascribe to themselves a property: I am that person whose legs are crossed. An implicit *de se* thought involves no such identification. Recanati says that 'implicit *de se* thoughts are identification-free, and they are *de se* only externally: no concept EGO occurs as part of the lekton [roughly, the content]. The lekton is a personal proposition, without any constituent corresponding to the person to whom a property is ascribed' (2007: 176). What this means is that in an implicit *de se* thought, one simply thinks of one's legs as crossed, a thought that is true because it is indeed one's own legs which are crossed. (The distinction is reflected in language: contrast the anaphoric construction 'He expects that he will be late' with the gerundival construction 'He expects to be late'. See also Perry 1998.) Recanati's point is that it is precisely because no identification of a subject is involved that implicit *de se* thoughts are immune to error through misidentification.

Recanati argues that the concept EGO involved in the notion of an explicit *de se* thought is itself explained by this notion of an implicit *de se* thought. He says:

The notion of an implicit *de se* thought in which the self is not represented is important..., to understand the concept of self that occurs in explicit *de se* thoughts. Indeed, the ability to entertain implicit *de se* thoughts is arguably a necessary condition for anyone to evolve the concept EGO. That is so because, as suggested by Evans, Perry, and myself following them, the concept EGO is best construed as a repository for information gained in a first person way...Now a piece of information is gained in the first person way if and only if it is the content of an implicit *de se* thought. It follows that the first step in an elucidation of the concept of self is a correct analysis of the functioning of implicit *de se* thoughts.

(2007: 177).

The notion of *manas*, as introduced by Asaṅga and developed by Vasubandhu, seems to me to be rather close in spirit to Recanati's notion of implicit *de se* thought. It certainly contains no representation of the self, and it has as its 'foundation' (*ālambana*) all the information contained in the store-consciousness. It is a first personal way of thinking about (*manana*) that information. The description 'repository for information gained in a first person way' might seem like a very good description of the joint contribution of *manas* and store-consciousness.[10]

Moreover, as we have seen, Vasubandhu speaks of a 'transformation' of *manas* into a concept of self, and that echoes with the claim Recanati is making about the evolution of the concept EGO. Finally, Recanati claims that the ability to entertain implicit *de se* thoughts is a necessary—though not necessarily a sufficient—condition for the evolution of the concept EGO, and this too is something Asaṅga and Vasubandhu are keen to stress; indeed, it is the primary motivation for introducing the notion of *manas* in the first place. For, as Asaṅga says in the *Yogācārabhūmi*, 'That [*manas*] has the mode of taking the store-consciousness as its object and conceiving it as "I am [this]" (*asmiti*) and "[this is] I" (*aham iti*)' (quoted in Waldron 2002: 42). Note that the concept EGO, as a repository of information gained in a first person way, does individuate thinkers, for no two such repositories will be alike. This concept of self is much less 'minimal' than Zahavi's.

So where is the difference? Both agree that there are explicit *de se* thoughts involving the concept EGO, but while Recanati thinks that the truth conditions of such thoughts are such that they are often true, Vasubandhu thinks that they are always false. He thinks this because he thinks that the concept EGO, which has certainly evolved in the manner described, is an empty concept, like the concept PHLOGISTON or the concept PEGASUS.

---

[10] The history of the Yogācāra concept of the store-consciousness is rather complicated. Originally conceived merely as a vehicle for the perpetuation of mental forces when the normal six types of awareness are absent, it was a technical solution to what would otherwise be a difficulty in the Yogācāra theory of individual persistence. Dreyfus and Thompson (2007: 112) say of it that '[t]his continuously present subliminal consciousness is posited by some of the Yogācāra thinkers to provide a sense of continuity in the person over time. It is the repository of all the basic habits, tendencies and propensities (including those that persist from one life to the next) accumulated by the individual'. Reaffirming this description in his article in this volume, Dreyfus offers the translation 'basic consciousness', and discusses an illuminating range of associations and resonances. The detailed studies by Lambert Schmithausen (1987) and Hartmut Buescher (2008) have revealed much greater complexity in the use of the notion in early Yogācāra than scholars had previously acknowledged. Schmithausen comments that 'it may well be that *ālayavijñāna* was, initially, conceived as a kind of 'gap-bridger', but hardly in such a way that its occurrence in ordinary states had been denied' (1987: §2.13.6). Items in the store do not themselves carry a feeling of mineness, but ground the feeling of mineness which attaches itself to the stream's conscious self-attention. They comprise a sort of database for the mind, information which can be drawn upon in the activity of bringing the states of the stream into conscious attention.

Our Buddhists think that the evolution of the concept EGO brings with it all manner of moral defilements, and one form of justification for that claim is that the concept rests in this way on an error. Sthiramati's comment on the first of the *30 Verses* bears the point out: he says that the concept of self presents only an apparent (*nirbhāsa*) referent, just as the perception of someone with an eye-disease presents only apparent hairs and circles. It is 'metaphorically designated' (*upacaryate*) because it is said to be there when it is not, as if one were to use the word 'cow' when there is an ox. Sthiramati's example, incidentally, shows that the notion of *upacāra* is much closer to metonymy than to metaphor, as traditionally understood.[11]

With P. F. Strawson's assertion that 'no use whatever of any criteria of personal identity is required to justify [a person's] use of the pronoun "I" to refer to the subject' (P. F. Strawson 1966: 165), Vasubandhu would appear to dissent. For his view seems to be that the use of the pronoun 'I' never refers to a subject of experience. Strawson's point is that we don't need any extra conceptual resource in order to make explicit self-references, and in particular we don't need a criterion of identity. The pronoun 'I' is not a term which we can correctly use only if we have successfully identified its referent, because if it were then there would be the possibility of error through misidentification relative to it. Strawson infers that 'I' refers to its subject without there being a criterion of identity. Perhaps what Vasubandhu would do would be to agree with this argument but contrapose it. His point would then be that all genuine reference involves the identification of a referent, and given that there is no question of such an identification in the case of the first person, the pronoun 'I' cannot be a genuine referring term. In saying that it is instead a 'metaphor' (*upacāra*), there seems to be a gesture at the possibility of a different, non-referential, account of its use. To say 'I feel hopeful' is, it might to be thought, to speak non-referentially of the existence of a hope which presents itself pre-attentively as mine. I will argue that, although this is not actually Vasubandhu's strategy, it is nevertheless a viable one.

---

[11] *tam ātmādinirbhāsam rūpādinirbhāsam ca tasmād vikalpād bahirbhūtam ivopādāyātmādyupacāro rūpādid-haropacāraś cānādikālikaḥ pravartate vināpi bāhyenātmanā dharmaiś ca | tadyathā taimirikasya keśondukādyupa-cāra iti | yac ca yatra nāsti tat tatropacaryate | tad yathā bāhike gauḥ | (Sthiramati, Trimśikāś-vijñapti-bhāṣya; see Buescher 2007).*

4. Two Uses of 'I'

Can one hear an echo of the Buddhist idea in the following remark?

One of the most misleading representational techniques in our language is the use of the word 'I', particularly when it is used in representing immediate experience, as in 'I can see a red patch'. It would be instructive to replace this way of speaking by another in which immediate experience would be represented without using the personal pronoun.

(Wittgenstein 1975: 88)

In another place, Wittgenstein speaks of 'two different cases in the use of the word "I" (or "my")', the 'use as object' and the 'use as subject' (1960: 66–7). The 'use as object' is the use to which it is put when we refer to ourselves as human beings, embodied entities in a public space, the use it has when, for example, one person says to another, 'I am just going to the shops to get the paper', or 'I have twisted my ankle'. Having distinguished between these two uses, one strategy would be to identify one of these uses as the primary use, and analyze the other use as being in some way derivative upon the first. Indeed, it is more in keeping with Indian theory about non-literal language to speak in this way of primary and derivative uses, rather than in terms of a distinction between literal and metaphorical use. The derivative use is metonymic rather than metaphorical: that is, the term is used to refer to something else, which stands in some relation to the primary referent. Among the contemporaries of Asaṅga and Vasubandhu are Vaiśeṣika philosophers, who argue that the primary use of 'I' is to refer to a self (ātman), and that its use to refer to oneself as an embodied being, in statements like 'I am fat', is an act of derivative reference, that is, reference to something which stands in an 'is the body of' relation to the primary reference.[12]

A variant on this approach is advocated by Galen Strawson. Strawson argues that the two uses are both genuinely referential, and neither is primary, in short, that 'I' is not univocal. One use is to refer to what he describes as a 'thin subject', a thin subject being 'an inner thing of some sort that does not and cannot exist at any given time unless it is having experience at that time' (2008: 156; cf. 2009: 331–8). The other use is to refer to 'the human being considered as a whole':

---

[12] See the discussion under *Vaiśeṣika-sūtra* 3.2.9–14.

Are we thin subjects? In one respect, of course, we are thick subjects, human beings considered as a whole. In this respect we are, in being subjects, things that can yawn and scratch. In another respect, though, we are in being subjects of experience no more whole human beings than hands or hearts: we are—literally—inner things, thin subjects, no more things that can yawn or scratch than eyebrows or thoughts . . . — But 'What then am I?' Am I two different sort of things, a thin subject and a thick subject? This is ridiculous . . . My answer is that 'I' is not univocal. We move naturally between conceiving of ourselves primarily as a human being and primarily as some sort of inner subject (we do not of course naturally conceive of ourselves as a thin subject). Sometimes we mean to refer to the one, sometimes to the other; sometimes our semantic intention hovers between both, sometimes it embraces both.

(G. Strawson 2008: 157–8)

Elsewhere, G. Strawson (2007) is clear that the relation between the two uses is one of metonymy, and indeed that the underlying relation is one of whole to part:

I think that we do at different times successfully use 'I' to refer to different things, to human beings considered as a whole and to selves. In this respect the word 'I' is like the word 'castle'. Sometimes 'castle' is used to refer to the castle proper, sometimes it is used to refer to the ensemble of the castle and the grounds and associated buildings located within the perimeter wall, sometimes it can be taken either way. The same goes for 'I', but 'I' is perhaps even more flexible, for it can sometimes be taken to refer to both the self and the whole human being, indifferently. Our thought (our semantic intention) is often unspecific as between the two.

(G. Strawson 2007: 543)

Vasubandhu, although he does not say so here, would perhaps be content to endorse as 'conventional' the use of the first person in statements like 'I am going to the shops', a use governed by the token-reflexive rule that 'I' refers to the speaker. When 'I' is used in the expression of first person psychological judgment, however, his claim is that the reference to an inner self fails, that this use erroneously imports a subject-predicate model and imposes it upon one's inner experience. In other words, his view of this use of 'I' is that there is a combination of metonymy and error-theory. When 'I' is used metonymically to refer to the inner subject, something goes wrong, and what goes wrong is that there is nothing at the far end of the metonymic relationship for it to refer to. This, indeed, is a view which G. Strawson (2007: 543) considers and rejects:

If it turns out that the best thing to say about selves is that there are no such things, then the best thing to say about 'I' may well be that it is univocal after all, and that the apparent doubleness of reference of 'I' is just the echo in language of a metaphysical illusion. If this is right, then 'I' is not in fact used to refer to selves as distinct from human beings even when its users intend to be making some such reference and believe that they are doing so. On this view, the semantic intentions of 'I'-users sometimes incorporate a mistake about how things are. I disagree.

According to the interpretation of Vasubandhu we have reached, then, 'I' does not function as an expression of genuine reference. but is rather one of *disingenuous reference*: it is a referring expression without a referent, its use creating the false impression that there is one. That is, I suggest, the best way to understand Vasubandhu's claim that it is a 'metaphor'.

There is another possibility, though. It might be the case that the mistake which 'I'-users make is not a metaphysical one, but rather a mistake about the semantic role of 'I' itself. Perhaps what goes wrong in the use of 'I' in representing immediate experience is that speakers take themselves to be making a referential use of an expression, and in doing so mistake its true logical role. It would be as if someone thought that 'perhaps' is a referring expression, and then imagined that there must be something in the world that it designates. This view is attractive, because it does not make the argument hinge on a prior metaphysical claim about the reality of selves, which then stands in need of further, extra-linguistic, justification. Rather, once we are clear about the logical role of 'I', we see that looking for a referent is as misguided as looking for the referent of 'perhaps'. And indeed, this is what Wittgenstein seems to say about the 'use as subject' of the word 'I', its use in a sentence such as 'I have a pain'. For Wittgenstein, denying that 'I', when used as in first person psychological judgments, is a referring expression, is the only way to explain the phenomenon of immunity to error through misidentification:

[T]here is no question of recognizing a person when I say I have a toothache. To ask 'are you sure that it's you who have pains?' would be nonsensical . . . And now this way of stating our idea suggests itself: that it is as impossible that in making the statement 'I have toothache' I should have mistaken another person for myself, as it is to moan with pain by mistake, having mistaken someone else for me. . . . To say, 'I have pain' is no more a statement about a particular person than moaning is.

(1960: 66–7)

The suggestion that there is a non-referential account of the use of 'I' was developed in one direction by Anscombe (Anscombe 1975). Anscombe, however, does not distinguish two uses, and argues that the first person does not refer, even in cases like 'I have a broken arm'. Other writers have tried, following the lead of P. F. Strawson, to argue that immunity of error does not commit one to a non-referential account of 'I', and indeed to reconcile immunity with the idea that 'I' refers univocally to the embodied human being (see for example Campbell 2004; McDowell 2009). In an insightful remark about Anscombe, Campbell suggests that the best way to understand her position is as claiming that the patterns of use involving the first person do not require justification in a semantic foundation:

An alternative reaction would, of course, be to say that we ought to abandon the search for a semantic foundation for our use of the first person. There are only the patterns of use, and no explanation to be given of them. This was essentially G. E. M. Anscombe's position in her famous paper, 'The First Person', in which she claimed that the first person does not refer. This claim is generally rejected, simply because philosophers have thought that when there is a use of the first person, there is, after all, always someone around who can be brought forward as the referent. But this is an extremely superficial response to Anscombe's point. Her claim is best understood as making the point that the ascription of reference to the first person is empty or idle; it does no explanatory work.

(Campbell 2004: 18)

I have argued at length elsewhere that something along these lines is just the move made by the Mādhyamika philosopher Candrakīrti (Ganeri 2007, ch. 7). His position, I have claimed there, is that we can give a fully explanatory use-theoretic account of the role of the first person in performances of self-appropriation, an account in which it is otiose to assign a reference. Asaṅga and Vasubandhu, on the other hand, say that in the movement from a pre-attentive self-awareness to an explicit use of 'I', a transformation of some sort is involved, one which involves conceptual work (*vikalpa*), and that the use of 'I' is metaphorical or metonymic. Their view is that the use of 'I' is indeed referential, and that the use as object and the use as subject are to be understood as making reference to, on the one hand, the human being, and on the other, an inner subject of experience, this second use being derivative from the first. There is, however, no subject of experience, and so the subjective use of the first person is an error.

5. Conclusion

I have argued that the new theory of Asaṅga and Vasubandhu consists in an account of the first-person perspective. Their further claim that the first person itself, the word 'I', is used 'metaphorically' in reporting the contents of the first-person perspective, rests on a prior commitment to the non-existence of an inner subject of experience. Only this permits them to claim that its use is one of what I have called 'disingenuous reference'. I have distinguished a different strategy, which is to begin with the observation that such reports are immune to error through misidentification, and to argue that it follows that in the proper account of the use in first person psychological judgments of the word 'I', the assignment of a referent is explanatorily superfluous. Some of the parts of this strategy are to be seen at work in various thinkers. Anscombe argues that 'I' is not a referring expression, but does not distinguish the two uses of the term. Candrakīrti explains the use of 'I' in a way that makes the assignment of a referent superfluous, through an appeal to the thought that its role has to do with self-appropriation (upā-dāna), but he does not base this claim on the phenomenon of immunity. The full strategy being defended here emerges only as a 'fusion' of components drawn from our various sources.[13]

References

Anacker, S. (1984), *Seven Works of Vasubandhu, the Buddhist Psychological Doctor,* Religions of Asia Series (Delhi : Motilal Banarsidass).

Anscombe, G. E. M. (1975), 'The first person', in Samuel Guttenplan (ed.), *Mind and Language* (Oxford: Clarendon Press).

Buescher, H. (2007), *Sthiramati's Triṃśikāvijñaptibhāsya: Critical Editions of the Sanskrit text and its Tibetan Translation,* Sitzungsberichte / Österreichische Akademie

---

[13] In his contribution to this volume, Matthew MacKenzie argues that the performativist model which I find in Candrakīrti needs to be supplemented rather with embodied and enactivist elements. Such a move "fuses" the Buddhist theory with ideas drawn from recent phenomenological literature, a theme of many of the contributions to this volume. I have tried instead to 'fuse' the Buddhist theory with elements taken from the recent analytical tradition, and the existence of both such possibilities suggests to me that Indian theory might well serve to create the intellectual space for a *rapprochment* between those hitherto separated strands of Western thought.

der Wissenschaften, Philosophisch-Historische Klasse (Wien : Verlag der Öster-reichischen Akademie der Wissenachaften).

——(2008), *The Inception of Yogācāra-Vijñānavāda* (Wien: Verlag der Österreichischen Akademie der Wissenachaften).

Campbell, J. (2004), 'What is it to Know what "I" Refers to?' *The Monist* 87.2: 206–18.

Dreyfus, G. and Thompson, E. (2007), 'Asian Perspectives: Indian theories of mind', in Morris Moscovitch, Evan Thompson, and Philip David Zelazo (eds.), *The Cambridge Handbook of Consciousness* (Cambridge: Cambridge University Press).

Galloway, B. (1978), '*Vijñāna, samjñā* and *manas*', *The Middle Way* 53.2: 72–5.

——(1980), 'A Yogācāra Analysis of the Mind, Based on the *Vijñāna* Section of Vasubandhu's *Pañcaskhandaprakaraṇa* with Guṇaprabha's Commentary', *Journal of the International Association for Buddhist Studies* 3.2: 7–20.

Ganeri, J. (1999), 'Self-Intimation, Memory and Personal Identity', *Journal of Indian Philosophy* 27.5: 469–83.

——(2007), *The Concealed Art of the Soul: Theories of Self and Practices of Truth in Indian Ethics and Epistemology* (Oxford: Clarendon Press).

——(forthcoming), *Mind's Own Nature: The Reconciliation of Naturalism with The first person perspective*, ch. 7.

Kramer, J. (2008), 'On Sthiramati's *Pañcaskandhakavibhāṣā*: a Preliminary Survey', *Nagoya Studies in Indian Culture and Buddhism: Saṃbhāṣā*. 27: 149–72.

McDowell, J. (2009), 'Referring to Oneself', in *The Engaged Intellect* (Cambridge. MA: Harvard University Press).

Perry, J. (1998), 'Myself and I', in Marcelo Stamm (ed.), *Philosophie in Synthetischer Absicht* (Stuttgart: Klett-Cotta).

Potter, K. H. (2003), *Buddhist Philosophy from 350 to 600 A.D., Encyclopedia of Indian Philosophies*, vol. 9 (Delhi: Motilal Banarsidass Publishers).

Recanati, F. (2007), *Perspectival Thought: A Plea for Moderate Relativism* (New York: Oxford University Press).

Sartre, J. (1957), *The Transcendence of the Ego: An Existentialist Theory of Consciousness* (New York: Noonday Press).

Schmithausen, L. (1987), *Ālayavijñāna: On the Origin and the Early Development of a Central Concept of Yogācāra Philosophy, Studia Philologica Buddhica, 2 v. (Tokyo: International Institute for Buddhist Studies)*.

Shoemaker, S. (1984), 'Self-Reference and Self-Awareness', in *Identity, Cause, and Mind* (Cambridge: Cambridge University Press).

——(1996), *The First-Person Perspective and Other Essays* (Cambridge: Cambridge University Press).

Strawson, G. (2007), 'Selves', in Brian P. McLaughlin and Ansgar Beckermann (eds.), *The Oxford Handbook of Philosophy of Mind* (Oxford: Oxford University Press).

——(2008), *Real Materialism and Other Essays* (Oxford: Clarendon Press).

——(2009), *Selves: An Essay in Revisionary Metaphysics* (Oxford: Clarendon Press).

Strawson, P. F. (1966), *The Bounds of Sense: An Essay on Kant's 'Critique of Pure Reason'* (London: Methuen).

Waldron, W. S. (2002), 'Buddhist Steps to an Ecology of Mind: Thinking about "Thoughts Without a Thinker"', *Eastern Buddhist* 34.1: 1–52.

Wittgenstein, L. (1960), *Preliminary Studies for the 'Philosophical investigations', Generally Known as the Blue and Brown Books* (Oxford: Blackwell).

——(1975), *Philosophical Remarks* (Chicago: University of Chicago Press).

Zahavi, D. (1999), *Self-Awareness and Alterity: A Phenomenological Investigation* (Evanston, IL: Northwestern University Press).

——(2005), *Subjectivity and Selfhood: Investigating the First-Person Perspective* (Cambridge, MA: MIT Press).

7

'I Am of the Nature of Seeing':

Phenomenological Reflections on the Indian Notion of Witness-Consciousness

WOLFGANG FASCHING

1. Introduction

Irrespective of the often considerable differences between their metaphysical doctrines, many of the major philosophical schools of India agree in their basic assumption that, in order to become aware of one's own true nature, one has to *inhibit* one's self-consciousness in the usual sense, namely one's 'ego-sense' (*ahaṃkāra*, literally 'I-maker'). The normal way we are aware of ourselves—that is, our self-awareness as a distinct psychophysical entity with particular characteristics and abilities, formed by a personal history, standing in manifold relations to other things and persons, etc.—is in this view really the construction of a *pseudo*-self that obscures what we really are. One has to come to realize with regard to all aspects of one's personality that 'this is not mine; this am not I; this is not the Self of me', as the Buddha puts it (*Saṃyutta Nikāya* XXII.59, Rhys Davids/Woodward 1972–79, vol. III: 60) and as, for example, Advaitins and proponents of classical Yoga could affirm without reservation.

Yet, whilst for Buddhism this means that the spiritual aim is to realize that it is an illusion that something like a self exists at all, for 'orthodox' schools such as Advaita Vedānta or Sāṃkhya and Yoga, liberation lies, on the contrary, in *becoming aware* of the true self (*ātman* or *puruṣa*).

In this paper, I would like to cast, from a phenomenological point of view, some reflections on what this overcoming of the ego-sense strived for by these traditions could possibly mean, and will try to vindicate the view of

Advaita Vedānta that it does not amount to a dissolution of oneself into a mere flux of substrate-less transient phenomena, but rather to a realization of one's self as something that changelessly underlies this flux.[1]

This 'self' is of course radically different from what we normally experience as 'ourselves': It has no qualities at all, can never become an object of consciousness (but is nonetheless immediately self-revealed), is identical neither to the body nor to the mind (qua mental goings-on we can introspectively observe), and neither does, nor wants, anything.

What should this be? It is characterized as the 'seer' (draṣṭā) or 'witness' (sākṣin)—that is, as that which sees (that which is conscious). Yet this is not supposed to mean that the self is a 'something' that performs the seeing or is in a state of seeing: Rather, it is, as Advaita Vedānta (just as, e.g. Sāṃkhya) stresses, in explicit contrast to Nyāya and Vaiśeṣika, nothing but seeing (consciousness) itself. 'The perceiver', as, for example, the classical Advaitin Śaṅkara says, 'is indeed nothing but eternal perception. And it is not [right] that perception and perceiver are different' (Upadeśasāhasrī II.2.79, Mayeda 1992: 241; addition in brackets by Mayeda). Sākṣin is, as Tara Chatterjee formulates, 'the never-to-be-objectified principle of awareness present in every individual' (Chatterjee 1982: 341).

So the claim against the Buddhists is not that there has to be some entity in addition to, and behind or beyond, our experiential life as its substrate, but that there is a stable element within it—yet not as some invariant content or content-constellation we could experience (such a thing is indeed not to be found), but as the very process of experiencing itself, as the permanence of 'witnessing', in which everything we experience has its being-experienced, and which is the constant ground of our own being. It is this notion of witness-consciousness that I wish to make some sense of in the following.[2]

---

[1] Although my main point of reference is the Advaitic understanding of the self, I will primarily focus on aspects it shares with Sāṃkhya/Yoga and many other Indian schools, i.e. independent of its monistic commitments. (For an attempt to make sense of the Advaitic idea that ultimately only one self exists, cf. Fasching 2010.)

[2] I must stress that I intend to pursue, as the subtitle says, 'phenomenological reflections' on the Advaitic understanding, and not engage in a staunch exegesis of the details of the various Advaitins' theories. I wish to discuss philosophically what I take to be a basic intuition about the nature of consciousness that seems to provide something like a foundation of the Advaitic speculations.

2. Self vs No-Self: The Buddhist Challenge

The central question of Advaita Vedānta is that of the nature of one's own self as the subject of experience. I evidently have manifold constantly changing experiences at each moment, and it is no big problem to observe them introspectively; but who am *I* who *has* all these successive experiences? It is the nature of this *experiencer of the experiences* that the whole thinking of Advaita revolves around—not in the sense of some reputed 'experience-*producer*' (so that today one could be tempted e.g. to assume the brain is the 'true self'), but in the sense of a subject-'I' as belonging to the nature of experiencing as such, however it may causally come about.

Buddhism famously denies the existence of such an experiencing 'I'. In *Saṃyutta Nikāya* XII.12, for example, the Buddha answers the question of *who it is who feels* by saying: 'Not a fit question ... I am not saying [someone] feels. And I not saying so, if you were to ask thus: "Conditioned now by what, lord, is feeling?" this were a fit question' (Rhys Davids/Woodward 1972–79, vol. II: 10; bracketed addition by the translators). So, in the Buddhist perspective, the mental life is to be characterized as a flux of permanently changing substrate-less mental events, each caused by some other, previous event, rather than in terms of a persisting experiencing self (an *ātman*). Experiences take place, but there is no one who experiences them.

It goes without saying that in the various schools of Buddhism the *anātman* doctrine has seen numerous interpretations (not all implying an outright *denial* of the existence of a self;[3] indeed, in Mahāyāna and Tibetan Buddhism one can find views that are quite compatible with the Advaitic concept of witness-consciousness[4]). However, for the sake of contrast I here construe the no-self thesis primarily in the sense of a strictly reductionist theory, as espoused by the Abhidharma schools. Even in this reading, the denial of the existence of an experiencing subject is not meant to deny, at

---

[3] For example, MacKenzie (this volume) argues that the Madhyamaka school holds—in contrast to the reductionism of the Abhidharma—that the self is not *reducible* to more basic phenomena, but 'is an emergent phenomenon that, while real, is not a substantial separate *thing*' (ibid.: p. 258). (Whether or not this makes a crucial ontological difference naturally depends on the precise definition of 'emergence'.)

[4] Miri Albahari even interprets the Pali Canon as implicitly, but centrally, assuming the existence of a witness-consciousness—'a reading', as she admits, 'that aligns Buddhism more closely to Advaita Vedānta than is usually acknowledged' (Albahari 2006: 2; cf. also Albahari this volume).

least on a conventional level, the existence of something like a unitary 'person' (*pudgala*), just as Buddhists would not deny that there are chairs or states. Yet a chair is wholly constituted by its parts and the way they are assembled, and is nothing over and above this, and similarly, the existence of a person does not involve the existence of a self over and above the manifold ephemeral phenomena that form, if sufficiently integrated, what we call 'one person'. A person is, in the Buddhist view, nothing but a certain 'psychophysical complex', that is, an 'appropriately organized collection of *skandhas*'[5] (MacKenzie 2008: 252). A person in this sense 'has' her experiences only in the sense that a whole 'has' parts, and not in the sense of some self-identical 'I'-core as the 'bearer' of its experiences, that is, as an *experiencer*.[6]

The account of persons in classical Indian Buddhist Abhidharma texts is, in its rejection of a substantial self, quite in accord with the (at least by implication) dominant modern Western view on this topic (cf. Siderits 2003): it corresponds to what Derek Parfit calls the 'reductionist view of personal identity', that is, the thesis that a person's enduring existence consists in (and is therefore reducible to) more fundamental facts, namely certain relations of connectedness and continuity between physical and mental events (Parfit 1987: 210–214)—and that in no way is the trans-temporal identity of a person due to the continued existence of something like a 'self' as a 'separately existing entity' (ibid.: 210). The many experiences of one person are not unified by each being connected to one enduring subject, but by being connected with *one another*, and the very 'oneness' of the subject is, the other way around, *constituted* by this (longitudinal) unification of the experiences.

This sounds plausible enough: What should there be in addition to the physical and mental events and their interrelations? What else should a person be but a 'psychophysical complex' of some sort? Nevertheless the 'orthodox' schools of India vehemently challenge the Buddhist *anātman* ('no-self') thesis, and insist on precisely what the Buddhists reject: that

---

[5] The term *skandhas* refers to the five types of phenomena (*dharmas*) that constitute the person according to Buddhism.

[6] Expressions like 'Devadatta's desire', as the Buddhist argues in Bhaṭṭa Rāmakaṇṭha's *Nareśvaraparīkṣā*, do not imply that there is something beyond the desire as its agent, but are 'just indicating that [the desire] is connected with a particular stream of cognition, like [such expressions] as "the flow of the Vitastā [river]"' (Watson 2006: 190; bracketed additions by Watson).

there is more to the existence of a person than this complex of *skandhas*, that there exists a 'self' in addition to the body and the experiences, which is the 'who' of experiencing.

Is this more than just a dogmatic assumption? Can anything be said in favor of this view? I think, on closer consideration, one has indeed to admit that it is hard to avoid feeling a certain unease about a purely 'selfless' account of one's own existence. Is it really true that there is no experiencing 'I'? Are there really only experiences, but no one who experiences them? Undeniably there seems to be a clear difference between an experience being experienced by me and an experience not being experienced by me. Speaking only of mental events, connected by some interrelations on the basis of which a permanent 'I' is constructed, deals with experiences more or less as if they were just objective occurrences, without taking their subjective mode of being—their 'first-person ontology' (Searle 1992: 16)—sufficiently into account. After all, experiences do not just lie about like stones or chairs, equally accessible in principle to everyone: Experiences only exist *in being subjectively experienced*, and that seems to mean: in being experienced *by a respective subject*. And obviously, all of my experiences, no matter how different they may be, have this one thing in common: that *I* experience them. In this sense, experiences are not thinkable as being 'ownerless': they are essentially experiences of an experiencing 'I'. And the big question of Advaita Vedānta is precisely what this 'I' that experiences its experiences (this 'first person' of their 'first-person ontology') is.

Yet, the *anātmavādin* (denier of a self) might reply that even if one concedes this subjective character of experience, this does not at all necessitate positing an additionally existing subject. Rather, the subject searched for (the 'experiencer') is simply the experience itself and not something 'behind' it (cf. e.g. Strawson 2003). The experiences, as the taking place of subjective appearance (as 'events of subjectivity', as Strawson puts it: 2003: 304), constitute the respective 'inner dimension' of a subject, and are therefore not 'had' by an additionally existing self.

This is indeed the position advanced by Yogācāra Buddhism and the school of Dignāga: This line of Buddhist thought expressly acknowledges the subjectivity (the being-subjectively-experienced) of experience, but rejects interpreting this fact as the experience's being experienced by a subject—rather it is supposed to refer to its self-givenness (*svasaṃvedana*) belonging to the very nature of experience:[7] An experience, in revealing its object, is simultaneously revealing itself, 'self-illuminating' (*svaprakāśa*) (just as a lamp does not need to be illumined by a second lamp in order to be visible). '*Svasaṃvedana* thus provides a continuous, immediate, and internal first-person perspective on one's own stream of experience' (MacKenzie 2008: 249), without presupposing a 'first person' in addition to experience itself. The stream of experience is given to *itself* and not to *a self*.[8]

Of course I do not experience myself *qua* experiencer as just being the present experience experiencing itself, but as someone who, as one and the same, lives through permanently changing experiences, and hence is to be distinguished from them. Yet for the Buddhist/reductionist account, this apparent diachronic identity of the subject is wholly constituted by relations between the experiences (most prominently memory-relations): The experiential life of a person is, in this view, a series of causally connected mental events without any underlying enduring self, and an important part of the relevant causal connections that constitute the unity of one person is that the contents of one experience leave memory-traces in the succeeding one. Nothing more (especially not an enduring self) is necessary to account for my remembering 'my' past experiences (and hence my experience of my continued existence) (cf. Dreyfus this volume p. 133; Siderits this volume pp. 314–15; Watson 2006: 153–165). It is true that I do not just remember that, anonymously, experiences have occurred, but *my* past experiencing them[9]—but this is simply due to the fact that the very meaning of the sameness of the self, of 'one person', is co-constituted by these very memory-connections (cf. Siderits 2003: 25): I remember my experiences as mine not because I remember my 'I' experiencing them, but because they *are* mine precisely *insofar as* I can remember them (i.e. insofar as they stand in the right form of causal connection to my present experience).

Advaita Vedānta, in contrast, insists that the subjectivity of experience refers to an experiencing subject. Just like Yogācāra Buddhism, it rejects the Nyāya thesis that an experience of an object only becomes itself manifest by becoming the object of another, subsequent experience (comparable to

---

[7] Cf. MacKenzie 2007: 47–49; MacKenzie 2008; Dreyfus 1997: 339–340, 400–402; and the contributions of Dreyfus, Krueger and Thompson in this volume.

[8] This view is comparable to non-egological accounts in phenomenology, for example by Sartre, Gurwitsch and the Husserl of the *Logical Investigations*.

[9] As Śaṅkara stresses against the Buddhist view: *Brahmasūtrabhāṣya* II.2.25, Deussen 1920: 353–354.

modern 'higher-order representation theories'): rather, for an experience, to be *means* to be conscious.[10] But at the same time they reject the Yogācāra idea that it is each experience that is conscious of itself, 'self-illuminating' (*svaprakāśa*)—rather *I*, the subject, am immediately aware of my experiences as they come and go (cf. Timalsina 2009: 20–21).[11] For example, if I am in a melancholy mood, this mood is not *conscious of itself*—for Vedānta this does not make much sense—rather the mood exists in virtue of *my experiencing it* (cf. Chatterjee 1982: 343).

And indeed, one might question whether it is really sufficient to account for the subjectivity of experience—its being-experienced-by-me (respectively)—in terms of its phenomenal self-givenness (*svasaṃvedana*), as 'an awareness of what one's experience is like both in the sense of how the experience represents its object and how it feels to undergo the experience' (MacKenzie 2008: 249). The question is *for whom* there is something it is like to be in a particular mental state. And it is far from clear that it really makes much sense to say that it is *for the mental state itself* to be (in) this state.

This 'who' of experiencing is an additional fact with regard to the experience and its phenomenal character: No facts whatsoever about an experience or its 'what-it-feels-like-ness' can ever imply its being experienced *by me* (except, precisely, that it is *I* who experiences it). It appears to be perfectly conceivable that this very experience with all its relations to other experiences of the same stream of consciousness, to this body and to the rest of the world, could have existed without the 'I' which experiences it being *me*. This seems to be a contingent (and even, as Thomas Nagel states, 'outlandish' (Nagel 1986: 55)) fact (as I argue in Fasching 2009; cf. also Madell 1981; Klawonn 1987).

This quite enigmatic additionality of the being-experienced-*by-me* with regard to all other properties of an experience, changes, I believe, the perspective on the question of the diachronic unity of the subject. It seems

---

[10] Cf. Chatterjee 1982: 342: 'The Advaitists say, that when we have an awareness of an object, the object is indeed manifested, but it is not the only thing revealed; here we have an automatic awareness of the awareness too. The two awarenesses are simultaneous, but they are not of a similar structure, in fact they are the two aspects of the same awareness.'

[11] Śaṅkara argues against the Yogācārins that even if the experience, like a lamp which need not be illuminated by a second lamp in order to be visible, is revealed by itself, it still has to be revealed *to a subject* (otherwise it would be 'like lamps, and be they thousands, burning in the midst of a mass of rocks' (*Brahmasūtrabhāṣya* II.2.28, Deussen 1920: 361–362), i.e. without anyone seeing them). Cf. Ingalls 1954: 301.

that *what happened once can happen again*: that an experience happens as the taking place of me. This refers to something radically different from the question of whether there are experiences that are *connected* to, or *continuous* with, my present one. When I ask whether I will still exist tomorrow, I do not ask whether there will be experiences that, for example, have a first-personal access to my present one. I do not refer to any aspects of the contents of some experiences in the future at all, but simply and irreducibly to the question of whether these experiences will be experienced *by me*.[12] And this seems to be logically compatible with a complete loss of memory or any other kind of psychological change (cf. Williams 1973).

3. Self as Consciousness

What, then, *is* this 'me'? Interestingly, for Advaita Vedānta[13] the true 'I' (or rather 'self': cf. Ram-Prasad this volume) is in no way some trans-experiential entity (as is the view of Nyāya and Vaiśeṣika), but is in a certain sense nothing but experience itself. For Advaita, 'the self *is* the object-experiencing ... , i.e., 'experiencing of something', and is not only becoming manifest in it as something which stands, as it were, behind or beyond it' (Hacker 1978: 275). So in this view experience does not take place *for* a subject, but simply *as* the subject.

Where, then, is the dissent from Buddhism and its rejection of an experiencing self in addition to experience? The crucial difference is that 'experience' is meant here in the sense of *consciousness* (*cit* or *caitanya*), which in Advaita Vedānta is strictly distinguished from the *mind* (in the sense of the changing mental states). When, for example, Advaitins speak of *jñāna* ('cognition' or, in the terminology of this paper, 'experience') as being

---

[12] Cf. *Brahmasūtrabhāṣya* II.2.25 where Śaṅkara stresses that my continued existence refers to strict numerical *identity* and not to some *similarity* (Thibaut 1962: 415; this sentence is missing in Deussen's translation)—and observes that while, with regard to external things, it is admittedly possible to mistake similarity with identity, this is impossible with regard to oneself as the subject (which today is called the 'immunity to error through misidentification').

[13] Just as for Sāṃkhya and Yoga, and, by the way, for the Śaiva Siddhāntin Bhaṭṭa Rāmakaṇṭha: cf. the interesting study by Alex Watson (2006). In his *Nareśvaraparīkṣāprakāśa*, Bhaṭṭa Rāmakaṇṭha initially lets the Buddhist win over Nyāya and Vaiśeṣika, which assume the existence of a self as a further entity beyond cognition. But while Buddhism concludes that there actually is no self, only the cognitions, Rāmakaṇṭha holds that cognition itself *is* the self (ibid.: 213–217). He thereby repeats earlier debates between Buddhism and Sāṃkhya (whose view of the self he largely inherits) (ibid.: 93).

the essence of the self, they expressly distinguish it from what they call the *vṛtti-jñānas*, that is, the manifold transient mental states (Chatterjee 1982: 342; cf. also Hiriyanna 1956: 344 and Timalsina 2009: 17).[14]

So, in Advaita Vedānta, consciousness is not equated with the single ephemeral experiences or with some property of them. Rather, it is understood as something that abides as that wherein the coming and going experiences have their manifestation (being-experienced). Consciousness is, so to speak, the *witnessing* (experiencing) of the experiences, and while the experiences change, experiencing itself abides. After all, the succession of the experiences consists precisely in one experience after another becoming experientially present, which *presence as such* therefore does *not* change.

Just like Yogācāra Buddhism, Advaita Vedānta espouses the idea of the 'self-luminosity' (*svaprakāśatva*) of experience—yet not as a feature of the individual mental states—these are things that become manifest *in* experience (*qua* consciousness)—but rather of consciousness itself (cf. Chatterjee 1982: 342–344, 349).[15] Consciousness, like light, is the medium of visibility of all things and does not have to be illuminated by *another* light (i.e. become the *object* of consciousness) in order to be revealed—it is the shining itself as the principle of revealedness.[16] Light is not visible in the way illuminated objects are, but at the same time, it is not concealed:[17] It *is* present, and it is precisely its presence that is the medium of the presence of everything—first

---

[14] Quite similarly, Bhaṭṭa Rāmakaṇṭha differentiates between two meanings of *jñāna*, namely on the one hand the many transient cognitions, and on the other, the one abiding cognition which is our very self (and which he also terms, when it comes to contrasting the two senses of *jñāna*, *prakāśa* = 'illumination' or *samvit* = 'consciousness'): the latter being a permanent witnessing or experiencing of the passing cognitions (Watson 2006: 354–373).

[15] In *Brahmasūtrabhāṣya* II.2.28, Śaṅkara lets the Buddhist ask whether, with his stressing of the self-revealedness of the cognizer, he is not actually adopting, only in other words, the Buddhist's own view of the self-givenness of cognition, and answers: 'No! Because cognition is to be distinguished [from the cognizing subject] insofar as it is originating, passing away, manifold, etc.' (Deussen 1920: 362, addition in brackets by Deussen).

[16] Cf. e.g. Śaṅkara's *Upadeśasāhasrī* I.15.40–41: '[It] has the light of knowledge as Its nature; [It] does not depend upon anything else for [Its] knowledge. Therefore [It] is always known to me. The sun does not need any other light for its illumination' (Mayeda 1992: 145–146, bracketed additions by Mayeda).

[17] Cf. *Upadeśasāhasrī* I.15.48 and 50: '*Ātman* Itself ... is by nature neither knowable nor not knowable'. 'Just as there is neither day nor night in the sun, since there is no distinction in the nature of light, so is there neither knowledge nor ignorance in *Ātman*, since there is no distinction in the nature of knowledge' (Mayeda 1992: 146). 'Though light is an illuminator, it does not illumine itself [since it has in itself no difference as between illuminator and illuminated] ... In like manner *Ātman* [which has homogeneous knowledge] never sees Itself' (ibid.: I.16.12, Mayeda 1992: 150, bracketed additions by Mayeda). Cf. Ram-Prasad this volume, section 5, and Ram-Prasad 2007: 78–79.

and foremost of the experiences whose very existence consists in their being-present.[18]

Hence for the Advaitins—although they hold that mental states are manifest *essentially*, and not by virtue of being the object of some further, higher-order mental states—it is not adequate to say that they are immediately *self-aware*. Rather, they exist in manifesting themselves *in* the medium of the luminosity of consciousness, which is immediately self-revealed. Experiences have their very being in their being-consciously-present (in being manifest in 'primary presence', as Erich Klawonn (1987, 1998) calls it), and while these experiences are permanently fleeting, conscious presence as such abides (Klawonn 1998: 59; cf. Zahavi 1999: 80; Zahavi this volume: p. 59).

So, in this view, the manifold transient experiences have their manifestation in one consciousness. Yet why should we assume this? Why should we draw a distinction between the individual experiences and consciousness, thereby obviously hypostasizing consciousness into a 'something' in addition to experience? Why should we assume an irreducible sameness of consciousness, if, quite evidently, constantly *new* consciousness-events are transpiring? Conscious experiences admittedly share the feature of being conscious, but it seems to be an obvious fallacy to speak here of something like a persisting consciousness-*entity*. So is there any justifiable sense in which consciousness is to be distinguished from the individual experiences and in which a multitude of experiences can be the taking place of the same consciousness?

I think there is. Already in a purely synchronic perspective, consciousness comprises *many* experiences, that is, I am actually seeing, hearing, thinking, etc. manifold things at the same time. The question is how one should account for this oneness of the experiencing 'I' across its manifold simultaneous experiences (i.e., what binds these experiences together as 'mine'). Naturally, the reductionist cannot explain the synchronic unity of experiences by their being experienced by one subject (by me). For, in her view, there *is* simply no subject one could presuppose as *explanans*; rather, it's the other way around: just like diachronic unity, the unity of being-experienced-by-one-subject at a time is to be explained by the being-unified of the experiences by unity relations that hold between them.

---

[18] For an insightful discussion of the understanding of consciousness as 'luminosity' in Indian philosophy, cf. Ram-Prasad 2007: 51–99.

Yet what sort of relations could these be? One must not forget that it is not just *any* relation, *any* unity between experiential contents that is at stake here, but the unity of being-present-in-one-consciousness. Certain experiential contents can be more strongly associated than others, and thereby bound together to form experiential 'fields' (experiential unities) in contrast to a background; they can be coordinated as constituting one coherent space, and the like—but all such relations that might bind together experiences into 'total experiences' actually *presuppose* their being-present-together (cf. Dainton 2006: 240–244). Only what is co-present in this sense can be associated.

And this presence is nothing other than the being-experienced of the experiences in which, in the sense of their 'first-person ontology', the experiences have their being. So they do not exist and *additionally* become somehow unified. Rather, it is their very being (namely their being-experienced) wherein they have their unity.

One could counter that it was inadequate to speak of many simultaneous experiences in the first place. Rather, it is one total experience with an inner complexity.[19] But the crucial question is precisely wherein the unity of this 'one total experience' lies. Nothing on the content-side can do this job. So one obviously has to distinguish between the one experience and the many experiential contents that manifest themselves within it. And if one wishes to call the latter 'experiences', it is important to understand that the one experience is not a *sum* or a *composition* of these many experiences (*qua* experiential contents), but rather it is 'experience' in the sense of the *experiencing* of the experiences (cf. Zahavi 1999: 80): that wherein they have their being-experienced, their primary presence—quite in the sense of the Advaitic notion of *jñāna* (or *sākṣi-jñāna*, as it is occasionally called) in contrast to the *vṛtti-jñānas*. So when we speak of many simultaneous experiences, their difference lies in *what* is present, not in presence itself.

This, I would suggest, is how the talk of 'witnessing' in Advaita Vedānta should be interpreted: We stated that the 'witness' (*sākṣin*) is not understood as an observing entity standing opposed to what it observes, but as the very taking place of 'witnessing' itself, and 'witnessing' is nothing other than the taking place of the experiential *presence* of the experiences, in which the experiences have their very being-experienced and thereby their existence.

---

[19] Cf. the suggestion of Bayne and Chalmers in Bayne, Chalmers 2003: 56–57.

In this sense, consciousness can be understood as the *existence-dimension* of the experiences (cf. Klawonn 1987; Zahavi 2005: 131–132; Zahavi this volume: p. 58; Fasching 2009: 142–144). A dimension comprises a multitude of elements that stand in manifold relations to each other, yet it is not the *sum* of these elements or a result of their interrelations, but what makes them, together with all their relations, possible in the first place. In this sense, 'the self' *qua* consciousness is to be distinguished from its experiences, but not as a 'separately existing entity'—just as space is not a separately existing entity in addition to the spatial objects, yet also not identical to them or reducible to their relations (since any spatial relations *presuppose* space).[20]

So the unity of being-experienced-together is irreducible to the many experiences and their relations, being rather that wherein they have their being, and this is nothing other than what Advaita Vedānta calls the *ātman* as 'the immediately co-experienced unity of experiencing' (as Paul Hacker characterizes Advaita's *ātman*, using a formulation of Scheler's about the 'person': Hacker 1978: 274; cf. ibid.: 275).

When Advaita Vedānta equates the self with consciousness, this is not supposed to mean that the subject is composed of the many contents of consciousness. I *qua* consciousness am not an agglomeration of phenomenal contents, properly organized, but rather their *thereness*, their presence (and that is the *one* presence of the manifold contents).[21]

---

[20] Cf., e.g. *Upadeśasāhasrī* II.2.58 and I.14.50: '*Ātman*, like space, is by nature not composite'; 'there is no distinction at any time in the Seeing which is like ether' (Mayeda 1992: 237 and 140–141).

[21] In her very lucid paper on the concept of witness-consciousness, Miri Albahari (2009) rigorously distinguishes it from the 'for-me-ness' or 'mineness' (i.e. 'first-personal givenness'), which Dan Zahavi posits as the core sense of self. While mineness is a property of experience, witness-consciousness is 'the *modus operandi* of the subject that has them' (Albahari 2009: 68), i.e. of a 'separate me' (ibid.: 73) (whereas for Zahavi 'the self ... does not exist in separation from the experiences, and is identified by the very first-personal givenness of the experiences': Zahavi 2005: 132). I agree that experiences and consciousness have to be *distinguished* in a certain sense (this being the very idea of 'witness-consciousness'), yet I disagree with breaking them apart as if they were separate existences, as Albahari seems to do. Witness-consciousness is, according to Albahari, the 'mode-neutral awareness' that is supposed to account for the experiences' accessibility to reflection, and for the unity of consciousness across manifold experiences (Albahari 2009: 71–72), thus obviously our pre-reflective awareness of our own experiences. Yet this is precisely what Zahavi calls 'mineness' *qua* first-personal givenness. To 'witness', according to my understanding of the term, does not literally mean that the subject 'observes' the experiences (as Albahari formulates: ibid.: 68), as if the witness were a separately existing entity that watches experience-objects existing outside of it. Rather, it should be understood as the experiencing of the experiences in which they have their very being. It is simply not the case that the being-present (first-personal givenness, for-me-ness) of the experiences and the witnessing as the *modus operandi* of the subject are two different things. And according to the Advaitic (and my) understanding, the 'me' of the for-me-ness (i.e. the *self*)

Now the question is: What is the nature of the temporal abiding of experiential presence through the permanent succession of experiences? Does a new presence with new contents not take place each moment? Is there a succession of presences together with the succession of contents (after all, the presence-of-this now and the presence-of-that then are obviously *different* presence-events)? Or is it, rather, not one and the same consciousness, in which the experiences have their coming and going? In other words: Can two presence-events at different times be the taking place of the *same* presence, that is, is there an irreducible sense in which two such presence-events can be the taking place of (one and the same) *me*? Vedānta insists that what changes when one experience follows the other (presence-of-this being succeeded by presence-of-that), are actually the *contents* of consciousness, not consciousness itself (cf. Sinha 1954: 329). And indeed, as soon as one distinguishes consciousness from the experiences, the assumption that the diachronic identity of consciousness has to consist in unity relations between the experiences appears less compelling. And if one takes a closer look at the nature of the presence of the momentary experience, it becomes outright implausible: The 'primary presence' (the current being-experienced) of an experience always and essentially is the presence of the temporal *streaming* of experience transpiring right now. And that means: presence is irreducibly presence of the current taking place of *temporal transition*. (Otherwise no time-experience, no experience of change and persistence, would ever arise.)

So the indubitable evidence of my experiences in their very being-experienced is always their evidence as passing the thereby 'abiding dimension of first-personal experiencing' (Zahavi 2005: 131). And, therefore, the absolute evidence of my present existence is the evidence of *my present living through* these streaming experiences. The being-experienced

is—quite in agreement with Zahavi—not something to be posited *in addition* to this presence (for-me-ness), but something that consists in nothing other than the witnessing/experiencing itself. Furthermore, Albahari holds that this for-me-ness is, as an aspect of experience, something introspectively detectable, and also in this respect stands in contrast to witness-consciousness which, as 'built into the very act of being aware', can never become an *object* of awareness (Albahari 2009: 68–69). I have my doubts about the former claim. 'Mineness' is about as much a 'real predicate' as is 'being' according to Kant. It is in no way a content towards which one could direct one's attention, no introspectively examinable quality (no 'feeling': Albahari 2009: 70) my experiences have in addition to other qualities (such as the specific character of my pain) (cf. also Zahavi this volume: p. 59)—it is rather precisely the first-personal *thereness-for-me* of my experiences, together with all their qualities.

of the streaming experiences as streaming implies the permanence of the actuality of experiencing itself, which is the being of my 'I'.[22] Therefore I, *qua* consciousness, am not the passing experiences, but rather their manifestation *as* passing, which does not pass with them: the abiding experiencing of the changing experiences (Fasching 2009: 144–145).[23]

So the question of whether the subject is something that can exist, in an irreducible sense, as one and the same at different times, must, I believe, be answered in the affirmative: It only *exists* as now-transcending from the start; in contrast to the fleeting experiences it abides as the presence of the streaming experiences as streaming. Experiences only exist in being experienced, that is, experientially present, and they are essentially present as streaming, which implies the abidance of this presence itself. This abidance cannot be constituted by relations between momentary 'experience-stages', because there simply *are* no experience-stages that would not have their primary presence as temporally passing. That is: There is no experiential evidence prior to the evidence of the 'standing' of the experiencing 'I'.

This abidance of the 'I' cannot properly be conceived of as the enduring of an *object* in time that derives its persistence from unity relations between its temporal stages. For presence is not so much something that takes place *in* the respective present, but rather it is this very present itself—not in the sense of the objective time-point that is now present and then sinks into the past, but in the sense of the *presentness* of the respective present moment:[24] What marks a particular moment as being *now* is no objective feature of this special point on the timeline (cf. Nagel 1986: 57), rather it is the 'now' only in relation to the experiential presence of the subject (cf. Husserl 2006: 58, 390, 406). Consequently, the abiding of the 'I' is not so much the enduring

---

[22] Cf. Śaṅkara in *Upadeśasāhasrī* II.2.75 (in answering the question of how the perceiver, perceiving now this, then that, can be said to be changeless): 'If indeed you were subject to transformation, you would not perceive the entire movement of the mind...Therefore, you are transcendentally changeless' (Mayeda 1992: 240). 'There must be some constant continuous principle to see their [the cognitions'] origin and destruction...And this continuous consciousness is *sākṣin*' (Chatterjee 1982: 349).

[23] Along comparable lines, Rāmakaṇṭha argues against the Buddhists that there is no need to assume that the change of the objects of consciousness implies a change of consciousness itself. For even the Buddhists cannot deny that many objects are conscious in one single consciousness at one point in time (and it is of no help for the Buddhist to hold that this is due to a unifying cognition: it is still necessary to appeal to the possibility of a single cognition having many objects). So, Rāmakaṇṭha argues, if the multiplicity of objects at one time does not affect the singleness of consciousness, why should the multiplicity of objects *over* time? It is the contents of consciousness that change, not consciousness itself (Watson 2006: 335–348).

[24] Cf. Husserl 1966: 333: '...the now-consciousness is not itself now'.

of an inter-temporal object (with its coming and going temporal 'object-stages'), but should rather be conceived of in terms of the 'standing' of the present itself, in which the very passing of time (the permanent becoming-present of ever-new time-points and object-stages) consists:[25] that is, of the phenomenon *that it is always now*. While the temporal stages of an object one is conscious of continually sink into the past, consciousness itself does *not* elapse: '... even though the object of knowledge changes', says Śaṅkara, 'the knower, being in past, future, and present, does not change; for his nature is eternal presence' (i.e. the presentness of the present) (*Brahmasūtrabhāṣya* II.3.7, Deussen 1920: 389). So the evidence of the abiding of the subject is not the experience of some object-persistence, but the *condition of the possibility* of any experience of persistence.[26]

4. The Presence of the World and the Subject in the World

What Advaita Vedānta soteriologically aims at as the realization of the 'self' is nothing other than becoming aware of experiential presence (consciousness) as such. So far, we have characterized this consciousness as the presence of the experiences. Yet this should not be misunderstood as meaning the presence of merely mental contents, of some subjective interiority in contrast to the outer

---

[25] Cf. *Upadeśasāhasrī* I.5.3: 'Just as to a man in the boat the trees [appear to] move in a direction opposite [to his movement], so does *Ātman* [appear to] transmigrate ... ' (Mayeda 1992: 114; bracketed additions by Mayeda).

[26] In my interpretation of the notion of witness-consciousness, I owe much to Dan Zahavi's views on consciousness and the self. However, I am not sure whether we fully agree regarding the nature of the diachronic identity of the self. Zahavi states 'that it is the shared mode of givenness that makes two experiences belong to the same subject, i.e. ... it is their exposure in the same field of primary presence which makes different experiences of one and the same self' (Zahavi 1999: 144). I find this formulation ambiguous. It could mean that a past experience is mine insofar as it is *in my present experiencing* given in a first-person mode, 'as mine', or it could mean that the experience, *when originally experienced*, had its manifestation in the same field or dimension of first-personal givenness. Hence, the question is: Is a past experience mine insofar as, and because, it is first-personally accessible to me (in the present), or is it first-personally accessible to me because it was experienced by me? The first reading ultimately amounts to a reductionist view in Parfit's sense, and Zahavi appears to tend towards this approach (cf., for example, the final section of his contribution to this volume). On the other hand, he speaks of an 'abiding dimension of experiencing' (Zahavi 1999: 80), which would allow a view of the 'sameness' of the 'same field of givenness' in the second sense (the view I favor). Formulations such as, 'Not only is the first experience retained by the last experience, but the different experiences are all characterized by the same fundamental first-personal givenness' (this volume: p. 58) may also be interpreted along these lines.

world. Rather, consciousness exists as the presence of anything we could ever refer to, be it 'inner' or 'outer'. The presence of the experiences *is* the presence of the world.[27] The presence of sensuous contents, for example, is *ipso facto* the sensuous presence of the respective perceived object; my thinking is nothing but the successive presenting-itself of some meaning-constellation (some 'thought' in the noematic sense); the moods I live through are aspects of the way the world is there for me, etc. So experiences are manifestation-events—they exist as appearing-of-something, and appearance as such has its existence in its being-present (being-experienced)—namely its existence *as* appearance-*of*. The presence of experience means that appearance-of-something takes place, and so the presence of experience is *ipso facto* the presence of this something.

Therefore my being *qua* presence means that all sorts of things are present to me. I can investigate these things given to me in manifold ways, and I can also reflect on their modes of givenness. Yet what can be said about the presence itself as such of what is present to me? This presence (consciousness) is notoriously elusive. It has no observable properties of its own, is no particular and distinguishable content we encounter, and can never stand before us as an object. Therefore the self in the Advaitic sense is not one of the 'seen' things but the 'seeing' itself: 'I am neither this object, nor that, I am That which makes all objects manifest' (Śaṅkara, *Vivekacūḍāmaṇi* verse 493, Prabhavananda/Isherwood 1978: 115). Presence is not a phenomenon of its own that I could find in addition to other phenomena, but simply the taking place of thereness of any phenomena. This is the sense of the so-called 'transparency' of consciousness, that is, the fact that when one tries to attend to the *consciousness* of an object, one can hardly help ending up attending to what it is conscious *of*.[28]

---

[27] Cf. Śaṅkara's *Brahmasūtrabhāṣya* II.2.28: 'We are obliged to assume objects apart from cognition, namely on the ground of cognition itself. For no one cognizes a post or a wall as mere cognition, but as objects of cognition everyone cognizes the post or the wall' (Deussen 1920: 359).

[28] Consciousness is no object we could find anywhere and is in this sense 'invisible'. But this does not mean that it is *concealed*. The transparency of consciousness does not mean that the cognitive processes through which we represent objects are not themselves again represented and thereby normally unknown to us (as Metzinger understands it: Metzinger 2003: 163–177), but rather that there simply *is* nothing to represent, because consciousness is nothing but the thereness of whatever it happens to be consciousness *of* and nothing beyond that: It is not an object we fail to be conscious of, but no object at all.

So the presence itself of what is present can never be an observable *object*, yet at the same time it is the most familiar thing in the world: It is that wherein everything we experience has its being-experienced, the medium of all phenomena (the taking place of their phenomenality). And the soteriological aim of Advaita Vedānta—the realization of *ātman*—is nothing but simply becoming explicitly aware of this taking place of presence as such.

Of course, in a certain sense we are constantly conscious of our being conscious. After all, we are not living in a permanent state of complete self-forgetfulness, fully absorbed in the objects: we are not only conscious of the objects we see but also—at least implicitly—of our seeing them. But evidently, this is not the form of self-awareness Advaita Vedānta strives for—rather, it is, in their view, precisely a form of self-*forgetfulness*, that is, of obscuration of the fundamental dimension of our own being *qua* subjectivity: It is *ahaṃkāra* ('ego-sense'), the awareness of a distinct 'I' (*aham*) as an inner-worldly subject with particular empirical (psychophysical) properties (a *jīva*, 'person').

To say that I am not only conscious, for example, of this desk I see, but also of my seeing it actually means that I am aware of myself sitting here and looking at the desk and of the fact that the desk appears in this particular way precisely because it is given to me as someone viewing it from this particular angle, with these particular sense-organs, and so on. So that which I am aware of here, is my localization in the world, and of my own body to which I relate the rest of the appearances. When I experience an unchanging object in changing modes of givenness, I experience this change as being due to the changing relations between the experiencing subject and the experienced object: that is, together with the object, experienced in changing modes of givenness, a 'subject' is experienced for whom the manifestations are manifestations, a 'subject' which is itself something that is objectively located within the objective world, standing in manifold—physical and psychical—relations to other things.

And this is essential to object-givenness in general. Objectivity means appearance-transcendence: We apprehend the subjective appearance as not being the object itself, but as only being an *aspect* of this object, that is, this object as seen from a certain viewpoint, in certain respects. Hence the from-where of seeing is necessarily co-constituted with the seen object—co-constituted as a 'subject' that is itself part of the objective world (cf.

Husserl 1952: 56, 109–110, 144; Albahari 2006: 8–9, 88). So in a way the experience of objects is *ipso facto* also *self*-experience, in the sense of the self-localization of the subject within the realm of the objects.

This not only holds for our being conscious of ourselves as a *body*, but also with regard to the mental aspects of what we experience as our 'I': For example, the field of givenness is never a mere homogeneous plane, but features an attentional relief which indicates a mental 'I' to which certain things are attentionally 'nearer' than others: I can direct my attention to this or to that *within* the field of what is consciously there for me, so that my 'I' is obviously to be *distinguished* from this field (cf. Husserl 1952: 105–106), an 'I' with particular personal interests and the like.

This 'self-experience' as a particular psychophysical being means that we identify a certain special sphere of what is experientially given to us as 'ourselves': that is, we constantly distinguish *within* the realm of phenomenal contents between what belongs to 'ourselves'—one's body, one's thoughts, and so on—and what is located 'outside of ourselves' (cf. Albahari 2006: 51, 56–60, 73[29]). This is what is called *adhyāsa* ('superimposition') in Advaita (see below).

So object-givenness implies the givenness of the subject (an indicated and experienced from-where of experiencing) as a necessary moment of the structure of the field of the objectively given. Now the point is that the *experiencing itself*—consciousness—is *not* a structural moment of what is given, but is *the very taking place of givenness itself*. The whole inner/outer (self/not-self) distinction constitutes itself within the realm of experiential contents—and consequently experiencing itself is not located within some 'inner sphere'. My consciousness is not to be found on one side of this inner-outer distinction in which what we experience is necessarily structured, but is, again, the taking place of experience itself. The viewpoint is part of the structure of the field of presence and therefore not presupposed, but constituted by it.

Hence consciousness of myself as an 'inside' as opposed to an 'outside' is not a way of being aware of consciousness as such, which is not a special inner realm opposed to the outer objects, but the *thereness* of these objects,

---

[29] Albahari 2006: 57: The identification of the subject with certain aspects of the body or mind involves 'the subject—the witnessing as it presents from a psycho-physical perspective—identifying with those very *khandhās* [= *skandhas*] (objects of awareness) that contribute … to the impression of a hemmed-in perspective from which the world is witnessed'.

the appearing of what appears (be it 'inside' or 'outside'). This 'pre-interior' consciousness is what Advaita Vedānta means by 'self': '[T]he self which is of the nature of consciousness … [is] the witness of both the seer and the seen' (Śaṅkara, *Ātmajñopadeśavidhi* III.7, quoted in Gupta 1998: 38), therefore it is 'the pure "subject" that underlies all subject/object distinctions' (Deutsch 1969: 49), 'the "field" of consciousness/being within which the knower/knowing/known distinctions arise' (Fort 1984: 278).

5. The Process of De-Superimposition

In order to become aware of the self in this sense it is necessary to stop identifying oneself with what presents itself as 'I' and 'mine': the 'annihilation of the ego-sense' (Ramana in Osborne 1997: 19). Normally we are not explicitly aware of consciousness as such, since we are totally lost in the *objects* of consciousness and can also understand ourselves only as one of the objects. This erroneous self-understanding as one of the objects is what is called *adhyāsa* in Advaita Vedānta, the 'superimposition' of self and not-self: Certain experienced contents are appropriated as belonging to one's own self, as an 'inner' opposed to what is located 'outside' the self (cf. Fort 1984: 278) as it articulates itself in our 'saying, for example, "that am I", "that is mine"' (Śaṅkara, *Brahmasūtrabhāṣya*, Introd., Deussen 1920: 3).

Accordingly, the way of becoming aware of one's true nature consists in a 'process of desuperimposition' (Indich 1980: 16, 10), that is, a process of de-identification from anything one objectively encounters as one's purported self (cf. Fasching 2008). One stops identifying oneself with the inner-objective 'subject', the psychophysical entity (*jīva*) one normally takes oneself to be. Instead of identifying certain configurations of *experienced contents* as being 'oneself', one begins to experience oneself as the abiding *experiencing itself* (the taking place of *presence*) of any contents. De-superimposition means radically distinguishing oneself from all objects by no longer delimiting oneself (as an 'inside') as opposed to the objects 'out there'. One stops considering anything as being 'oneself' or 'one's own': 'He to whom both "I" … and "my" … have become meaningless, becomes a knower of *Ātman*', as Śaṅkara puts it (*Upadeśasāhasrī* I.14.29, Mayeda 1992: 138).

In the 'de-identified' mode of experiencing that is strived for, one completely lets go of 'oneself' and becomes nothing but 'seeing', without any distinct 'seer' standing apart from the 'seen'. This amounts to a profound transformation of one's self-experience and of the way of being in the world. To experience oneself as the 'witnessing' leads to a sense of detachment, a loosening of one's involvement in the concerns, desires, and fears of the ego.[30] One experiences oneself as an inner stillness in the midst of all motion, and as non-acting even when engaged in action.[31] Instead of simply identifying oneself with a particular configuration of experiential contents, standing in permanently changing relations of activity and passivity to other experienced contents, one simultaneously experiences oneself as the abiding experiencing itself, as the motionless and non-acting dimension of manifestation of all movements and activities, of any 'inside' and 'outside' and all relations between them. One no longer apprehends oneself as a subject-pole in opposition to an object-pole, being affected by it, reacting to it, dealing with it, but as the event of presence of any subject and object. 'I (= *Ātman*) am of the nature of Seeing, non-object … , unconnected [with anything], changeless, motionless … [Touch] does not produce for me any change of gain and loss … , since I am devoid of touch, just as a blow with the fist and the like [does not produce any change] in the sky' (*Upadeśasāhasrī* III.3.115, Mayeda 1992: 252; bracketed additions by Mayeda).

With the dropping of the notions of 'I' and 'mine', in a way nothing remains for oneself, and in this sense it could be seen as a dissolution of the self. Yet for Advaita Vedānta this 'nothing' actually just means no-*thing*, that is, non-objectivity. The modern Advaitic author Arvind Sharma answers the question of whether 'the sense "I am" [is] real or unreal' with the words: 'Both. It is unreal when we say: "I am this, I am that". It is real when we mean "I am not this, nor that"' (Sharma 1993: 96–97).[32] One becomes aware of oneself precisely when one ceases to find oneself anywhere.

---

[30] Cf. e.g. Śaṅkara's descriptions in *Vivekacūḍāmaṇi* verses 428–442, Prabhavananda/Isherwood 1978: 104–106; Osborne 1997: 31.

[31] '… he who, though acting, is actionless—he is the knower of *Ātman*' (*Upadeśasāhasrī* I.10.13, Mayeda 1992: 124); cf. also Osborne 1997: 32.

[32] Cf. *Upadeśasāhasrī* I.6.6: 'The learned should abandon the "this"-portion in what is called "I", understanding that it is not *Ātman*' (Mayeda 1992: 116). (Formulations like this seem to contradict the claim, such as Ram-Prasad (this volume) makes, that in Advaita Vedānta the term 'I' does not at all refer to the *ātman*.)

6. Conclusion

In opposition to Buddhism, Advaita Vedānta insists on the existence of an abiding self, a self which consists in nothing but consciousness ('seeing' or 'witnessing') and as such is the non-object *kat' exochen*, since seeing is not itself something visible. I have argued that this view does indeed capture something essential about the nature of experience.

Buddhism and Advaita Vedānta agree that it is necessary to inhibit the identification with the 'I' and the clinging to what is 'mine' to achieve liberation. The theoretical interpretation of this process is where they disagree. Now it is my opinion that the notion of witness-consciousness allows for a more faithful description of what actually happens in this process than the idea of no-self (at least in its reductionist interpretation).

Buddhism invites us to reflect on our own being and holds that what we will find are all kinds of transient phenomena (the five *skandhas*), but nothing like a stable 'self'. With regard to each of the *skandhas* one should understand: 'this is not mine; this am not I; this is not the Self of me' (*Samyutta Nikāya* XXII.59). This insight leads us to the liberation from the illusion of self. Yet the question is: If there is nothing but these transient phenomena that constitute our being (in other words: if this simply *is* what we are)—*who* is it then that is not identical to all this? Who is it who can say of her body, her thoughts, etc. 'this am not I'? This 'who' is, I wish to suggest, nothing but the experiencing consciousness in which all the passing phenomena have their manifestation and which Advaita Vedānta regards as our 'self'.[33]

References

Albahari, M. (2006), *Analytical Buddhism: The Two-Tiered Illusion of Self* (Basingstoke: Palgrave Macmillan).

——(2009), 'Witness-Consciousness: Its Definition, Appearance and Reality', *Journal of Consciousness Studies* 16/1: 62–84.

[33] This article was conceived and written in the framework of the Austrian Science Fund (FWF) research project *Experiential Presence* (P21327). I wish to thank Himal Trikha, Chakravarthi Ram-Prasad and the editors for their comments and suggestions.

Bayne, T. and Chalmers, D. J. (2003), 'What Is the Unity of Consciousness?' in Axel Cleeremans (ed.), *The Unity of Consciousness: Binding, Integration, and Dissociation* (Oxford: Oxford University Press).

Chatterjee, T. (1982), 'The Concept of Sākṣin', *Journal of Indian Philosophy* 10: 339–356.

Dainton, B. (2006), *Stream of Consciousness: Unity and Continuity in Conscious Experience* (London: Routledge).

Deussen, P., trans. (1920), *Die Sutra's des Vedānta oder die Çārīraka-Mīmāṅsā des Bādarāyaṇa nebst dem vollständigen Commentare des Çankara* (Leipzig: Brockhaus).

Deutsch, E. (1969), *Advaita Vedānta: A Philosophical Reconstruction* (Honolulu: University of Hawaii Press)

Dreyfus, G. B. J. (1997), *Recognizing Reality: Dharmakīrti's Philosophy and Its Tibetan Interpretations* (Albany, NY: State University of New York Press).

Fasching, W. (2008), 'Consciousness, Self-Consciousness, and Meditation', *Phenomenology and the Cognitive Sciences* 7: 463–483.

——(2009), 'The Mineness of Experience', *Continental Philosophy Review* 42: 131–148.

——(2010), 'Fremde und eigene Gegenwart: Über Anderheit, Selbst und Zeit', in Matthias Flatscher and Sophie Loidolt (eds.), *Das Fremde im Selbst-das Andere im Selben* (Würzburg: Königshausen & Neumann).

Fort, A. O. (1984), 'The Concept of Sākṣin in Advaita Vedānta', *Journal of Indian Philosophy* 12: 277–290.

Gupta, B. (1998), *The Disinterested Witness: A Fragment of Advaita Vedānta Phenomenology* (Evanston, IL: Northwestern University Press).

Hacker, P. (1978), *Kleine Schriften*, ed. Lambert Schmithausen (Wiesbaden: Franz Steiner).

Hiriyanna, M. (1956), *Outlines of Indian Philosophy* (London: George Allen & Unwin).

Husserl, E. (1952), *Ideen zu einer reinen Phänomenologie und phänomenologischen Philosophie. Zweites Buch: Phänomenologische Untersuchungen zur Konstitution*, ed. Marly Biemel (The Hague: Nijhoff (Husserliana IV)).

—— (1966), *Zur Phänomenologie des inneren Zeitbewußtseins (1893–1917)*, ed. Rudolf Boehm (The Hague: Nijhoff (Husserliana X)).

——(2006), *Späte Texte über Zeitkonstitution (1929–1934): Die C-Manuskripte*, ed. Dieter Lohmar (Dordrecht: Springer (Husserliana Materialien VIII)).

Indich, W. M. (1980), *Consciousness in Advaita Vedānta* (Delhi: Motilal Banarsidass).

Ingalls, D. H. H. (1954), 'Śaṃkara's Arguments against the Buddhist', *Philosophy East and West* 3/4: 291–306.

Klawonn, E. (1987), 'The "I": On the Ontology of First Personal Identity', *Danish Yearbook of Philosophy* 24: 43–75.

——(1998), 'The Ontological Conception of Consciousness', *Danish Yearbook of Philosophy* 33: 55–69.

MacKenzie, M. D. (2007), 'The Illumination of Consciousness: Approaches to Self-Awareness in the Indian and Western Traditions', *Philosophy East and West* 57/1: 40–62.

——(2008), 'Self-Awareness without a Self: Buddhism and the Reflexivity of Awareness', *Asian Philosophy* 18/3: 245–266.

Madell, G. (1981), *The Identity of the Self* (Edinburgh: Edinburgh University Press).

Mayeda, S., ed. and trans. (1992), *A Thousand Teachings: The Upadeśasāhasrī of Śaṅkara* (Albany, NY: State University of New York Press).

Metzinger, T. (2003), *Being No One* (Cambridge, MA: MIT Press).

Nagel, T. (1986), *The View from Nowhere* (New York: Oxford University Press).

Osborne, A., ed. (1997), *The Collected Works of Ramana Maharshi* (Boston, MA: Weiser Books).

Parfit, D. (1987), *Reasons and Persons* (Oxford: Clarendon Press).

Prabhavananda, S. and Isherwood, C., trans. (1978), *Shankara's Crest-Jewel of Discrimination (Viveka-Chudamani)* (Hollywood, CA: Vedanta Press).

Ram-Prasad, C. (2007), *Indian Philosophy and the Consequences of Knowledge: Themes in Ethics, Metaphysics and Soteriology* (Aldershot: Ashgate).

Rhys Davids, C. and Woodward, F. L., ed. and trans. (1972–79), *The Book of the Kindred Sayings (Samyutta-Nikāya)*, 5 vols. (London: Routledge & Kegan Paul).

Searle, J. R. (1992), *The Rediscovery of the Mind* (Cambridge, MA: MIT Press).

Sharma, A. (1993), *The Experiential Dimension of Advaita Vedānta* (Delhi: Motilal Banarsidass).

Siderits, M. (2003), *Personal Identity and Buddhist Philosophy: Empty Persons* (Aldershot: Ashgate).

Sinha, D. (1954), 'The Concept of Sākṣin in Advaita Vedānta', *Our Heritage* 2: 325–332.

Strawson, G. (2003), 'What Is the Relation between an Experience, the Subject of the Experience, and the Content of the Experience?' *Philosophical Issues* 13: 279–315.

Thibaut, G., ed. (1962), *The Vedānta-Sūtras with the Commentary by Śaṅkarācārya*, 2 vols. (Delhi: Motilal Banarsidass).

Timalsina, S. (2009), *Consciousness in Indian Philosophy: The Advaita Doctrine of 'Awareness Only'* (London: Routledge).

Watson, A. (2006), *The Self's Awareness of Itself: Bhaṭṭa Rāmakaṇṭha's Arguments against the Buddhist Doctrine of No-Self* (Wien: Sammlung de Nobili).

Williams, B. (1973), 'The Self and the Future', in *Problems of the Self: Philosophical Papers 1956–1972* (Cambridge: Cambridge University Press).

Zahavi, D. (1999), *Self-Awareness and Alterity: A Phenomenological Investigation* (Evanston, IL: Northwestern University Press).

——(2005), *Subjectivity and Selfhood: Investigating the First-Person Perspective* (Cambridge, MA: MIT Press).

8

Situating the Elusive Self of Advaita Vedānta[1]

CHAKRAVARTHI RAM-PRASAD

I. Introduction: Advaita and the Question of What is Denied When Self is Denied

In this essay, I will explore some ambiguities concerning what it is to affirm or deny the self, through the view of the Hindu school of Advaita Vedānta on the nature of the 'I' and its relationship to the reflexivity of consciousness. In particular, I will seek to situate this elusive self between my understanding of Dan Zahavi's notion of the minimal self (Zahavi 2005; 2009; and this volume) and one reading of the significance of Thomas Metzinger's brief but provocative comparisons of his denial of self with Advaita and Buddhism (Metzinger 2003: 549–50; 566).

As Zahavi (like others in this volume) observes in Section 4 of his essay, the boundaries between self and no-self theories depend on what the self is taken to be. Exposition of Buddhist denials of self in this volume range from Siderits' uncompromising reductionism all the way to Albahari's defence of a unitary and perspectival witness consciousness, which Zahavi points out appears to preserve many of the defining characteristics of theories of self. So it is clear that in the classical Indian traditions, within Buddhism itself, what it means to deny self is a highly disputed matter. So it is with the Hindu school of Advaita. As both Fasching's paper and mine show, the Advaitic assertion of self is not a straightforward matter, for other senses of self are denied by them that look intuitively necessary for a theory of self.

[1] I would like to thank Miri Albahari, Wolfgang Fasching, Jonardon Ganeri and, especially, Mark Siderits for responses to an earlier draft of this paper.

Let me begin to situate my reading of Advaita by first commenting on Albahari's position (this volume; and 2006). Drawing on the early Buddhist texts of the Pali Canon, Albahari argues that when the Buddhists deny 'self', they deny the ontological independence of a bounded consciousness tied to ownership. She proposes that we understand insight as leading to recognition of the constructedness of this sense of self, leaving only what, she maintains, is nirvana-consciousness—a perspectival, unitary, impersonal witness-consciousness. Such consciousness will be consistent with the intellectual conclusion that the subject of consciousness always eludes us, being its own object.

Some might argue that this sounds remarkably close to the witness-consciousness of Advaita explored in phenomenological terms by Fasching in this volume. Of course, that in itself is not a philosophical criticism of Albahari's position: it merely alerts the reader to the complexity of the debate about the borders of self/no-self. Later on, agreeing with Zahavi even while distinguishing the Advaitic position from his, I will make the point that Albahari's distinction between subjectivity and selfhood is one that Advaita rejects.

Although Fasching and I do not always use the same terminology to frame the Advaitic position, we agree on the elusiveness of the Advaitic self: the Advaitins reject both the generally understood Buddhist denial (*contra* Albahari) of the unity of consciousness, as well as the insistence on individuated or bounded inwardness that other Hindu schools require of self (*ātman*). Fasching provides a phenomenological critique of what he takes to be the Buddhist view that consciousness is momentary, by focusing on arguments for a continuous conscious presence which has changing experiences. I look more closely at a point he touches on, namely, the analysis of the use of the first-person in Advaita, and the role that analysis plays simultaneously in the denial of some senses of self and in the affirmation of a more mimimal unitary conscious presence. So, in a sense, my paper follows up on Fasching's, looking at the way in which unitary presence is, in some sense, 'self' for Advaitins.

2. The *ātman* as Self: Hindu Debates

The concept in Advaita that is going to be discussed in this essay is what may be called a formal self—the *ātman*. In the West, much later, Kant is the starting point for the discussion about formal selfhood, that is, selfhood that is not filled in by the specific content of experience (in short, personhood). His distinction between 'empirical apperception' (or 'inner sense' or 'inner experience') and 'transcendental apperception' which precedes all experience, sets in motion the tradition of analysis that distinguishes between the specific features of any person's sense of themselves as such-and-such a person, and the impersonal consciousness of self that is the ground for the possibility of the former (e.g. Kant: B132). In a very general sense, the Hindu thinkers are somewhat akin to Kant. They too hold that what one takes onself to be (the 'sense of self' or literally, '"I"-ness', *ahaṃkāra*), through experiences of psychological states and bodily conditions, is always shifting; Kant talks of 'empirical consciousness' that 'depends on circumstances or empirical conditions' (Kant: B140). Their concern is with something akin (in its function, rather than any explanatory feature) to Kant's 'pure apperception', namely, the *ātman*'s priority to empirical consciousness. There are, however, major disagreements among the Hindu or brahmanical schools themselves about what that *ātman* is, such that it is metaphysically distinguishable from shifting personhood.

David Velleman has made a distinction that, terminologically, and to a large extent conceptually, parallels mine. He comments that if two thinking substances share thoughts they are one *person*, whereas if there is access to (presumably to the content and perspective of) one another's first-personal thoughts, they are one and the same *self* (Velleman 1996: 75, n. 40; emphasis Velleman's). This is part of his larger distinction between what he calls identity and reflexivity, the first holding between persons at different times, the latter between subjects sharing first-personal terms (Velleman 1996: 65).[2] In any case, it is the perspectival presence, a consciousness of subjective unity, that is the point of disagreement in Indian philosophy. The question for the Indians is whether what is phenomenologically given—the experience, and the sense of a subject that is the ground condition for experience—is best explained by a genuine unity of consciousness, or whether that unity is itself a

---

[2] However, I approach the distinction with different concerns. Velleman calls the selfhood that holds between persons across times a metaphysical relation, and that which holds between first-person-sharing subjects a psychological one. To me, it seems as if it is the other way around: What makes for a person, through identification, are psychological ties, together with other factors such as narrative and social relationality, and what makes for subjective selfhood is the metaphysics by which a unity of consciousness holds across time. I am unsure whether this means we are talking of different things, whether this is purely terminological, or whether there is some important difference in approach here.

construct of experience, and if it is agreed that there is unity of consciousness, whether that points to a unified self. Buddhists, of course, generally deny that there is a unified self which generates unity of consciousness; through a wide range of positions, they maintain that that felt unity is constructed. Broadly, Hindu realists, like the Nyāya and Mīmāṃsā schools, hold that there is a unified self to which phenomenology points, which is the condition for the construction of the empirical person (although there are different theories abut how the nature and existence of that self is affirmed). The Advaita school holds that there is a unity of consciousness, but not that there is a unified self that happens to possess the quality of consciousness.

Nyāya and Mimāṃsā (as also the schools of Jainism) clearly assert the existence of a plurality of *ātmans*, understood as non-physical simple entities with the quality of consciousness, with each being (human or otherwise, whether a person or not) animated by an *ātman*. In short, while the *ātman* does individuate each person, its identity is purely formal, in that each *ātman* is ontologically distinct but has no further contentful distinctions, which latter are all tied to the specific features of the person. For Nyāya, the *ātman*, while the owner of the consciousness that thinks of *ātman* in the first place, is at the same time an object in the world, one of the categories (*padārtha*) that constitute reality.[3] In the rest of the essay, we will focus on Advaita, which also asserts the existence of *ātman*, and therefore falls under those who believe in 'self' against the Buddhists, but turns out to have a very different explanation for what that *ātman* is.

Advaita holds that consciousness can be understood in three ways. (One could say metaphorically, that the latter two are 'allotropes' of the first—of the same stuff ontologically, but with different structures and functions.) There is *brahman*, which is simply the name for consciousness as the universal and singular basis for all reality, and from which, in some sense, all reality is no different. Then there is *ātman*, which is the general name for

---

[3] In many ways, Nyāya's robust metaphysical realism about the *ātman* is closer to Thomas Nagel's idea of an objective self, in which, while it is contingently true that the self has a perspective on the world, it is itself only an element in that very world, so that the perspective it seeks is completely objective (the famous 'view from nowhere') (Nagel 1986). Even more pertinently, its position in some ways resembles Richard Swinburne's 'simple self' (1984), although we have to be careful about mapping the details of Swinburne's dualism onto the Hindu schools.

consciousness understood as the ground of every individuated being. Finally, there is the *jīva*, which, through its egoity (*ahaṃkāra*) is the empirical consciousness in the locus of every individuated being. The gnoseological project is the cultivation and disciplining of *jīva*-consciousness through analyzing away the inauthentic features of self found in egoity, so that the phenomenology of consciousness is purified to the point when only *ātman* as formal consciousness is left to, and for, itself; at the point of formal presence alone, the non-difference between the hitherto limited consciousness and that of the universal consciousness is realized.

We are not concerned here with either the gnoseological discipline or the cosmic ontology of Advaita. Rather, the focus will be on how consciousness as we know it, that phenomenal undergoing whose presence is the starting-point of investigation into selfhood, is understood in Advaita. In what follows, we will concentrate on the interplay between (i) the concept of *ahaṃkāra*—the construction of an 'I'—in the individuated consciousness of the *jīva* and (ii) the concept of *ātman* that is peculiar to Advaita. I want to locate this exploration within the context of the denial and affirmation of self found in Zahavi and Metzinger.

3. Metzinger's No One and Zahavi's Core Self

The contemporary research around which I want to build this analysis is a juxtaposition of Thomas Metzinger's denial of self and Dan Zahavi's assertion of a core self available in phenomenological consciousness. Let me begin with Zahavi, starting with his interpretation of the phenomenologists (Zahavi 2009). Zahavi reads Husserl and Heidegger as working with a distinction between (i) a self which is not a person as such and (ii) the personal self. Husserl says that the phenomenology of every possible subject of experience has only a peculiar mineness (*Meinheit*), different from the proper individuality of the person whose origin is in social life (Husserl 1989). Again, although this is a notoriously difficult topic, there are elements in Heidegger's concept of selfhood (*Dasein*) that appear to be getting at a core conception of the self in the phenomenological mineness of consciousness, when he distinguishes this from the everyday *Dasein*, which is an objectual form. For him, selfhood has these different modes, the first addressed by the question of 'who', which speaks of existence itself, and the other by 'what', which is that person who is present, or to hand, as the object of any investigation (Heidegger 1962: 62–77).[4] It would seem here that in both cases, the phenomenological core of being is a self that does not contain the constitutents of personal identity, the first-personal nature of awareness being the minimal structure of phenomenal consciousness. In this, all the brahmanical systems, barring Advaita, have a somewhat similar attitude toward the *ātman*, which is picked out by the 'I' (*aham*).

Drawing on phenomenology, Zahavi has eloquently made the distinction between a phenomenologically constitutive minimal self which is the perspectival subject, and a more extended sense of self, constituting personhood, given by a richer and more robust psycho-social being (Zahavi. 2005). Zahavi argues for a minimal conception of self, based on the phenomenology of mineness: he derives this conception from his interpretation of the German phenomenologists' notion of in-each-case-mineness (*Jemeinigkeit*), which he reads as 'formal individuation'. Again, although this leads to specific aspects of phenomenological interpretation, it has striking parallels with my reading of the nature of *ātman*, especially in the non-Advaitic brahmanical schools, as having only formal identity. For the Advaitins, this applies to the *jīva*, the *ātman* being the impersonal reflexivity of persistent consciousness, as we will see below.

The idea that consciousness is primarily about phenomenality–the what-it-is-likeness that conscious beings undergo–and the idea that that phenomenality contains within it the sense that a self undergoes it, were barely recognized in Anglophone philosophy twenty years ago. But now, even those who take their philosophy to derive from close study of cognitive science, like Thomas Metzinger, agree on these two points. But Metzinger has an interesting claim regarding the phenomenality of self, or the sense within consciousness that such consciousness is that of a self. His scepticism about the self starts with an examination of whether a study of the stable physical world can reveal anything that might count as a self. His claim, which has quickly become well known in the field, is that, 'nobody ever was or had a self' (Metzinger 2003: 1).

---

[4] There is also the further, very tricky issue of Heidegger's distinction between authentic and inauthentic modes of being the self, which has some resonance with the brahmanical search for a similar-sounding difference.

It seems to me that there are two approaches to take to Metzinger. One concerns his theory of the basis of consciousness (from which the illusion of self is said to derive), and it is broadly physicalist. Another concerns his account of how consciousness (howsoever constituted) generates a sense of self that is somehow illusory. It is the latter in which I am interested. Of course, this means that one can look at his entire book as a physicalist reduction of self. But that these issues can also be read separately can be seen in the fact that Metzinger himself explicitly compares his claims about self with Plato, Śaṅkara, and the Buddhists—none of whom, he will know very well, could possibly be physicalists about consciousness. Surely it is with some deliberation that he makes these comparisons, and that seems sufficient for my purpose of bracketing possible issues about the basis of consciousness (i.e. whether it be physicalist or not), and looking at the way a self is presented in phenomenality. (Despite his own effort at comparison, nothing I say here implies that I read Metzinger as agreeing with the ontological claims of Advaita, or most traditional Buddhist positions for that matter.) My focus, then, is on Metzinger's view that a model of self is generated in and by consciousness, such that there appears to be an owner for phenomenality.

Now, Metzinger cites both the Buddhists and, importantly for my purposes, Śaṅkara (the founder of Advaita Vedānta), as holding a position comparable to his own (Metzinger 2003: 550; 566), so far as the illusion of self is concerned. With regard to the former, he compares his conception of selflessness with the Buddhist conception of 'enlightenment'; with the latter, he finds a common concern to argue that what is identified as self is in some metaphorical sense a 'shadow' of self-consciousness. I take it, then, that he himself is not too concerned with the differences between his scientific concerns and the gnoseological ones of the Indians.

Turning then to some details of Metzinger's position, one line of his argument against belief in a self is that the self-identification with body and the rest by phenomenal awareness—that is to say, the identity that consciousness takes by associating itself with its content—generates an illusion. Insofar as both Śaṅkara and the Buddhists maintain that what consciousness constructs or generates as an individual self, from out of its phenomenal inputs, is an illusion at some level, then Metzinger is right in citing them both. He argues that the phenomenology of consciousness is itself wrong when it appears to yield a self to whom that consciousness belongs. His complex and ground-breaking book is impossible to summarize but the relevant argument (Metzinger 2003: 547–99) is that consciousness is a system whose function of transparently representing the world includes building into itself a perspectival grasp of that world, and that perspectival quality consists in a model of a phenomenal self whose construction is transparent (i.e. not apparent) to the conscious system. In other words, just so the conscious organism can function for survival, it requires representing the world from a (its) perspective; and the way to do that is to generate a sense that there is someone, a subject from whose perspective the world is experienced, and to whom that experience happens. In that way, all the distinctions and lack of confusion between 'you' and 'me' that ordinary consciousness possesses are delivered. But there is no real self which is the subject of experience, if by subject is meant a metaphysical entity whose capacity to be conscious explains the perspectival nature of consciousness' presence to itself. There is only a model of a phenomenal self built into the representational functions of consciousness. It is impossible to both preserve that sense of self and become convinced that intuitively there is no such self. Either 'I' continue to function with that illusion necessary for perspectival functioning or—radically—the consciousness 'here' reconfigures its entire global model of what it is to be phenomenal and enters a cognitively lucid way of functioning in which there is no self-ascription of experience at all (Metzinger 2003: 626–7).

It is this latter possibility that prompts Metzinger to suggest that there are similarities in his view with Asian notions of enlightenment. In short, Metzinger is not only reducing away the social dimensions of personhood, he is also saying that the I-ness of phenomenal consciousness is just a model and not 'real'—by which he means not a metaphysical object.

Zahavi, in contrast, reads phenomenal consciousness as that of a self: he affirms 'the subject(ivity) of experience' (Zahavi 2005: 146), in effect arguing that subjectivity simply is the presence of a subject in, and of, awareness. The self that Zahavi is interested in asserting as minimal but real is precisely what is provided in phenomenal consciousness (or 'experience'): a persistent presence in its own occurrence (Zahavi 2005: 128). But this indicates that he may not necessarily be involved in a metaphysical disagreement with Metzinger so much as a conceptual one. If Metzinger starts by granting that the phenomenality of the self is given—that consciousness contains consciousness that it is/appears to be a self's consciousness—then Metzinger has granted enough for his, Zahavi's, purposes.[5] Zahavi is not interested in defending conventional Western theories of a substantial self that Metzinger rejects.

Two main points relevant to my interpretation of Advaita emerge: First, there is a self-model in phenomenal consciousness, which is not a self (Metzinger 2003: 550); under this model, where presence is transparent to consciousness, phenomenality is represented as a relationship between a perspectival subject (the 'self') and its objects. In that sense, Metzinger does bear similarity to Advaitins and Buddhists, in charging that the self built out of the interaction of consciousness and world (howsoever their ontological status is conceived) is illusory, and not a legitimate type of selfhood.[6] Secondly, however, in stating that, if phenomenal consciousness does not depend on an independent self whose consciousness it is, then there is no self at all, Metzinger is only denying particular conceptions of selfhood, which require 'an "individual" in the sense of philosophical metaphysics' (Metzinger 2003: 563). That would include such theories as those of the Hindu schools of Nyāya or Mīmāṃsā, for whom consciousness is a quality of the ātman, and therefore secondary to its existence. For Naiyāyikas or Mīmāṃsakas, if phenomenal consciousness has perspective (i.e. is structured as being from some specific perspective, that of the self) that is only because there is actually a self which possesses that consciousness. For them, the transparency of consciousness to its objects is explicable through there being a subject-self which directly grasps those objects at all only because it possesses the determinative quality of consciousness (Ram-Prasad 2001: chs. 1 and 2).

In arguing that consciousness is not intrinsically that of an individual self, even a minimally phenomenological one, Metzinger does offer a view that has something in common with Advaita and with (most conventional interpretations of) Buddhism. Zahavi might simply decide that that is sufficient to call that consciousness a minimal self, just because that is how

---

[5] Zahavi in correspondence.

[6] Zahavi, by contrast, wants a different account of this sort of self, an extended and richer self which is equally real, but on an account different from the strict phenomenological one. Incidentally, there is much in the classical Indian material on such a view, in which the socially embedded person, regardless of his or her constructivity, is still an ethically relevant and real entity, whose metaphysical status does not alter the significance of virtue and conduct. This is the so-called 'human-ends' (puṣārtha)-oriented view concerned with dharma or the ordered, virtuous life.

experience phenomenologically represents it. There is then an ambiguity over how the very idea of a 'self' (in the ātmanic sense) should be understood. This ambiguity over whether what is left as core consciousness is a self or not is precisely what is evident in the Advaitic use of *ātman*.

For the Advaitins, authentic self (*ātman*)—the core, undeniable presence that is the ground of phenomenological content—is not about individuality. The sense of an individual locus of consciousness—consciousness as *jīva*—is not the final stage of analysis. This is because, according to them, *jīva* consciousness functions through the instruments (*kāraṇa*) and objects (*kārya*) of embodiment (*śarīratva*) (Śaṅkara 1917: 254–5). Perception and other cognitive activities that are structured in the subject–object relation are, of course, possible only in consciousness individuated through its psychophysical apparatus of mental operations, senses, etc. But that sense of individuated selfhood is consciousness functioning (*kṛtam*) through 'adjuncts' (*upādhi*-s), that is, the intellectual faculty (*buddhi*) of conceptualization, the perceptual organs, etc.; consciousness is not that of an individual self (Śaṅkara 1913: 487). The Advaitin rejects the idea of an individual self which happens to possess the capacity for consciousness. Rather, what the Advaitin calls *ātman* is not the 'seeing of the seen'—because that would simply imply a subject in relation to its object—but the 'seer of the seeing' itself (Śaṅkara 1914: 161–2)—in short, reflexive subjectivity as such. Advaita therefore has a complex and ambiguous view of the perspectival nature of consciousness: on the one hand admitting that that is constitutive of subjectivity, and on the other denying that that implies an individual subject. It is in its analysis of the 'I' of consciousness that we perhaps find a radical way of cutting across the apparently rival accounts of Metzinger and Zahavi.

4. Exploring the 'I' and its Peculiarities in Advaita

We now turn to looking at the details of the Advaitic analysis of 'I' and the way in which this analysis shows how it may be possible to deny egology, even while affirming a unified consciousness that can be termed 'self'. Philosophical systems committed to a metaphysically robust self routinely relate it to the reflexive pronoun; whatever the precise details of their theory, they tend to see the 'I' as somehow naming a self. In the classical Indian schools, there is a common gnoseological concern to determine features of selfhood that mislead the seeker into continued entanglement with the world of suffering and metaphysical misunderstanding. Carefully delineating the many features of bodily, psychological, ethical, relational, and social existence that make up a sense of selfhood, the philosophers argue that these are not, in fact, truly constitutive of one's being, and that it is only through profoundly transformative realization of this truth that there is liberation from the conditions of suffering. Of course, the Buddhist schools deny there is anything ultimately constitutive of being at all, although they disagree amongst themselves as to how such a misleading constitution of selfhood occurs and how it should be discarded. The brahmanical schools, including the other main Vedānta schools, Viśiṣṭādvaita and Dvaita, generally tend to distinguish between these misleading senses of selfhood—which they term egoity (ahaṃkāra, the made-up-'I')—and the authentic self—which is picked out in some way by the reflexive pronoun 'I' (aham).

In order to appreciate the strangeness of the Advaitic position, we can compare it to more intuitive accounts given by other Hindu schools. In the school of Mīmāṃsā (or rather, within it, a sub-school called the Bhāṭṭa), for example, Kumārila argues for two things at the same time: the self makes infallibly veridical reflexive reference to itself through 'I'-thoughts which take it as their object, yet, the features to which these 'I'- thoughts relate the self, like bodily qualities and activities, are themselves not part of the self. On the one hand, the very locution 'my self' (mamātmeti) indictates that the primary meaning (mukhyārtha) of the first-person cannot apply to anything other than the self. On the other, locutions regarding my body indicate a distinction between the self and the body (Kumārila: 125–134). Pārthasārathi Miśra defends this combination of claims. He says that the cognizing subject is the object of the 'I'-thought (ahampratyaya). When one apprehends (parāmṛśati), one apprehends two things: the self as 'I' and something else as 'this'. At the same time, when the apprehension is of the form, 'I am thin' or 'I go', the being thin and the going are distinct from the self. This is grammatically indicated by the use of the genitive case, for what is actually implied is, 'this, my body, is thin', and what is mine (the being thin or the going) is not me. The 'detrimental effect of intimacy' (saṃsargadoṣa) between self and its embodiment creates the illusion that, in the case of qualities pertaining to the embodied self (the person), those qualities are somehow constitutive of the ātmanic self (Pārthasārathi: 121). The Bhāṭṭa

Mīmāṃsakas maintain that awareness requires embodiment: without body, there is no consciousness for the self.[7]

The Naiyāyikas have a somewhat similar view of the matter. The 'I' picks out the self. The self (i.e. *ātman*) cannot have experience (*bhoga*) without embodiment (Vātsyāyana: 1.1.22; 35). Vātsyāyana also states that the fundamental erroneous cognition (*mithyājñānam*) consists in taking what is not the self as the self; this is the delusion (*moha*) of egoity. Egoity consists in taking the body (*śarīra*), the senses (the *indriya*-s), the mind (*manas*), feelings (*vedanā*-s) and the intellectual faculty (*buddhi*) to be self (Vātsyāyana: 4.2.1, p. 288) This is not to say that these thinkers reject any association of selfhood with psychological states or the conception of their body as an object in the world. They understand, to repeat the point made at the beginning of the essay, that this extended sense of self is intimately connected with the rich features of the life of a person, that only the direct way of referring to the embodied person is possible in ordinary language. All conduct and experience require understanding oneself to be a person who takes a trajectory through the world. But the gnoseological interest in these features of extended selfhood—emotions, attachments, revulsion, relationships, physical features, bodily activities—lies in analysing their separateness from the irreducible self, the *ātman*, which they believe is picked out by the referential use of the 'I', independently of the ascriptions of personhood.

I have given these other views in order to demonstrate that many brahmanical thinkers tend to do three things simultaneously: (i) They assert that what the 'I' designates, without ascription of particular states or qualities, is the *ātman*, that is, the authentic self. (ii) They deploy, in contrast, the concept of egoity—'I'-ness—as a fraudulent (*sopadha*) sense of selfhood (Udayana: 377) which, for all its psychological and social vitality (or, indeed, precisely because of that), needs to be analyzed insightfully in the gnoseological project of attaining liberation. (iii) At the same time, they allow any and every conscious state—those that actually occur in life—invariably to take the form of associating the 'I' with qualities (sick, sad, tall). So the condition of life consists in the ascription of a sense of self that is always extended beyond what the self truly is. (That the analytic distinction

---

[7] J. L. Mackie makes a similar distinction (although, of course, for very different purposes), saying that there are two different rules for the use of 'I': one linking it directly to the human being, and the other, to the subject, whatever it may be (Mackie 1980: 56).

between the transcendental 'I' and all its ascribed qualities is in fact a meta-physical one between true and inauthentic selves is a further argument within that project. But finally, both Bhāṭṭas and Naiyāyikas argue that the 'I', when stripped of all ascriptions, is the self free of all personal qualities.)

The Advaitins, on the other hand, say something much more radical: the 'I' itself is part of egoity, everything about it is made up. The 'I' simply does not pick out *ātman*. They are sensitive to the actual function of the ego in the life of human beings, but given their interpretation of *ātman*, the individuation denoted by the 'I' is precisely what they must reject.

Śaṅkara notes that there can be no account of the epistemic life which does not involve the use of the reflexive pronoun in all its psychological complexity. Without the appropriation (*abhimāna*—a possessive pride) that 'I' and 'mine' deliver, there can be no epistemic subject (*pramātṛ*) and the operation of the epistemic instruments (the *pramāṇas*). Vācaspati, in his commentary on Śaṅkara, explains how this extended and gnoseologically misleading sense of self functions through two types of paradigmatic asser-tions: 'I am this' and 'this is mine'. The first, primary claim of identity between *ātman* and the bodily apparatus individuates the self, and distin-guishes it from other loci of such identification. The secondary claim is an appropriation of relationships, in which the individuated being's identity becomes extended socially; 'this is my son' is Vācaspati's example. The self's two-fold (*dvividha*) appropriation sustains the march of the world (*lokayā-tram*), including the means for the attainment of liberation (Vācaspati:154).

The Advaitins go so far as to say that all uses of the reflexive pronoun only pick out the extended self, the person, and not the authentic, 'innermost *ātman*' (*pratyagātman*). The Mīmāṃsaka might say that the misleading inti-macy that leads to erroneous identification is between the 'I' and the qualities attributed through the 'this'. But the Advaitin says this intimacy is in fact between consciousness as such and the 'I' (which are co-present like fire and wood are burner and burnt, in Sureśvara's picturesque analogy). The 'I' too is truly just a 'this' for the seer (Sureśvara: 3.59, 3.61). This suggests that even the barest awareness of individuation—howsoever stripped of specific thoughts or feelings or perceptions—does not desig-nate the *ātman*; it only designates the individuated self represented in consciousness (i.e. *jīva*-consciousness).

In common with the other schools, the Advaitins agree that the 'I' picks out an object idiosyncratically: the user of the 'I' succeeds in referring to that very user and it alone. They agree with their brahmanical interlocutors that the states the 'I'-usage represents the subject as being are not themselves part of the authentic self. But they part company with the others when it comes to the claim that the bare consciousness of self present in the 'I' is in fact the *ātman*. Here we must be very careful in seeing just what is going on. The Advaitins do not disagree with the others that the 'I'-form picks out something uniquely and idiosyncratically, and that, moreover, there is a plurality of such entities, each with its own locus of awareness. But whereas the others call this the *ātman*, and take it as an element in the ultimate order of metaphysical existence, the Advaitins call it the form of consciousness-as-*jīva*. In other words, they argue that 'I' only designates a constructed self, namely, a representation of consciousness individuated by and through its psychophysical locus. What the Advaitins call *ātman*, however, is not the self of individuated consciousness. For them, *ātman* is simply the consciousness itself that does the taking (we can say, using the Metzingerian term, 'the modeling') of itself as an individual. Consciousness as such is not designated even by the bare 'I'.

If by the use of the word 'self' we mean necessarily an individuated locus of consciousness idiosyncratically designated by the 'I', then the *ātman* of the Advaitins is not a self at all, for they reject mineness as a fundamental feature of reality, arguing that appropriation is a mark of the inauthentic self. At the same time, there is a more nebulous usage of 'self', which adverts to the quintessential nature, the very basis of a being's reality, which is what makes it what it is. Now, our standard view of the fundamental nature of a being is construed in terms of distinguishing it from what it is not. In the other brahmanical systems, the 'I' functions admirably to thus distinguish the *ātman* which uses it idiosyncratically from all others who use it in their own way. So we find it reasonable to think that the *ātman* should be translated as 'self' for them, howsoever different this usage is from the richer notions of personhood found in the larger tradition. But if the whole point of the Advaitic *ātman* is to deny ultimate distinction between individual loci of consciousness and treat it simply as the generic name for reflexive presence, then it does seem strange to use the word 'self' for it.

What then does the 'I' pick out (because, after all, it does function to designate something idiosyncratically)? The 'I' in fact refers to the mind, for the Advaitins. The mind for them is an internal organ or mechanism (*antaḥkaraṇa*), in itself part of the physical functions of the body. The classical Indians, of course, had no knowledge of the microstructures of the brain, but by taking the mind to be some sort of 'subtle' (*sūkṣma*) but physical internal cognitive organ, they treat it very physicalistically, as something that can be described entirely through its content. Consciousness is truly only that aspect of phenomenology which is reflexive, that is, the constant accompaniment of being present, which renders an event something that the subject undergoes. But what consciousness takes to be happening to its (constructed) subject is in fact a process represented in the content of the mental processes with which it is associated. The analytic separation of awareness from, say, my feeling of sadness and its ascription, is phenomenologically occluded: I feel sad and recognize it thus; the consciousness here is not aware that the sadness is only associated with a sense of mineness which is itself constructed. There are three elements for the Advaitin here: the 'I'; the sadness as a state of the subject, as detected by the internal organ; and the awareness that this is so ascribed to the superimposed 'I'. The Advaitins urge us to recognize that the occlusion is because of egoity. Egoity is that function of the mind whereby the (non-aware) mind's contents are associated with the (ātmanic) awareness, in that awareness is not aware that it has constructed a first-person ascription: in other words, the constructed self is transparent to consciousness.

The 'I', then, lies in the domain of objective usage, albeit in the specially restricted indexical sense that it can be used truthfully only by each user him/herself, where this user-specificity is determined by the location of consciousness within a body. In fact, in Sureśvara's formulation (Sureśvara: 3.60), first-personal ascriptivity is a specific mental function: it is the operation of the internal organ (*antaḥkaraṇa*) as delimited (*avacchinna*) by the 'I'-state (*ahaṃvṛtti*). As he puts it, 'putting on the cloak of the "I" (*ahaṃkañcukaṃ paridhāya*), the self associates itself with things external to it, whether they be helpful or harmful' (Sureśvara: 3.60). Mental functions occur in two ways: first, they operate in the 'revealer-revealed' (*avabhāsaka-avabhāsya*) relationship with the self, in which consciousness reveals (or takes itself to relate to) the 'I'-function of the mind; this is why consciousness has the illusion that it is familiar with an object called 'itself'. The mind becomes the idiosyncratically possessed object of consciousness, through the unique use of the 'I' in ascribing its contents to that consciousness. Second, mental functions operate in a helped–helper (*upakārya-upakāraka*) relationship with objects, in that the objects help to structure 'I'-thoughts ('I want this pen'; 'I do not want that poison'). It thereby allows consciousness to take itself to relate meaningfully with the world, even if erroneously.[8]

The Advaitins themselves obey the normal grammatical uses of the first-person pronoun, although they do mark out their special usage of the 'I' as mind-wrought object too. For the former, they use the conventional cases (*vibhaktyaḥ*) for the first person, for example the genitive is 'mine' (*mama*). But when signifying the use of the 'I' as a metaphysically important object— that which is associated with, but is not the self (*ātman*) as such—they are capable of treating it as a special sort of proper name, so that, with the genitive case, they use the locution 'I's' (*ahamasya*) like one would use 'Rāma's' (*rāmasya*).[9] Sureśvara also says that the self (*ātman*) is the secondary meaning (*lakṣyārtha*) of 'I' by virtue of its association with the mind. The 'I' is extremely helpful for self-realization (*ātmadṛṣṭya*), and the self should therefore be seen to be implied by the use of the 'I' (Sureśvara: 2.55).

5. The Elusive Advaitic Self

What this account shows is a position that interestingly combines features of Metzinger and Zahavi. Regarding the former, for the Advaitin too there is no *one* indeed. For Metzinger, there is consciousness here that generates a sense of 'I', as that which picks out an individual self; phenomenal self-consciousness represents mineness, a sense of ownership whose construction is not spotted by the consciousness which constructs it, because its modeling is transparent (Metzinger 2003: 562). For the Advaitin, consciousness of individuality is an illusion: *ātman* is not one particular entity but the consciousness which mistakenly generates individuality.[10]

Regarding Zahavi, the Advaitin shares the notion of core consciousness with him. Zahavi's argument is that phenomenological investigation simply presents the 'subjectivity of experience', the denial of which (by Metzinger)

---

[8] *Ibid.*; Balasubramanian's editorial commentary here is extremely helpful.

[9] I must thank Nirmalya Guha for his insightful understanding of this usage in Advaita.

[10] Of course, this consciousness is also transcendental for the Advaitin, for in the manner of Kant, it is the prerequisite, the ground, for the phenomena of individual consciousness. Incidentally, Metzinger is dismissive of Kant, and resolutely avoids the terminology of transcendental metaphysics, but one could ask whether his 'system', which models the phenomenal self, is not in some sense a transcendental requirement. The possible response that reductive physicalisms do not require transcendental arguments requires a discussion that will take us beyond the remit of this essay.

seems 'unnecessarily restrictive' (Zahavi 2005: 128). He is aware that his minimal self is 'overly inclusive' and the comparison with Advaita's insistence on its notion of consciousness being also one of self certainly seems very lax too. In general, his careful distinction between core and extended self also fits my interpretation of Advaita comfortably. In his essay in this volume, he reiterates his view that the 'givenness' of the unity of consciousness is also a 'mineness'. But, unlike Zahavi, the Advaitins will resist seeing this reflexivity as a perfectly natural appropriative and ascriptive 'mine'. For them, any mineness is empty unless it is about some specific quality or representation—but then, that is not the core consciousness that provides the very possibility of phenemology but is itself not found in phenomenological content. Earlier Advaitins did not recognize immediately that the combination of denying the 'I' and affirming the presence of unified consciousness requires more understanding of how consciousness relates to perspectival phenomenology. Later Advaitins concentrated on this via the theory of 'auto-luminosity' (*svataḥ-prakāśa vāda*). We will now turn briefly to this theory, in order to see how they seek to approach perspectival presence without first-personal usage.

6. The Reflexivity of Consciousness

Analytic philosophers have sometimes thought that the phenomenal presence of consciousness to itself (what the phenomenologists had talked about as the essential mark of the self) is actually about the self-consciousness of any particular conscious state. The Indian debate that can address the mix-up of the phenomenology of mineness and the analytic self-consciousness of consciousness is actually the one about whether, whatever the way in which self-consciousness is secured, the consciousness that possess that feature is a persistent entity or not. The question of whether a stream of self-conscious states—that is, whether phenomenal continuity—implies a self, is now being tackled in the philosophy literature (Dainton 2005: 1–25). An extended and elaborate debate on this, of course, is central to the Buddhist-Hindu debates of classical India. The outline of a specific Advaitic critique of the Buddhist position therefore also shows the potential of that hoary debate to contribute to current inquiry into the relationship between individual moments of self-consciousness and the possibility of a conscious self.

The classical Indians do not conflate these two debates. They have a separate debate on the constitutive nature, the presence as it were, of consciousness. This takes the form of auto- and hetero-luminosity (*svataḥ* and *parataḥ prakāśa*) theories, on how consciousness 'illuminates', that is, in what phenomenality consists. This debate is initiated with the terminologically different, but conceptually similar, *svasaṃvedana* doctrine of the Buddhist Dignāga. In effect, it looks at the self-consciousness of consciousness, but clarifies that it is not about the question of the self (even if intimately connected to it).

In general, earlier Advaitins simply assert the self-evident nature of (the phenomenality of) consciousness to consist in its reflexive access to itself: the self's intrinsic nature is of being ever-present (*sarvadā vartamānasvabhā-vatvāt*) (Śaṅkara 1917: 2.3.7; 585). (Fasching too, in this volume, deals with the notion of presence in Advaita.) In short, the self has nothing to mediate its access to itself. By contrast, knowledge of things is mediated by transactions involving epistemic instruments and their objects (*pramāṇaprameyavyavahāra*). To say that something is known is for there to be (i) the subject of knowledge (*pramātā*), (ii) its object and (iii) the mediation of epistemic instruments such as perception and its organs. But the self has no such distinction between itself and its awareness of itself. So the self is not an object of knowledge (Sureśvara: 2.98; *ātmano aprameyatvam*). By 'object', the Advaitins mean precisely that—things in the world that are accessible to epistemic instruments. The Naiyāyikas would hold that that exhausts all the elements of any ontology. But the Advaitins cannot mean quite that: indeed, quite the opposite, because in their ontology, there ultimately and irreducibly exists only universal consciousness—precisely that which is not an object! So they must be distinguishing between that entity alone which is real—consciousness—and objects of knowledge, which have some sort of sub-real, provisional, transactional existence.[11] In that sense, they are committed to cognitive closure, a denial that epistemic states can ever take the subjectivity of the epistemic agent—that is, consciousness as such—as their content.

---

[11] On the Advaitic position on the status of the world of objects through a variety of concepts, see Ram-Prasad 2002.

As it became clear that others—especially the Naiyāyikas and the different sub-schools of the Mīmāṃsakas—interpreted the nature of the self and its consciousness very differently, later Advaitins sought to define more precisely their understanding of the presence of consciousness to itself as its 'autoluminosity'.[12] The aim of these later works[13] is to clarify that the distinctive and constitutive feature of consciousness is its transparency to itself: all content is presented as if to the perspective of a particular subject, while in reality, consciousness is the 'pure' presence of itself to its own occurrence, which does not in fact enter into the content of specific mental states. Following the earlier Advaitic position, the most important feature of the definition of the autoluminosity of consciousness is that it is unknowable (avedyatva). This is not the self-defeating claim that nothing can be known about consciousness, since that very fact could be known about it. Madhusūdana points out that what is known is the theoretical claim about the nature of consciousness as unknowable in the strict sense in which knowable things are objects of epistemic procedures like perception and inference, but consciousness itself is that which is aware (i.e. that which is only ever the subject) of the claims regarding its nature and never the actual object.

The Advaitins therefore deny many different sorts of self, and what they affirm is hardly self in any recognizable way, apart from the reflexivity of consciousness being, in some very abstract sense, the essence of consciousness, the 'self' of consciousness. In effect, they assert a stable subjectivity, or a unity of consciousness through all the specific states of individuated phenomenality, but not an individual subject of consciousness. What we see here is that, unlike Zahavi (in this volume, section 4, response 2), the Advaitins split immanent reflexivity from 'mineness'. At the same time, like him, they do not think selfhood can be distinguished from subjectivity. They therefore insist that they are committed to self and reject no-self views.

---

[12] A more detailed and systematic taxonomy of position, looking at Yogācāra-Madhyamaka (the Yogācārins being the first to comment on the constitutive nature of consciousness), Bhāṭṭa and Prābhākara Mīmāṃsā, Nyāya and Advaita is given in chapter 2 of Ram-Prasad 2007.

[13] The locus classicus is Citsukha's *Tattvapradīpikā* (Citsukha: 1–5) with Madhusūdana Sarasvatī's clarifications on the same topic in the *Advaitasiddhi* (Madhusūdana Sarasvatī: 767–9).

7. Conclusion

Metzinger's argument that the constructedness of the individual self is transparent to consciousness appears to apply equally to both Advaita and most schools of Buddhism. If we set aside the historical development of a Buddhist commitment to the view that all elements of reality, consciousness included (or consciousness alone if it constructs the rest of reality), are momentary, then Metzinger might be made to fit some reinterpretations of both Advaita and Buddhism. After all, in this volume, Albahari sets aside the reality of momentariness within a Buddhist denial of self. However, if more conventional interpretations of Buddhism preserve the doctrine of momentariness, then a Metzingerian account that does not appear to require any denial of a unified system of consciousness, nor ask explicitly for consciousness to be a sequence of momentary states, appears more easily to allow of a cross-cultural comparison with Advaita than with Buddhism. This is because the heart of the Advaitic critique of Buddhism is a two-fold argument: one in support of the unity of consciousness, and the other against the doctrine of momentariness (Śaṅkara 1917: 2.2.18–25). (Fasching has more to say about both these Advaitic arguments, albeit from another text attributed to Śaṅkara.) But in the end, the interesting point about Metzinger is that he seems to offer possibilities for cross-cultural articulations (both Advaitic and Buddhist) of how our most robust and intuitive sense of self might be an illusion, intrinsic though it may be to how consciousness functions in relation to the world.

Zahavi certainly yields riches for the cross-cultural philosophy of self, his concept of the minimal self being very amenable to being read through Advaitic lenses. The slight differences in emphasis between my paper and Fasching's—especially my argument that the Advaitic position is somewhat more radical than Zahavi when it comes to the first-person—drives home the point that there is still much to be done with such genuine cross-cultural philosophical engagement.

Advaitins, then, within the specific debate about the nature and existence of the formal subject-self (*ātman*) of phenomenal consciousness, while seeming to side against the Buddhists in affirming the existence of *ātman*, mean something very different about it than the objective self with the quality of consciousness espoused by Nyāya or Mīmāṃsā. Their insistence that the irreducible essence of being is subjectivity, rather than an objective self with the quality of being conscious, seems somewhat akin to some versions of Buddhist denial of *ātman*. Advaitins also take that subjectivity to be unified, not consisting of a process of momentary events, while yet denying that the use of the 'I' accurately picks out such a unified consciousness. The ātmanic self of Advaita is indeed an elusive one. That was its gnoseological attraction to the tradition and that is its philosophical interest today.

Bibliography

Albahari, M. (2006), *Analytical Buddhism* (New York: Macmillan).

Baker, L. (1998), 'The first-person perspective: A test for naturalism', *American Philosophical Quarterly* 35: 327–47.

Citsukha (1956), *Tattvapradīpikā*, ed. Swami Yogindrananda (Varanasi: Udasina Samskrta Vidyalaya).

Dainton, B. (2005), 'The Self and the Phenomenal', in Galen Strawson (ed.), *The Self?* (Oxford: Blackwell).

Duerlinger, J. (2003), *Indian Buddhist Theories of Persons: Vasubandhu's 'Refutation of the Theory of a Self'* (London: RoutledgeCurzon).

Ganeri, J. (2007), *The Concealed Art of the Soul* (Oxford: Oxford University Press).

Heidegger, M. (1962), *Being and Time*, trans. John Macquarrie and Edward Robinson (Oxford: Blackwell).

Husserl, E. (1989), *Ideas Pertaining to a Pure Phenomenology and to a Phenomenological Philosophy—Second Book: Studies in the Phenomenology of Constitution*, trans. R. Rojcewicz and A. Schuwer (Dordrecht: Kluwer).

Kant, I. (1933), *The Critique of Pure Reason*, trans. Norman Kemp Smith (London: Macmillan).

Kumārila Bhaṭṭa (1899), *Ślokavārttika*, ed. Ramasastri Tailanga (Benares: Chowkambha Sanskrit Series).

Locke, J. (1979), *An Essay Concerning Human Understanding*, ed. P. Nidditch (Oxford: Clarendon Press).

Mackie, J. L. (1980), 'The Transcendental "I"', in Zak van Straaten (ed.), *Philosophical Subjects: Essays Presented to P. F. Strawson* (Oxford: Clarendon Press).

Madhusūdana Sarasvatī (2005), *Advaitasiddhi*, ed. N. S. Ananta Krishna Sastri (Delhi: Parimal Publications).

Metzinger, T. (2003), *Being No One* (Cambridge, MA.: MIT Press).

Nagel, T. (1986), *The View from Nowhere* (Oxford: Oxford University Press).

Pārthasārathi Miśra (1915), *Śāstradīpikā*, ed. Dharmadatta Suri (Bombay: Nirnaya-sagar Press).

Ram-Prasad, C. (2001), *Knowledge and Liberation in Classical Indian Thought* (Basingstoke: Palgrave).

——(2002), *Advaita Epistemology and Metaphysics: An Outline of Indian Non-Realism* (London: RoutledgeCurzon).

——(2007), *Indian Philosophy and the Consequences of Knowledge* (Aldershot: Ashgate).

Śaṅkara (1913), *Katha upaniṣadbhāṣya*, ed. Rajavade Sarma (Poona: Anandashrama Sanskrit Series).

Śaṅkara (1914), *Bṛhadāraṇyaka upaniṣadbhāṣya*, ed. Kasinatha Sastri Agase (Poona: Anandashrama Sanskrit Series).

Śaṅkara (1917), *Brahmasūtrabhāṣya* with Vācaspati's *Bhāmatī*, ed. N. A. Krishna Shastri and V. L. Sastri Pansikar (Bombay: Nirnayasagar Press).

Sureśvara (1988), *Naiṣkarmyasiddhi*, ed. R. Balasubramaniam (Madras: Madras University Press).

Swinburne, R. (1984), 'Personal Identity: the Dualist Theory', in Sydney Shoemaker and Richard Swinburne, *Personal Identity* (Oxford: Blackwell).

Udayana (1995), *Ātmattvaviveka*, ed. N. S. Dravid (Shimla: Indian Institute of Advanced Study).

Vācaspati, *Bhāmatī*. See Śaṅkara 1917.

Vātsyāyana (1939), *Nyāyabhāṣya* to Gautama's *Nyāyasūtra*, ed. Ganganatha Jha (Poona: Poona Book Agency).

Velleman, D. (1996), 'Self to Self', *The Philosophical Review* 105.4: 39–76.

Zahavi, D. (2005), *Subjectivity and Selfhood. Investigating the First-Person Perspective* (Cambridge, MA.: MIT Press).

——(2009), 'Is the self a social construct?' *Inquiry* 52.6: 551–73.

9

Enacting the Self: Buddhist and Enactivist Approaches to the Emergence of the Self

MATTHEW MACKENZIE

I. Introduction

The conception of the self as a substance separate from the body and the rest of the natural world (e.g. the Cartesian ego) is widely rejected today. Yet many accounts of the self are developed based on assumptions, such as substantialism and objectivism, that arguably remain basically Cartesian (cf. Dennett 1991; Metzinger 2003). In contrast, both Buddhism and en-activism present fruitful alternatives to broadly Cartesian approaches to cognition, subjectivity, embodiment, and the nature of the self. Indeed, the enactive approach to cognition and its allied method of neurophenomenology explicitly and systematically draw from Buddhist thinkers, ideas, and practices in order to move beyond Cartesianism. In this paper, I take up the problem of the self through bringing together the insights, while correcting some of the shortcomings, of Indo-Tibetan Buddhist and en-activist accounts of the self. I begin with an examination of the Buddhist theory of non-self (*anātman*), and the rigorously reductionist interpretation of this doctrine developed by the Abhidharma school of Buddhism. After discussing some of the fundamental problems for Buddhist reductionism, I turn to the enactive approach to philosophy of mind and cognitive science. In particular, I argue that human beings, as dynamic systems, are character-ized by a high degree of self-organizing autonomy. Therefore, human beings are not reducible to the more basic mental and physical events that constitute them. In a similar vein, Francisco Varela argues that the self emerges through the processes of self-organization, and that the self is thus merely *virtual* (Varela 1999). I critically examine Varela's enactivist account of the self as virtual, and his use of Buddhist ideas in support of this view. I argue, in contrast, that while the self is emergent and constructed, it is not merely virtual. Finally, I sketch a Buddhist-enactivist account of the self. I argue for a non-reductionist[1] view of the self as an active, embodied, embedded, self-organizing process—what the Buddhists call 'I'-making (*ahaṃkāra*). This emergent process of self-making is grounded in the fundamentally recursive processes that characterize lived experience: *autopoiesis* at the biological level, *temporalization* and *self-reference* at the level of conscious experience, and conceptual and narrative *construction* at the level of intersubjectivity. In Buddhist terms, I will develop an account of the self as dependently originated and empty, but nevertheless real.

2. Non-Self

The doctrine of non-self (*anātman*) is perhaps the best known and most controversial aspect of Buddhist thought. On the Buddhist view, phenomena arise in dependence on a network of causes and conditions. This is the fundamental Buddhist notion of dependent co-arising (*pratītyasamutpāda*). The Buddhist analysis of any particular entity, event, or process will focus on the dynamic patterns of interaction within and through which it arises, has its effects, and passes away. It is against the backdrop of this basic analytical and ontological commitment that we can understand the Buddhist account of the self.

First and foremost, the doctrine of non-self is a rejection of the *ātman*, the enduring substantial self. On this view, the 'self' (*ātman*) is not just another term for the empirical person (*pudgala*), but is rather the substantial, essential core of the person—the inner self whose existence grounds the identity of the person. Within the Brahmanical religious and philosophical tradition,

---

[1] 'Reductionism' is often used very liberally in the literature on personal identity, such that an account of personal identity is reductionist so long as it does not rely on either a Cartesian ego or a brute 'further fact'. My view does not easily fit into these categories, but rather is an emergentist self-constitution view of the self.

the *ātman* is generally given a strongly metaphysical interpretation. It is the unitary, essentially unchanging, eternal, spiritual substance that is said to be one's true self. However, the ultimate target of the Buddhist theory of non-self is not the rarified spiritual conception of self commonly defended by various Brahmanical schools. Most fundamentally, the Buddhist target is a much more widely held and more deeply entrenched conception of the self. Galen Strawson's account of our basic sense of self fits well with Buddhist characterizations of the *ātman*. He writes:

I propose that the mental self is ordinarily conceived or experienced as:

(1) a *thing*, in some robust sense
(2) a *mental* thing, in some sense
(3, 4) a *single* thing that is single both *synchronically* considered and *diachronically* considered
(5) *ontically distinct* from all other things
(6) a *subject of experience*, a conscious feeler and thinker
(7) an *agent*
(8) a thing that has a certain character or *personality*

(Strawson 1999: 3).

Compare Strawson's view to Miri Albahari's account of the *ātman* (Pāli: *atta*) in early Buddhism:

A self is defined as a bounded, happiness-seeking/*dukkha* [suffering]-avoiding (witnessing) subject that is a personal owner and controlling agent, and which is unified and unconstructed, with unbroken and invariable presence from one moment to the next, as well as with longer-term endurance and invariability.

(Albahari 2006: 73)

Here we find the self understood as an experiencing subject, owner, and controller that is bounded (or, in Strawson's terms, 'ontically distinct') and enduring. Albahari also usefully distinguishes between the subject and the self. A subject is '*witnessing* [awareness] *as it presents from a psycho-physical (hence spatio-temporal) perspective*' (Albahari 2006: 8, emphasis in original). Thus, while perspectival experience implies a subject, it does not necessarily imply a self. For a self is a particular *type* of subject: bounded, enduring, controlling, and so on. Central to the Buddhists, the self in the above sense does *not* exist, and our deeply entrenched sense that we are such an entity is at the root of our existential and spiritual bondage (*saṃsāra*).

Rejecting the existence of the substantial self, the Buddhists argue the existence of a person (*pudgala*) consists in the existence of the five *skandhas* (bundles or aggregates) organized in the right way. The five *skandhas* are:

1. *Rūpa*: the body or corporeality
2. *Vedanā*: affect and sensation
3. *Saṃjñā*: perception and cognition
4. *Saṃskāra*: conditioning and volition
5. *Vijñāna*: consciousness

These five *skandhas* are not to be taken as independent things, but instead are seen as interdependent aspects of a causally and functionally integrated psycho-physical (*nāma-rūpa*) system or process (*skandhasantāna*: an 'aggregate-stream' or 'bundle-continuum').

The *rūpa-skandha* (material form) refers to the corporeal aspect of the human being, including the organizational structure of the person as an organism. The *vedanā-skandha* denotes affective dimensions of the person and their experience (pleasant, unpleasant, or neutral). The *saṃjñā-skandha* denotes the more fully cognitive faculty of perception, including the ability to identify and re-identify objects of experience.[2] The operation of this capacity depends on sensory contact (*sparśa*) with the environment as well as sensory-motor skills (such as exploratory behavior) and is often taken to involve the use of concepts. Next, the *saṃskāra-skandha* (conditioning) includes the various dispositions, capacities, and formations—such as sensory-motor skills, memories, habits, emotional dispositions, volitions, and cognitive schemas—that both enable and constrain the person and her experiences. This category also includes our basic conative impulses—attraction, repulsion, and indifference—which are in turn closely tied to our feelings and the affective modalities (*vedanā*) of experience. On the Buddhist view, typically one's whole being in the world is driven by this sedimented conditioning—and not always for the better. Indeed, the basic conative impulses often manifest in pathological ways, as the 'three poisons' of greed, hatred, and ignorance. As Dan Lusthaus remarks, 'such predilections are always already inscribed in our flesh, in our very way of being in the world, even while we

---

[2] The term *saṃjñā* (*sam*: 'together' + *jña*: 'knowledge') is cognate to 'cognize' and can have the sense of 'synthesis' as well as 'association'. Lusthaus translates *saṃjñā* as 'associational knowledge' (Lusthaus 2002: 47).

ignore—or remain ignorant of—the causes and conditions that have given rise to them' (Lusthaus 2002: 49). Finally, the *vijñāna-skandha* denotes discerning or discriminating intentional consciousness.

Therefore, in the standard Buddhist analysis, the person is not an entity that can exist independently of the five *skandhas*. Take away the complex, impermanent, changing *skandhas* and we are not left with a constant, substantial self: we are left with nothing. Moreover, the diachronic identity of a person consists in the appropriate degree of continuity and connectedness of the *skandhas*—that is, it is a matter of there being a causally and functionally integrated series or stream of *skandhas*.

Having briefly sketched the theory of non-self, let us examine two lines of argument against the existence of the self (*ātman*): the *criterial* argument and the *epistemic* argument. First, it is argued that none of the *skandhas* individually, nor the whole complex of *skandhas* could be the self—that is the independent, substantial, enduring, inner controller and owner of the *skandhas*. Upon examination, none of the five *skandhas* meets these criteria of selfhood.[3] The various mental factors (*nāma-skandha*) are simply too transitory, too mutable to constitute the stable, enduring essence of the person. Moreover, the mental factors are revealed in experience as a stream (*santāna*) or flow, rather than as a substance or object. The body is perhaps more stable, but the fundamental problem is the same: like any complex phenomenon, the body is in perpetual flux. How should we specify the persistence-conditions of the body? One might attempt to identify the body's unique ontological boundary or some essential part of the body that explains its persistence. But neither of these strategies looks particularly viable. The physical boundaries of the body are vague, and even if one could find the essential part of the body, it is doubtful that this essential part could meet the other criteria of selfhood. Thus it appears that none of the *skandhas* individually, neither mental factors nor the body, could be the substantial enduring self.

What, then, of the *skandhas* taken together, the *nāma-rūpa* or psycho-physical complex? Could this be the self? One problem with this response is that the psycho-physical complex is the empirical person, whereas the self is being posited as the essence of the person which grounds and explains the

---

[3] The classic version of the criterial argument occurs in *Samyutta Nikāya* 3.66–68. Cf. Holder (2006) for a translation.

persistence of the person. The empirical person, like the individual *skandhas*, is in flux, and therefore its endurance is equally problematic. Therefore, to simply identify the self with the person as a whole would be to conflate the *explanans* with the *explanandum*. Secondly, the relationship between a whole and its parts is problematic, and the Buddhists deny that a complex could be the *independent* owner and controller of its parts. Therefore, the substantial, essential self is not found among the *skandhas*, individually or collectively.

The second, and later, line of argument builds on the first. According to the Buddhist philosopher Vasubandhu (fourth century CE), we must apprehend the self either through direct acquaintance or through inference.[4] But we do not apprehend the self through either means. Therefore, we have no epistemic warrant for the existence of the *ātman*. The self is not a direct object of the five external senses or introspection. And while human beings typically have a *sense* of self, it does not follow from this that the sense of self provides direct acquaintance with an enduring, substantial self. Moreover, while it is certainly possible for 'the self' to be an object of thought, again it does not follow that the self exists.

So if the self is not known through direct acquaintance, then perhaps it is known through inference. Vasubandhu examines a valid inference to the existence of the unobservable sense faculties, and then asserts that there is no such valid inference to the existence of the unobservable self. In the case of the sense faculties, there is some reasonable way to tell whether the sense faculties are present or absent (e.g. in the case of the blind person versus the sighted person). Can the same be said for the *ātman*? One might, for example, posit the existence of distinct substantial selves in order to individuate persons A and B. But because the substantial self is supposed to retain its identity independently of the ever-changing stream of mental and physical events associated with A and B, how are we to establish anything about these posited selves? As it stands, the empirical evidence—for example, distinct bodies, various uses of names, and 'I'—is consistent with both the presence and the absence of the posited self, as well as a single shared self or a new substantial self each moment. Hence, the inference to the existence of the *ātman* looks weak. Vasubandhu's assertion here is not decisive, but the underlying argumentative strategy is to shift the burden of proof onto the

---

[4] This argument occurs in the 'Refutation of the Theory of the Self' 1.2. Cf. Duerlinger (2003) for a translation.

proponent of the substantial self. Is there inferential warrant for positing an enduring substantial self or can the phenomena (e.g. memory) be accounted for in terms of the systematic relations between various mental and physical events and processes? The Buddhists, of course, opt for the latter approach on grounds of epistemic and ontological parsimony. We are, they argue, *selfless persons* (*pudgalanairātmyā*).

3. Buddhist Reductionism

The account of human beings as selfless persons is held by all major Buddhist schools, but there has been a great deal of disagreement as to the full ontological implications of the rejection of a substantial self. For the Abhidharma or Buddhist reductionist schools, the doctrine of *anātman* is at the center of a radically reductionist, anti-substantialist empiricism. Everyday entities such as pots and people are not ontologically basic (*dravyasat*), but rather are reducible to aggregations of basic entities. On this view, the seemingly objective, mind-independent unity of everyday composite objects is illusory—these entities have only a secondary, conceptual existence (*prajñaptisat*). The ontologically basic entities to which everyday things are reducible are called *dharmas*. These are simple, fleeting events individuated by their intrinsic defining characteristic (*svalakṣaṇa*). Moreover, the Abhidharma's basic ontology is fairly austere—according to one school, there are only seventy-five types of *dharmas*. As the Abhidharma philosopher Vasubandhu explains the view:

> That of which one does not have a cognition when it has been broken is real in a concealing way (*saṃvṛti-sat*); an example is a pot. And that of which one does not have a cognition when other [elemental qualities (*dharmas*)] have been excluded from it by the mind is also conventionally real; an example is water. That which is otherwise is ultimately real (*paramārtha-sat*).
>
> (Ganeri 2007: 170)

This view constitutes a type of anti-realism about everyday composite entities, including persons. Such entities may be pragmatically or conventionally real (*saṃvṛtisat*), but they are not ultimately real (*paramārthasat*). The being of these entities is fully accounted for in terms of more basic entities: they are fully analytically and ontologically decomposable. Thus, they have a merely derived nature (*parabhāva*), rather than their own irreducible intrinsic nature (*svabhāva*). Further, conventionally real entities must be epiphenomenal because, if they were to have their own causal powers, they would not be completely reducible. Hence, according to the Ābhidharmikas, all causation is microcausation—that is, real causation occurs only between simple, momentary *dharmas*. Further, the genuine causal powers of these entities are determined by their intrinsic natures. Notice, then, that this two-tiered ontology rests on a radical dichotomy between the entities with a purely extrinsic nature (*parabhāva*) and those with a purely intrinsic nature (*svabhāva*).

Given such a revisionist ontology, one can see the importance of the Buddhist doctrine of two truths. On the Abhidharma view, conventional truths (*saṃvṛtisatya*) are those truths that quantify over reducible or conventionally real (*saṃvṛtisat*) entities, whereas ultimate truths (*paramārthasatya*) only quantify over irreducible or ultimately real (*paramārthasat*) entities. When using conventional discourse, one is not ontologically committed to anything but the entities mentioned in the ultimate discourse, even if conventional discourse is not analytically reducible to ultimate discourse. Further, the discourse of ultimate truth is the Abhidharma's 'philosophically favored discourse'—that is, the discourse in terms of which all other discourses are ultimately to be explained (Arnold 2005).

Persons, then, are organized, temporally extended systems of mental and physical events characterized by dense causal and functional interconnectedness, including complex physical and psychological feedback loops. Psycho-physical systems are also seen as deeply intertwined with, and dependent upon, the larger environment. Indeed, for the Buddhist reductionist, there is no sharp dividing line between the collection of events labeled 'person' and the collection of events labeled 'environment'. These terms do not carve the world at its joints: they are pragmatic, interest-relative categories. In order to understand the psychological dynamics that give rise to and perpetuate suffering, one does not look for a substantial mental self or an enduring substantial person. Instead, the Buddhist analyst attempts to understand the complex interrelations between mental and physical events over time. The rigorous Abhidharma analysis, though, goes beyond the early Buddhist shift in perspective from personal to impersonal analysis and defends a strict mereological reductionism—this position,

I argue in the next section, is in significant tension with the more general Buddhist analysis of sentient beings.

4. Four Problems for Buddhist Reductionism

While Buddhist reductionism offers a powerful critique of, and a sophisti-cated alternative to, substantialist views of the self, this radical view of the human person did not go unchallenged. Indeed, both Buddhist and non-Buddhist philosophers vigorously disputed the Abhidharma or Buddhist reductionist approach. In this section, we will examine four interconnected problems for Buddhist reductionism, and for strongly reductionist theories of the person in general. These four problems are: personal and experiential continuity, first-person consciousness, mereological reductionism, and the reification of *dharmas*. I argue that a turn to the enactive approach will contribute to the development of an anti-substantialist account of the person that overcomes these problems.

The first problem for the Buddhist reductionist has to do with personal continuity and, even more fundamentally, the continuity of the pre-personal body–mind stream that is the ground of personal continuity. An advocate of the self (*ātmavādin*) will want an account of diachronic personal identity (or at least personal continuity)[5] in the absence of a self. And as we have seen, the Buddhist reductionist holds that personal continuity is reducible to psycho-logical continuity (memory, skills, habits, personality traits), which is in turn reducible to causal connections between impermanent mental and physical events. One problem for this approach is that there are just too many causal connections. By their own view, the world is taken to be a causally interde-pendent network of events. How are we to individuate different streams of events?

The Buddhist reductionist has a two-part response to this problem. At the conventional (*saṃvṛti*) level, streams are individuated by the *density* of causal connections and by the way in which some sets of interconnected mental and physical events are able to ground relatively stable capacities or functions,

---

[5] Continuity is a weaker relation than identity in that continuity comes in degrees, while identity is all or nothing. Non-substantialist theories of the person typically account for diachronic personal identity in terms of continuity.

such as perception and motility.[6] Furthermore, at the ultimate (*paramārtha*) level, there simply is no ontologically correct way to individuate streams. Individuating streams (carving them out of the causal manifold) is an inherently pragmatic and interest-relative activity, and thus at this level of analysis, there is no fact of the matter about the identity of streams.

However, there is a deeper problem here, pointed out by the Vaiśeṣika philosopher, Śrīdhara (c.990 CE):

[Buddhist:] As a result of there being a causal connection, a later memory [is a memory] of what was experienced at an earlier moment. The son does not, however, remember what was experienced by the father; this is because there is no causal connection between the cognitions of a father and son, and their bodies, though admittedly so [connected], are not [themselves constituted of] consciousness.

[Śrīdhara:] This is not well-reasoned, for in the absence of self, there would be no determinate notion (*niścaya*) of a causal connection. At the time of the cause, the effect has yet to occur, and when its time comes, the cause has gone. Aside from the two of them, some unitary perceiver is denied; so who would observe the causal connection between those two things occurring in sequence?

(Ganeri 2007: 177)

In order to form a determinate notion of a causal sequence or stream, Śrīdhara argues, one must be able to *experience* a causal sequence.[7] And yet, on the radically reductionist view of the Ābhidharmikas, there are only momentary (*kṣaṇika*) events in causal interaction.[8] How could a series of discrete mental events come to form a concept of a causal sequence if no mental event lasts more than a single moment? The continuity problem, then, is whether *experiential* continuity can be reductively explained in terms of

---

[6] Though the reductionist still owes us an account of how to get from causal connections to the kind of semantic and (broadly) narrative connections that seem to play an important role in any plausible account of psychological continuity.

[7] It might be argued that the concept of a causal sequence is innate, but this response is not available to the empiricist Ābhidharmikas. Even if it is claimed that the concept of a causal sequence is inherited from a past life, the concept, at some point, must have been derived from experience. Thus the move to an innate concept of causal sequence simply pushes back the problem.

[8] There is in fact a debate about whether *dharmas* have only momentary existence, as argued by the Sautrāntikas, or whether, as argued by the Sarvāstivādins, *dharmas* exist in the past, present, and future. In either case, though, *dharmas* are only causally efficacious in the fleeting present. Thus there remains a problem of continuity on either view.

causal continuity. If it cannot, the Buddhist reductionist view looks to be self-undermining.[9]

The second problem for Buddhist reductionism involves I–consciousness, or first-person experiences and thoughts. If a particular token of the first-person pronoun 'I' does not refer to the utterer's self, what, if anything, does it refer to? It seems obvious that when an individual correctly uses 'I', she is referring to herself. But, as the Buddhist reductionist will quickly point out, from this it does not follow that when she uses 'I' she refers to a substantial self. Self-reference is not necessarily reference to an ontologically independent self. So even if one rejects the existence of such a self, one can still give an account of first-person self-reference. Perhaps the first-person pronoun is not a genuine referring term, or perhaps, as for Vasubandhu, 'I' refers to the continuum in which it occurs, rather than the self. The deeper problem here concerns the centrality and continuity of the sense of self (*ahaṃkāra*) and its connection to self-consciousness, or what Western phenomenologists term 'the first-person mode of givenness' of experience.[10]

The great Nyāya critic of Buddhism, Uddyotakara, presses the difficulty in the following passage:

> The consciousness of 'I', which conforms to the distinctions of the nature of the object, and which does not depend upon memory of marks, the possessor of the marks, and their relationship, is direct acquaintance just as is the cognition of physical form. Concerning what you yourself, with perfect confidence, establish to be direct acquaintance, in virtue of what is it that it is [said to be] direct acquaintance? You must establish it as being consciousness alone, which does not depend upon the relationships among marks, etc., and which is self-presenting. So then you think there is an I-cognition, but that its object is not the self? Well, then show us its object!
>
> (Kapstein 2002: 98)

As Uddyotakara points out here, first-person self-reference must be anchored in a non-criterial, non-inferential mode of self-acquaintance. But if there is no self, what are I-cognitions directly acquainted with? What is the subject of experience? As Uddyotakara himself mentions, one later Buddhist

---

[9] Śrīdhara intends this argument to establish the necessity of an enduring substantial self. However, as I argue below in my discussion of time-consciousness, what is required is not a substantial self, but a more robust account of the experiential continuity.

[10] 'First-personal givenness' is often used interchangeably with 'subjectivity'. Cf. Zahavi (2005) for a discussion of this.

response to this problem is to argue that consciousness is inherently reflexive or self-presenting (*svasamvedana*), and that this inherent reflexivity is the basis of both explicit I-cognitions and the more inchoate diachronic sense of self (*ahaṃkāra*). That is, as in Sartre's view, consciousness is always consciousness of *itself*, but not necessarily consciousness of a *self* (Sartre 1957). Later developments aside, however, it is unclear that the ruthlessly reductive, impersonalist causalism of the Abhidharma can accommodate the first-personal givenness or the first-personal continuity of human experience.[11]

The third problem for Buddhist reductionism arises from the commitment to mereological reductionism. The properties of a whole, including causal properties, are thought to be reductively determined by the intrinsic properties of its components. Yet the thoroughgoing reductionism of Abhidharma seems to be in tension, not just with non-Buddhist substantialism, but also with the dynamic, processual, and multi-level analysis of human beings found in early Buddhism. Dependent co-arising (*pratītyasamutpāda*) is a multi-level account of interdependence, ranging from the arising of a single moment of experience to the entire cycle of rebirth. The radical interpretation of dependent origination and anti-substantialism found in Buddhist reductionism may not have the resources required to account for the dependent origination of the human person. And, in any case, as I argue below, there are good reasons to question mereological reductionism, at least with regard to some systems.

The fourth problem for Buddhist reductionism, namely the reification of *dharmas*, is closely related to the third. Recall that Abhidharma ontology rests on a sharp dichotomy between, on the one hand, those entities that have a dependent nature (*parabhāva*) and are therefore merely conventionally real and, on the other hand, those ultimately real entities that have an independent intrinsic nature (*svabhāva*). Clearly, mereological reductionism requires an irreducible reduction-base and, as the Ābhidharmikas insist, the entities that form the reduction-base for everyday things must not themselves borrow their nature from other things. That is, macro-level properties, including the properties of wholes, must reductively supervene on the intrinsic, non-relational properties of the base level. Thus, ultimately real entities must be independent and basic, as well as individuated by their unique and intrinsic, non-relational properties. Ultimate reality,

---

[11] But see Siderits (this volume) for an attempt to address this problem.

then, is understood in terms of substance (*dravya*) and essence (*svabhāva*).[12] Therefore, the worry is that this picture constitutes an unwarranted reification of some phenomena (basic *dharmas*) and, at the same time, an unwarranted nihilism about other phenomena (conventional entities).[13] Moreover, as with the Abhidharma's merelogical reductionism, we will argue that there are good reasons to question this reified account of phenomena. Indeed, if the Buddhist Mādhyamikas are right, the Abhidharma view is not just unwarranted, but also incoherent.

5. The Dependent Origination of Autonomous Systems

Given the shortcomings of the Abhidharma theory of persons, what is required is a middle way between their reductionist fictionalism and the substantialism of *ātman* and Cartesian ego theories. Moreover, developments in complex systems theory and biology call into question strongly reductionist approaches such as that of the Abhidharma. For, unlike flames or chariots (two of the common analogues to the human person), biological systems display a high degree of self-organized autonomy. On the enactive approach discussed below, living beings are neither enduring substances, nor merely aggregative systems, but rather self-regulating unities. Of course, as we have seen, the Abhidharma analysis recognizes that psycho-physical systems are self-perpetuating, and characterized by functional integration and feedback loops. Yet this traditional Buddhist analysis is combined with a strict mereological reductionism that must, in the end, deny genuine causal status to macro-level entities or structures. Therefore, to avoid this problem, in this section I will turn to the theory of autonomous systems, an integral component of the enactive approach, for support in developing an anti-substantialist, but non-reductionist, account of persons.

According to both Buddhist and enactivist accounts, sentient beings are organized dynamic systems. Hence an understanding of the system requires

---

[12] A *dharma* is substantial, not because it is the substratum of properties, but because it is ontologically basic and independent. It is these latter features that are rejected by Madhyamaka.

[13] Of course, the Buddhist reductionist will resist these claims. The charges of reification and nihilism depend on a certain account of the relationship between the two truths that will be explored below.

that we pay close attention, not just to the system's components, but also to its organization.[14] We may begin with the distinction between *heteronomous* and *autonomous* systems. A heteronomous system is exogenously controlled, and can clearly be modeled as an input–output system. In contrast, an autonomous system primarily will be understood in terms of its 'endogenous, self-organizing and self-controlling dynamics', and 'does not have inputs and outputs in the usual sense' (Thompson 2007:43). Instead of an input–output model, autonomous systems are understood in terms of perturbation and response. External factors perturb the ongoing endogenous dynamics of the system, yielding a response that must be understood in terms of the system's dynamics and its overall organization. More specifically:

> In complex systems theory, the term *autonomous* refers to a generic type of organization. The relations that define the autonomous organization hold between processes (such as metabolic reactions in a cell or neuronal firings in a cell assembly) rather than static entities. In an autonomous system, the constituent processes (i) recursively depend on each other for their generation and their realization as a network, (ii) constitute the system as a unity in whatever domain they exist, and (iii) determine a domain of possible interactions with the environment
>
> (Thompson 2007: 44; cf. Varela 1979)

In biochemistry, Maturana and Varela (1980) call this type of autonomy 'autopoiesis' (self-production). Autopoiesis involves what Varela terms a 'logical bootstrap' or 'loop' in which a network or process creates a boundary and is subsequently constrained by that boundary. This is the system's *organizational closure* ((ii) above). For instance, at the cellular level, a self-organizing process of biochemical reactions produces a membrane that, in turn, constrains the process that created it (Varela 2001). The completion of this loop gives rise to a distinct biological entity that maintains its own boundary in its environment. This new level of coherence is a 'virtual identity' that is to be understood in terms of both boundary-maintenance or organizational closure and a new mode of interaction with the environment. In addition, autopoietic systems are characterized by *operational closure* ((i) above): 'the property that among the conditions affecting the operation

---

[14] The following discussion of autonomous systems closely follows Thompson (2007) and Varela (1999, 2001).

of any constituent process in the system there will always be one or more processes that also belong to the system' (Di Paolo 2009: 15). Furthermore, autonomous systems are always coupled to their environments ((iii) above). As Thompson explains, 'Two or more systems are coupled when the conduct of each is a function of the conduct of the other' (Thompson 2007: 45). When two systems (organism and environment) develop a history of recurrent interactions leading to a 'structural congruence' between them, we have *structural coupling* (Thompson 2007; Maturana 1975; Maurana and Varela 1987).

Sentient beings, on this view, are understood not as heteronomous, mechanical input-output systems, but rather as dynamic, autonomous systems—necessarily coupled to the environment, but also self-controlling. In addition, autonomous systems, in particular living and sentient systems, involve *emergent processes*. As Thompson describes, 'An emergent process belongs to an ensemble or network of elements, arises spontaneously or self-organizes from the locally defined and globally constrained or controlled interactions of those elements, and does not belong to a single element' (Thompson 2007: 60). Emergent processes, and the systems in which they arise, exhibit two forms of determination. Local-to-global determination involves the emergence of novel macro-level processes and structures based on changes in the system components and relations. Global-to-local determination involves macro-level processes and structures constraining local interactions. Thus self-organizing systems display *circular causality*: local interactions give rise to global patterns or order, while the global order constrains the local interactions (Haken 1983).

The type of self-production and self-maintenance found in living systems goes beyond the type of self-organization seen in non-living systems. The degree of autonomy found in living beings is, according to the enactive approach, a form of *dynamic co-emergence*.

Dynamic co-emergence best describes the sort of emergence we see in autonomy. In an autonomous system, the whole not only arises from the (organizational closure of the) parts, but the parts also arise from the whole. The whole is constituted by the relations of the parts, and the parts are constituted by the relations they bear to one another in the whole. Hence, the parts do not exist in advance, prior to the whole, as independent entities that retain their identity in the whole. Rather, part and whole co-emerge and mutually specify each other.

(Thompson 2007: 65)

A candle flame (a common Buddhist analogy for non-substantial personal continuity) or a Bénard cell, as dissipative systems, will display self-organization and self-maintenance to a degree, but the key boundary conditions that keep these systems away from equilibrium are exogenous. In contrast, in truly autonomous systems, 'the constraints that actually guide energy/matter flows from the environment through the constitutive processes of the system are endogenously created and maintained' (Ruiz-Mirazo and Moreno 2004: 238).

Returning to Buddhist reductionism, recall that Vasubandhu's criterion for the mere conventionality of a phenomenon was its actual or analytical decomposability. Moreover, the issue of decomposability, on the Abhidharma approach, is closely tied to reducibility. Full decomposability requires that the components of a complex entity are fully specifiable independently of their relations to one another and within the whole. Full reducibility further requires that the properties and (apparent) causal powers of the whole be determined by the intrinsic properties and causal powers of the independent and irreducible components.

However, in complex dynamic systems with *nonlinear* interactions, such as multicellular organisms, the immune system, and the brain, full decomposability is not possible. Nonlinear systems are characterized by non-additive and non-proportional interactions—that is, nonlinear interactions—and thus the system's properties cannot be aggregatively derived from the properties of its parts (Thompson 2007). As Thompson points out:

An autonomous system is at least minimally decomposable, if not nondecomposable. More precisely, when one adopts an autonomy perspective, one *ipso facto* characterizes the system as at least minimally decomposable. The reason is that an autonomous system is an organizationally and operationally closed network; hence it is the connectivity of its constituent processes that determines its operation as a network.

(Thompson 2007: 421)

If this view is correct, sentient beings, as living autonomous systems, are not amenable to the reductive analysis of the Abhidharma. Sentient beings are not sufficiently decomposable (if decomposable at all) to be exhaustively analyzed and explained in terms of the intrinsic properties and causal powers of independently specifiable components. In addition, the self-organizing, self-maintaining, and self-regulating capacities of living beings rely on both local-to-global and global-to-local influence, and therefore the causal capacities of the system *qua* system are both real and not determined by the intrinsic properties of their most basic components. In the case of autonomous systems such as human beings, we have mereological dependence without strict mereological reduction. On the other hand, it is important to note that the enactive approach is not a return to substantialism. Autonomous systems are not static, ontologically independent substances. Rather the autonomy and irreducibility of living beings derives from dense networks of relationality and interdependence. That is, autonomous systems are dependently originated (*pratītyasamutpanna*).[15]

6. Emptiness and the Virtual Self

A turn toward the enactive approach and its autonomy perspective can help to find a middle way between substantialism and reductionism about persons. Persons can be understood in dynamic-relational terms as autonomous systems. So far, however, the focus has been on persons as sentient beings—that is, as embodied and embedded biological systems. I will now turn to the importance of the deeply entrenched human sense of self. In addition, just as I have used the enactive approach to expand upon and modify a Buddhist analysis, I will in turn use later developments in Buddhist thought (in particular the Madhyamaka school) to correct what I take to be shortcomings in Francisco Varela's enactivist account of the self.

Varela (1999, 2001), explicitly drawing on Buddhist philosophy, argues that the human self is both emergent and *virtual* or *empty* (*śūnya*). He therefore rejects the existence of a substantial, bounded, enduring self. The self, he argues, emerges from the human organism's endogenous neurobiological dynamics and from its embeddedness in its natural and social-linguistic environment. Thus we create and re-create ourselves from moment to moment through the dynamic interaction of brain, body, language, and world. He writes:

[15] See Siderits (this volume) for a reductionist response. It is worth reiterating that if there are autonomous systems, they would not be somehow outside the network of cause and effect. That is, even if merelogical reductionism is false for autonomous systems, those systems are still dependently originated.

Why do emergent selves, virtual identities, pop up all over the place creating worlds, whether at the mind/body level, the cellular level, or the transorganism level? This phenomenon is something so productive that it doesn't cease creating entirely new realms: life, mind, and societies. Yet these emergent selves are based on processes so shifty, so ungrounded, that we have an apparent paradox between the solidity of what appears to show up and its groundlessness.

(Varela 2001)

These systems behave *as if* a central agent or controller is directing them— yet no such central agent can be found. This is what Varela means by the virtual or empty self: 'a coherent global pattern that emerges from the activity of simple local components, which seems to be centrally located, but is nowhere to be found, and yet is essential as a level of interaction for the behavior of the whole' (Varela 1999: 53).

Of course, it is natural to think that while an ant colony or an amoeba may have only a *virtual* self, surely we humans are the real deal. But Varela is avowedly in agreement with the Buddhist theory of non-self. On his account, 'either we are unique in the living and natural world, or else our very immediate sense of a central, personal self is the same kind of illusion of a center, accountable by more of the same kind of analysis [i.e. in terms of autopoiesis]' (Varela 1999: 61). Moreover, 'what we call "I" can be analyzed as arising out of our recursive linguistic abilities and their unique capacity for self-description and narration' (Varela 1999: 61). Indeed, this linguistically constructed self serves as what he terms a 'virtual interface' between the body and the natural and social environment in which it is embedded.

Now the virtuality or emptiness of the self can be taken in a weaker or a stronger sense, and it is not always clear which sense Varela intends. In the weaker sense, the emergent self is virtual merely because it is distributed or not localized, and thus insubstantial. The self is not an illusion, but its supposed singularity and localizability is a fiction or projection. This would rule out naive homuncular or substantialist accounts of the self, without entailing fictionalism about the self per se. In the stronger sense, the self is virtual in that it is an illusion or useful fiction. The insect colony behaves *as if* someone were in charge, *as if* it had a unified perspective, and so on, but this is an illusion. Likewise, our sense of self, our sense of having (or being) a unified first-person perspective, and being a center of agency are also illusions.

Despite some ambiguity in Varela's characterization of the virtual self, I take him to be arguing for the stronger sense of virtuality. First, he repeatedly points out the ways in which mainstream findings in cognitive science challenge the notion of the self as a unified and coherent point of view— that is, not just inner homunculus *explanations* of a unified perspective, but also the very existence of such a perspective is challenged (Varela 1999: 36–41). Second, Varela notes that he and Daniel Dennett—the arch-fictionalist—have come to the same conclusions regarding the self (Varela 1999, 2001). Thus, on Varela's view, the self is a virtual or fictional construct that emerges from the distributed activity of a natural, autopoietic system and, in the case of the human self, the system's use of language and its embeddedness in a linguistic community.

Now the resonance between Varela's account and Buddhism should be obvious. And, of course, Varela draws heavily from Buddhist ideas and practices in the formulation and defense of his account of the virtuality of the self, especially the concept of emptiness (*śūnyatā*) as developed in the Madhyamaka, or Middle Way, school of Buddhism. Indeed, he argues that the emptiness of the self 'is the golden thread that unites our self-understanding with an external and scientific account of mental functioning', and further that ethical wisdom rests on first-hand acquaintance with the empty nature of the self (Varela 1999: 36). However, a proper understanding of emptiness casts doubt on Varela's account of the self as merely virtual.

As mentioned at the outset of this paper, the account of human beings as selfless persons (*pudgalanairātmya*) is held by all major Buddhist schools, but there has been a great deal of disagreement as to the full ontological implications of the rejection of a substantial self. In contrast to the reductionists, some Mādhyamika thinkers allow for an ontologically deflationary account of the self. The self is said to have an experiential and practical reality, while they still insist that this minimal self is not to be reified. As the Dalai Lama explains the latter view, 'both body and mind are things that belong to the I, and the I is the owner, but, aside from mind and body, there is no separate independent entity of I. There is every indication that the I exists; yet, under investigation, it cannot be found' (Gyatso 2000: 65). This minimal self—what is called the 'mere I' or 'mere self' (Tibetan: *nga tsam*)—

is an emergent phenomenon that, while real, is not a substantial separate *thing*, and therefore disappears under analysis.[16]

The difference between the Abhidharma reductionist fictionalism and the later Buddhist deflationary non-reductionism turns on competing accounts of the concept of emptiness. To be empty, on the reductionist view, is to lack ontological independence and an intrinsic nature and, therefore, to be nothing more than a conceptual construct or convenient fiction. In contrast, the Madhyamaka school—which Varela, Thompson, and Rosch claim as one basis of their thought in *The Embodied Mind* (1991: 217–235)— takes a different approach to the concept of emptiness. The Mādhyamikas agree that to be empty is to lack *svabhāva* or inherent existence, but go on to argue that the notion of *svabhāva* is itself untenable. Rather than arguing that conventional phenomena can only be accounted for in terms of ultimate phenomena, the Mādhyamikas argue that positing ultimate, non-empty phenomena actually *precludes* a coherent account of the conventional world.[17] The Mādhyamikas, therefore, argue for the selflessness of persons (*pudgalanairātmya*) *and* the selflessness (i.e. emptiness) of all phenomena (*dharmanairātmya*).

But what does it mean to say that all things are empty, that they lack *svabhāva*? Of course, within the Abhidharma framework, to say this amounts to nihilism. To be conventionally real is to be purely derivative, indeed to be a mere convenient fiction. Yet, how could *everything* be a mere convenient fiction? Within the Mādhyamika framework, in contrast, for a thing to be empty is not for it to be unreal, but rather for its existence and nature necessarily to depend on other things. There is a three-way implication between emptiness, dependent origination, and conventional reality. As Jay Garfield explains:

When we say that a phenomenon is empty, we mean that when we try to specify its essence, we come up with nothing. When we look for the substance that underlies the properties, or the bearer of the parts, we find none. When we ask what it is that gives a thing its identity, we stumble not upon ontological facts but upon conventions. For a thing to be non-empty would be for it to have an essence discoverable upon analysis; for it to be a substance independent of its attributes, or a bearer of

---

[16] The analysis here is the type of ontological analysis that looks for the substantial reality of the object. Thus, insofar as the self has no substantial reality, it is not found in this type of analysis.

[17] It is in this sense that the Ābhidharmikas can be accused of nihilism, despite the fact that their reductionism is not intended to be a form of eliminativism.

parts; for its identity to be self-determined by its essence. A non-empty entity can be fully characterized nonrelationally.

(Garfield 2002: 38)

So, according to the Mādhyamikas, any thing that exists depends on other things for its existence and nature, and depends (in part) on our practices of individuation for its identity-conditions.[18]

Returning to the question of the self, one can see why Varela's identification of virtuality with emptiness is problematic. On the Mādhyamika account of emptiness, which Varela himself endorses, emptiness simply does not entail virtuality in either its weaker or stronger senses. To call the self virtual is to imply that it is either unreal or less real than other things. But showing that the self emerges from, and depends on, lower-level processes, that it is not an independent substance, that in trying to specify its identity-conditions we make reference to our interests and practices, or that it has no absolute ontological primacy, does not cast doubt on its existence. Rather, it shows that the self is empty, *just like everything else.* To think otherwise, on the Madhyamaka view, is to accept an ontological foundationalism and essentialism that they argue is incoherent.[19]

The larger point here is that, insofar as all phenomena are embedded in a network of relations (causal, mereological, emergence, etc.), there is nothing especially *virtual* about the emergent self. In aligning his account of the emptiness of the self with the fictionalist views of the Abhidharma schools (Varela, et al. 1991: 58–81) and Dennett, Varela implicitly reifies lower levels of stable organization, while simultaneously negating the conventional reality of the emergent self. In contrast, Thompson is in agreement with the Madhyamaka school when he insists that, 'Phenomena at all scales are not [independent] entities or substances but relatively stable processes, and since processes achieve stability at different levels of complexity, while still interacting with processes at other levels, all are equally real and none has absolute ontological primacy' (Thompson 2007: 441). To claim, as Varela seems to do, that the emergent global pattern is virtual, but that the components from which it emerges are actual, is to miss the full implications of the dynamic-relational ontology at the heart of both Buddhism and the enactive approach.

---

[18] Hence, the Mādhyamika holds that all phenomena are interdependent and also rejects the idea of the 'ready-made world' characteristic of metaphysical realism.

[19] See Garfield (1995), Siderits (2003), and Westerhoff (2009) for in-depth discussions of Madhyamaka arguments.

7. The Minimal Self

Mādhyamikas argue that the self is empty, but that it is neither a mere fiction, nor reducible to the body–mind continuum.[20] The great Tibetan Madhyamaka philosopher, Tsongkhapa, distinguishes three approaches to the question of the self: (1) the substantialism of non-Buddhist schools, (2) Buddhist reductionism, and (3) the view of his tradition of Prāsaṅgika Madhyamaka (Jinpa 2002: 109). The first type of view holds that the self is a kind of entity that exists independently of the *skandhas*, and combines non-reductionism and realism. The second type of view holds that the self does not exist at all and that persons are fully reducible to the *skandhas*. Terms such as 'I', 'self', and proper names, in fact, refer to the impermanent mental and physical elements. This type of view, according to Tsongkhapa, combines realism (about the elements as the reduction base) with reductionism. Finally, the Prāsaṅgika Madhyamaka school holds that the self is dependent upon, but not reducible to, the *skandhas*. This view combines ontological deflationism (i.e. all things are empty of inherent existence) with non-reductionism. As Tsongkhapa writes:

There are two senses of the term 'self': a self conceived in terms of intrinsic nature that exists by means of intrinsic being, and a self in the sense of the object of our simple, natural thought 'I am'. Of these two, the first is the object of negation by reasoning, while the second is not negated, for it is accepted as conventionally real.

(Jinpa 2002: 71)

Unlike their reductionist forebears, therefore, some Mādhyamikas accept the *minimal self* as the object of the natural sense of self or I-consciousness.[21] Here we see a Madhyamaka answer to Uddyotakara's challenge to identify the referent of I-consciousness. I-thoughts *do* refer to the self rather than a mere bundle of physical and mental events, but this minimal self is not an enduring substance.

But once one has rejected the substantialist account of the self, why not identify the self with the psycho-physical continuum? According to the

---

[20] The Mādhyamikas do say that the self is illusion-*like* in that it appears to have substantial existence, but is in fact empty. But, again, according to this view *all* phenomena are illusion-like in this sense.

[21] There is controversy both within the Madhyamaka school and in the Western literature on whether and how Madhyamaka may differ from Abhidharma on the nature of the self. Thus the view I explore below should be seen as *a* Madhyamaka view, but not *the* Madhyamaka view.

Mādhyamikas, the self cannot be identified with the aggregates, first because they have incompatible properties. The self is, by hypothesis, single and persisting, while the aggregates are multiple and fleeting.[22] Identifying them would lead to a multiplication of selves within the life of a single person—a result taken to be absurd. Moreover, the self and the aggregates have different persistence-conditions, and therefore cannot be identical. Secondly, it is argued that memory presupposes the continuity of a first-person perspective or I-consciousness that cannot be accounted for in impersonal, reductionist terms. That is, the first-person perspective needed to account for genuine memory disappears from the impersonal causalism of reductionism.[23] Thirdly, Tsongkhapa argues that our conventions and practices, such as assigning moral responsibility, take the notion of a person and the 'mere I' as basic (Jinpa 2002). Finally, the Mādhyamikas argue that both substantialist and reductionist approaches to the self fail to account for the inherently indexical, perspectival nature of the minimal self. Āryadeva argues: 'That which is self to you is not self to me; from this fixed rule it follows that that is not self. Indeed, the construction (*kalpanā*) [of a sense of self] arises out of the impermanent things' (Ganeri 2007: 191). Candrakīrti expands on this argument in his commentary on Āryadeva:

> That which is self to you, the focal point of your sense of 'I' (*ahaṃkāra*) and self-interest (*ātmasneha*), that indeed is not self to me; for it is not the focal point of my sense of 'I' and self-interest. This then is the fixed rule from which it follows that it is not [a real thing]. There is no essence to such a self as it is not invariably present. One should give up the superimposition of [such] a self, for it is something the content of which is unreal (*asadartha*).
>
> (Ganeri 2007: 192)

Having a sense (or concept) of self entails being able to draw a distinction between self and other, and to experience things as mine and not mine. However, substantialitist or entitative views of the self, according to Āryadeva, cannot ground this indexical, perspectival distinction because they take the self to be a kind of *thing*.

---

[22] Mādhyamikas reject the 'pearl' view of the self (cf. Strawson 1999)—the view that the person consists of a series of short-lived selves—and maintain, on phenomenological and pragmatic grounds, that the self is persistent. But, since the self is a process, it perdures rather than endures.

[23] On this point, the Mādhyamikas agree with the Nyāya critics of Buddhist reductionism.

Yet the reductionist view, despite denying the existence of the self, fares no better. The project of Buddhist reductionism is to account for persons in impersonal terms, that is, in terms of causal connections between fleeting mental and physical events. In shifting to an impersonal and non-perspectival standpoint, the reductionist loses sight of the first-person perspective, and it is unclear in this case how to derive the perspectival from the non-perspectival. There appears to be an explanatory gap between the first- and third-person standpoints. Of course, for the reductionist, the fact that the minimal self is not found when one shifts to a non-perspectival, third-person discourse is grounds to deny its real existence. However, the Mādhyamikas deny that this discourse has any absolute metaphysical or explanatory priority. The problem with reductionist accounts of personal identity, then, is that they deny the importance of the first-person perspective.

One helpful and important aspect of the Madhyamaka approach is that it shifts the discussion from a concern with third-person, metaphysical issues about the existence of selves and persons to a concern with the first-person, lived sense of self (ahaṃkāra). The attempt to find a metaphysical *ground* for the existence of the self either in a mental substance or in a reduction to impersonal aggregates is eschewed by the deflationist Mādhyamikas as merely two instances of the error of reification. Instead, the Madhyamaka account of the empty minimal self is given in terms of its experiential and practical reality. It is fundamentally a matter of the structure and continuity of the first-person perspective.

In discussing Tsongkhapa's approach to the minimal self Thupten Jinpa remarks:

One of the fundamental premises of Tsongkhapa's thought . . . is that an individual's sense of self, or I-consciousness, is innate. It is instinctual and natural. It is neither linguistic nor even conceptual, if by conceptual one presupposes [reflective] self-awareness. It is a natural, reflexive consciousness, almost like an underlying sense of one's own existence.

(Jinpa 2002: 123)

Our most basic sense of self is pre-conceptual, pre-linguistic, and natural.[24] But we must proceed with caution here. Despite holding that the sense

---

[24] Thompson defines sentience as 'the feeling of being alive' (2007: 161), while neuroscientists Damasio (1999) and Panksepp (1998) posit a primitive 'feeling of self'.

of self is natural and pre-linguistic, Tsongkhapa denies that each moment of consciousness is self-presenting (*svaprakāśa*). Like Mādhyamikas such as Candrakīrti and Śāntideva, he rejects the idea that all consciousness inherently involves pre-reflective self-consciousness (*svasaṃvedana*).[25] The 'mere I' (Tibetan: *nga tsam*) here refers to the *ahaṃkāra*, not *svasaṃvedana*.[26] Here again, Tsongkhapa's view of the self differs from Varela's. Recall that, on Varela's account, the 'I' arises from our 'recursive linguistic abilities and their unique capacity for self-description and narration' (Varela 1999: 61), whereas the minimal self in Tsongkhapa's account is experientially prior to linguistic construction.[27]

Furthermore, on Tsongkhapa's view, the minimal self has a diachronic dimension.[28] He explains:

> The self that is the focus of Devadatta's instinctual sense 'I am' when not thinking of a specific temporal stage [of his existence] is the mere I that is within him since beginningless time. The individual selves [of Devadatta] when he appropriated the body of a celestial being and so on are only instances of the former [mere I]. Therefore, when an I-consciousness arises in Devadatta focusing specifically on a particular form of existence [e.g., as a human], the object of his I-consciousness is a particular instance of Devadatta's self.

(Jinpa 2002: 123)

The idea here is that the mere I is not confined to the present, but rather provides a basic form of continuity throughout the different phases or temporal stages of one's life. Indeed, it is precisely the continuity of this basic first-person perspective that explains why the various forms of existence are parts of the same life history. Each of the 'individual selves' is based upon the minimal self, each tokening of an I-thought is a particular instance or expression of this mere I.

Tsongkhapa further argues that the minimal self allows us to explain the coherence of our personal plans and projects. When we plan for the future

[25] See Dreyfus (1996), Garfield (2006), MacKenzie (2007), MacKenzie (2008), and Williams (1997) for further discussion.

[26] Unlike, Tsongkhapa, I *do* accept the notion of *svasaṃvedana*. On my view, the minimal self (*ahaṃkāra*) emerges from the more basic inherent reflexivity of consciousness. Thus my view is closer to the Madhyamaka of Śāntarakṣita (in India) or the Kagyu and Nyingma traditions (in Tibet).

[27] This is not to say that linguistic construction plays no role in Tsongkhapa's account, but only to point out that the minimal self is pre-linguistic.

[28] The Madhyamaka account of the minimal self, therefore, differs from Antonio Damasio's notion of the core self in that the core self has no long-term temporal extension.

or undertake a particular project, he argues, we do not 'make distinctions between the self of this time or that time. Rather, these endeavors are motivated by the simple wish for the self to be happy and overcome suffering. And since the self as a generality does pervade all temporal stages [of a person's existence], these acts also cannot be said to be deluded' (Jinpa 2002: 124). For the Prāsaṅgika Mādhyamika such as Tsongkhapa, these pragmatic, experiential considerations concerning the self are central.

8. Self-Appropriation

On a Madhyamaka account, the empty self is neither independent of, nor reducible to, the five *skandhas*. What, then, is the dependence relation between the pre-personal *skandha-santāna* and the self? A common analogy for the relation between the self and the *skandhas* is the mutual dependence of fire and fuel.[29] Just as the fire appropriates (*upā* + *dā*) the fuel to perpetuate itself, the self appropriates as its own the various mental and physical events that make up the *skandha-santāna*. Further, as Jan Westerhoff notes in this context:

Not only does the self depend for its existence on the constituents, but the constituents acquire their existence as distinct parts of the stream of mental and physical events only by being associated with a single self, which, regarded as a constitutive property, produces the basis for postulating the individual in which the various properties of the self inhere. It is precisely this reason which keeps the Mādhyamika from regarding the constituents as ultimate existents (*dravya*) and the self as merely imputed (*prajñāpti*).

(Westerhoff 2009: 163)

Moreover, as Candrakīrti comments on Nāgārjuna's use of the analogy:

That which is appropriated is the fuel, the five [types of] appropriated element. That which is constructed in the appropriating of them is said to be the appropriator, the thinker, the performing (*niṣpādaka*) self. In this is generated [the activity of] 'I'-ing, because from the beginning it has in its scope a sense of self.

(Ganeri 2007)

[29] See Nāgārjuna's MMK X: 15 on the relevance of the analogy and X: 10, and X: 12–14 on the issue of mutual dependence.

The self, then, is the appropriator (*upādātṛ*), and the various elements are the appropriated (*upādāna-skandha*), and yet Candrakīrti insists 'the self is not a real, existent thing'. That is, the self lacks inherent existence (i.e. it is empty), and it is not any kind of thing or object. Rather, the self is 'I'-ing (*ahaṃmāna*) or ongoing self-appropriative activity (Ganeri 2007). Furthermore, 'I'-ing is an inherently perspectival activity: it appropriates phenomena as 'me' and 'mine', incorporates them into its own ongoing dynamic, by *indexing* (or tagging) them to the I. Appropriation, then, functions as a self-referential loop.

According to Jonardon Ganeri, the Madhyamaka theory is a *performativist* theory of the self (2007). On his interpretation,

When I say 'I am in pain', I do not *assert* ownership of a particular painful experience; rather, I *lay claim to* the experience within a stream. This is a performativist account of the language of the self, in which 'I' statements are performative utterances, and not assertions, and the function of the term 'I' is *not* to refer.

(Ganeri 2007: 202)

Of course, with its emphasis on self-appropriation, Ganeri's performativist reading is congenial to my enactivist account of the self, but it differs in two ways. First, I do not want to deny that 'I' statements can refer. Second, while I agree with Ganeri (and Varela) that language is central to the full constitution of the self, I also agree with Tsongkhapa that the minimal self has its roots in the pre-linguistic structure of lived experience.

More specifically, the root of the minimal self is the *recursive* nature of lived experience. A recursive process is one wherein the results of the process are fed back into the process itself. On the Buddhist view, the vicious cycle of *saṃsāra* is understood in terms of the recursive process of dependent origination. Indeed, living itself is a recursive process. As Hans Jonas remarks, 'organisms are entities whose being is their own doing... the being that they earn from this doing is not a possession they then own in separation from the activity by which it was generated, but is the continuation of that very activity itself' (Jonas 1996: 86). In order to survive, the organism must maintain its own dynamic organization in the face of, but also in virtue of, continuous matter-energy turnover. The viable organism, through its organizational and operational closure, is able to subsume or appropriate both bits of the environment and elements of the organism itself. Thus, 'I'-ing is perhaps more like the organic process of metabolizing than it is like inorganic combustion.

In addition to the recursivity of biological processes, the stream of experience has its own recursive structure.[30] The 'stream' of experience is a temporal flow. Yet, as Śrīdhara pointed out in his criticism of the Abhidharma, it is hard to see how a series of discrete momentary experiences could constitute the type of ongoing point of view required to even form the concept of a causal sequence. Furthermore, the problem involves not only external objects and processes, but also how we can be aware of our own experiences as forming a unified temporal flow. Without this, we will be unable to account for the emergence of the minimal self through self-appropriation. What is required is an account of how impressions are retained within the temporal flow of experience—that is, we must have an account of time-consciousness (Husserl 1991).[31]

The basic unit of temporal experience for Husserl (as for James) is not a durationless point, but rather a moment with temporal thickness. The structure of this 'duration-block' is *protention-primal impression-retention*. As Husserl explains:

In this way, it becomes evident that concrete perception as original consciousness (original givenness) of a temporally extended object is structured internally as itself a streaming system of momentary perceptions (so-called primal impressions). But each such momentary perception is the nuclear phase of a continuity, a continuity of momentary gradated retentions on the one side, and horizon of what is coming on the other side: a horizon of 'protention', which is disclosed to be characterized as a constantly gradated coming.

(Husserl 1977: 154)

The primal impression is restricted to the now-phase in a sequence. In listening to a melody, the primal impression is directed to the currently sounding note. Retention is directed toward the just-elapsed note. The elapsed note is not actually present in consciousness, but is retained intentionally. Protention is directed toward the future, the next note about to be heard. Whereas the currently sounding note is given in the vivid immediacy

---

[30] Though of course, we do not want to make too sharp a distinction between the biological and the experiential here. These are two aspects of one process of *living*.

[31] See Zahavi (2005) for an illuminating discussion of these issues.

of the present, and the just past note is determinately retained, the upcoming note is not given in a fully determinate manner.

This three-fold structure forms a unified whole, the continuous operation of which allows for the experience of temporal continuity. The structure constitutes the living present within which temporal experience 'wells up'. Further, on Husserl's view, the primal impression-protention-retention structure of consciousness accounts for the temporal unification of the stream of consciousness itself. Retention retains the prior phases of the stream, while protention reaches out toward future moments of consciousness. It is through this process, which Husserl calls *longitudinal intentionality*, that consciousness is self-affecting, or temporally given to itself. Furthermore, longitudinal intentionality makes possible what Husserl calls *transverse intentionality*. It is the transverse intentionality of time-consciousness that allows for the continuous experience of a temporal object, such as melody or a spoken sentence. Because the now-phase of consciousness takes an object (e.g. a note) and is retained in the stream, so too is the object of the now-phase of consciousness. In sum, the threefold structure of time-consciousness is the condition of the possibility of both the diachronic unification of the stream of consciousness and the experienced continuity of temporal objects.

Husserl's analysis of time-consciousness shows that consciousness is itself recursive. Consciousness takes in its impressions and retains them, marking the impression as past, and making the past impression available for the ongoing flow of consciousness. Indeed, the process of retention is iterative, in that not only 'pastness', but the degree of 'pastness' is marked within the flow of experience. The temporal flow of consciousness involves retentions of retentions, thereby allowing the experience of a temporal *sequence*. Moreover, this recursive process is self-referential. As James Mensch observes:

In retention the subject does not just have the experience of the retained, it experiences itself having this experience, i.e., as retaining the retained. Accordingly, when it grasps an object through a series of retained contents, it prereflectively grasps itself in its action of retention. This grasp is a grasp of itself as having experience, i.e., of itself as a subject. Such self-experience implies that the self-referential character of retention grounds the subject as nonpublic, i.e., as referring (or being present) only to itself.

(Mensch 2001: 107)

The upshot of these brief Husserlian considerations is that self-making (*ahaṃkāra*) (what Tsongkhapa calls the object of our 'simple, natural thought "I am"') is grounded in, and emerges from, the recursive temporality of the stream of consciousness (*citta-santāna*). Moreover, this analysis of experiential continuity answers Śrīdhara's objection. Even without a substantial self, one can form the concept of a causal sequence because the stream of experience is characterized by longitudinal and transverse intentionality.[32] The root of the minimal self, then, is not in linguistic self-appropriation, but in temporal self-appropriation within an inherently reflexive flow of consciousness. The 'I', or rather 'I'-ing, emerges from self-grasping, and in this sense we are, in Ganeri's phrase, 'whirlpools of self-appropriating action' (2007: 204).

Yet, while temporal self-appropriation is necessary for a diachronically extended minimal self, it is not clear that it is sufficient. What else might be required? One type of view holds that language or concepts are required for the emergence of even the minimal self. Another type of view, in contrast, holds that pre-linguistic awareness of the body and action are required. In support of this latter view, one may cite, for instance, recent research on neonatal imitation. As Shaun Gallagher summarizes the significance of this research:

> Neonates less than an hour old are capable of imitating the facial gestures of others in a way that rules out reflex or release mechanisms, and that involves a capacity to learn to match presented gesture. For this to be possible the infant must be able to do three things: (1) distinguish between self and non-self; (2) locate and use certain parts of its own body proprioceptively, without vision; and (3) recognize that the face it sees is of the same kind as its own face (the infant will not imitate non-human objects). One possible interpretation of this finding is that . . . the human infant is already equipped with a minimal self that is embodied, enactive and ecologically tuned.
>
> (Gallagher 2000: 18)

Furthermore, as ecological psychologists point out, the visual field affords information about the perceiver's environment as well as self-specifying information. In seeing the cup, one is also gaining information about one's own position in relation to the cup, information that is crucial to coordinating perception and action. Thus, on this account, the minimal self is embodied and enactive, as well as temporal.

---

[32] Husserl thought that temporality was central to the nature of the transcendental ego. However, it is not at all clear that Husserl's notion of a transcendental ego would constitute a substantial self. Moreover, like Sartre and other phenomenologists, I take Husserl's account of time consciousness to be consistent with a non-egological view of consciousness.

Finally, to move beyond the minimal self to a more robust form of personhood requires long-term memory, concepts, language, and social embeddedness. Indeed, on the Buddhist-enactivist account I have sketched here, the robust self or person is a complex conceptual, linguistic, and social *construction* (*abhisaṃskāra*). In particular, the robust self involves narrative construction. As Zahavi remarks, 'human activities are enacted narratives; our actions gain intelligibility by having a place in a narrative sequence' (Zahavi 2005: 107). This narrative conception of persons fits well with traditional Buddhist accounts that emphasize the conventional nature of personhood. Indeed, the narrative construction of the self can be seen as a further extension of the basic dynamic of self-appropriation discussed above.

On the downside, however, from a Buddhist point of view, this narrative is the tale of a being trapped in *saṃsāra*. And a central factor that perpetuates this vicious cycle is the conceit 'I am' (*asmimāna*). This conceit is the hub around which the wheel of *saṃsāra* turns. It is grounded in self-grasping (*ātmagraha*) and the recursive, open-ended proliferation of concepts (*prapañca*) made possible by language. We have already seen how the emergence of an embodied self through organizational closure brings with it an intimate, but precarious relation to the environment. At this basic level, closure creates identity, but also *need* and *danger*. At the level of the narrative self, the conceptual and linguistic resources that make possible the fully articulated narrative self also create a form of conceptual-linguistic closure (through self-reference) which, in conjunction with deeply ingrained afflictive tendencies (*kleśa*), amplifies and perpetuates the suffering and dysfunction that characterizes *saṃsāra*. Simply put, we become *self-centered*: grasping after what is self-serving, suppressing and denying what goes against the self, and being ignorant of, or indifferent to, what does not serve the self. Moreover, because the conceit 'I am' emerges along with the narrative self itself—that is, the conceit is the default mode of the narrative self—its status as a construction is occluded. The emergent, dependently originated, empty self—the 'whirlpool of self-appropriating action'— mistakes itself for a bounded, enduring, substantial entity.[33]

---

[33] It is worth noting that my view of consciousness is remarkably similar to George Dreyfus' in this volume. We both agree (as does Krueger) that consciousness is inherently reflexive, but is not, at its most basic level, egological. Rather, the sense of self arises from a more basic flow of reflexive consciousness. This sense of self or minimal self is illusion-like in the sense that sentient beings with a sense of self take themselves to be enduring, bounded, substantial selves when they are not. Dreyfus, Krueger, and I agree that there are no substantial selves. However, Dreyfus seems to reserve the term 'self' for the substantial

Our deeply engrained tendencies to self-centeredness and self-forgetfulness—that is, forgetting the ways in which the self is constructed and can be reconstructed—lead us to enact *saṃsāric* narratives individually and collectively. Therefore, while it might be heartening to realize that the narrative self makes a difference, that it is not simply an epiphenomenon, it may be less heartening to realize that the self causes and perpetuates real suffering. Buddhist thinkers are so focused on understanding the nature and emergence of self-making precisely because they see with such great clarity the deep connection between selfhood and suffering.

9. Conclusion

The Buddhist-enactivist conception of the self explored here provides, I argue, a middle path between substantialism and reductionism, between treating the self as either an independent entity or a mere fiction. The fundamental problem for substantialism is *change*: positing a fundamentally unchanging substratum of our identity in the face of incessant change ultimately alienates the self from experience and the world. Nothing in our experience—neither body, nor mind, nor world—has the kind of permanence and stability attributed to the substantial self. One might take the substantial self as an explanatory posit, but it remains unclear whether this posit is necessary or even whether it could do any real work.

On the other hand, the fundamental problem for reductionism is the centrality of subjectivity, of the first-person perspective. According to the Buddhist-enactivist view I have sketched, a living sentient being is not a mere aggregate or bundle of components, and cannot fully be understood from a purely external, third-person perspective. The living organism displays the interiority of its own immanent purposiveness and its needful and precarious relations to its (enacted) milieu. The stream of experience is inherently reflexive, given to itself in pre-reflective self-awareness (*svasaṃvedana*) and through the recursive structure of time-consciousness. The

---

self. On the other hand, Krueger and I allow for a dependently originated, empty self. The mistake involved in the sense of self, then, is twofold: first, one mistakes the empty self for a substantial self; second, one mistakes the sense of self for the most basic level of subjectivity when it in fact emerges from the egoless reflexivity of consciousness.

embodied being is pre-reflectively aware of itself in and through its active, striving body (Thompson 2007). On my view—and here I am in basic agreement with both Krueger and Dreyfus as articulated in this volume—the minimal self (*ahaṃkāra*) emerges from the more basic inherent reflexivity of consciousness. A more robust self is constructed through the self-referential resources of language and narrative (Zahavi 2005). In each of these ways (and others) the phenomena of subjectivity resist reduction. The common themes here are recursivity, self-organization, and self-reference. The key to understanding (or beginning to understand) self-making, I suggest, is to see how dynamic processes enact themselves through self-organizing, self-appropriating activity—biologically, experientially, and socially. For, if the Buddhists and the enactivists are right, we *are* this activity.

References

Albahari, M. (2006), *Analytical Buddhism: The Two-Tiered Illusion of Self* (Houndsmills, NY: Pallgrave Macmillan).

Arnold, D. (2005), *Buddhists, Brahmans, and Belief: Epistemology in South Asian Philosophy of Religion* (New York: Columbia University Press).

Damasio, A. (1999), *The Feeling of What Happens: Body and Emotion in the Making of Consciousness* (New York: Harcourt Brace).

Dennett, D. (1991), *Consciousness Explained* (Boston: Little, Brown).

Di Paolo, E. (2009), 'Extended Life', *Topoi* 28: 9–21.

Dreyfus, G. (1996), *Recognizing Reality: Dharmakīrti's Philosophy and Its Tibetan Interpretations* (Albany, NY: State University of New York Press).

Duerlinger, J. (2003), *Indian Buddhist Theories of Persons: Vasubandhu's 'Refutation of the Theory of a Self'* (London: Routledge/Curzon Press).

Gallagher, S. (2000), 'Philosophical Conceptions of the Self: Implications for Cognitive Science', *Trends in Cognitive Science* 4: 14–21.

Ganeri, J. (2007), *The Concealed Art of the Soul: Theories of Self and Practices of Truth in Indian Ethics and Epistemology* (Oxford: Oxford University Press).

Garfield, J. (1995), *Fundamental Wisdom of the Middle Way: Nāgārjuna's Mulamadhyamakakakārikā* (NY: Oxford University Press).

——(2002), *Empty Words: Buddhist Philosophy and Cross-Cultural Interpretation* NY: Oxford University Press.

——(2006), 'The Conventional Status of Reflexive Awareness: What's at Stake in the Tibetan Debate?' *Philosophy East and West* 56: 201–228.

Gyatso, T. (2000), *The Meaning of Life: Buddhist Perspectives on Cause and Effect* (Somerville, MA: Wisdom Publications).

Haken, H. (1983), *Synergetics: An Introduction* (Berlin: Springer-Verlag).

Hamilton, S. (2000), *Early Buddhism: A New Approach: The I of the Beholder* (London: Routledge/Curzon Press).

Holder, J. (2006), *Early Buddhist Discourses* (Indianapolis: Hackett Publishing Company).

Husserl, E. (1977), *Phenomenological Psychology: Lectures, Summer Semester, 1925,* trans. John Scanlon (The Hague: Martinus Nijhoff).

——(1991), *On the Phenomenology of the Consciousness of Internal Time (1893–1917),* trans. J. B. Brough (Dordrecht: Kluwer Academic Publishers).

Jinpa, T. (2002), *Self, Reality, and Reason in Tibetan Philosophy: Tsongkhapa's Quest for the Middle Way* (London: Routledge/Curzon Press).

Jonas, H. (1996), *Mortality and Morality: A Search for Good After Auschwitz* (Evanston, IL: Northwestern University Press).

Kapstein, M. (2002), *Reason's Traces: Identity and Interpretation in Indian and Tibetan Buddhist Thought* (Boston: Wisdom Publications).

Lusthaus, D. (2002), *Buddhist Phenomenology: A Philosophical Investigation of Yogācāra Buddhism and the Ch'eng Wei-shu lun* (London: Routledge/Curzon Press).

MacKenzie, M. 2007. 'The Illumination of Consciousness: Approaches to Self-Awareness in the Indian and Western Traditions', *Philosophy East and West* 57: 40–62.

——(2008), 'Self-Awareness without a Self: Buddhism and the Reflexivity of Awareness', *Asian Philosophy* 18: 245–266.

Maturana, H. (1975), 'The Organization of the Living: A Theory of the Living Organization', *International Journal of Man-Machine Studies* 7: 313–332.

——(1980), *Autopoiesis and Cognition: the Realization of the Living,* Boston Studies in the Philosophy of Science, vol. 42 (Dordrecht: D. Reidel).

Maturana, H. and Varela, F. (1987), *The Tree of Knowledge: The Biological Roots of Human Understanding* (Boston: Shambhala Press/New Science Library).

Mensch, J. (2001), *Postfoundational Phenomenology: Husserlian Reflections on Presence and Embodiment* (University Park, PA: Pennsylvania State University Press).

Metzinger, T. (2003), *Being No One: The Self-Model Theory of Subjectivity* (Cambridge, MA: MIT Press).

Panksepp, J. (1998), *Affective Neuroscience: The Foundations of Human and Animal Emotions* (Oxford: Oxford University Press).

Ruiz-Mirazo, K., and Moreno, A. (2004), 'Basic Autonomy as a Fundamental Step in the Synthesis of Life', *Artificial Life* 10: 235–259.

Sartre, J-P. (1957), *Transcendence of the Ego: An Existentialist Theory of Consciousness*, trans. F. Williams and R. Kirkpatrick (New York: Noonday).

Siderits, M. (2003), *Personal Identity and Buddhist Philosophy: Empty Persons* (Aldershot: Ashgate).

Strawson, G. (1999), 'The Self', in S. Gallagher and J. Shear (eds.), *Models of the Self* (1–24) (Thorverton: Imprint Academic).

Thompson, E. (2007), *Mind in Life: Biology, Phenomenology, and the Sciences of Mind* (Cambridge, MA: Harvard University Press).

Varela, F. (1979), *Principles of Biological Autonomy* (New York: ElsevierNorth Holland)).

——(1999), *Ethical Know-How: Action, Wisdom, and Cognition* (Palo Alto, CA: Stanford University Press).

——(2001), 'The Emergent Self', *Edge*, vol. 86, www.Edge.org. (accessed 27 February 2006).

Varela, F., Thompson, E., and Rosch, E. (1991), *The Embodied Mind: Cognitive Science and Human Experience* (Cambridge, MA: MIT Press).

Westerhoff, J. (2009), *Nāgārjuna's Madhyamaka: A Philosophical Introduction* (Oxford: Oxford University Press).

Williams, P. (1997), *The Reflexive Nature of Awareness: A Tibetan Madhyamaka Defence* (London: Routledge/Curzon Press).

Zahavi, D. (2005), *Subjectivity and Selfhood: Investigating the First-Person Perspective* (Cambridge, MA: MIT Press).

10

Radical Self-Awareness*

GALEN STRAWSON

I. Experience

I want to consider the claim that the subject cannot in the present moment of awareness take itself as it is in the present moment of awareness as the object of its awareness. In the first two sections I'll set out some assumptions.

First, I'll assume that materialism is true. By 'materialism', though, I mean real or realistic materialism, that is, materialism that is wholly realist about the *experiential-qualitative character* or *what-it's-likeness* of our conscious mental goings on—I'll call this 'experience'—and accordingly takes it to be wholly physical. When real materialists say that experience—colour-experience, pain-experience—is wholly physical, they're not saying that it's somehow less than we know it to be in having it; that wouldn't be real materialism, realistic materialism, because it would involve the denial of something that obviously exists. Rather, they're saying that the physical must be something more than it's ordinarily supposed to be—given that it's ordinarily supposed to be something entirely non-experiential—precisely because experience (what-it's-likeness considered specifically as such) is itself wholly physical.

Experience is necessarily experience-*for*—experience for someone or something. I intend this only in the sense in which it's necessarily true, and without commitment to any particular account of the metaphysical

---

* §§IV–VII of this paper develop ideas in Strawson 1999: 498–502; see also Strawson 2009: 176–81. When I cite a work I give the date of first publication, or occasionally the date of composition, while the page reference is to the edition listed in the bibliography.

nature of the someone-or-something. To claim that experience is necessarily experience-for, necessarily experience-for-someone-or-something, is to claim that it's necessarily experience on the part of a subject of experience. Again I intend this only in the sense in which it's a necessary truth, and certainly without any commitment to the idea that subjects of experience are persisting things. Some say one can't infer the existence of a subject of experience from the existence of experience, only the existence of subjectivity, but I understand the notion of the subject in a maximally ontologically non-committal way—in such a way that the presence of subjectivity is already sufficient for the presence of a subject, so that 'there is subjectivity, but there isn't a subject' can't possibly be true.[1]

Consider pain, a regrettably familiar case of experience. It is, essentially, a feeling, and a feeling is just that, a *feeling*, that is, a feel-ing, a being-felt; and a feel-ing or being-felt can't possibly exist without there being a feel-er. Again I'm only interested in the sense in which this is a necessary truth. The noun 'feeler' doesn't import any metaphysical commitment additional to the noun 'feeling'. It simply draws one's attention to the full import of 'feeling'. The sense in which it's necessarily true that there's a feeling and hence a feeler of pain if there is pain, is the sense in which it's necessarily true that there's a subject of experience if there is experience and, hence, subjectivity. These truths are available prior to any particular metaphysics of object or property or substance or accident or process or event or state. (Descartes is very clear about this in his *Second Meditation*.)

Some like to think that there can be subjectivity or experience without a subject. That's why it's important to bring out the full import of the notion of subjectivity or experience by stressing the fundamental sense in which it can't exist without a subject. But there's a no less important point in the other direction. If all you need to know, to know that there is a subject, is that there is subjectivity or experience, then you can't build more into the notion of a subject than you can know to exist if subjectivity or experience exists. I think, in fact, that the object/property distinction is metaphysically superficial—that there is no 'real distinction' between (a) the being of an object, considered at a given time, and (b) the being of that object's proper-tiedness, that is, its whole actual concrete qualitative being at that time, that

---

[1] See further Strawson 2009: 274, 414.

is, everything in which its being the particular way it is at that time consists. But that is a difficult issue for another time.[2]

2. The Thin Subject

I propose to take the unchallengeable, ontologically non-committal notion of the subject of experience in a minimal or 'thin' way. By 'subject', then, I don't mean the whole organism (the whole human being, in our own case). I mean the subject considered specifically as something 'inner', something mental, the 'self', if you like, the inner 'locus' of consciousness considered just as such.

One way to think of this inner subject or self is as some complex persisting neural structure or process.[3] Another still more minimal way to think of it is this. Consider the neural activity that is the existence of your current experience right now. Imagine that this neural activity somehow exists on its own—nothing else exists. In this case a subject of experience exists. It must exist, because experience exists. This last claim is not just the epistemological claim that we can know that a subject exists because we know that experience exists. It's the metaphysical claim that whatever constitutes the existence of your experience must already suffice to constitute the existence of a subject of experience. Otherwise it couldn't suffice to constitute the existence of your experience, which it does by hypothesis.

The conception of the subject as a persisting neural structure or process is probably the most common materialist conception of the inner subject, but I prefer the more minimal 'thin' conception of the subject. According to the thin conception, the presence of experience is not only sufficient for the existence of the subject but also necessary. No experience, no subject of experience. There's a new subject of experience every time there's a break in experience. There's no subject of experience when one is dreamlessly asleep. We already have it as a necessary truth that [existence of

---

[2] See Strawson 2008d, and references there to Descartes, Nietzsche, Ramsey, and others.
[3] Or else, perhaps, as a subject in Dainton's sense, 'a collection of experiential powers', a subject-constituting 'C-system' (Dainton 2008: 252).

experience → existence of subject of experience]. Now we add the converse [existence of subject of experience → existence of experience].

This is the thin subject. According to the present proposal, this isn't just a way of thinking of the subject, a way of isolating an aspect of the subject, where the subject proper must be supposed to be the whole human being, or a persisting neural structure, or some such. Rather, when we consider the subject as defined by the thin conception of the subject we have to do with something that is, whatever its metaphysical category, at least as good or solid a candidate for qualifying as an entity, a thing, an object (a substance, if you like) as the whole human being, or a persisting brain structure.

This is not to say that reality contains anything that actually makes the grade as a thing or object or substance. The Buddhist doctrine of 'dependent origination' suggests that nothing does. An alternative view is that only one thing does—the universe. On this view, Parmenides and a number of leading present-day cosmologists are right. There's really only one A-Grade thing or object or substance: the universe. (Nietzsche and Spinoza agree that nothing smaller will do.)

That's one important view. The present claim is neutral on this issue. It's simply that the claim thin subjects are as good, as candidates for thinghood, as anything else. In fact I think they're better candidates than a persisting brain structure, or any ordinary physical object, and indeed any supposed fundamental particle.[4] I'm stressing the point to counter the thought that thin subjects are somehow not real things, ontologically worse off than persisting brain-structures, for example. This view isn't sustainable, I think, when metaphysics gets serious and stops spending its time trying to square ordinary language and ordinary thought categories with reality.

Having said that, I should add that most of the claims I'm going to make will apply to the persisting-brain-structure subject as well as to the thin subject. The difference between these two conceptions of the inner subject isn't really at issue when it comes to my main present purpose, which is to consider the old claim that the subject can't in the present moment of awareness take itself as it is in the present moment of awareness as the object of its awareness. The thin subject is my favourite candidate for the title 'self', if we're going to talk of selves at all, but this issue too—the issue between

---

[4] I support this claim in Strawson 2009: 294–320, 379–88.

those who agree with me about this and those who feel that any candidate for the title 'self' must be something more enduring—may be put aside for the purposes of this paper.

I'm going to use various numbers and letters to set things out, and apologize to those who don't like this sort of thing. I hope that my approach to the issues I discuss may contrast helpfully with some of the Indian approaches considered in this book precisely because of my ignorance of the Indian approaches.

3. Present-Moment Self-Awareness

Some claim that the subject can no more take itself as the object of its awareness than the eye can see itself, or, putting aside the word 'taking', that

(i) the subject can no more be the object of its awareness than the eye can see itself.

Some make the more restricted claim that the subject cannot in the present moment of awareness take itself as it is in the present moment of awareness as the object of its awareness, or, putting aside 'taking' again,

(ii) the subject in the present moment of awareness cannot be the object of its awareness in the present moment of awareness,

being, in Ryle's memorable phrase, forever and 'systematically elusive' to itself (1949: 186).

(i) and (ii) express an ancient view. I think it's mistaken in both forms. A quick if unimportant point against (i) is that subjects that persist for appreciable periods of time can have themselves as object of awareness, in the fullest sense, when they remember themselves experiencing something yesterday, or a moment ago. Against that, it may be said that it's part of the meaning of the word 'aware', used to denote a state of conscious experience, that 'awareness of x' can refer only to apprehension of x as it is in the present moment, modulo whatever time lapse is integral to the mode of awareness in question (visual, auditory, inner self-awareness).

So be it. I'm going to concentrate on (ii), the case of present-moment awareness, and argue that there are two distinct ways in which

[1] the subject of awareness can be aware of itself as it is in the present moment of awareness.[5]

First, less controversially, and in line with Phenomenological orthodoxy, I'll argue that the subject can be present-moment aware of itself in a *non-thetic* way, where to be aware of something *x* in a non-thetic way is to be aware of *x* although one isn't specifically attending to *x*. Secondly, less familiarly, I'll argue that subjects of experience can also (if exceptionally) be present-moment-aware of themselves in a *thetic* or attentive way.[6] I take this second claim to be a more direct challenge to the ancient view, which seems to rely on the idea that the reason why the subject can never truly grasp itself as it is in the present moment of awareness is that it must in so doing take (have) itself as a thetic object of thought in some way that means that the thing that it is taking (that it has) as object can't really be the thing that is doing the taking, that is, itself as it is in the present moment of awareness.

I'm going to use 'present-moment' rather than 'immediate', at least for now, because 'immediate' also carries the non-temporal sense 'not mediated'. Temporal immediacy may imply non-mediatedness, but I want to leave the issue open.

I'll begin by considering a popular source of support for the non-thetic case which licenses a much stronger claim than [1]. On this view

[2] the subject of awareness is *always* aware of itself as it is in the present moment of awareness

whenever it's aware in any way at all.[7] We can rephrase this as

[2] Present-Moment Self-Awareness is Universal

and rephrase its weaker sibling as

[1] Present-Moment Self-awareness is Possible.

---

[5] I use 'awareness', 'experience', and 'consciousness' interchangeably.

[6] I use 'thetic' in the Sartrean way to mean simply 'in the focus of attention', rather than in the Husserlian way, insofar as the latter implies belief.

[7] The thin notion of the subject makes the words 'whenever it's aware in any way at all' redundant; but the thin notion is of course at odds with the standard dispositional use of 'subject of awareness', which allows that a subject of awareness (whole human being, persisting brain structure, whatever) can exist in a state of dreamless sleep.

Taking 'SA' to be short for 'present-moment self-awareness', we can call [2] the Universal SA thesis, 'USA' for short, and we can call [1] the possible SA thesis, 'PSA' for short.

According to [2], it isn't possible for a subject to be aware of anything without being present-moment-aware of itself. This is true of every subject of awareness, however lowly. If sea snails have any sort of awareness, then they're (necessarily) aware of themselves in the present moment of awareness. I take [2] to be endorsed by many in the Phenomenological tradition. Husserl, for example, writes that 'to be a subject is to be in the mode of being aware of oneself' (Husserl 1921–8: 151; see also Zahavi 2006, as well as this vol, pp. 58–60).

As it stands, the ancient view rejects both [1] and [2], both PSA and USA, in both their non-thetic and thetic versions.[8] I'm going to start by putting the case for non-thetic USA and thetic PSA, beginning with the former. Since non-thetic USA entails non-thetic PSA, only thetic USA will be unsupported—as it should be.

It may be objected that it's best to stop now, because it's obvious that USA and PSA can't be true, simply because the neuronal processes that constitute awareness (at least in our own case) take time: there's an inevitable time lag that rules out all present-moment self-awareness. I'll leave this objection until later. It may turn out that rejecting USA and PSA for this reason is like holding that we never experience pain as it is in the present moment, even if the two cases seem at first disanalogous.

4. The AOI Thesis (All Awareness Comports Awareness of Itself)

Why should anyone assert [2], that is, USA? I'm going to assume the truth of the following two general principles:

[P1] awareness is (necessarily) a property of a subject of awareness,

which has already been argued for (and is in any case evident, given that it is legitimate to talk of properties at all), and

---

[8] 'As it stands': as far as I know the ancient view isn't really concerned with the non-thetic versions.

[P2] awareness of a property of x is *ipso facto* awareness of x.[9]

[P1] and [P2] entail

[3] any awareness, A1, of any awareness, A2, entails awareness of the subject of A2

and we can get [2] = USA from [3] if we add

[4] all awareness involves awareness of awareness

or rather (the key premiss)

[5] all awareness involves awareness of that very awareness

that is,

[5] all awareness involves awareness of itself.

[5] is in fact the only defensible version of [4]—as Aristotle pointed out—given the threat of an infinite regress of awarenesses of awarenesses that [4] poses as it stands.[10] I'll call [5] the AOI thesis, 'AOI' for 'awareness of itself', 'AOI' for short.

The claim is, then, that AOI plus the two principles [P1] and [P2] entails USA. More briefly: AOI and [3] entail USA. The argument isn't formally valid as it stands, but the idea is clear.

It may be allowed that [5] all awareness involves awareness of itself, but doubted that

[6] all awareness is or involves *present-moment* awareness of itself

on the grounds that there is always a time lag, or an episode of what Ryle calls 'swift retrospective heed' (1949: 153). But it seems that this is not possible, if [5] is true at all, because the last moment in any episode of awareness couldn't in this case involve awareness of itself (all streams of awareness would have to last for ever).

---

[9] 'For purposes of argument': I take it that [P1] and [P2] say something true, even if there is in the final metaphysical analysis no fundamental (categorial) ontological division corresponding to the distinction between object and property.

[10] See Aristotle *De Anima* 3.2. 425b12–17. Compare Reid: 'I cannot imagine there is anything more in perceiving that I perceive a star than in perceiving a star simply; otherwise there might be perceptions of perceptions in infinitum' (1748: 317). For an excellent recent discussion of these questions in the context of Indian philosophy, see e.g. Mackenzie 2007. Note that [4] makes no explicit reference to the present moment.

The substantive premiss is AOI. The question is, why believe AOI? Why—to strengthen it slightly—believe

[7] all awareness essentially involves awareness of that very awareness,

or again, more heavily,

[8] all awareness essentially, constitutively, and intrinsically involves awareness of that very awareness

('intrinsically' and 'constitutively' aim to block the possibility, arguably left open by 'involves', that the awareness A1 of the awareness A2 might be something ontologically separate from A2), or more lightly, to the same effect,

[9] all awareness is at least in part awareness of that very awareness,

or, to rephrase [8],

[10] all awareness comports awareness of that very awareness,

or, reintroducing the subject of awareness,

[11] all awareness on the part of any subject comports awareness, on the part of that same subject, of that very awareness

or again, reintroducing multiply redundant explicit reference to the present moment,

[12] all awareness on the part of any subject at any moment comports awareness, at that moment, on the part of that same subject, of that very awareness at that very moment

or, shortening [10] to what I hereby designate as the canonical version of AOI,

[13] all awareness comports awareness of itself?[11]

Good question, about which there is a lot to say. I think AOI is initially difficult, but compelling on reflection. It's endorsed by many, including

---

[11] One can rewrite [13] as [13a] *all awareness comports self-awareness*—so long as one is clear that the occurrence of 'self-' in 'self-awareness' is merely reflexive, so that [13a] means exactly the same as [13], and doesn't imply any awareness of something called a self.

Descartes, Arnauld, Locke, Brentano, Husserl, Sartre, and most thinkers in the Phenomenological tradition.[12] All of them insist that the awareness of awareness that is held to be partly constitutive of all awareness mustn't be thought of as involving some 'higher-order' mental apprehension, A1, say, bearing on an ontically distinct, separate, 'lower-order' mental apprehension, A2 (for this triggers an infinite regress). The relevant awareness of awareness is, rather, an intrinsic feature of any episode of awareness considered independently of any other, given which it is correct to say that [13] = AOI is true.[13]

One might say that [13] = AOI can be re-expressed by talking of

[14] the self-awareness of awareness

but [14] is paradoxical, at least initially, in a way that [13] isn't, because it seems clear that awareness is, necessarily, a property of a subject of awareness (as [13] still allows, given the word 'comport'), and can't properly—or indeed possibly—be said to be a property of awareness itself. That said, I think that [14] is an acceptable way of putting things. First, it's an acceptable shorthand for [11]: all awareness on the part of any subject comports awareness, on the part of that same subject, of that very awareness. Secondly, and more strongly, the fact that all awareness is, necessarily, awareness on the part of a *subject* of awareness—the fact that reference to a subject must enter into any fully articulated description of what is going on when there is awareness—does not in any way undercut the truth of [14], according to which it is a constitutive feature of the phenomenon of awareness itself that it comports awareness of itself. Thirdly (a much stronger and much more difficult point), I think that there is a metaphysically fundamental conception of the subject (by which I mean the thin subject) given which

[15] the subject of awareness (that which wholly constitutes the existence of the subject of awareness) isn't ontically distinct from the awareness of which it is the subject

---

[12] See, e.g. the quotations from Sartre in Zahavi, this volume, p. 56.

[13] Among Descartes's endorsements of AOI are the following: 'we cannot have any thought of which we are not aware at the very moment when it is in us' (1641: 2.171) and 'the initial thought by means of which we become aware of something does not differ from the second thought by means of which we become aware that we were aware of it, any more than this second thought differs from the third thought by means of which we become aware that we were aware that we were aware' (1641: 2.382).

or in other words

[16] the subject of awareness is identical with its awareness.

I'll call [16] the Subject of Awareness/Awareness Identity thesis or S=A thesis, 'S=A' for short.[14] It's endorsed, interestingly, by Descartes, Leibniz, Kant, and Nietzsche, among others, in the Western tradition,[15] and if one accepts it, then [14], the further proposed version of AOI, can be understood to be fully equivalent to [2] = USA. That is,

[[AOI & S=A] → USA].

If S=A is too strong for you, you may be able to accept the weaker claim that

[[AOI & [P1] & [P2]] → USA].

If you think [P1] & [P2] are trivially true, you can shorten this to

[AOI → USA].

All I've done, in moving from [5] to [13] ± [14], is re-express AOI in a number of different ways, but one might also say that all I've done is re-express USA in a number of different ways. (The AOI thesis is focused on the nature of awareness, whereas the USA thesis is focused on the nature of the self or subject, but they are of course closely connected.)

Arnauld puts AOI well when he writes that 'thought or perception is essentially reflective on itself, or, as it is said more aptly in Latin, *est sui conscia*', is conscious of itself.[16] In endorsing the AOI thesis, as he does here, he also endorses USA, given that he follows Descartes in accepting the S=A thesis.

---

[14] I argue for S=A in Strawson 2003b, revised in Strawson 2009: 345–9, 405–19. It entails the 'thin' conception of the subject, while making an even stronger claim about the relation between the subject and its experience.

[15] In his famous letter to Herz, Kant writes that 'the thinking or the existence of the thought and the existence of my own self are one and the same' (1772: 75). Although Descartes, Leibniz, and Spinoza often write as if the subject is ontically distinct from its states of experience or awareness, they're all committed to the view that the concrete being of a substance (considered at any given time) is not ontically distinct from the concrete being of its attributes at that time (whatever modes of the attributes are currently instantiated).

[16] 1683: 71; he uses 'thought or perception' to cover all conscious mental goings on.

Ryle also puts it well, although with disparaging intent, when he speaks of the idea that consciousness is 'self-intimating' in some constitutive way, or 'self-luminous', or 'phosphorescent' (1949: 158–9; see also 162–3, 178). Frankfurt is also helpful, although parts of this passage are potentially misleading:

what would it be like to be conscious of something without being aware of this consciousness? It would mean having an experience with no awareness whatever of its occurrence. This would be, precisely, a case of unconscious experience. It appears, then, that being conscious is identical with self-consciousness. Consciousness *is* self-consciousness. The claim that waking consciousness is self-consciousness does not mean that consciousness is invariably dual in the sense that every instance of it involves both a primary awareness and another instance of consciousness which is somehow distinct and separable from the first and which has the first as its object. That would threaten an intolerably infinite proliferation of instances of consciousness. Rather, the self-consciousness in question is a sort of *immanent reflexivity* by virtue of which every instance of being conscious grasps not only that of which it is an awareness but also the awareness of it. It is like a source of light which, in addition to illuminating whatever other things fall within its scope, renders itself visible as well (Frankfurt 1987: 162).[17]

The claims that are most likely to mislead in Frankfurt's passage are.

[a] consciousness *is* self-consciousness.

and the immediately preceding

[b] being conscious is identical with self-consciousness,

but [a] doesn't I think say more than [13], the AOI thesis that all awareness comports awareness of itself, and [b], which may presumably be adjusted to (or at least entails) *being conscious is identical with being self-conscious*, may be understood to be the same as to [2], USA, the key thesis that the subject of awareness is always present-moment-aware of itself. The—in my opinion correct—suggestion is (once again) that USA falls out of the AOI thesis as a necessary consequence of it, given principles [P1] and [P2] on pp. 280–1

---

[17] On the claim that consciousness is self-consciousness, compare again the quotations from Sartre in Zahavi, this vol. p. 56. Among Indian philosophers, Dignāga, Dharmakīrti, Śaṃkara, and others regularly use the trope of the light that illuminates itself. See e.g. Dreyfus and Ram-Prasad, this vol., pp. 120, 234.

above. If one also accepts [16], the S=A thesis, the ultimate identity of the subject and its awareness, then [a] and [b] come to the same thing.

5. Ground of the AOI Thesis

There's a lot to say about the metaphysical grounding of AOI. I take the central metaphysical question to be the following. Given that AOI is true—given that all awareness (necessarily) comports awareness of itself—why is this so? There seem to be two main options.

[O1] AOI is true because it's a necessary *consequence* of the intrinsic nature of awareness; and this intrinsic nature can none the less be specified independently of AOI in such a way that we can see why AOI is true.

[O2] The fact that AOI is true is *constitutive* of the intrinsic nature of awareness in such a way that that intrinsic nature can't be specified independently of the fact that AOI is true.

Locke endorses the second view, when he writes that 'thinking consists in being conscious that one thinks'.[18] Arnauld's position in the quoted passage is I think compatible with [O1], although it doesn't exclude [O2]. Descartes's position (see note 13) seems at first compatible with [O1], but the fact that the necessity of AOI is for him grounded in the *identity* of the awareness with the awareness of the awareness makes this less clear.

   This is a question for another time. My present aim is simply to lay out the way in which the non-thetic version of PSA, that is,

[1] the subject can be aware of itself as it is in the present moment of awareness

taken in its strong universal form, that is, as USA that

[2] the subject is always aware of itself as it is in the present moment of awareness

is seen to follow from a substantive thesis, the AOI thesis, which I've put through a series of formulations, beginning with

[4] all awareness involves awareness of awareness,

passing through

---

[18]   1689: 2.1.19; he uses 'thinking' in the broad Cartesian sense to cover all experiential goings on.

[11] all awareness on the part of any subject at any moment, comports awareness, at that moment, on the part of that same subject, of that very awareness at that very moment,

and ending with

[13] all awareness comports awareness of itself.

The move made here, from the claim that the subject is necessarily aware of its awareness to the claim that it is necessarily aware of itself, is guaranteed given [P1] and [P2] (*sc.* [3]). AOI itself may still need defence, and even when its truth is granted questions about its fundamental metaphysics will remain. But these are matters for another occasion.

6. Non–Thetic Present–Moment Self–Awareness

Does the plausibility of USA depend essentially on AOI? I'm not sure, and I'm now going to consider some other ways of expressing non-thetic present-moment awareness of self. According to Louis Sass,

The most fundamental sense of selfhood involves the experience of self not as an object of awareness but, in some crucial respects, as an unseen point of origin for action, experience, and thought.... What William James called...the 'central nucleus of the Self' is not, in fact, experienced as an entity in the focus of our awareness, but, rather, as a kind of medium of awareness, source of activity, or general directedness towards the world.

(Sass 1998: 562)

Bernard Lonergan remarks that

Objects are present by being attended to, but subjects are present [to themselves] as subjects, not by being attended to, but by attending. As the parade of objects marches by, spectators do not have to slip into the parade to be present to themselves.

(Lonergan 1967: 226)

In Samuel Alexander's words:

In knowing the object I know myself, not in the sense that I contemplate myself, for I do not do so, but in the sense that I live through this experience of myself.

(Alexander 1924: 1.xiv)

Arthur Deikman makes the same point: 'we know the internal observer not by observing it but by *being* it ... knowing by being that which is known is ... different from perceptual knowledge' (1996: 355).[19] This is knowledge 'by acquaintance'. There's a narrow, philosophically popular, independent-justification-stressing conception of knowledge that makes it hard for some to see this is really knowledge, but the claim doesn't really need defence. Rather the reverse: this particular case of knowledge, self-knowledge in non-thetic self-awareness, shows the inadequacy of the narrow conception of knowledge. The general point is backed up, most formidably, by the fact that knowledge of this kind must lie behind all knowledge of the narrower justification-involving sort, as a condition of its possibility. This is because it's a necessary truth that all justification of knowledge claims is relative to something already taken as given.

Certainly the eye can't see itself (unless there is a mirror). The knife can't cut itself (unless it is very flexible), and the fingertip can't touch itself. The idea that the subject of experience can't have itself as it is in the present moment as the object of its thought—the idea that 'my today's self', in Ryle's words, 'perpetually slips out of any hold of it that I try to take' (1949: 187)—has many metaphorical expressions. Laycock says that it is part of 'perennial Buddhist wisdom' (1998: 142), and so it is, considered as a truth about the limitations of a certain particular sort of thetic, object-posing self-apprehension. But it is, so taken, fully compatible with the claim that there's another non-thetic form of occurrent self-apprehension in which the subject can be directly aware of itself in the present moment, for example in the way just indicated by Lonergan, Sass, Alexander and Deikman. Dignāga and Dharmakīrti also hold that a cognition cognizes itself, and is in the present terms non-thetically aware of itself, although they don't in this context distinguish explicitly between thetic and non-thetic awareness.[20]

Does it follow, from the fact that this form of occurrent present-moment self-awareness is *non-thetic*, that it isn't *explicit* in any way? Is it

---

[19] Plainly 'knowing by being that which is known', or rather, perhaps, knowing (oneself) by being that which is knowing, does not require knowing everything there is to know about that which is known. On a standard materialist view, one may grant that that which is known, in this sort of self-presence of mind, has non-experiential being whose nature is not then known at all.

[20] See e.g. Dreyfus, this vol, p. 120. On the terms of the thin conception of the subject and the S = A thesis, then, Dignāga and Dharmakīrti can also be said to agree that the subject can be non-thetically aware of itself.

some sort of *implicit* awareness? No: there's a key sense in which the implicit/explicit distinction lacks application when 'awareness' is used to refer to occurrent experience, as here. 'Awareness' also has a dispositional use, as when we say of someone who is dreamlessly asleep that she's aware of your intentions, and this makes it seem natural enough to contrast implicit awareness with explicit awareness, just as we contrast implicit with explicit understanding, and implicit with explicit belief. The implicit/explicit distinction applies naturally enough in the dispositional realm, as when we say of a dreamless sleeper that she explicitly believes or understands or is aware that p, given that she has actually consciously entertained and assented to the thought that p at some time, or that she implicitly believes or understands or is aware that q, given (say) that she would assent to q but hasn't ever actually consciously thought or realized that q. The fact remains that there's no such thing as implicit occurrent awareness, because 'awareness' is currently defined (p. 247) as something that involves what-it's-likeness, which 'implicit' rules out.[21] Non-thetic occurrent awareness can't be said to be implicit occurrent awareness, then: it's simply awareness of content that isn't in the focus of attention, or rather, more simply, in attention.[22] We can also call it background awareness, perhaps, for background awareness isn't 'implicit' awareness either, any more than dim or peripheral awareness is.

Another way to put the point, perhaps, is to say that all occurrent awareness is *ipso facto* and *eo ipso* explicit awareness just in being, indeed, awareness, occurrent awareness, genuinely given in awareness, part of the actual content of experience that is experienced by the subject. This is, admittedly, a non-standard use of 'explicit', inasmuch as it allows that explicit awareness can be very dim, but one can use the word 'express' to do most of the work usually done by 'explicit', and the basic distinction is in any case clear: it's the undeniably real, if soft-bordered, distinction between express, foreground, attentive, thetic awareness, on the one hand, and more or less dim, peripheral, non-attentive, background, non-thetic awareness on the other.[23]

[21] This is not to say that one couldn't give sense to a notion of implicit awareness.

[22] 'In attention' is often better than 'in the focus of attention', because the notion of focus seems to contain the foreground/background distinction, and to exclude the possibility that there may be nothing more to one's experience, when one is attending, than what is in attention.

[23] One can even talk of unconscious occurrent awareness when considering things like blindsight; see, e.g. Rosenthal 2005. Note that although 'peripheral awareness' has a good use in describing visual

The distinction can be refined. There's a sense in which self-awareness of the sort described by Sass, Lonergan, and Deikman can be said to be *in the foreground* even though it isn't *thetic*. Such self-awareness is, or can be, a centrally structuring part of experience, in such a way that it's rightly classified as a foreground aspect of experience, even though there's also a respect in which it normally passes unnoticed, being entirely non-thetic. In the penultimate paragraph I suggested that we can equate 'non-thetic' with 'background', but I'm now inclined to overrule this by introducing a wider notion of foreground and claiming that

experiential elements may be constitutive of the nature of the foreground while not being thetic.

At this point we have five distinct expressions, and the terminology is threatening to go out of control. But the idea should be discernible to a sympathetic eye. On the present terms [i] all awareness is indeed *explicit* in the weak sense, since this now simply means is that it is genuine awareness, genuinely given in awareness. [ii] Some explicit awareness is *background*, and not at all thetic or express. [iii] Some explicit awareness is *foreground*, but still not *thetic* or *express*. [iv] Some foreground awareness is in addition thetic or express.

These matters need careful treatment (a careful terminology), and I won't say much more here, except to note a parallel with the case of the qualitative character of the sensation of blue when one looks at the sky. There's a clear respect in which the qualitative character of one's sensation of blue is in the foreground of experience—it floods one's experience—as one looks at the blue sky. But it is at the same time wholly 'diaphanous', in the sense that one sees 'through' it, as it were, in seeing the blue sky. It is to that extent wholly non-thetic, not in the (cognitive) focus of attention in any way, considered specifically as a sensation.[24] This being so, I'm now tempted to split 'express' from 'thetic', just as I previously split 'foreground' from 'thetic', and to say that the awareness of the sensation of blue is express but not thetic. I'll return to this idea on p. 294 below; I think these distinctions capture real differences

experience, and perhaps experience in other sensory modalities, the spatial metaphor is potentially misleading when giving a general characterization of elements of awareness that are out of (the focus of) attention.

[24] The use of 'diaphanous' to characterize sensation is not the same as Moore's famous use to characterize 'bare' consciousness (1901: 450). See e.g. Vam Cleve (2005). The place to start, when considering these questions, is with Reid 1785: 193–6 (§2.16); see also Montague 2009: 501–2.

although they need careful further work. Experience is an extraordinarily complex part of reality, and this is one dimension of its complexity.

7. Thetic Present-Moment Self-Awareness.

The form of present-moment self-awareness described by Sass and others is plainly non-thetic. This means that it isn't in conflict with the ancient eye objection, if the eye objection can be expressed as the claim that the subject of experience can't take itself as it is in the present moment of experience as the thetic object of its attention. As already remarked, I think that present-moment (no time lag) self-awareness can also be thetic, so that the eye objection is false even in that formulation, and I will now try to say why.

—This is hopelessly vague. Plus you haven't answered the 'systematic elusiveness' objection. You may think *I'm now thinking a puzzling thought,* or *I'm looking down on India,* or just *Here I am,* in an attempt to apprehend yourself as mental self or subject or thinker in the present moment, but in entertaining these contents you necessarily fail to apprehend the thing that is doing the apprehending—the entertainer of the content, the thinker of the thought, that is, yourself considered as the mental subject at that moment. Ryle is right. Any mental performance 'can be the concern of a higher-order performance'—one can think about any thought that one has—but it 'cannot be the concern of itself' (1949: 188–9). When one thinks an I-thought, this performance 'is not dealt with in the operation which it itself is. Even if the person is, for special speculative purposes, momentarily concentrating on the Problem of the Self, he has failed and knows that he has failed to catch more than the flying coat-tails of that which he was pursuing. His quarry was the hunter' (1949: 187). William James, whom you favour, quotes Comte's statement of the same point, and agrees with him that 'no subjective state, whilst present, is its own object; its object is always something else' (1890: 1.190).

It's arguable, though, that to think *this very thought is puzzling,* or *I'm now thinking a puzzling thought,* is precisely to engage in a performance that is concerned with itself; in which case a certain kind of seemingly immediate self-presence of mind is possible even in an intentional, designedly self-reflexive, and wholly cognitive act—a point quite independent of considerations of the sort adduced by Lonergan, Sass, Alexander, Deikman and many others. On this view, it's *only when one tries to apprehend expressly that one has succeeded* that one triggers the regressive step. Nor is it clear that hunters can't catch the quarry when the quarry is themselves. A detective with partial amnesia, sitting in her chair and reasoning hard, may identify herself as the person who committed the crime she is investigating. Wandering in the dark, I may get increasingly precise readings regarding the location of my quarry from a Global Positioning System, program my noiseless grabber robot to move to the correct spot, press the Grab button—and get grabbed.[25]

It may be said that concentration on cognitively articulated thoughts such as *I'm now thinking a puzzling thought* or *Here I am* can't deliver what is required, or provide a compelling practical route to appreciation of the point that it's possible to have express awareness of oneself apprehended specifically as the mental subject of experience in the present moment of experience. I agree. The best route to this point is much more direct. It doesn't involve any such discursively articulated representations, although it does require being in some sort of meditative condition. Then it's simply a matter of coming to awareness of oneself as a mental presence (or perhaps simply as: mental presence) in a certain sort of alert, but essentially unpointed, global way. The case is not like the eye that can't see itself, or the fingertip that can't touch itself. These old images are weak. A mind is rather more than an eye or a finger. If Ryle had perhaps spent a little more time on disciplined, unprejudiced mental self-examination, or had tried meditation, even if only briefly, and in an entirely amateur and unsupervised, Senior Common Room sort of way, he might have found that it's really not very difficult—although it's certainly not easy—for the subject of experience to be aware in the present moment of itself-in-the-present-moment. It's a matter of first focusing on the given fact of consciousness and then letting go in a certain way. As far as the level of difficulty is concerned, it's like maintaining one's balance on a parallel bar or a wire in a let-go manner that is relatively, but not extremely, hard to attain. One can easily lose one's

---

[25] There is also the case of Winnie the Pooh, Piglet and the Heffalump (Milne 1928).

balance—one can fall out of the state in question—but one can also keep it, and improve with practice.[26]

The attainment of such self-awareness, for brief periods in the unpractised (and the incompetent, such as myself), seems to involve a state that has no particular content beyond the content that it has in so far as it's correctly described as awareness or consciousness of the awareness or consciousness that it itself is, awareness that includes in itself awareness that it is awareness of the awareness that it itself is, but does so without involving anything remotely propositional (contrary to what the word 'that' suggests to many) or thetic in the narrow and apparently necessarily distance-involving, ob-ject-of-attention-posing way. The route to it that I have in mind involves a preparatory focusing on the fact of consciousness that stops the ordinary flow of content; it isn't just a matter of meditative awareness of breathing, say, or of whatever is passing in the mind, although these practices may on occasion precede and facilitate the same result. It may be a route to, or form of, what people have in mind when they speak of 'pure consciousness experience': consciousness that is consciousness of the consciousness that it itself is, and that includes consciousness that it is consciousness of the consciousness that it itself is.[27]

Something like this is, if only fleetingly, an early and rather routine step in certain meditative practices, and there's a pretty robust consensus about its reality, precise character, and (relative) ease of attainment, as there is also about the more often stressed point that it involves an experience of 'selflessness', an experience it's natural to express by saying that it seems that there is just subjectivity, rather than a subject, although there is still—necessarily—a subject in my metaphysically non-committal sense of the term, since all experience is necessarily experience-*for*, and although a subject in my sense of the term is still experienced. One mustn't be misled by the fact that this thetic present-moment self-awareness involves a sense of selflessness, or by the fact that I've characterized it with the impersonal mass terms 'awareness' and 'consciousness', into thinking that it isn't after all a genuine case of the phenomenon whose reality I'm trying to establish:

[26] One such method is Patricia Carrington's Clinically Standardized Meditation (1998).

[27] See, for example, Forman 1998, Shear 1998. See also Parfit 1998. It may be what Karme Chagme is describing in the passage quoted by Dreyfus (this vol., pp. 121–2).

awareness on the part of the subject of experience of itself in the present moment of experience.

The proposal, then, is that

[17] the subject of awareness can be fully thetically aware of itself as it is in the present moment of awareness,

which earns the laborious title

[17] the Possible Thetic Present-Moment Self-Awareness Thesis

—the Thetic PSA thesis, for short. It claims that thetic SA (present-moment self-awareness) is possible. It incorporates the idea that the neural time lag objection mentioned at the end of §2 doesn't apply. In Yogācāra, it classifies as a case of 'objectless cognition', a phenomenon whose possibility was much debated in that tradition.

8. Doubts about Thetic Present-Moment Self-Awareness

Can the claim that present-moment self-awareness (SA) can be fully thetic be maintained? It certainly seems right to say that the awareness of oneself can in this case be fully *express*, no less express than any awareness of anything is when one's awareness of it is thetic, even though there is in this case no sort of posing or positing or positioning of oneself for inspection of the sort that may seem to be built into the meaning of the word 'thetic'. I think, in fact, that it can also be said to be *thetic*, taking the core meaning of 'thetic' to be just: genuinely in the field of attention, genuinely in attention, and rejecting the idea that attention requires articulation or construction of such a kind that the subject is bound to present to itself in such a posed or set-up way given which one can't be said to be aware of it as it is at that moment. On this point, I think Ryle and a host of others are simply wrong. Their model of awareness is too rigid, insofar as it pushes the subject—the 'now-subject', one might say—into being necessarily cut off from its (attempted) object—itself. It hasn't been shown that there's an insuperable difficulty in the matter of present-moment or immediate (im-mediate) self-awareness—in apprehending the subject 'live'. This is certainly something special, but it seems that I can engage in it with no flying coat-tails time lag. The eye can't see itself, but the I isn't much like an eye.

If we take 'thetic' to entail some kind of structured operation of positing or positioning of an object of attention, a focusing that typically requires some sort of effortful maintenance, some sort of intellectual upkeep, then we may do best to distinguish 'thetic' from 'express', and fall back to 'express', leaving 'thetic' to denote an essentially time-lagged and distancing, cognitively articulated operation. On this understanding of 'thetic', present-moment self-awareness of the sort I have in mind can still be said to be foreground and express, but can't strictly speaking be said to be thetic. My inclination, however, is to resist this move, on the ground that an adequate and therefore broad understanding of *cognition* needs to allow for— acknowledge—the genuinely cognitive nature of this present-moment self-awareness. We need perhaps to try to wean our understanding of 'thetic' away from too narrow a conception of what cognition is, to allow that one can achieve a fully thetic state of awareness by a certain sort of letting go. and so assert the Thetic PSA thesis outright. I'm prepared to retreat to

[18] the subject of awareness can be fully expressly aware of itself as it is in the present moment of awareness

that is,

[18] the Possible Express Present-Moment Self-Awareness Thesis

(the Express PSA thesis, for short) if the word 'thetic' is judged to be irretrievably out of bounds. In the rest of this paper, though, I'm going to continue to defend the Thetic PSA thesis: I'm going to take the word 'thetic' to be principally tied simply to the idea of attention, attentiveness, full attention, and attempt to cultivate a sense of how attention (and cognition) can have forms that don't involve anything like discursively structured operations of positing or positioning things as objects of attention.

9. Defence of Thetic Present-Moment Self-Awareness

The fundamental objection to the Thetic PSA thesis, perhaps, is that thetic awareness is necessarily a *mediated* form of awareness, where this means not only that there is necessarily a time lag, but also that one inevitably has to do with a *representation* of the phenomenon one is aware of which is not the phenomenon itself. Here we come up against some very general questions about knowledge, and I'll limit myself to a few remarks.

'Cognitive' means 'of or pertaining to . . . knowing'. It follows immediately that the standard distinction between cognition and emotion is illegitimate, because our emotions, however fallible, are one of our main sources of knowledge of how things are. Putting that aside, the claim is that we need, when thinking about cognition, to acknowledge the reality as knowledge or cognition—knowledge or cognition in the fullest sense—of knowledge by direct acquaintance. This is how I know the nature of the pain that I feel now. Such knowledge by direct acquaintance is, one might say, perfect. (Knowledge of a priori truths can be no less perfect.) There's a crucial aspect of reality, one's experience (= the experiential-qualitative character or what-it's-likeness of one's experiences) that one knows as it is in itself, simply because 'the having is the knowing', and in such a way that there is no time lag.

—Suppose I accept this as an example of knowledge or cognition by direct acquaintance. It isn't going to be enough to illustrate what's supposed to be going on in Thetic SA. There are at least two objections.

[1] The notion of direct acquaintance seems clear enough when we consider sensory or feeling (sense/feeling) aspects of experience, but the direct acquaintance is standardly *non-thetic* in these cases, however express it is—however much it is in the overall experiential foreground. So it provides no model for *thetic* direct acquaintance.

[2] You've given us a proposed case of direct acquaintance for *sense/feeling* aspects of experience, but Thetic SA—if it exists at all—is presumably some kind of *non-sense/feeling* or *cognitive* direct acquaintance with oneself as subject; in which case, presumably, it has no experiential-qualitative feeling aspect at all. Even if you could come up with a model of thetic direct acquaintance in the sense/feeling case (which you haven't yet done), it wouldn't help with the case you're aiming at, which is a case of the non-sense/feeling direct acquaintance of the subject with itself.

First: I completely reject the equation of experiential-qualitative phenomena with sense/feeling phenomena. There is, in addition to sense/feeling phenomenology, sense/feeling experience, cognitive phenomenology, cognitive experience. Our experience has cognitive experiential-qualitative character in every sense in which it has sense/feeling experiential-qualitative character (for the purposes of argument I take 'sense/feeling' and 'cognitive', broadly understood as above, to be mutually exclusive, and jointly exhaustive of the field of experience). I've argued for this in other places and will take it for granted here.[28] There is, furthermore, a fundamental sense in which *all* experience as currently defined, that is, all what-it's-likeness, is a matter of direct acquaintance, be it sense/feeling or cognitive. So far, then, there's no reason to think that the idea of cognitive-experiential direct acquaintance is any more problematic than the idea of sense/feeling direct acquaintance. Some philosophers may find the idea of direct acquaintance with cognitive what-it's-likeness alarming, but it's backed by a point parallel to the point about knowledge made on p. 288: if there is any kind of cognitive experience at all, this kind of direct acquaintance must exist as a condition of its possibility.[29]

Second: I agree that the direct present-moment acquaintance involved in sense/feeling experience is standardly non-thetic. Sense/feeling experience is a huge part of our overall experience, for example, when we perceive things, but we very rarely focus on it.[30] So it's unclear how we can work a passage from the understanding of direct acquaintance given to us by non-thetic sense/feeling cases to Thetic SA, a subject's direct thetic present-moment acquaintance with itself, assuming that this involves some essentially non-sense/feeling and hence cognitive element, some cognitive apprehension of self.

Let me try to take an intermediate step. My having-is-the-knowing direct acquaintance with my headache is usually non-thetic—even when I'm painfully aware of it, so that it's in the overall experiential foreground. I find, though, that I can bring it about that I have it as thetic object of attention and *also* have having-is-the-knowing direct acquaintance with it. At the least, I can bring the pain sensation to (thetic) attention, and then, having done so, fall into experiencing it in the direct way in which I ordinarily take myself to experience objects in the world. And because what I am experiencing in this case is in fact my own sensation, this way of experiencing it can be having-is-the-knowing direct acquaintance.

---

[28] See, e.g. Strawson 1994: 5–13, Strawson forthcoming 2011.

[29] There is I think a connection here with Searle's notion of the Background. See Searle 1983.

[30] This is the truth in the 'transparency thesis', which is often inflated into a larger and false thesis.

This 'falling' is a relatively delicate operation, relative to ordinary everyday full-on thetic attention. For in everyday full-on thetic attention, I take it, the fact that the object of attention is being taken as object of attention is part of what is given in the overall character of the experience. But it is—I propose—precisely this aspect of everyday full-on thetic attention that can lapse, leaving the pain *in full attention* without there being any awareness of oneself as taking it as object of attention. When this happens, the fact that the object of attention is being taken as object of attention is no longer part of what is given in the overall character of the experience. Only the pain is. This can also occur more naturally, without being engineered for purposes of philosophical research, as it is here. It can happen in cases when one passes from thetic concentration to a state of absorption, artistic or otherwise.

One can do the same with the sensation of blue that one has when one looks at the blue sky. One can take the sensation of blue as thetic object of attention even as one continues to look at the sky (Reid and Moore make related but different points),[31] When one does this in a standard way, as a philosophical exercise of the sort prescribed by Reid, one's awareness of the sensation of blue will comport some sort of awareness of the fact that the sensation of blue is being taken as object of attention. But one can also go beyond this, I propose, into a state of direct thetic having-is-the-knowing acquaintance, a state of holding the sensation of blue in full attention, in which one's experience ceases to have, as any part of its content, the structure of subject-attending-to-something.[32]

If this is right, we now have a model of thetic direct acquaintance in the sense/feeling cases, and it's not clear why we should suppose that some huge, further gulf must appear when we turn from such cases—pain, or blue-experience—to the case of the subject. In fact, if the S = A thesis is correct, as

---

[31] It's not easy: it requires practice, as Reid pointed out: 'it is indeed difficult, at first, to disjoin things in our attention which have always been conjoined, and to make that an object of reflection which never was before, but some pains and practice will overcome this difficulty in those who have got into the habit of reflecting on the operations of their own minds' (1785: 196). See also James: when we consider perception, we see 'how inveterate is our habit of not attending to sensations as subjective facts, but of simply using them as stepping-stones to pass over to the recognition of the realities whose presence they reveal' (1890: 1.231). Some philosophers of perception mistakenly think that it is a mark of philosophical sophistication to hold that this can't be done.

[32] This isn't possible in Reid's model of attention to sensation, in fact, in which attention can only be paid to sensation that is—however fractionally—already past. See Yaffe 2009.

I think it is, then direct thetic acquaintance with pain or blue-experience is already direct thetic acquaintance with the subject. Relative to such cases, the special, alert, unpointed way of coming to awareness of oneself as a mental presence (or as mental presence) described in §7 is special only in that it doesn't involve any particular content like pain or blue-experience, and is therefore a candidate for the title 'pure consciousness experience'.[33]

—Even if you've now secured a case of thetic present-moment direct acquaintance, you've done it only for the sense/feeling case, and you still need to show how there can be non-sense/feeling present-moment direct acquaintance.

Well, again it's not clear that we need to build a bridge from the proposed cases of direct and thetic present-moment acquaintance with sense/feeling content in order to understand, or at least acknowledge the possibility or reality of, Thetic SA: direct, present-moment acquaintance of the subject with itself. Thetic SA must presumably be a non-sense/feeling matter, hence a cognitive matter, in some sense of cognitive—at least in part. But we already have it that there is such a thing as cognitive experience (it pervades every moment of our lives), and there is, as observed, a fundamental sense in which it's essentially constitutive of something's being experiential content at all that its subject or haver is in a relation of direct acquaintance with it— whether it be sense/feeling content or cognitive-experiential content.[34]

I've claimed that Thetic SA must be an essentially non-sense/feeling matter, at least in part, but I'm not sure quite what this amounts to, if only because currently standard classifications of what one may call the *experiential modalities* are extremely crude. Many assume that all experiential modalities are sensory or sense/feeling modalities: they exclude the idea that there are cognitive experiential modalities from the start. And even those who admit that there is a distinctively cognitive experiential modality may wish to

---

[33] It's still pretty special. Hume gives a correct (if widely misunderstood) report of the results of ordinary reflective mental self-examination when he denies that he ever has any such experience: 'when I enter most intimately into what I call *myself*, I always stumble on some particular perception or other.... I never can catch *myself* at any time without a perception, and never can observe any thing but the perception' (1739/40: 252).

[34] Remember that cognitive-experiential content is wholly internalistically understood. It's what you have wholly in common with your philosophical Twins, whether they're on Twin Earth, or in a vat, or have just popped miraculously into existence. See Strawson 2008c: 294–5, forthcoming 2011.

exclude the idea that there may be a *non-propositional* or *non-discursive* experiential modality which is nonetheless a non-sense/feeling experiential modality, and indeed a genuinely cognitive experiential modality. They're also likely to assume that the division between sense/feeling content and cognitive experiential content is absolute, as I have done for purposes of argument (without committing myself to the view that either can occur wholly without the other).

These are difficult issues, about which I feel unsure. I do, however, feel sure about the Thetic PSA thesis, the possibility of having direct thetic (in the wider sense) awareness of oneself as subject in the present moment of awareness. And I'm strongly inclined to think that this is, precisely, a non-propositional, non-discursive form of awareness, which is nonetheless properly said to be a matter of cognition.

10. Can the Subject Know Itself as it is in Itself?

In the last section I shifted from talking about present-moment *awareness* to talking about present-moment *direct acquaintance*, without explicitly acknowledging that this is a substantive move. As it stands, the Thetic PSA thesis doesn't, in speaking of awareness, make any claim about *knowledge* of the nature of the subject as it is in itself, still less about complete knowledge of the nature of the subject as it is in itself, of a sort that may seem built into the idea of direct acquaintance. And this, so far, may seem agreeable, because the picture of the subject as some kind of active principle lying behind all its experience, in such a way that one can't know its essential nature, even if one can be present-moment-aware of it as existing, remains beguiling. And given that it's beguiling, it seems good that it should be, so far, compatible with the Thetic PSA thesis.

I think, though, that the Thetic PSA thesis must accept its responsibilities; it must square up and take on the burden of implying that the subject have at least some acquaintance with itself as it is in itself. Supporters of the Thetic PSA thesis like myself should, in other words, accept that any argument that as-it-is-in-itself self-awareness is impossible is an argument against the Thetic PSA thesis.

The first thing to do, perhaps, is to ask why the picture of the subject as some kind of active principle lying behind all its experience is beguiling.

Part of the explanation is that the metaphysics of subject and predicate forces itself on us almost irresistibly, demanding that we distinguish between the subject of awareness and its various states of awareness in a way that I believe we must ultimately reject (quite independently of any commitment to the S = A thesis), and opening the way to the idea that we are at best aware of its states and so not of itself as it is in itself.[35] More respectably, our sceptical instincts are active, as they should always be, and they too invite us to acknowledge that we could perhaps be present-moment-aware of something and yet not know anything of its essential nature. They then suggest that absolutely all awareness of anything, other than the what-it's-likeness of experience, is *mediated* by a *representation* of that thing. So if the subject is aware of anything other than the what-it's-likeness of experience, then even if that other thing is itself, itself considered specifically as subject, still there is an affecting relation, albeit a self-affecting relation. The Kantian conclusion is then triggered: 'nothing which emerges from *any* affecting relation can count as knowledge or awareness of the affecting thing as it is in itself'.[36]

Kant famously takes the subject itself to be, for this reason, unknowable by itself as it is in itself, to be knowable only as it appears to itself (if only because it can only be encountered in the spatiotemporal—in particular temporal—form of sensibility).[37] The present suggestion is precisely that this isn't so—that it's possible to be aware of the subject of awareness in an immediate, but nonetheless express and indeed thetic (in-full-attention) way, that is parallel, at least in respect of immediacy, to the immediate (im-mediate) awareness we have of experiential what-it's-likeness. Usually, representation/mediation gets in the way, leaving us with 'mere appearance', but not in this case. On this view, Fichte's principal objection to Kant, which he expressed by saying that the subject can apprehend itself as subject in 'intellectual intuition', is quite correct, even if he has quite different reasons for it.[38]

---

[35] On this, and the dubiousness of the 'so', see e.g. Strawson 2008d.

[36] P. F. Strawson (1966: 238), summarizing Kant. See also Langton 1998.

[37] Consider, for example, his remark that 'I do not know myself through being conscious of myself as experiencing/thinking, but only when I am conscious of the intuition of myself as determined with respect to the function of experiencing/thinking' (1781/7: B406).

[38] Fichte 1794–1802. The notion of 'intellectual intuition' is precisely an attempt to characterize a kind of knowledge-of-x-involving *relation* with x that does not involve being *affected* by x in a way that inevitably limits one to knowledge of an *appearance* of x. Note that if one goes into a state of Thetic SA, one's awareness is bound to be genuinely awareness of oneself, the subject that one is—by the nature of the case.

Here, then, I boost the Thetic PSA thesis into being committed to the thesis that present-moment self-awareness is, and must, involve some sort of awareness of the nature of the subject as it is in itself, a step I'm happy to take for other Cartesian-Kantian-Jamesian reasons (the S=A thesis, the ultimate identity of subject and experience, experiencer and experiencing). Note, as a final reflection, that phrases like 'the subject's awareness of itself considered specifically as subject' can be taken in a stronger and a weaker sense. The stronger sense takes 'as subject' to mean that the subject's awareness of itself involves its bringing itself under the concept SUBJECT. The weaker sense requires only that what the subject is in fact concerned with is itself in so far as it is a subject, and allows that it may not, in being so concerned, be deploying anything recognizable as a concept of itself as subject. Here I have the weaker sense in mind. It allows for the idea, which seems necessary, that although all ordinary adult human beings possess the concept SUBJECT, it simply lapses—is not deployed in any way—in immediate thetic self-awareness. It also allows that children may be capable of immediate thetic self-awareness prior to possessing anything that can be dignified by the name 'concept'.[39]

11. Conclusion

I've proposed that the mental subject can be immediately relationally aware of itself, both in the non-thetic, everyday Sass-Lonergan-Deikman way, and also, exceptionally, in the express, thetic 'pure consciousness experience' way.[40] Evidence? Each must acquire it for himself or herself *in foro interno*. This doesn't mean it isn't empirical: it's wholly empirical. It does mean that it isn't publicly checkable, and it will always be possible for someone to object that the experience of truly present self-awareness is an illusion produced—say—by Rylean flashes of 'swift retrospective heed' (1949: 153). I think, though, that this notion of heed has the flying coat-tails

[39] Is one present-moment aware of oneself as being *oneself*? One might think 'Yes, but in some non-conceptual way', or, 'No, inasmuch as nothing that really qualifies as a sense of individuality remains.'

[40] According to Fasching, Indian soteriological traditions, such as Advaita Vedānta and Sāṃkhya-Yoga, equate this with realization of the 'self' —'which is nothing other than becoming aware of experiential presence (consciousness) as such' (Fasching, this vol., p. 207).

error built into it, and there is another larger mistake that can I think be decisively blocked.

Suppose that it's in the nature of all naturally evolved forms of experience/consciousness that they are, in the usual course of things, incessantly and seemingly constitutively in the service of the perceptual and agentive survival needs of organisms. It doesn't follow that this is essential to the nature of consciousness, that experience/consciousness must be defined in terms of adaptive function or perceptual content, even in part. The notion of pure consciousness experience is incompatible with any such conception of the nature of experience, but it's certainly not in tension with naturalism, properly understood, or with anything in the theory of evolution by natural selection.[41]

This is another topic that needs separate discussion. Here I simply want to note that even if experience isn't a primordial property of the universe,[42] and even if it came on the scene relatively late, there's no good reason—in fact it doesn't even make sense—to think that it first came on the scene because it had survival value. Natural selection needs something to work on, and can only work on what it finds. Experience/consciousness had to exist before it could be exploited and shaped, just as non-experiential matter did. The task of giving an evolutionary explanation of the existence of consciousness is exactly like the task of giving an evolutionary explanation of the existence of matter: there is no such task. Natural selection moulds the phenomena of experience it finds in nature into highly specific adaptive forms in exactly the same general way as the way in which it moulds the phenomena of non-experiential matter into highly specific adaptive forms.[43] The evolution by natural selection of various very finely developed and specialized forms of experience (visual, olfactory, etc.) is no more surprising than the evolution by natural selection of various finely developed and specialized types of bodily organization.[44] Even if (even though) evolved forms of experience have come to be what they are because they have certain kinds of content that give them survival value, kinds of content

---

[41] Naturalism, by which I mean real naturalism, acknowledges experience or consciousness as the most certainly known natural fact.

[42] I think it must be; see, e.g. Strawson 2006a.

[43] It may be that everything physical is experiential in some way, but I'll put this point aside.

[44] To speak of such forms of consciousness is not to reject the possibility that functional equivalents of, e.g., visual and auditory experience could exist in the complete absence of consciousness.

which are (therefore) essentially other than whatever content is involved in pure consciousness experience, it doesn't follow that pure consciousness experience is some sort of illusion. On the contrary: evolution gives us an explanation of how anything other than pure consciousness ever came to exist. Pure consciousness experience, as we can know it, may become possible only after millions of years of EEE-practical forms of consciousness, but it may for all that be uniquely revelatory of the fundamental nature of experience.[45]

References

Alexander, S. (1924), 'Preface to New Impression', *Space, Time and Deity* vol. 1 (London: MacMillan).

Aristotle (*c*.340 BCE/1936), *De Anima*, trans. W. S. Hett (Cambridge, MA: Harvard University Press).

——(*c*.340 BCE /1963), *Rhetoric*, ed. W. D. Ross (Oxford: Clarendon Press).

——(*c*.340 BCE /1963), *Categories* and *de Interpretatione*, ed. and trans. J. L. Ackrill (Oxford: Clarendon Press).

Arnauld, A. (1683/1990), *On True and False Ideas*, trans. with introduction by Stephen Gaukroger (Manchester: Manchester University Press).

Carrington, P. (1998), *Learn to Meditate: The Complete Course in Modern Meditation* (Rockport, MA: Element).

Dainton, B. (2008), *The Phenomenal Self* (Oxford: Oxford University Press).

Deikman, A. (1996), ' "I" = Awareness', *Journal of Consciousness Studies* 3: 350–356.

Descartes, R. (1641/1985), *Meditations*, in *The Philosophical Writings of Descartes* vol. 2, trans. J. Cottingham et al (Cambridge: Cambridge University Press).

——(1641–2/1985), *Objections and Replies* in *The Philosophical Writings of Descartes* vol. 2, trans. J. Cottingham et al (Cambridge: Cambridge University Press).

Fichte, J. (1794–1802/1982), *The Science of Knowledge*, ed. and trans. P. Heath and J. Lachs (Cambridge: Cambridge University Press).

Forman, R. (1998), 'What Does Mysticism Have to Teach Us About Consciousness?' in *Journal of Consciousness Studies* 5: 185–201.

Frankfurt, H. (1987/1988), 'Identification and Wholeheartedness', in *The Importance of What We Care About* (Cambridge: Cambridge University Press).

[45] My thanks to Mark Siderits for his very helpful comments.

Gurwitsch, A. (1941/1966), 'A non-egological conception of consciousness', in *Studies in Phenomenology and Psychology* (Evanston: Northwestern University Press).

Hume, D. (1739–40/1978), *A Treatise of Human Nature*, ed. L. A. Selby-Bigge and P. H. Nidditch (Oxford: Oxford University Press).

——(1748–51/1999), *An Enquiry Concerning Human Understanding*, ed. T. L. Beauchamp (Oxford: Oxford University Press).

Husserl, E. (1921-8/1973), *Zur Phänomenologie der Intersubjektivität, Texte aus dem Nachlass. Zweiter Teil: 1921–8* (The Hague: Martinus Nijhoff).

James, W. (1890/1950), *The Principles of Psychology*, 2 volumes (New York: Dover).

Kant, I. (1772/1967), Letter to Marcus Herz, February 21, 1772, in *Kant: Philosophical Correspondence 1759–99*, ed. and trans. Arnulf Zweig (Chicago: University of Chicago Press).

Langton, R. (1998), *Kant's Humility* (Oxford: Oxford University Press).

Laycock, S. (1998), 'Consciousness It/Self', *Journal of Consciousness Studies* 5: 141–52.

Locke, J. (1689–1700/1975), *An Essay Concerning Human Understanding*, ed. P. Nidditch (Oxford: Clarendon Press).

Lonergan, B. (1967), *Collection*, ed. F. Crowe (New York: Herder and Herder).

MacKenzie, M. (2007), 'The Illumination of Consciousness: Approaches to Self-Awareness in the Indian and Western Traditions' *Philosophy East and West* 57: 40–62.

Milne, A. A. (1928), *The House at Pooh Corner* (London: Methuen).

Montague, M. (2009), 'Perceptual experience', in *Oxford Handbook in the Philosophy of Mind*, ed. A. Beckermann and B. McLaughlin (Oxford: Oxford University Press).

Moore, G. E. (1903), 'The Refutation of Idealism', *Mind* 12: 433–53.

Nietzsche, F. (1885–8/2003), *Writings from the Last Notebooks*, trans. Kate Sturge, ed. Rüdiger Bittner (Cambridge: Cambridge University Press).

Parfit, D. (1998), 'Experiences, Subjects, and Conceptual Schemes', in *Philosophical Topics* 26: 217–70.

Ramsey, F. (1925/1997), 'Universals', in D. H. Mellor and Alex Oliver (eds.), *Properties* (Oxford: Oxford University Press).

Reid, T. (1748/2000), 'On the self', in *An Inquiry into the Human Mind on the Principles of Common Sense*, ed. D. Brookes (Edinburgh: Edinburgh University Press).

——(1785/2002), *Essays on the Intellectual Powers of Man*, ed. D. Brookes (Edinburgh: Edinburgh University Press).

Rosenthal, D. (2005), *Consciousness and Mind* (Oxford: Oxford University Press).

Ryle, G. (1949), *The Concept of Mind* (New York: Barnes and Noble).

Sartre, J.-P. (1936–7/2004), *Transcendence of the ego* trans. Andrew Brown, introduced by S. Richmond (London: Routledge).

——(1943/1969), *L'être et le néant* (*Being and Nothingness*), trans. H. Barnes. (London: Methuen).

——(1948/1967), 'Consciousness of Self and Knowledge of Self', in N. Lawrence and D. O'Connor (eds.), *Readings in Existential Phenomenology* (Englewood Cliffs, NJ: Prentice-Hall) 113–142.

——(1948), 'Conscience de soi et connaissance de soi,' *Bulletin de la Société Française de Philosophie* 42: 49–91.

Sass, L. (1998), 'Schizophrenia, Self-consciousness and the Modern Mind', *Journal of Consciousness Studies* 5: 543–65.

Searle, J. (1983), *Intentionality* (Cambridge: Cambridge University Press).

Shear, J. (1998), 'Experiential Clarification of the Problem of Self', *Journal of Consciousness Studies* 5: 673–86.

Strawson, G. (1994), *Mental Reality* (Cambridge, MA: MIT Press).

——(1999), 'The Self and the Sesmet', *Journal of Consciousness Studies* 6: 99–135.

——(2003a), 'Real materialism', in L. Antony and N. Hornstein (eds.), *Chomsky and his Critics*, ed. (Oxford: Blackwell).

——(2003b), 'What is the relation between an experience, the subject of the experience, and the content of the experience?', *Philosophical Issues* 13: 279–315, revised version see (2008b).

——(2005/2008), 'Intentionality and Experience: Terminological Preliminaries', in G. Strawson *Real Materialism and Other Essays* (Oxford: Clarendon Press).

——(2006a), 'Realistic Monism: Why Physicalism Entails Panpsychism', in A. Freeman (ed.), *Consciousness and its Place in Nature* (Thorverton: Imprint Academic).

——(2006b), 'Reply to Commentators, with a Celebration of Descartes', in A. Freeman (ed.), *Consciousness and its Place in Nature* (Thorverton: Imprint Academic).

——(2008a), *Real Materialism and Other Essays* (Oxford: Clarendon Press).

——(2003/2008b), 'What is the Relation between an Experience, the Subject of the Experience, and the Content of the Experience?' in G. Strawson *Real Materialism and Other Essays* (Oxford: Clarendon Press), revised version of Strawson (2003b).

——(2008c), 'Real Intentionality 3', in *Theorema* 27, and in G. Strawson *Real Materialism and Other Essays*, (Oxford: Clarendon Press).

——(2008d), 'The Identity of the Categorical and the Dispositional', *Analysis* 68/4: 271–82.

——(2009), *Selves: An Essay in Revisionary Metaphysics* (Oxford: Oxford University Press).

——(2011), 'Cognitive Phenomenology: The Sixth Āyatana', in T. Bayne and M. Montague (eds.), *Cognitive Phenomenology* (Oxford: Oxford University Press).

Strawson, P. (1966), *The Bounds of Sense* (London: Methuen).

Van Cleve, J. (2005), 'Troubles for Radical Transparency', http://www-ref.usc. edu/~vancleve/

Yaffe, G. (2009), 'Thomas Reid on Consciousness and Attention', *Canadian Journal of Philosophy* 39/2: 165–94.

Zahavi, D. (2006), 'Thinking about Self-Consciousness: Phenomenological Perspectives', in U. Kriegel and K. Williford (eds.), *Consciousness and Self Reference* (Cambridge, MA: MIT Press).

11

Buddhas as Zombies:

A Buddhist Reduction of Subjectivity

MARK SIDERITS

1. Introduction

In the phenomenological tradition, the two questions,

Does subjectivity require a self or subject?

and,

Is consciousness intrinsically reflexive?

have come to be linked.[1] As other contributors to this volume have pointed out, one part of the Buddhist tradition likewise saw a connection here. Certain Buddhist philosophers held both that the first question required a negative answer, and that this in turn required them to answer the second question in the affirmative. A non-egological account of consciousness is vulnerable to the objection that the phenomenal character of conscious states requires a conscious subject: it is incoherent to claim that there is what-it-is-likeness and yet no such thing as that-for-which-it-is-like. The Buddhist philosophers in question embraced the reflexivity thesis as part of a strategy that was meant to answer this objection. The idea, roughly, was that a non-dual account of cognition, one on which awareness of content is really just a cognition's cognizing itself, would preserve phenomenality

[1] I have greatly benefitted from discussions with Georges Dreyfus, Galen Strawson, Evan Thompson, and Dan Zahavi on the topics discussed here.

while not endangering the core Buddhist claim that the self is no more than a reification.

Not all Buddhist philosophers accepted this strategy, however. The reflexivity thesis was accepted only by the Yogācāra-Sautrāntika school;[2] it was rejected by all the Abhidharma schools,[3] as well as by Prāsaṅgika Madhyamaka and those Svātantrika Mādhyamikas who followed the Sautrāntika line.[4] What I should like to do is explore what this Buddhist alternative might look like, and what it might tell us about our options when we theorize consciousness. I shall begin with a brief sketch of the history of Buddhist non-egological accounts of consciousness. The point of this sketch is to isolate and clarify what may be an interesting Buddhist alternative to the Buddhist position described elsewhere in this volume. This alternative Buddhist position contains the following three elements:

1. Subjectivity (= phenomenality) requires a subject or self.
2. There is no self.
3. Consciousness is irreflexive.

The upshot, given certain plausible assumptions concerning the nature of cognition, is that consciousness cannot be ultimately real. In the remainder of the essay following the historical sketch, we shall see what resources the Buddhist philosophical tradition might contain for defending such an outlandish claim.[5]

---

[2] Yao (2005: 6–41) claims that the Mahāsāṃghikas also accepted the thesis that all cognitions are reflexive or self-cognizing. The evidence he cites is equivocal, however. The context in which this claim is attributed to them is a discussion of the knowledge of a liberated person. The question is whether such a person knows the nature of all ultimately real entities at one time. While other Abhidharma schools claim that such knowledge occurs serially, the Mahāsāṃghikas say there can be a single cognition that cognizes all *dharmas* or ultimate reals. Since this cognition is itself a *dharma*, this means it is included in the set of all *dharmas* whose nature is cognized. What is unclear is whether the cognition involved here is perceptual in the strong sense of what Nyāya calls non-conceptual perception. Only if it is would we have in this claim an anticipation of Dignāga's view.

[3] By 'Abhidharma' I mean what is also sometimes called Śrāvakayāna, the teachings of the so-called 18 schools of 'Hearers'. Representative works of Abhidharma thought include the Theravāda compendium *Visuddhimagga* by Buddhaghosa, and *Abhidharmakośabhāṣya* by the Sautrāntika philosopher Vasubandhu. (Strictly speaking Sautrāntika is not an Abhidharma school, but its project is sufficiently like that of the 18 schools that it may usefully be put under that rubric here.)

[4] For Bhāviveka's rejection of reflexivity see Eckel 2008: 288, 437.

[5] I should say in advance that this outlandish position was not to my knowledge held by any Indian Buddhist school. I arrive at it through a combination of rational reconstruction and speculation based on positions actually held by various Indian philosophers. I engage in this exercise because I think there may be interesting things we can learn when we take seriously the resources provided by the Indian philosophical tradition.

2. The Buddhist Reductionist Understanding of Non-Self

The Buddha said that suffering arises because of our ignorance about our identity. We are each trapped on the wheel of *saṃsāra* because we have a false view about what the 'I' truly is. Thus far his teachings are not unlike those of other Indian emancipatory projects (see Fasching and Ram-Prasad, this volume). What sets his apart is the doctrine of non-self (*anātman*). The Indian philosophical tradition, both Brahmanical and Buddhist, took this to be the ultimate rejection of any entity that might serve as referent of the 'I', as owner of the states of the person.[6] Of course the Buddha did not deny that persons experience such things as pleasure and pain. Indeed one of the Buddha's core teachings is that there is suffering, and it is virtually axiomatic that suffering is adjectival on a sufferer, or more generally that experience requires an experiencer. In his teachings, the Buddha follows the common-sense way of understanding such things when he attributes such states to persons. This appears to conflict with his teaching of non-self. The tradition sought to resolve this conflict by claiming that, in such teachings, the Buddha is merely using the common parlance, that such teachings are merely 'conventionally true' and not 'ultimately true'. It is out of this hermeneutical device that there emerges the articulation of the non-self doctrine that I call Buddhist Reductionism.

Buddhist Reductionism is based on the claim that if 'I' is a referring expression then its referent might be one of two things: it might be the self, defined as that one part of the psycho-physical complex that is its essence, or it might be the person, the whole that is constituted by the psycho-physical elements when properly arranged in a causal series. Buddhist Reductionists claim that there is no self, and that the person is only conventionally, and not ultimately, real. To say that the person is only conventionally real is to call it a kind of useful fiction. The idea is that, strictly speaking, there are

---

[6] Some modern scholars (e.g. Albahari 2006) claim that the Buddha meant to deny only an empirically accessible self, not the self *tout court*. While I am skeptical that the Buddha intended to affirm a transcendent self, or even to leave his teachings open to the interpretation that there is such a thing, this is not the place to engage in a dispute over 'what the Buddha really meant'. What is, I think, beyond dispute is how the Indian philosophical tradition subsequently took the Buddha's teaching of non-self, namely as the straightforward denial that anything ultimately real might serve as experiencer, controller, and ground of diachronic personal identity.

only impersonal psycho-physical elements in a causal series, but the cognitive economies achieved by thinking of such a series as a single thing serve significant interests. It is important to note that this makes Buddhist Reductionism importantly different from eliminativism about persons. The Eliminativist would agree that persons are not ultimately real, but they would add that persons are use*less* fictions. Reductionists claim instead that given what is ultimately real (impersonal psycho-physical elements in complex causal relations), there is considerable utility for creatures like us in thinking and acting as if such things do exist. On this analysis, suffering comes from mistaking this useful fiction for something ultimately real, and thus coming to see what is strictly speaking just a causal series of psycho-physical elements as that single entity for which events in the series have meaning and value.[7]

A key move in the construction of this fiction is what is called appropriation (*upādāna*), a disposition whereby different parts of a series are taken as 'I' or 'mine'. Note that this construction is held to be useful up to a point (namely the point at which, by taking it too seriously, we generate existential suffering). It follows that constructionist views of the self and of personal identity, such as the narrative self theory, may be compatible with Buddhist Reductionism despite the latter's explicit denial of a self. For the reasons that make it useful (up to a point) to believe that there are persons might be best served if persons were organized heuristically around a narrative structure. Seeing one's life as a sort of self-authored narrative might, for instance, serve the important purpose of helping in the maximization of overall well-being in a given causal series over time, by rationalizing present sacrifices as serving longer-term interests. In that case, a Buddhist Reductionist could claim that the narrative self is conventionally real.

No such self could, however, be ultimately real according to Buddhist Reductionism. This is because its view is grounded in a thorough-going mereological reductionism, according to which anything analyzable into a multiplicity of distinct constituents is not ultimately real. A narrative self must be so analyzable in order to serve its function. The richer the life, the more varied must be the ends intrinsic to the self. And on the sort of mereological reductionism at work here, even an allegedly simple entity

---

[7] I discuss the distinction between Reductionism and Eliminativism in more detail in chapter 1 of Siderits 2003.

turns out to be partite and thus reducible if it has more than one intrinsic property (AKBh *ad* AKB VI.4. See Abbreviations at the end of this essay.). So while belief in a self for whom events in this life have meaning and value may be useful (up to a point), such a self can at best be a useful fiction.

The point beyond which this fiction ceases to be useful is, of course, the point at which the well-being promoted by its adoption is outweighed by the suffering that results from taking it as more than a useful fiction. This suffering is, paradigmatically, the frustration, alienation, and despair that come with the realization of one's own mortality. This realization typically threatens to drain one's life of all significance by revealing the happiness-seeking project to be unsustainable in the long run: How can the events in my life have meaning if in the long run that for which they have value will cease to exist? The Buddhist soteriological project may be seen as at bottom an attempt to show how to reap the benefits of the useful fiction of the person, without paying the steep price exacted when we take it literally.[8]

This gives us an important criterion in assessing proposed accounts of cognition from a Buddhist perspective. Buddhist philosophers tend to be wary of anything that might be taken to be a self. Collins once claimed that this represents no more than a linguistic taboo on words like 'I' and 'self' (Collins 1982: 183). This wariness may instead stem from a genuine concern that there be nothing that could serve as the basis for suffering-inducing appropriation. In assessing accounts of cognition, the Buddhist philosopher will want to know whether the appeal of a given account stems, covertly, from its appearing to affirm such things as human value and dignity, or the richness of a fully human life. As other contributors to this volume have pointed out, there are any number of different sorts of self on offer, with varying degrees of thinness or thickness.[9] It is conceivable that some sort of self is necessary for an adequate account of human cognition. Perhaps subjectivity does require a subject, not only conventionally (as the Buddhist

---

[8] For more on what it might mean to live in this mode, see Siderits 2006, Goodman 2009.

[9] For instance, the sort of 'embodied self' that is required to explain motor control (discussed by Thompson, Krueger, and MacKenzie, this volume) is probably too thin to arouse Buddhist suspicions. That an animate organism must be able to tell its body from the surrounding environment, to locate its movable parts within that environment, and to predict the results of motion of its body parts, is indisputable. But as neuroscience uncovers more about the brain mechanisms that support these abilities, it becomes increasingly clear that they involve no more than the most straightforward of feedback loops, and thus nothing that could provide much solace to those seeking the basis for a sense of rich narrative depth. It seems unlikely that sea slugs experience existential suffering.

Reductionist readily grants) but ultimately as well. The Buddhist simply cautions that acceptance of such an entity should be based on compelling evidence, and not just on the desire that it be possible for our lives to have value and dignity.

Buddhist philosophers were, of course, familiar with the view that the self is just of the nature of consciousness (found in the Upaniṣads, and held by Sāṃkhya, and later by Vedānta—see Fasching, this volume), or that consciousness is one of the qualities of the self (held by Nyāya). One very early response is that consciousness cannot be the self since it is impermanent. Consciousness is here acknowledged as among those psychophysical elements (skandhas) that make up the person, and as thus itself real. But, it is claimed, since consciousness arises in dependence on contact between sense faculty and sensible object, and the senses of vision and smell are distinct, the consciousness that takes the color of the flower as object must be distinct from that which takes its smell as object a moment later. The assumption at work here is that the self is meant to be the ground of diachronic personal identity, and as such would have to endure as long as the person endures.

A different assumption about the self is the target of another argument developed later in the Abhidharma tradition. This assumption is that the act-object model is appropriate for understanding the nature of consciousness. That this assumption would prove useful in trying to establish the existence of a self is evident from its role in the Cartesian cogito. In the hands of Nyāya and Mīmāṃsā philosophers it is deployed by way of the grammatical point that a construction involving a verb and an occurrence of the accusative case requires an occurrence of the nominative: the cutting (verb) of the tree (accusative) requires that there be a cutter (nominative). So consciousness requires a subject, which is understood to be just the self.

One Abhidharma response to this argument builds on the thesis that all existents are not just impermanent (as the Buddha claimed) but momentary, lasting but an instant before perishing and being replaced by others. This thesis has the interesting consequence that there can be no such thing as the performance of an action. To speak of someone or something performing an action is to presuppose that an entity can continue to exist through three distinct times: when the action is yet to be performed, when the action is being performed, and when the action has been completed. If all existing things are momentary, then nothing endures through two times, let alone three. Applied to the case of consciousness, this not only undermines the argument for the self as the agent of the action of being conscious. It also subverts the view, implicit in Sāṃkhya and explicit in Advaita Vedānta, that the self is not a substance, but just the pure activity of witnessing. As Vasubandhu puts it, consciousness 'does nothing whatever... it simply arises in conformity with its object' (AKBh IX, 472).

To this it is objected that we are conscious not only of the smell of the flower, but also that the flower we now smell is the same flower that we saw a moment ago. This common experience of diachronic synthesis is said to require an enduring conscious subject. To this it is replied that the apparent awareness of continuity is like the appearance of a circle of fire in the case of a whirling firebrand. This analogy requires careful unpacking. Part of the point, of course, is that there is no circle of fire, only a rapid succession of occurrences of fire at the different points in the arc traveled by the torch. The example derives additional force from the fact that, on the assumption of momentariness, there is no continuous fire traveling around the arc, just distinct occurrences of fire at each point. The wheel we seem to see is actually a series of successive flames. And on the mereological reductionism that is central to Abhidarma, a series can at best be a conceptual fiction, something that is conventionally, but not ultimately, real. For a series is like the chariot in that any effect we ascribe to it (such as, in the case of the wheel of fire, appearing to be two meters wide) is to be explained in terms of the effects of its parts (this flame occurring here, the next occurring there, etc.). Since causal efficacy is the hallmark of the real, and the wheel lacks autonomous explanatory power, it cannot be ultimately real. Like the chariot, it is something we take to be real due to our interests and cognitive limitations.

This reply might seem to miss the real point of the objection. The opponent might grant that the wheel of fire is a sort of mental construction, but still deny that the consciousness that takes there to be such a wheel could be any such thing. Now on the assumption that a given occurrence of consciousness arises in dependence on sense faculty and object, the consciousness that is aware of fire at one point is distinct from the consciousness that is aware of fire at any other point in the arc (since the two consciousnesses have distinct objects and so distinct causes). So the Abhidharma view will be that it is a series of successive consciousnesses that constructs the wheel. But the opponent will object that it is absurd to suppose a succession of distinct consciousnesses could do any such thing. For on this view there is nothing that is aware first of fire at this point, then of fire at the next point. Awareness of continuous succession requires either an enduring conscious-ness (the Sāṃkhya and Vedānta view), or an enduring subject as owner and synthesizer of distinct consciousness episodes (the view of Nyāya and Mīmāṃsā).

The Abhidharma response will be that a given cognition can inherit information from earlier cognitions in the series, with the result that it and its neighbors can cognize the series of flames as making up a wheel in the specious present. To see the plausibility of this reply, consider the case of the motion detector that turns on the yard lights when a stray raccoon passes by. The processor that performs this feat does so by retaining information from the immediately preceding scan of the area while performing a new scan. When the two resulting wave patterns match, they cancel each other out and no further result follows, save that information from the current scan is stored in short-term memory. When they do not match, the disparity causes the light switch to be tripped. Here it is a single enduring processor that performs the sequence of scans. But one could achieve the same result using a new processor for each scan. All that matters is that the processor that scans at t_n cause there to be, in the processor that scans at t_{n+1}, a standing wave that represents the scan input at t_n. Comparison of the states at t_n and t_{n+1} does not require an enduring 'witness' of both states. Synthesis is compatible with a series of ownerless, momentary, but causally connected, consciousnesses.

The Buddhist Reductionist stance on consciousness and the self depends crucially on mereological reductionism, the view that the composite entities of our folk ontology are conceptual fictions, conventionally but not ulti-mately real.[10] To this it is sometimes objected (e.g. Thompson 2007, Mackenzie this volume) that the 'linear' conception of causality at work in mereological reductionism is inadequate. As Merricks (2002) nicely illustrates, mereological reduction goes through on the grounds that causa-tion in the matter at hand is bottom-up and not top-down: the effects that we attribute to the bicycle are all produced by the suitably arranged parts. It

---

[10] For more on the mereological reductionism of Buddhist Reductionism, see Siderits 2009. It is crucial to bear in mind that the sort of reduction in play here is ontological, not semantic. The question is not whether it is possible to give a complete semantic analysis of ordinary ways of talking that is couched in a language containing no terms for complex entities. The question is whether the world itself contains, independently of the ways we talk and think, complex entities.

will be said that while this might be true of artifacts like chariots and bicycles, it is not true of certain complex dynamic systems such as organisms, which exhibit a kind of system causality that cannot be captured with a linear, bottom-up model. This idea, that novel causal powers emerge at higher levels of complexity, has a long history. And as that history illustrates, caution is required in assessing it. The fact that we can 'compute the embryo' (Rosenberg 1997) certainly suggests that we can predict macro-level properties of the organism from micro-level knowledge of its causal antecedents. The feedback loops of such organic processes as immune system functioning are also readily decomposable, along the lines of such models as audio (mike-amp-speaker) feedback, and the self-controlling home heating system. Once we prise apart ontological and semantic reduction, we may come to see that the appearance of system-level causation often stems from our need to treat the system as one big thing in order to manage our cognitive economies. It is sometimes claimed that since RNA is a self-assembling structure, its causal powers cannot be reduced to those of its constituent molecules. But this consequence does not follow from the structure's being self-replicating. It would only follow that RNA has irreducible causal powers if the structure could not have first appeared through the unprecedented combination of molecular components. There is ongoing research into the question whether terrestrial processes could have brought this about. It would be presumptuous to make any claim about this in advance of definitive research results. But given the past history of emergentism, it would surely be rash to take our current lack of knowledge about how it might have happened as evidence that it cannot have happened.[11]

---

[11] What is most fundamentally at issue in the dispute between the Buddhist Reductionist and those critics who favor emergentist or non-reductive supervenience approaches is the direction of the constraint arrow between causation and explanation. Reductionists claim that an acceptable explanation must appeal to causal laws. Their opponents claim that it is the other way around, that what counts as an acceptable causal law is constrained by what serves as an adequate explanation. It is possible that this dispute might be resolved through appeal to Dennett's notion of the intentional stance, but I shall not attempt to do that here. All of this proceeds on the realist assumption that there is a ready-made world. If the anti-realist arguments of Madhyamaka are valid, then all bets are off: since causation would itself then be a conceptual construction, there could be no question as to whether causation is ultimately bottom-up, top-down, circular, loopy, or none of the above. For discussion of what Madhyamaka anti-realists might have to say about the conventional status of causation, see Siderits 2010.

3. Subjectivity without Subjects?

A new phase in the development of Buddhist Reductionist thinking about consciousness begins with the Sautrāntika school. While there was considerable controversy among Abhidharma thinkers concerning the proper analysis of cognitive processes, the tradition before Sautrāntika was united in holding to the direct realist view of perception that was most likely the Buddha's own view (Dhammajoti 2007: 136–44). Sautrāntika rejects that view in favor of representationalism, on the grounds that there is a time lag between the contact of sense faculty with sensible object and the occurrence of sensory cognition. Since the object lasts only a moment, it no longer exists when the cognition occurs, so it cannot be the object of that cognition. The direct object of sensory cognition must instead be a mental image or representation. Now it was open to Sautrāntika to retain the old model of sensory cognition as a mental act operating on a distinct object, only 'internalize' the object by making it a separate mental state that then serves to represent the external object with which the perceptual process began. But this was not the path they ultimately chose. And perhaps with good reason, since a representationalism of this sort invites an understanding of the mind as Cartesian theater, with consciousness as spectator viewing the images brought in by the senses. Instead, in later Sautrāntika we find the claim that awareness of sensory content occurs through the arising of a cognition that bears the form of the physical object. The experience of seeing blue is just the occurrence of a cognition that has blue color as its form. Consequently, a cognition cognizes itself.

Dignāga is widely held to have first developed this reflexivity claim, but it seems likely to have originated somewhat earlier, in Sautrāntika.[12] Dignāga is the founder of the Yogācāra-Sautrāntika school of Buddhist epistemology, the aim of which is to develop a theory of knowledge acceptable to both the representationalist-realist Sautrāntika and the subjective idealist Yogācāra. Yogācāra took the logical next step following Sautrāntika's representationalism, playing Berkeley to their Locke. But Yogācāra also developed some interesting views about the nature of consciousness (discussed in

---

[12]   Yao (2005: 97–118) discusses the evidence for the claim of a Sautrāntika origin.

greater detail by Dreyfus and by Ganeri, this volume). Of particular importance here is their claim that consciousness is ultimately non-dual in nature.
This first comes out in their assertion that subjective idealism is soteriologically effective in the quest for nirvana because the feeling of interiority
that is central to the sense of self depends on contrast with an external world,
so that all sense of self must dissolve once one realizes that there is no
external world. This suggests that Buddhist Reductionists had begun to
worry about the problem of subjectivity—the problem that the phenomenal
character of cognitive states seems to require that there be a subject for
which they have this character. This might then be part of the motivation
behind Dignāga's formulation of the reflexivity claim. Also worth noting is
that this defense of Yogācāra subjective idealism involves an explicit disavowal of the perspectival self argued for by Albahari (this volume). If one
attains the ideal state by dissolving all sense of interiority, then the ideal state
cannot involve the sense that the presentations of consciousness are from a
perspective.[13]

Dignāga is famous for his claim that consciousness is self-illuminating,
that it illuminates both its object and itself, just as light makes visible not
only the objects in a room but itself as well. He also claims that each instance
of consciousness has two forms, the form of the intentional object and its
own form as cognizer, but that these two forms are ultimately non-distinct,
it being only the demands of conceptuality that lead us to see a difference
here. And he formulates this view in defense of the Yogācāra claim that
consciousness is ultimately devoid of the subject-object dichotomy.
Dignāga might then appear to be responding to the problem of subjectivity.
For his reflexivity claim is treated as an answer to the question how
consciousness is cognized, and this seems to be a way of addressing the
perspectival nature of consciousness. Dignāga's answer to this question—
that consciousness cognizes itself in cognizing its object—looks like it could
have been designed to show the compatibility of Reductionism with that
nature. It would nonetheless be surprising, given that no Brahmanical critic
of Buddhist Reductionism raises the question of subjectivity per se. Their
objections continue to be those discussed above, having to do with the

---

[13] This of course invites the objection that Yogācāra must therefore embrace solipsism. The late
Yogācāra thinker Ratnakīrti agrees, but holds that this is no fault. See Kajiyama 1965.

synthetic unities required for phenomena like experience-memory, cross-modal perception, and the karma–fruit link.[14]

Be that as it may, there would seem to be a genuine problem for the Reductionist here. Reductionism about things of kind K typically involves showing that our belief that there are Ks is perfectly understandable despite there being, strictly speaking, no such things, in that this is how things will naturally appear to us given the facts about the im-K-ish things that do exist, plus the facts about our interests and cognitive limitations. This may make perfectly good sense when the Ks are heaps, or chariots, or ships. But when the K in question is the person, one will naturally ask just who the 'us' is to whom the impersonal entities and events appear. Reductionisms try to demote their targets to a second-tier ontology of entities that are in some sense 'subjective'. But when the target is the person, such demotion may seem problematic, in that it is unclear how there can be such a status in the absence of a real subject. Shoemaker (1985) may have had something like this difficulty in mind when, in his review of Parfit's *Reasons and Persons*, he claimed that the ontological reduction of persons that Parfit seemed to wish for would require a reduction of the mental as well, to either the physical or to events characterized functionally. So whether or not Dignāga had this problem in mind when he formulated his reflexivity claim, it is still worth inquiring whether his view offers Buddhist Reductionism any aid on this score.

Might Dignāga's approach succeed in answering the subjectivity objection? Strawson's (2008) discussion of the relation between experiential content and (thin) subject sheds some helpful light here. Now Strawson does call it 'a necessary truth' that there is a subject whenever there is subjectivity (2008: 183). And what Dignāga must give the Buddhist Reductionist is a way of affirming subjectivity or what-it-is-like-ness that does not require an experiencing subject. Strawson's thin subject exists only for a moment, and so would be considered unobjectionable by Abhidharma standards. But we are supposing Dignāga is concerned that even a fleeting subject of experience can serve as grounds for existential suffering, and wants to show that phenomenal content is possible without even this thinnest of subjects. Strawson's claim must be read with caution however, for this comes in the context of a

---

[14] That is, Indian realists about the self wanted an enduring subject of experience, and would not rest content with the 'pearl self' of Strawson 1997. The central focus of debate continued to be the Buddhist Reductionist contention that consciousness is necessarily impermanent or episodic. For an interesting attempt on the part of an Indian realist to circumvent this objection to the self, see Watson 2006.

sustained argument for the conclusion that the distinction between subject and content of experience is at best only conceptual, not real. And this sounds very much like Dignāga's claim that cognition's two forms (the form of the object and the form of its nature as cognizing) are only conceptually and not ultimately distinct. It seems then that Strawson's 'necessary truth' holds only conventionally—which for Dignāga means for purposes of discourse, the ultimate truth being inexpressible. Ultimately, cognition is non-dual, but this non-duality being inexpressible, it cannot be stated and so cannot be the content of any sort of true statement.

This identity of subject and content would go some way toward explaining the much-touted immunity from error through misidentification allegedly possessed by our awareness of our own conscious states. That we cannot be wrong in thinking that a given state is our own is sometimes seen as evidence, not only for the existence of a subject of experience (as Fasching, this volume, interprets it), but also for reflexivity. It could thus serve as support for the self-illumination view (though Dignāga did not so use it). The idea is that since subjective states are simply and immediately given as one's own, it must be the case that in undergoing such a state one is immediately aware, not only of its content but of its being experienced as well. If, as Dignāga and Strawson seem to be saying, cognizing and content are only conceptually and not ontologically distinct, then it follows that cognizing of content just is cognizing of the cognizing. So it is hardly any wonder that one cannot go wrong in identifying an experience as belonging to this (thin) subject. But now the reflexivity claim begins to look a little odd. If the cognition of cognition is no more than the occurrence of phenomenal content, in what sense can it be said that some operation is being carried out on that content by that very content itself? The demand for a subject began with the claim that what-it-is-like-ness requires that for which it is so like. We are taking Dignāga to have sought to answer this with his reflexivity claim. One begins to suspect that the 'for' in 'that for which it is so like' reflects the functional role of cognition, not its intrinsic nature: content presents itself to the system for which it serves a role in action guidance. And of course this system is a complex series, not something ultimately real.[15]

---

[15] Perhaps Dignāga would agree that cognition is self-illuminating only in the weak sense that cognitive content presents itself to the system without the need for any other source of illumination. According to Williams (1998), certain Tibetan exegetes took Dignāga and Dharmakīrti this way. But this

In any event, Dignāga's view is not without its philosophical difficulties. First, Indian philosophers generally accept a principle of irreflexivity, to the effect that an entity cannot operate on itself. Even the most skilled acrobat, it is said, cannot stand on their own shoulders. The alleged counter-example of light, that supposedly illuminates itself while illuminating other things, is questionable. Strictly speaking what is visible when we say we see a beam of light is dust motes illuminated by the light, not the light itself.[16] Likewise, mereological reductionism shows how to dispose of such other alleged counter-examples as the sentence that refers to itself, or the doctor who heals herself. Proper analysis shows such cases to invariably involve one part of a larger system operating on another part. It is our belief in real wholes that leads us to suppose there are genuinely reflexive operations in the world.

Moreover, Dignāga's arguments against the alternative other-illumination view, that a consciousness is only cognized by a distinct consciousness, are flawed. He claims that the view leads to an infinite regress: if a given cognition requires a second occurrence of consciousness to apprehend it, the second will require a third, etc.[17] This is true, but it fails to refute the theory of other-illumination. The awareness of my awareness of a pot requires a second occurrence of consciousness, but the occurrence of this second consciousness does not require a third. Only the cognition of this second consciousness would require a third, and the opponent holds that there can be awareness of x without the awareness of the awareness of x. It would be question-begging to assume that there cannot be cognition of the cognition of the pot without cognition of that reflective cognition.[18]

Equally flawed is a second argument against other-illumination: that this view would have it that awareness of cognition always involves memory of a prior cognition, but one cannot remember what one has not experienced. This argument might be telling against the Nyāya version of other-illumination, which has it that the cognition of a cognition involves a kind of

can be confused with self-reflexivity only if one presupposes a certain sort of internalist model of cognition according to which one is aware that p only if one is aware that one is aware that p.

[16] But see Fasching, this volume, for an alternative way of taking the claim that light illuminates itself.

[17] For a survey of the debate between self-illuminationists and other-illuminationists, see Sinha 1958: 199–221. More recent discussions include Ganeri 1999, and Chapter 2 of Ram-Prasad 2007.

[18] Perrett 2003: 226f makes a similar point about Sartre's version of the argument. For further discussion, see Chatterjee 2008. For an analysis of Dharmakīrti's formulation of the infinite regress argument that reveals it to be equally question-begging, see Kellner (forthcoming).

internal perception of an already-completed cognition; such reflective awareness might be said to involve a sort of remembering of the immediately preceding cognition. But it does not pose a problem for the Bhāṭṭa Mīmāṃsā formulation of the other-illumination theory, according to which the cognition of the pot is cognized, not by reflection or memory, but through a kind of abductive inference (an inference to the best explanation). When one cognizes the pot one comes to be aware of the pot as qualified by cognizedness, and from this awareness one may abductively infer the occurrence of cognition of the pot. While it is true that one does not remember what one did not experience, on this account one is not remembering the cognizing of the pot, so the conceptual point about memory is irrelevant.

Thompson (this volume) proposes a phenomenological formulation of the argument from memory. On this version, the evidence for self-illumination comes not from the general phenomenon of cognition of cognition (something that can occur immediately after the occurrence of the target cognition) but from what is experienced as memory of an earlier cognition (in which there is a temporal gap between the target cognition and the memory cognition). The claim is that such experience-memory involves the remembering, not of the pot, but of the experience of seeing the pot. And since one cannot remember what one did not experience, memory of the experience of the pot requires that, at the time of the experience, one was aware, not only of the pot, but also of the experiencing of the pot: memory of prior cognition requires that the original cognition cognized itself.

To this, the response is that memory occurs through connection with the experienced object, and is thus of the object, not the experience of the object (BCA IX.24cd). From this awareness of the object in its absence there is the indirect cognition of the earlier experience of the object, by means of an abductive inference using the principle that one does not remember what one did not experience. While it may be true that experience-memory feels like the re-presentation of something as given in the past, the claim is that here, as elsewhere, the phenomenal feel of a presentation can be misleading: in memory it is the object that is given, its having been experienced in the past is the conclusion of an (automatic) abductive inference. To the objection that then there would be no difference between perceptual presentation of the pot and memory presentation of the pot, so that one would not have grounds for inferring that the pot was previously experienced, it will be replied that the two presentations differ in degree of acuity, the perceptual being more distinct or vivid (*spaṣṭa*).[19] The abductive inference in this case is based on the indistinctness of the memory image. Perhaps it will be objected that one can make such an inference only if one is aware of this indistinctness, and that this requires that one be aware of the present cognition of the memory image, hence that the present cognition be self-illuminating or reflexive. But to so object is to presuppose that information cannot bring about cognitive operations unless one is aware of oneself as possessing that information. And to make this assumption is to beg the question against the other-illumination theorist.

A similar strategy defeats Dignāga's argument for a cognition's having two forms. He claims that if a cognition had only a single form, either of itself or of its intentional object, then the cognition of the pot and the cognition of the cognition of the pot would be indistinguishable. But this follows only on the assumption that the form cognized by a cognition must be immanent to that very cognition—something denied by direct realists such as the Bhāṭṭas.

Finally, Dignāga's attempt to avoid a subject-object dichotomy involves some dubious metaphysics. He appears to want to say that the dichotomy is avoided by virtue of the fact that there is but a single entity involved, albeit one with two forms. But by the tenets of Buddhist Reductionism's mereological reductionism, an entity with more than one intrinsic property is just as lacking in ultimate reality as a partite entity. And the two forms Dignāga attributes to cognition certainly look like intrinsic properties. Of course Dignāga will claim that cognition's having two distinct forms is no more than a concession to the demands of conceptuality and does not reflect its ultimate nature. But then he will run up against the paradox of ineffability: his claim that the ultimate nature of cognition is inexpressible certainly looks like an attempt at expressing its ultimate nature. And why suppose that it is after all cognition that we are

---

[19] See, e.g., PV 3.10, PV 3.299, TSP *ad* TS 1120–1. There are good neuroscientific reasons to suppose that there must be discriminable differences between perceptual representations and representations generated internally (such as memory images and simulations). On the forward dynamic model of action control, the agent produces an 'efference copy' of the motor command which is then compared with the sensory consequences of one's action. As such, this forward copy must be perceptually attenuated. This explains why, e.g. a ticklish person cannot tickle themselves. See Choudhury and Blakemore 2006: 40–1. Perceptual attenuation might correspond to what the Buddhist authors mean by 'indistinct'.

talking about, and not some other candidate for the role of ultimate reality, if the nature of the ultimately real is inexpressible?

So it is not clear that Dignāga has an effective response to the subjectivity objection to Reductionism that avoids reinstating the subject–object dichotomy. It would be interesting to see if some other formulation of Buddhist Reductionism could do a better job of answering the subjectivity objection.

4. A Buddhist Reduction of Consciousness

Other Buddhist schools hold that one becomes conscious of a cognition only through a distinct cognition. This is the view of Theravāda, Vaibhā-ṣika, early Sautrāntika and Prāsaṅgika Madhyamaka. But I know of no systematic development and defense of the other-illumination view by any Buddhist philosopher. Now, because all these schools hold that consciousness is momentary but that a self must endure, they would not see a difficulty if it turned out that an occurrence of consciousness plays the role of subject in a particular cognition. But suppose we agreed with Strawson (1997) and the Yogācārins that anything that may be seen as playing the role of conscious subject is sufficiently self-like to threaten the Reductionist project. This would be reason to think that this minimal form of subjectivity poses a threat to Reductionism even when its base ontology is not physicalism but a kind of dualism. To respond to this challenge, the Buddhist Reductionist would need to develop a position on the question of how cognition is cognized. I propose that the best fit would be with the Bhāṭṭa Mīmāṃsā form of other-illumination theory.

Consciousness is, on this view, irreflexive, just like everything else in the universe. No more is consciousness aware of itself than a knife cuts itself or a fingertip touches itself. We can nonetheless be aware not only of a pot, but of our awareness of a pot. This must be achieved through a distinct cognition. But the cognition in question is not a case of reflection or inner perception. It is indirect. This makes it a case of what we would call inference. But for Indian epistemologists, 'inference' refers to a kind of indirect cognition that is mediated by cognition of a relation of invariable concomitance between the property to be proved and the inferential mark. Seeing smoke, one infers the existence of fire on the hill by virtue of one's having seen smoke and fire together in the kitchen. This makes it a requirement on inference that the property to be proved be amenable to direct cognition. If consciousness cannot be perceived, then its occurrence cannot be known through inference. This is why Bhāṭṭas claim that cognition is cognized through abductive inference (inference to the best explanation). Seeing that the obese Devadatta does not eat during the day, one abductively infers that he eats at night, despite the fact that we never observe co-occurrences of the property of being obese but not seen to eat, and the property of eating when unobserved. Likewise, they claim, we can abductively infer the occurrence of cognition from the occurrence of cognizedness in the object, despite the fact that we never perceive the co-occurrence of cognizedness and cognition (since we never perceive cognition).

A major difficulty for this view is that it is not at all easy to explain what the property of cognizedness is. The Bhāṭṭa claims that we notice this property in the pot and abductively infer from it the occurrence of a cognition that has taken the pot as its intentional object. But, the opponent objects, cognizedness is a relational property, and one does not cognize a relational property unless one cognizes both relata. One does not cognize Jill's property of being the same height as Jack unless one also cognizes Jack. So one cannot cognize cognizedness in the pot without first cognizing the pot and the cognition that has it as intentional object. Hence we arrive back at the need to countenance the direct cognition of cognition.

To this it is replied that the cognizedness in the object is just the property of the object's being available for speech and action: to say there is cognizedness in the pot is just to say that the pot can now be referred to and employed in various ways. To this it is objected (Sinha 1958: 210) that it is tantamount to denying the existence of cognition. The thought behind this objection is that if there is no more to cognizedness than the availability of the object for systems like memory, speech, desire, and action-guidance, then 'consciousness' comes to seem like an empty place-holder. And there is, I think, something to this objection. If all there were to cognizedness was being such as to be available to a single system, such as action-guidance, there would be no reason to posit anything like consciousness in order to explain the phenomena. For this is just what we find in cases of blind-sight: the subject navigates around obstacles while claiming to see nothing. In such cases we say that the object directly plays a causal role in the guidance of action, without consciousness as an intermediary. We do not think the thermostat is conscious of the temperature of the air in the room: the thermostat serves as an intermediary between the temperature of the air and the operation of the heating/cooling system. But why should things be any different where the object is available to multiple systems? The flow of information is more complex, but such flow is still along what are, after all, no more than causal pathways, just more of them. The suggestion is that if cognizedness is just global availability, then the abductive inference to consciousness fails to go through.[20]

A Buddhist Reductionist other-illumination theorist would no doubt want to resist this consequence of their view, that consciousness becomes a mere empty place-holder. First there are considerations of orthodoxy. To call consciousness an empty place-holder is in effect to call it a conceptual fiction. Yet the Buddha spoke of consciousness as one of the psychophysical elements (*skandhas*) to which the person is said to be reducible. So to call consciousness a conceptual fiction would be to call the Buddha's authority into question. But there are also considerations stemming from the role of meditation in Buddhist practice. For meditation looks like a kind of phenomenological investigation; in meditation one carefully examines the rise and fall of mental states, their structure and causal interactions. If consciousness is no more than an empty place-holder, then it seems there is nothing for phenomenology to investigate. Yet the practice of meditation is thought to be efficacious on the Buddhist path to the cessation of suffering. If the subjective realm is illusory, why should its analytic investigation have any useful consequences?

Yet I think the Buddhist Reductionist who wants to avoid the difficulties of Dignāga's view should embrace this consequence of the other-illumination position. To do so need not amount to abandoning the other-illumination view. One can instead put the objection just rehearsed to reductionist uses. It does, after all, appear to us as though we are aware of our own states of consciousness. This phenomenon is quite real, and requires explaining. How is it to be explained, given irreflexivity? By way of an abductive inference from the global availability of objects. Since global availability is just an aggregation of distinct causal pathways, it will come as no surprise that consciousness turns out to be a conceptual fiction, a single entity posited in order to simplify the task of data management. (Hence the abductive inference is valid, but only conventionally.) Just as it seems to us that there is a chair when the parts are assembled in a certain way, so it seems to us that there is the conscious state of seeing a chair in my path to the door

---

[20] For a useful discussion of the term 'global availability', see Metzinger (2003: 31).

when the chair is made available not only to the action-guidance system (as in blind-sight) but also to the memory system, the speech system, etc. We can thus understand why it is that, despite there being no such thing as what-it-is-like-ness, it would seem to us that there is such a thing. Subjectivity is a useful fiction.[21]

But is it at all coherent to claim that it seems to us as if there is such a thing as its seeming to us as if... when in fact there are no seemings? Two responses are possible. One is that the persistence of an illusion is no proof that it is not an illusion. One can know perfectly well that the lines in an illustration of the Ponzo illusion are of equal length, yet one will continue to see some as longer than others. The sense that there is the perspectival, it might be said, is just such an illusion. Of course this must count as the mother of all illusions, since without it there could be no gap between how things seem and how things are. But it nonetheless makes sense to speak of it as an illusion, since it leads the system in which it occurs to misrepresent its environment. There is no what-it-is-like-ness for the thermostat, yet we speak naturally of our fooling the thermostat into taking the room to be warmer than it is by holding a candle nearby. So we might say that the psycho-physical system misrepresents its environment as containing a subject to which things seem a certain way. One's grasping of this point may include an instance of just such a seeming. But this need not be paradoxical. Once we see how the illusion is generated, and why it persists (due to its utility for systems like these), we can understand that it is a misrepresentation, and why such a misrepresentation occurs.

A second possible response is that the illusion may be dispelled by knowledge of its source. In the Buddhist tradition one sometimes encounters the claim that when fully perfected enlightened beings exercise their compassion, they do not cognize the unenlightened beings who are the objects of their compassion, but nonetheless act appropriately toward them

---

[21] For a Buddhist Reductionist, saying that consciousness is a conceptual fiction would be tantamount to saying there can be unconscious mental functions. The orthodox Buddhist Reductionist view is that all mental functions are conscious: there can be no *caitta* without *citta*. This orthodoxy is the source of the Yogācāra notion of *ālayavijñāna* or 'storehouse consciousness', as well as the Theravāda notion of *bhavaṅga*, the continuum of consciousness. In both cases a seemingly unobservable consciousness is posited in order to explain continuities in mental functioning. But this orthodoxy was challenged by Sautrāntikas when they claimed that mental dispositions can be preserved over intervals when there is no cognition whatever. This was the original form of their 'seeds' theory. So there is precedent for a Buddhist Reductionist to hold a view that entails that mental functions can occur without consciousness.

in a purely spontaneous, intuitive fashion. One might dismiss this as the sort of hyperbole that is often generated when devotionalist sects compete over the relative merits of their ideal figures. But in this case there is at least something more going on. In Yogācāra thought all conceptualization is said to be deceptive in that it conceals the non-dual nature of reality. Since enlightened beings know the ultimate nature of reality, it follows that their grasp of the world must be non-conceptual. Yet unenlightened beings inhabit a world that is structured by a set of conceptual tools. And it would seem that the enlightened can help the unenlightened only by sharing in that distorted vision. One response to this dilemma is to claim that enlightened beings act directly on their perception without any intervening thought, yet their actions are ideally suited to benefit the unenlightened. This notion of a Robo-Buddha sounds implausible, but it might be worth looking to see if sense can be made of it in the present context.

The other-illumination theorist holds that a cognition need not itself be cognized in order to perform its function of illuminating the object. (Note that for the Buddhist Reductionist I have in mind, consciousness is a target for reduction, not elimination, and so is conventionally real: they hold the other-illumination theory to be part of the conventional truth.[22]) If the cognition of a cognition is always optional, what could be its point? A hint is to be found in the claim (TS 2959–62) that a truly novel perception is not accepted as veridical immediately, but only upon subsequent investigation. The context of this claim is the dispute over whether cognitions are initially taken to be veridical, with such credulity withdrawn only on the subsequent occurrence of disconfirming evidence, or whether instead cognitions are only taken as veridical upon the presentation of additional evidence. The claim here is that whereas a perception of something familiar is taken as 'intrinsically veridical' (svataḥprāmāṇya), perception in a novel context is taken to be veridical only 'extrinsically' (parataḥprāmāṇya). This means that while the stereotyped perception (e.g. of water in the irrigation pond one sees every day) functions directly on the relevant sub-systems, the novel perception comes to be taken as reliable only by being treated as a state of the system. Where we know our way about, the sensory state is taken as putting us in direct touch with the object (the cognition is transparent);

---

[22] For a clear statement of the difference between reductionism and eliminativism about the mental, see Kim 2004: 138.

where we are in cognitively new territory, the sensation is taken as producing an inner representation that may or may not be veridical, and so warrants further investigation (the cognition is opaque). We can then say that the cognizedness of the object is the mark that this yellow flag has gone up. We take perception to result in a cognition, an inner subjective state, when it would enhance the performance of the system to make perceptual content available to the fact-checker routines. But having done so on several occasions, we can make the process fully automatic. Seeing is like any other skill, something done deliberately and self-consciously at first, but in time done on auto-pilot.

The claim about the Robo-Buddha might, then, be no more than a way of saying that the skillful and highly practiced teacher will spontaneously and effortlessly give the student just the right bit of instruction on any given occasion. No thought being required, there is no need to generate the otherwise useful illusion of thought–the illusion that there is a private realm of subjectivity. For those of us who are not so skilled, it will prove useful to acquiesce in the illusion that there is consciousness, to accept the abductive inference as valid. But the existence of Robo-Buddhas would show that what we acquiesce in is not part of our ultimate ontology. There is no experiencing subject, not even a momentary one, nor is there the inner subjective realm. Consciousness is only conventionally and not ultimately real. That there are Robo-Buddhas would show that the difference between zombies and us is just one of our taking all too seriously the merely useful device of self-representation.[23]

---

[23] Dretske (2003) appeals to the evidence concerning early childhood acquisition of the concept of belief in arguing for the claim that one's thinking and experiencing are constituted by external, historical relations. A useful summary of this evidence is to be found in Gopnik (2009). On the resulting view, self-representation is not only an acquired skill, but also one the exercise of which introduces distortions into our view of ourselves. This might suggest an alternative reading of Dignāga's claim that the subject-object distinction results from conceptual superimposition. On this reading, phenomenality is the by-product of the useful practice of self-representation, a practice made possible by the use of concepts. And all conceptualization falsifies the nature of reality by making reality conform to our interests and cognitive limitations. One might, then, in turn interpret the methodological stance taken by Dreyfus (this volume), of conducting phenomenological investigation while steering clear of ontological questions, as a stance that is compatible with thoroughgoing ontological reduction. The idea would be that while the other-illuminationist is right that mental states are not intrinsically self-intimating, and thus that self-illuminationism is not ultimately true, the useful device of self-representation gives rise to the appearance of phenomenality and self-cognition, and careful exploration of this realm can be helpful in dispelling our belief in a subject of experience. Yogācāra would then represent a lesser form of conventional truth.

Abbreviations

AKBh = *Abhidharmakośabhāṣyam of Vasubandhu*. Edited by Prahlad Pradhan. Patna: Jayaswal Research Institute, 1975.

BCA = *Bodhicaryāvatāra* of Śāntideva with the commentary *Pañjikā* of Prajñākaramati. Ed. P.L. Vaidya. Darbhanga, India: Mithila Institute, 1960.

PV = S. *Pramāṇavārttikabhāṣya* of Prajñākaragupta. Edited by R. Sāṃkṛtyāyana. Patna: Kashi Prasad Jayaswal Research Institute, 1953.

TS = *Tattvasaṅgraha* of Śāntarakṣita. Edited with the *Pañjikā* of Kamalaśīla by Dwarkidas Sastri. Varanasi, 1968.

References

Albahari, M. (2006), *Analytical Buddhism* (New York: Macmillan).

Chatterjee, A. (2008), 'Intentional Consciousness and Higher Order Consciousness: An East West Perspective', in Suresh Raval, G. M. Mehta, and Sitanshu Yashaschandra (eds.), *Forms of Knowledge in India: Critical Revaluation* (Pencraft International, Delhi).

Choudhury, S. and Blakemore, S. J. (2006), 'Intentions, Actions and the Self', in Susan Pockett, William P. Banks, and Shaun Gallagher (eds.), *Does Consciousness Cause Behavior?* (Cambridge, MA: MIT Press).

Collins, S. (1982), *Selfless Persons* (Cambridge: Cambridge University Press).

Dhammajoti, Bikhu JL. (2007), *Abhidharma Doctrines and Controversies on Perception* (Hong Kong: Center of Buddhist Studies, University of Hong Kong).

Dretske, F. (2003), 'Externalism and Self-Knowledge', in Susan Nuccutelli (ed.), *New Essays on Semantic Externalism* (Cambridge, MA: MIT Press).

Eckel, M. D. (2008), *Bhāviveka and His Buddhist Opponents,* Harvard Oriental Series vol. 70 (Cambridge, MA: Harvard University Press).

Ganeri, J. (1999), 'Self-Intimation, Memory and Personal Identity', *Journal of Indian Philosophy* 27: 469–83,

Goodman, C. (2009), *Consequences of Compassion* (NY: Oxford University Press).

Gopnik, A. (2009), *The Philosophical Baby* (New York: Farrar, Straus and Giroux).

Kajiyama Y. (1965), 'Buddhist Solipsism: A Free Translation of Ratnakīrti's *Santānāntaradūṣaṇa*', *Journal of Indian and Buddhist Studies* XIII.1: 9–24.

Kellner, B. (forthcoming), 'Self-Awareness (*svasaṃvedana*) and Infinite Regresses: A Comparison of Arguments by Dignāga and Dhar-makīrti', *Journal of Indian Philosophy*.

Kim, J. (2004), 'The Mind-Body Problem at Century's Turn', in Brian Leiter (ed.), *The Future for Philosophy* (NY: Oxford University Press).

Merricks, T. (2002), *Objects and Persons* (NY: Oxford University Press).

Metzinger, T. (2003), *Being No One* (Cambridge, MA: MIT Press).

Perrett, R. (2003), 'Intentionality and Self-awareness', *Ratio* XVI: 222–35.

Ram-Prasad, C. (2007), *Indian Philosophy and the Consequences of Knowledge* (Aldershot: Ashgate).

Rosenberg, A. (1997), 'Reductionism Redux: Computing the Embryo', *Philosophy and Biology* 12: 445–70.

Shoemaker, S. (1985), 'Critical Notice of *Reasons and Persons* by Derek Parfit', *Mind* 94: 443–53.

Siderits, M. (2003), *Personal Identity and Buddhist Philosophy* (Aldershot: Ashgate).

—— (2006), 'Buddhist Reductionism and Buddhist Ethics', in P. Bilimoria, J. Prabhu, and R. Sharma (eds.), *Indian Ethics: Classical and Contemporary Challenges* (Aldershot: Ashgate).

—— (2009), 'Is Reductionism Expressible?' in Mario D'Amato, Jay L. Garfield, and Tom J. F. Tillemans (eds.), *Pointing at the Moon: Buddhism, Logic, Analytic Philosophy* (NY: Oxford University Press).

—— (2010), 'What the Gopis Know', in Jay Garfield (ed.), *Moonshadows* (NY: Oxford University Press).

Sinha, J. (1958), *Indian Psychology: Cognition*, vol. 1 (Calcutta: Sinha Publishing House).

Strawson, G. (1997), 'The Self', *Journal of Consciousness Studies*, 4: 405–28.

—— (2008), 'What is the Relation Between an Experience, the Subject of the Experience, and the Content of the Experience?', in *Real Materialism and Other Essays* (Oxford: Oxford University Press).

Thompson, E. (2007), *Mind in Life: Biology, Phenomenology, and the Sciences of Mind* (Cambridge, MA: Harvard University Press).

Watson, A. (2006), *The Self's Awareness of Itself: Bhaa Rāmakaṇṭha's Arguments against the Buddhist Doctrine of No-Self*, De Nobili Research Library XXXII (Vienna: Institut für Südasien-, Tibet- und Buddhismuskunde der Universität Wien).

Williams, P. (1998), *The Reflexive Nature of Awareness* (Surrey: Curzon Press).

Yao, Z. (2005), *The Buddhist Theory of Self-Cognition* (Abingdon: Routledge).

Index